...ooks including
Book of Prison Breaks and *That's What They* ...
well as guides to James Bond, Stephen King, Oz and *Doctor Who*.
He is a freelance editor for various UK and US publishers, as well as
running the genre website Sci-Fi Bulletin from his home in a small
village north of Brighton, England.

The Serial Killer Files

PAUL SIMPSON

ROBINSON

ROBINSON

First published in Great Britain in 2017 by Robinson

1 3 5 7 9 10 8 6 4 2

Copyright © Paul Simpson, 2017

The moral right of the author has been asserted.

A CIP catalogue record for this book
is available from the British Library.

ISBN: 978-1-47213-674-9

Typeset in Scala by Hewer Text UK Ltd, Edinburgh
Printed and bound in Great Britain by CPI Group (UK), Croydon CRO 4YY

Papers used by Robinson are from well-managed forests and other responsible sources.

Robinson
An imprint of
Little, Brown Book Group
Carmelite House
50 Victoria Embankment
London EC4Y 0DZ

An Hachette UK Company
www.hachette.co.uk

www.littlebrown.co.uk

For Chris Williams and Alexandra Luzzato,
without whom this would not have been possible

You feel the last bit of breath leaving their body. You're looking into their eyes. A person in that situation is God!

Ted Bundy

Contents

Introduction

....

What is a serial killer?

You'd think it might be one of the simplest questions to answer – yet plenty has been written over the last few decades that suggests that it's not that simple at all. Is a serial killer the same as a mass murderer? Both are deemed responsible for a number of deaths, but you can easily see the difference when you look at someone who can be seen as a 'typical' mass murderer – Anders Behring Breivik, who killed sixty-nine people in a single incident on the island of Utøya on 22 July 2011. A serial killer may not kill that many people – in fact, although there is a small handful whose stories will be recounted in this book who do achieve such high numbers, most kill significantly fewer before they are either caught or killed (sometimes dying by their own hand). The key difference is that a serial killer commits his acts over a period of time; he (and for the purposes of this discussion, I will use the male singular pronoun, although female serial killers and couples do exist and will be featured) may kill more than one person in a single incident, but the vast majority of his crimes are separated in space and time.

In 1998, the United States Congress passed a law that included a definition of serial killers: 'The term "serial killings" means a series of three or more killings, not less than one of which was committed within the United States, having common characteristics such as to suggest the reasonable possibility that the crimes were committed by the same actor or actors.' This was designed to help the US Federal Bureau of Investigation (FBI) decide whether a case fell under its purview or not.

Ten years later, in July 2008, the FBI published a monograph, based on the discussions they had held at a multi-disciplinary symposium in San Antonio, Texas, from 29 August to 2 September 2005. This monograph deals with many aspects of the pursuit and capture of serial killers – and is highly recommended reading to anyone with a serious interest in the topic – and begins with a definition of serial murder, which took as its basis the statutory definition, but aimed to refine it. After much discussion, the eventual outcome was that serial murder is defined as: 'The unlawful killing of two or more victims by the same offender(s), in separate events.'

More importantly, perhaps, than its definition of serial murder, the FBI symposium discussed the many urban myths that have grown up around serial killers (and which, it should be noted, too many thriller writers who have not bothered with their research have perpetuated) – or, as they put it, 'certain stereotypes and misconceptions take root regarding the nature of serial murder and the characteristics of serial killers'. These myths include the idea that serial killers are all dysfunctional loners; that they are all white males; they are only motivated by sex; they all travel and operate across a wide area; that they cannot stop killing; they are all insane or evil geniuses; and that they all want to get caught. Of course, there are some who fit into these categories, but as you will find in the pages that follow, the married 'Green River Killer' was not a dysfunctional loner; there are plenty of female and non-Caucasian serial killers; Dr Harold Shipman was certainly not motivated by sex; many serial killings (such as the Ipswich prostitute murders carried out by Steve Wright) happen within a confined area; the 'BTK Killer', Dennis Rader, stopped his activities in 1991 but wasn't caught until fourteen years later ... And as for 'evil geniuses' ... well, Thomas Harris has a lot to answer for in his creation of Dr Hannibal Lecter in his novel *Red Dragon*. Many may have a low animal cunning and be 'street smart', but they're not Mensa-level.

In *The Serial Killer Files*, I have not attempted to compile a comprehensive list of every serial killer globally – it would need dozens of volumes this size to do that. Some of the most prolific – such as the Indian serial killer Kampatimar Shankariya, who killed seventy people with a hammer in the late 1970s – have not made the list simply because of a paucity of material to make them stand out. I have tried to ensure that each of the thirty cases discussed here is unusual in some respect, perhaps in the way in which the killer carried out their crimes, the choice of victims, the way in which they were apprehended or the method of their execution. Some will fit the FBI's archetype; many do not. The cases are presented alphabetically by country, and then chronologically. They come from across history and from all over the world, and, as with my previous books on prison breaks and air disasters, I have gone back as far as possible to contemporary source material – newspaper accounts, trial evidence, interviews with perpetrators or survivors – rather than the increasingly blurred truth to be found in far too many collections.

While television documentaries often play up to their audience's expectations and can conflate or expand events in order to fit the story into their allotted running time, the best of them do incorporate interviews with the detectives involved in the cases, and often include footage of the killers, either during police interview or afterwards. Thanks to YouTube, these key pieces of archive footage are now available to researchers in a way that they simply were not, even a decade ago. Many of the cases come from non-English-speaking countries, and my thanks to all those who assisted with translations.

With a book like this there is an ever-present danger that the reader – and the author – can become hardened to the reality of what's being discussed, which in the vast majority of cases involves violent loss of life. The attention can sometimes be too firmly on the perpetrator of the crime rather than the victim, and those writing about the subject have to bear in mind the heartfelt plea of the family of one of Ted Bundy's victims: 'Any article or news report about Ted Bundy always included Caryn's name and the fact that "her nude and frozen body was found in a snowbank",' Caryn Campbell's sister, Nancy McDonald, wrote in a letter published in the *Detroit News* the week of Bundy's execution. 'It's been extremely difficult for us to accept Caryn's loss and the way her body was found, but we, her family, did not need to hear, see and read the same fact for 14 years.' Therefore, it is to the memory of the many hundreds of innocent people whose deaths are recounted in this volume, and to those they left behind, that this book is also dedicated.

CHAPTER 1

Australia: Ivan Milat

Everyone is entitled to a fair trial – it's a fundamental precept of the Western legal system, and one with which most people would agree, even in such horrendous cases as those being examined in this book. But at the same time, no one wants a serial killer to 'get off' through some form of legal chicanery or exploitation of a loophole. In the case of Ivan Milat, responsible for what became internationally known as 'the backpacker murders' between 1989 and 1994, the Australian Chief Judge at Common Law was unequivocal in his remarks after a guilty verdict was returned: 'The case against the prisoner at the conclusion of the evidence and the addresses was, in my view, an overwhelming one. Although his legal representatives displayed a tactical ability of a high order, and conducted his defence in a skilful and responsible manner, in my view the jury's verdicts were, in the end, inevitable. I agree entirely with those verdicts. Any other, in my view, would have flown in the face of reality.' The case continues to resonate today: the successful *Wolf Creek* franchise of horror films and TV series is centred on a serial killer who is based in large part on Ivan Milat.

Ivan Robert Marko Milat was one of fourteen children whose father Stjepan had emigrated from Yugoslavia to Australia and married a much younger local girl, Margaret. He was born on 27 December 1944 and brought up in a rural community on the outskirts of Sydney where such a large family was difficult for his parents to control. He loved hunting and guns, and he and his brothers would often find themselves in trouble with the local police. 'The Milats aren't a normal Australian family, I like to say

5

they're the sort of family you see in the southern states of America,' Clive Small, the head of Task Force Air who captured Milat, noted in a 2015 documentary about Australian crime families. More details of Milat's upbringing have recently been revealed by his nephew, Alistair Shipsey (who, it should be noted, believes his uncle was not responsible for the murders and is spearheading a campaign for a new appeal). 'They had 500 acres down at Wombeyan Caves and they used to go camping all the time, and shooting,' Shipsey explained.

> And in those days you were allowed guns, you didn't have gun licences. Most people had guns in the old days and you would if you had a few brothers. He had ten brothers, you'd have a few guns between ya. They used to get the black powder ones in kits and even make rifles and pistols.
>
> We'd go down hunting on the property and shooting targets. It was fun. Okay, we used to shoot the odd goat, there was lots of wild goats there. We had targets, we used to have barbecues and camp there on the river, and think about how much fun it was having a big family, camping, drinking, cooking barbecues and everybody being down there. That's what people did in the old days.

Some family members claimed that Milat's father was violent, breaking one of the boys' arms, but Shipsey and others have denied this.

Milat's brother Boris claimed that Ivan attacked a taxi driver when he was just seventeen in 1962, a crime for which someone else went to prison (because that person believed that his own brother was responsible, but took the blame). The taxi driver was shot in the back and was paralysed. Boris only made this claim in 2015; again, other family members have said it's a false accusation.

Ivan Milat was certainly known to the police for at least one crime of violence. He was acquitted of the rape of two female hitchhikers in 1971, after the prosecution failed to prove their case – the victims had claimed that he had driven them off the highway and used a knife against them during the attacks. He spent much of the 1960s in prison for theft, but there was no suspicion that he was involved in anything more serious – although now police believe that he was carrying out killings long before December 1989, and continue to regard him as a prime suspect in many cases. As recently as August 2016, coroner Peter Bain referenced Milat at the inquest for missing Cronulla teenagers Elaine Johnson and Kerry Anne Joel. 'Police inquiries show a number of young girls went missing in New South Wales in the late 1970s and early 1980s. A number of persons of interest with violent histories are suspected by police to have been active during this time.'

Milat has always claimed his innocence of the backpacker murders, but the evidence certainly seemed to stack up against him. The bodies of seven missing backpackers were found in the Belanglo State Forest, ten miles from the town of Berrima, close to Milat's home, and circumstantial evidence linked him to all seven – as well as to the attempted robbery of another backpacker, Paul Onions. It was Onions's testimony combined with the abundance of evidence that convinced the jury to convict – although Justice David Hunt noted that it was clear from the evidence that two people had been involved because of the way that the victims were killed, but it did not diminish Milat's part in the crimes.

On 19 September 1992, two runners found a decaying body while they were orienteering in the state forest, in an area informally known as Executioner's Drop. They reported this to the police, who carried out a search, and the next day Police Constables Roger Gough and Suzanne Roberts found a second body around thirty metres away. There was originally some debate as to the deceased's identities, as there were a number of reports of missing couples, but thanks to dental records they were soon revealed as a British pair, twenty-one-year-old Caroline Clarke and Joanne Walters, who was a year older. They had last been seen in the Kings Cross area of Sydney in April that year, and had told friends they were hoping to get seasonal fruit-picking jobs.

Joanne had been gagged, then stabbed twenty-one times in the back and fourteen times in the chest. Her spine had been severed, which paralysed her, with one blow. Her body was placed under a rock below a camp on the Longacre Creek Fire Trail; her killer had covered her with branches. Caroline had been marched ten metres away, blindfolded with her sweater (confusingly referred to as a 'Sloppy Joe' in the Australian news reports), and then shot ten times in the head (possibly being used for target practice) before being stabbed once in the chest. Ten Winchester 'Winner' cartridge cases were found nearby. The girls' parents made a public appeal for information about the 'animals' who had done this to their children. A forensic psychiatrist, Rod Milton, assessed the scene, and felt that the perpetrators knew the area and were hunters – the differences in the way the girls were killed made him suspect there were two different killers. The area was searched for further bodies, but after five days, nothing further was found, and the investigators believed they had found everything in the forest.

They hadn't. Over a year later, on 5 October 1993, local resident Bruce Pryor – who had, by his own admission, become obsessed with the case – was searching in a part of the forest only 600 metres from where Caroline and Joanne's bodies were discovered, and found a human skull and a thigh bone. He fetched police, and the skeletal remains of two more people were found, twenty-five metres apart: the female body was at the base of a tree, the male beside a fallen log. Both had been covered with leaf and stick debris; both had died from multiple stab wounds. (Pryor, perhaps not surprisingly, briefly became a suspect in the case.)

They were quickly identified as Melbourne residents Deborah Everist and James Gibson, both of whom were nineteen when they left Surry Hills in Sydney to hitchhike to Confest, a music festival 300 miles away at Albury, on the morning of 30 December 1989. The location of the bodies rather surprised police, as they had found a couple of items belonging to the pair by the side of the road at Galston Gorge, over 75 miles away from the forest, in the northern suburbs of Sydney. A camera was located on 31 December 1989, and a backpack – with James's name and address on its base – on 13 March 1990. Another backpack had been seen in the area in early January 1990.

A further intensive search by 300 officers was begun and, on 1 November 1993, Police Sergeant Jeff Trichter found the skull of twenty-one-year-old German tourist Simone Schmidl. She was last seen on 20 January 1991, carrying a distinctive multi-coloured backpack and a blue day bag: she had left Guildford planning to get a bus to Liverpool and then hitchhike down the Hume Highway to Melbourne. When her body was found, it was clear she had died from numerous stab wounds in the upper torso, including two that severed her spine. There was an elasticised band around her skull, and a gag of some sort in her mouth. There was some clothing at the scene, but it wasn't hers – it belonged to another missing person, twenty-year-old German backpacker Anja Habschied.

Three days after Simone's skull was located, the investigators discovered the bodies of Anja and her friend Gabor Neugebauer, who had only come to Australia for a brief holiday after spending time in Indonesia. As senior prosecutor Ian Lloyd explained at one of Milat's first hearings, 'Habschied's head had been severed at the neck, apparently in one blow and despite an extensive search the head has not been located. Habschied's body had no lower clothing.' The bodies were in shallow graves about fifty-five metres apart. Gabor's mouth had been gagged with cloth, and five spent bullets were found in his skull – once again, it seemed he had been used for target practice.

Police forensically searched the area, and about 165 metres away from Gabor's body, they found a treasure trove of evidence, which included Eley and Winchester 'Winner' cartridge cases and ammunition boxes, as well as a pair of pink jeans and a blue and yellow piece of Telecom rope. Nearer the body, items belonging to Gabor and Anja were found, as well as what the court described as 'a device suitable for use for restraining a person'.

'I think it's fair to say that given we now have seven bodies recovered, and notwithstanding that we don't have cause of death in the present case, that we do have a serial killer,' Inspector Clive Small announced. The police worked out a profile of the killer but had a huge amount of data with which to deal. According to a study by the Australian Institute of Criminology, 'at one stage during the Backpacker Murder Investigations it was estimated that the holdings of information increased from around seven to ten thousand pieces of information to around 1.5 million in just 12 weeks'. A report in the Australian press described the operation as 'the biggest dragnet for a serial killer in Australian history, reaching from Sydney and the Southern Highlands as far as Greece, Italy, Germany, the Netherlands and Britain. Up to 360 police at a single time have been employed in the search, and several million dollars spent.'

Police invented special computer software to try to cross-reference all of this evidence – over a million telephone calls came in. Even though link analysis technology was able to bring the suspect field down from 230 to 32, it really was getting almost impossible to see the wood for the trees . . .

Until a phone call came from the United Kingdom. Or rather, until the note about a phone call from the United Kingdom finally surfaced among the thousands of pieces of paper relating to the case. Paul Onions had contacted New South Wales police on 13

November 1993; his call wasn't followed up until exactly five months later.

Back in 1989, twenty-four-year-old Paul Onions had left his engineering job in Britain to backpack around Australia. The former sailor decided to hitchhike from Sydney to Victoria looking for fruit-picking work after Christmas that year. He was aware of the risks, but knew it would save him money. On the morning of 25 January 1990 he took a train to the Hume Highway and unsuccessfully tried to flag down passing motorists for about an hour. After taking a break at Lombardo's Shopping Centre at Casula, he was approached by a smiling man 'with a moustache like Merv Hughes' (the Australian cricketer who sported very distinctive and large facial hair), who asked if he needed a lift.

The man introduced himself as 'Bill', and they got chatting as they headed down the road in the man's four-wheel-drive. Bill didn't say much about his own job, although he told Paul his family came from Yugoslavia, but he established what Paul's plans in Australia were, before, about an hour into the journey, his attitude started to change. He began expressing 'vehement and controversial opin-ions' (the court's polite version) 'like a Jekyll and Hyde character', as Paul would later recall. Then Bill stopped the vehicle close to the entrance to Belanglo State Forest, claiming that radio reception was poor out on the highway, so he would sort out some music for them to listen to on the journey.

Bill got out, and started rummaging under the driver's seat, claiming he was looking for some cassette tapes. A little uneasy, Paul also got out and stretched his legs, then got back in when Bill did. However, Bill exited the vehicle again, and this time returned to his seat brandishing a black revolver and screaming at Paul, 'This is a robbery!' Paul tried to calm him down, but Bill then reached under his seat and pulled out a bag of rope, clearly intending to restrain the young Englishman.

Fearing for his life, Paul ran. There were cars coming towards him, but no one would stop. From behind, Bill shouted, 'Stop or I'll shoot!' and then Paul heard a gunshot. Bill caught up with him and pulled him to the ground. They wrestled for a moment before Paul managed to get up and this time 'threw myself into the path of an oncoming car to make it stop and, as it screeched to a halt, I just jumped into the back seat'. The woman driver, Joanne Berry, did a U-turn, and took Paul to Bowral Police Station. Paul's rucksack, containing a distinctive Next blue denim shirt, was still on the back seat of Bill's car.

Paul made his report to Constable Janet Nicholson who made detailed notes. Most of his description would later prove to match Ivan Milat – Paul overestimated his attacker's height, but Milat was known as Bill at the time, he drove a Nissan four-wheel-drive vehicle; he was a road worker; his father was from Yugoslavia; he was divorced; and despite denying it originally, at the time he did have a moustache (a passport photo from the previous year was tracked down). The offence was treated as assault with a firearm, but no arrests were made – for four years. Paul went back to Sydney the same day, where he was teased by a group of British former miners with whom he had been drinking – they had been confident he would be back from fruit picking within a week because it was hard work. 'I was like, "Look, some fucker just tried to kill me,"' Paul said.

After he returned to the UK, Paul was haunted by memories of his close call with Bill, and when he saw the newspaper and television reports of the Backpacker Murders in November 1993, he contacted the Australian High Commission in London. Eventually the task force seeking the backpacker murderer got in touch with him. On 5 May 1994, Paul was shown a video of thirteen still photos including Milat's passport shot – and he chose Milat, from his moustache, his 'narrow squinting eyes', hair and face. 'He is identical to the face I see that approached me at the news agency,' Paul testified. Joanne Berry independently got in touch with the task force and corroborated Paul's story.

The evidence provided by Paul added to the information the officers already had amassed about the tight-knit family of hunters. Not long after the bodies were found in November 1993, Alex Milat had come to police with a story about seeing two girls being abducted – some months earlier, he and a friend had been in the forest and seen a car with youths in it, and a couple of women tied up in the back. The story didn't ring true – why hadn't they said anything earlier, and why didn't they do anything to help? – and it had focused police attention on the family. The profilers suggested that such a family could fit the likely suspects (particularly as they believed that two people were working together), and suspicion focused on Ivan, particularly when police discovered that he was something of a control freak who presented a very different version of himself to the neighbours.

Investigations showed that Ivan and his brother Richard worked on road gangs along the highway; Milat had a property near the state forest park, and he had sold his Nissan four-wheel-drive not long after the initial bodies were found in 1992, accidentally leaving a .22 calibre bullet under the front seat. The brothers' alibis for the times of the disappearances of the backpackers were checked – and only Ivan was unaccounted for on the day of each of the murders. Milat's earlier acquittal for armed robbery also weighed against him when a hard copy of the charge was discovered by the task force. Alex Milat and his wife were questioned again, and, almost casually, mentioned that Ivan had given them a backpack – which belonged to Simone Schmidl.

In the early morning of 22 May 1994, teams of police, wearing bulletproof vests and armed with shotguns and submachine guns, surrounded Milat's home. He had been under surveillance for some time, and police were aware that he was asleep at the property with access to firearms. It took two phone calls and over thirty minutes before Milat surrendered himself to the police to be arrested for robbery and weapons offences. He appeared in court simply on those charges the next day, but didn't enter a plea. A week later, he was charged with the seven Backpacker Murders.

When Milat was arrested, police didn't just search his house: over 300 officers checked out the properties of his brothers Richard, Alex, Boris, Walter and Bill at the same time. The evidence that incriminated Ivan was found in three places: at Ivan's own house, at his mother's house, and at his brother Walter's. In his own home, police found a photo of Milat carrying Deborah Everist's sleeping bag, as well as the bag itself; Simone Schmidl's sleeping-bag cover and tent were in a cupboard – with a similar headband around the tent to the one found near her body; her water bottle and pouch (with the name still visible when infrared light was shone on it) were in his bedroom; Indonesian money believed to be from Gabor Neugebauer was by the bed; parts of firearms and knives were discovered in hidden places in the cavity walls and the roof. At his mother's home, police found Paul Onions's Next shirt in a box in the garage, as well as lengths of sash cord that matched the cord used on Gabor and Anja. Milat's girlfriend, Chalinder Hughes – who had no idea about Milat's murderous ways – had been given Caroline Clarke's Benetton shirt. Caroline's camera was in the kitchen at Milat's home, with a photo of Chalinder wearing the shirt. In total, more than 300 pieces of evidence were logged. Ballistics tests linked the cartridges found near Gabor's body with the parts of the rifle discovered in the cavity walls. DNA testing on a blood-stained piece of cord linked Milat to Caroline Clarke.

The trial began in March 1996 (after various discussions regarding Milat's eligibility for legal aid) and lasted three months, with the prosecution relying on the discoveries in the house as well as Milat's repair of his Nissan after a bullet caused damage to it, a week after Anja and Gabor's disappearance. The defence had to concede that 'there can be absolutely no doubt that whoever committed all eight offences must be within the Milat family, or very, very closely associated with it', and tried to shift the blame onto other family members. Milat himself made a poor witness, and on 27 July 1996 the jury returned from three days' deliberation to find him guilty on all charges. He received six years for the attack on Paul – and seven consecutive life sentences for the murders.

Ivan Milat tried to break out of Maitland Gaol on 17 May 1997 alongside drug dealer George Savvas, but the attempt was foiled. 'With the assistance of two other inmates,' the Minister for Corrective Services told the New South Wales legislative assembly, 'these men thought they would be able to scale an eight-metre wall which bristles with razor wire, guard wire and camera and microwave surveillance. They thought they could get through gates overlooked by guard towers and staffed by officers armed with Ruger rifles.' Savvas and Milat didn't realise their plan had been detected weeks before, and a 'squad of heavily armed officers' were waiting for them. Savvas was found hanged in his cell the next day, and Milat was transferred to the maximum security wing of Goulburn Prison. (Milat tried to claim that he was framed for the escape attempt.) He appealed against his sentence on numerous occasions, even going so far as to cut off his finger to try to get attention for his case. However, despite a Facebook campaign and other social media presence by his family members, it seems highly unlikely Ivan Milat will ever see the outside of a prison again.

CHAPTER 2

Australia: Paul Charles Denyer

....

'Can you explain why we have women victims?' the police interviewer asked the twenty-one-year-old suspect who had just confessed to three savage murders.

'I just hate them,' Paul Charles Denyer replied.

'I beg your pardon,' the officer said.

'I hate them,' Denyer repeated.

'Those particular girls or women in general?'

'General.'

That misogynistic hatred was clear to all those who dealt with Denyer in the criminal justice system. 'The apprehension that you have occasioned to many thousands of women in our community will be felt for a very long time,' the judge said at his sentencing. 'For many, you are the fear that quickens their steps as they walk alone or that causes a parent to look anxiously at a clock when a child is late.' And yet a decade after his conviction for the serial killings, Denyer was in the Australian press once more – because he was interested in finding out what the state government's policy was on sex change. 'I committed those disgusting crimes . . . not because I ever hated womankind,' he wrote in 2003. 'But because I have never really felt that I was male.'

There has been a large number of cases where violent films and images have been linked to violent acts by perpetrators; some of these may not have had the causal link that those wishing to ban them might assert. However, in the case of Denyer, the link seems justified. The film that influenced him was *Stepfather II* (also known as *Stepfather 2: Make Room for Daddy*), a 1989 horror movie written by John Auerbach and directed by Jeff Burr. It starred Terry O'Quinn – later to feature in *Lost* and *Hawaii Five-0* – as the murderous stepfather of the title, who breaks out of an asylum and attacks a family; the movie was deemed insufficiently bloody by studio executives Bob and Harvey Weinstein, who insisted on more gore being added. According to Denyer, a scene in the film where the stepfather stabs someone in the neck was his guiding pattern for his attacks.

Denyer can only have seen that image after the age of sixteen but he had a penchant for violence long before then, and admitted to police he had wanted to kill since he was fourteen. He was born in Campbelltown, New South Wales, Australia, on 14 April 1972, the son of British immigrants, Anthony and Maureen, who had entered Australia seven years earlier. He was one of their six children, and never quite settled when the family moved from the Sydney area to the Melbourne suburb of Mulgrave just before his ninth birthday. He studied at Northvale Primary School and Clayton Technical School before the family moved to Long Street in Langwarrin, just east of the area that he terrorised. As a child, he displayed aberrant behaviour – possibly following a blow to the head when he was very young – slashing the throats of his younger sister's toy bears in a horrible foreshadowing of the violence he would display later. He also cut the throat of the family's young cat and hung it from the branch of a tree, and was responsible for disembowelling another feline and slitting the throats of its kittens.

He didn't get on with his new fellow students after the move, and had self-confidence issues exacerbated by weight gain during adolescence. He claimed that his father was abusive, although other members of the family have denied that. He was arrested aged twelve for stealing a car, and two months later accused of theft, wilful damage and making a false report to the emergency services.

Aged fifteen, he was charged with a rather unusual form of assault – making another boy masturbate in front of a group of other children. He was stalking women for a few years in Frankston, the area just west of where he lived, an hour or so away from Melbourne, before his first attack, and threatened the lives of his own brother and sister-in-law in 1992, forcing them to flee the country.

Denyer wasn't able to hold down a job successfully, getting fired from both a supermarket and a marine workshop. He did manage to start a relationship with Sharon Johnson, whom he met in 1992. They moved in together to a flat in Frankston, but Denyer had time on his hands as he was unemployed. The next-door flat was vandalised, a peeping tom was reported around the neighbourhood, and then, in February 1993, there was an attack on the flat of other neighbours, young parents Les and Donna. The words 'Dead Don' were scrawled on the wall in blood in one room; their cat had been disembowelled and its blood used to paint the words 'Donna – You're dead' on the wall. The rest of the apartment had been vandalised, so Donna moved in with her sister – who lived next door to Paul Denyer.

Denyer's first victim, eighteen-year-old student Elizabeth Stevens, was killed around 7 p.m. on Friday, 11 June 1993. Denyer had walked over to Langwarrin and seen Elizabeth getting off a bus on her own. By his own admission, he wasn't targeting her specifically: he just wanted to kill someone. He followed Elizabeth down the road then grabbed her, pushing a fake gun – which he had made from some aluminium piping with a wooden handle – into her side. He then walked her along the road, as if they were a courting couple, then dragged her into Lloyd Park. He knew the wet rainy night would cover the sounds of her screams.

In the park, they walked for a while, and then Denyer allowed Elizabeth to urinate. Once they got near the goalposts in the park, he started to strangle her. When she was unconscious, he then stabbed her repeatedly in the throat. 'And she was still alive,' Denyer later confessed. 'And then she stood up and then we walked around and all that, just walking around a few steps and then I threw her on the ground and stuck my foot over her neck to finish her off.' He then dragged her into a drain, and left her there with two branches on her body. The blade of his homemade knife had broken, so he dumped the pieces beside the road.

Elizabeth was found the next day in the drain in the pouring rain, which meant that, as Denyer had calculated, police were automatically at a disadvantage. Blood and other trace evidence, as well as footprints, were all washed away. Denyer had left Elizabeth lying face up with what forensic examiners described as a 'very small tree branch' across her body. Her trousers and underwear hadn't been disturbed, but the upper body was exposed, and there were massive wounds on her throat. The autopsy showed she had abrasions and bruises on her arms and hands which Dr Tony Landgren, the Senior Forensic Pathologist at the Victorian Institute of Forensic Science at the time, thought might have been defensive wounds. He believed that the victim had been rendered unconscious before the killer used the knife on her so violently – distinctive petechial haemorrhages were present. After she died, Denyer had cut her on the chest with a distinctive cross pattern (four cuts from breast to navel, and four at right angles to them) – enough to worry police that Satanists could be involved. Once the rain had stopped, the police could examine the area more closely, and not far from the body, they found a blue and white sports bag with school books in Elizabeth's name.

Homicide detectives were baffled as there seemed to be no motive for Elizabeth's brutal killing. She had left a note for her uncle and aunt, with whom she lived, to say she was going to the library and would be back at eight. Police appealed for witnesses, using a mannequin dressed in similar clothes, and were able to deduce that she had got a bus from the Central Business District in Frankston back towards her home.

For a time, police thought they had solved the case quickly, after a door was slammed in officers' faces when they were carrying out a house-to-house enquiry. When they forced entry, there was blood throughout the property – but it turned out that the owner had simply mutilated himself.

The hunt was still ongoing when, on the night of 8 July 1993, Denyer struck again. Forty-one-year-old bank clerk Rosza Toth was grabbed near Seaford station (two stops north of Frankston) in the early evening as she made her way home from work. The attacker said he had a gun, which he put to her head. She tried to bribe him with an expensive ring, but he wasn't interested, and she knew she was in a fight for her life. Denyer was able to pull out clumps of her hair, but in return she bit his fingers to the bone. When she got an opportunity, she took it and broke free, running into the middle of the road trying to stop a passing vehicle. But no one stopped, and Denyer grabbed her by the hair and told her to shut up or he would blow her head off. She nodded in acquiescence, but managed to escape again. This time a car did stop and allowed Rosza to get in. Denyer ran away into the night.

Denyer wasn't satisfied. He returned to Seaford station and went one stop down the line to Kananook, picking out another victim quickly as he crossed the footbridge over the railway track. Young mother Debra Fream, who had only given birth less than a fortnight earlier, had gone out to get some milk, leaving her baby with a family friend who had come over for dinner. She left her car unlocked as she popped into the milk bar, not realising that the man who had been walking down the road towards her was going to get into her vehicle and hide behind the driver's seat. Paul Denyer waited for her to return with her purchase, and then revealed himself. Debra panicked and smashed her car into the side of the milk bar, but Denyer pulled his 'gun' once more, and told her to drive to an unmade road, Taylors Road, in Cranbourne. There he started to strangle her with a black tracksuit cord, and when she was barely conscious, he used a homemade aluminium knife to stab her multiple times in the neck and upper body. He then dragged her body into a clump of trees, and covered it with a couple of branches. His knife had broken again so he put the pieces in his pocket, then calmly drove the car away and dumped it. The next morning, he came back to the abandoned vehicle and stole Debra's purse and her shopping from it, burying her handbag in a nearby golf course.

Debra was reported missing by her partner, and her car was spotted where Denyer had left it, over a mile from her home. There was blood on a blade of grass found in the vehicle. On 12 July, Debra's body was found in grazing land near the unmade road, ten miles from her home. Denyer had not left any direct evidence – but there were enough clues that the same perpetrator was responsible for both Debra's and Elizabeth Stevens's deaths to have police worried there was a serial killer, particularly as there had been two other unsolved homicides in the area in the previous three years. Sarah MacDiarmid disappeared in 1990 from Kananook railway station, the same place that Denyer had travelled to when he attacked Debra; the only clue was a pool of blood, but her body has never been found. (Psychics hired by an Australian TV programme thought her body had been dumped on the Mornington Peninsula.) Twenty-five-year-old Michelle Brown's body had been found in March 1992.

The women of Frankston became frightened to go out at night (men complained there were no single women at the nightclubs), and the media was convinced that there was another killing coming. Witnesses started to come forward – a tall man had been seen taking items from Debra's vehicle – and the police consulted their profiler, Claude Minisini, over the two murders. Among his deductions, he believed the killer was local, aged between eighteen and twenty-four, and unemployed.

As the investigation continued, Denyer struck again. On the night of 30 July, the body of seventeen-year-old Natalie Russell was found. She had been reported missing eight hours earlier. This time Denyer hadn't just struck at random: he had decided to attack a young woman who was walking down the bike track between two golf courses. Earlier in the day he had cut holes in the wire fences on either side of the track, large enough for him to be able to pull a victim through and into the trees. At 2.30 p.m. he lay in wait, carrying his sharpened homemade aluminium knife and a leather strap. Shortly before 3 p.m. he saw Natalie start down the track, dressed in her blue school uniform. 'I stuck about 10 yards behind her until I got to the second hole,' Denyer later explained, 'and just when I got to that hole, I quickly walked up behind her and stuck my left hand around her mouth and held the knife to her throat.' Denyer then made what would prove to be his fatal mistake – he cut his thumb with his own blade, and didn't realise that the piece of skin had adhered to Natalie's.

Natalie struggled – the police officer who found her body was adamant that she had put up 'a hell of a fight' – but stopped when he threatened to cut her throat. She then offered to have sex with him if he would let her go, but this disgusted Denyer. He forced Natalie to kneel down in front of him, and held the knifepoint near her eye. Then he made her lie down on the ground and held her by the throat before cutting her face. Natalie desperately managed to break free and started screaming. Denyer bellowed at her to shut up and told her he would kill her if she didn't. 'And she said, "What do you want from me?" I said, "All I want you to do is shut up." ' She knelt down, and Denyer put the strap round her neck to strangle her, but it broke in half. He pushed her head back and cut her throat. 'I cut a small cut at first and then she was bleeding. And then I stuck my fingers into her throat . . . and grabbed her cords and I twisted them.' With Denyer's fingers in her throat, the dying girl fainted – at which point, Denyer 'grabbed the opportunity of throwing her head back and made one big large cut which sort of cut almost her whole head off. And then she slowly died.' He then kicked her body to make sure she was dead, slashed her face again with his knife and left her lying in the dirt.

Her mother became alarmed when Natalie didn't come home on the usual bus she would take if she had gone into Frankston after school. She called the police who started an intensive search around 9 p.m., looking along the bike track that the children used as a quick cut-through. They found the holes in the cyclone fence two hours later; the discovery of her body followed quickly after.

The police realised that the serial killer was becoming more brazen and more of a risk taker – this was a daytime killing, which he had prepared meticulously, on a well-used track. Around the scene, they found small leather straps, like those used on binocular cases, which were bloodstained, and within the largest neck wound on Natalie's body, there was a small piece of skin, 2.75 cm x 0.5 cm, that came from a hand – and not Natalie's. An appeal for witnesses was made for anyone seen loitering around the golf course and more than 150 detectives met up at the Bayside Police Station in Frankston the day after Natalie's murder to begin Operation Pulsar, a door-to-door enquiry around the area.

Two young constables told the task force about a call they had received from postwoman Vikki Collins the previous day about a suspicious vehicle. Around 3 p.m., Vikki had seen a yellow Toyota Corona parked opposite the bike track, with a man inside who was slouching down to try to hide. The constables who responded found the car, with no registration plates, but there was an interim registration label on the front windscreen which gave the number. There was no one inside. The driver therefore was likely to be either a 'first grade witness' – or a suspect. 'It was a perfect example of the community taking on responsibility and being our eyes and ears,'

Detective Charlie Bezzina wrote on the twentieth anniversary of the killings.

The car was registered to Paul Charles Denyer, whose flat was in the middle of the area police had been targeting for investigation. When detectives visited Denyer, he was eager to please and very cooperative, but when they noticed cuts on his fingers, he was invited to come back to the police station. At 9.23 p.m. the formal questioning under caution began (which was videoed). He confirmed he was twenty-one years old and unemployed before being asked to give his movements for 30 July. Twenty or so minutes into the questioning, he said that the temperature gauge on his car had been 'going high', and so he had pulled in opposite the golf course to let the engine cool down. Half an hour later, he was asked to explain the long cut on his hand, which he said had happened when he caught his hand on the fan in his car. It seemed as if he had an answer for everything and could remember precisely what he was doing throughout the days on each of the murders – which made the police more suspicious. He admitted that he was near each of the scenes but he maintained that it was pure coincidence. Just before 11 p.m., Denyer was asked point blank, 'Are you responsible for the deaths of any of these women?' He denied it.

While he was at the police station, his flat was searched. The officers brought back knives, a pair of pliers and pieces of clothing for checking, along with a set of strapless binoculars from his car. The pliers matched the striations on offcuts of wire found at the bike track.

Around half past eleven, the police told Denyer they would need a blood sample and other tissue, and then left him for a few minutes, during which time Denyer chatted with the detective on guard about the policeman's Christian faith. He then admitted – when the recording wasn't running – that he was responsible for the murders. On the record, around 3.45 a.m., he repeated the confession and over the next five hours he gave details of the women's deaths in almost a drab monotone. 'I just had the feeling, that's all,' he said when he was asked why he had killed Elizabeth. 'I just wanted to kill.' He was charged at 9 a.m.

He was as cooperative telling the truth as he had seemed to be when spinning his tale, going with police to the scene of Debra Fream's murder and explaining exactly what he did, and where he buried her purse – not far from where Natalie was murdered. Three weeks later, he returned to the bike track and showed how he had crept along the grass to attack Natalie.

During the time before his trial, forensic psychologist Ian Joblin examined Denyer and explained that Denyer 'has a grandiose sense of self-importance. He has a need for constant attention with feelings of entitlement, exploitativeness, self-centredness and self-absorption . . . He finds satisfaction in abusing, degrading, humiliating and destroying his captive.'

Paul Denyer pleaded guilty to three counts of murder and on 20 December 1993, he was sentenced to life in jail with no minimum term. He successfully appealed the sentence to the Supreme Court, arguing that a minimum period should be set and, despite state opposition, the court upheld the appeal and set a non-parole period of thirty years. In prison, he decided that he wanted to be known as Paula, and made an application to find out what the rules were about gender reassignment. He wrote to another inmate that he had 'put the pieces together', claiming – in a series of blunt statements that read more like a formula or instruction manual – that he had felt like a female from birth and his crimes were an attempt to destroy those feelings.

During 2004, Denyer tried to use anti-discrimination laws to force the authorities to allow him to wear make-up and, in June that year, he underwent a medical assessment by the Department of Human Services's director of mental health after applying for a sex change.

He tried to change his name legally to Paula Denyer, but this was not permitted and, according to Australian news reports, he was investigated over four prison rapes that took place in 2012. He was still adopting mascara, lip gloss and homemade nail polish made from paint and glue, as well as a hand-sewn bra in 2013. None of this is permitted in Australian prisons – officially.

Paul Charles Denyer will be eligible for parole in December 2023. He could be released aged just fifty-one if he is successful.

CHAPTER 3

Canada: Michael Wayne McGray

....

'Half of the fun for me is remembering the details,' claimed serial killer Michael McGray shortly after pleading guilty to a savage murder, and offering to share details of over a dozen more killings with Canadian authorities, providing closure for families of victims in Ottawa, Calgary and Saint John. He is someone who admits that he's ready to kill again – in 2000, he gave fair warning of this, and in November 2010, he killed his cellmate, despite believing that the man was a 'good guy'. The savagery that McGray demonstrated during two of his killings was so excessive that a special psychiatric unit had to be set up to assist the officers who attended the scene.

Michael Wayne McGray was born on 11 July 1965 in Collingwood, Ontario, but was brought up on the east coast of Canada. According to him, he was beaten as a child, and developed an interest in serial killers at an early age – which led him to unleash his own homicidal impulses. 'It's something that builds up, and gets stronger and stronger and stronger over the months. It starts out like an urge, but then it's so strong in the end that it's almost like a hunger. It's some-thing I need,' he told the Canadian *National Post* in 2000. 'When I kill it's a big high for me.'

McGray spent much of his childhood in group homes and reform schools. In his early teens, his father kicked him out, and he started a life as a drifter. McGray couldn't remember his own path across the country, but remembered that, by the age of sixteen, he was on his own and had started to attack those that were vulnerable.

A report from the Montreal prisons system noted that he had 'an extremely violent temper', was a risk to 'not only adults but to children' and was likely to reoffend – as he did with multiple property and robbery offences.

His first confirmed murder – to which he admitted during an interview with reporters after his life sentence was confirmed – was of seventeen-year-old Gale Tucker on 24 April 1985. He was just two years older than his victim, and was travelling across the continent in an old car. Gale was hitchhiking from her home in Dartmouth, Nova Scotia, across country to Meteghan, Digby County, on the west coast, where she hoped to be hired for a new job at a fish processing plant; she was so keen to get there that she wasn't willing to wait a day for her mother to lend her the money for the bus when the banks opened. She had sent her luggage on ahead with her friend Bonnie, and didn't take any money with her. Around 5 p.m. she got in a car from Dartmouth, the first of a number of rides that she took – until she reached the village of Weymouth, Nova Scotia. No one saw the vehicle she got into there.

It belonged to Michael McGray, who claims that he was travelling with a companion (although authorities don't believe him). As they went along, McGray asked Gale for oral sex, but she refused. McGray was angered by this, stopped the truck, pulled the girl out, ripped her clothes off, and then, when she refused to stop struggling, he stabbed her repeatedly in the side with a single-edged blade. He then dumped her body by the side of the road (possibly with the help of the accomplice). He drove off without a backward glance. 'Wasn't lots to remember,' he said later of his first murder.

Gale was reported missing by her mother after a few days, and police were able to track her movements as far as Weymouth. However, there the trail ran cold, and it was only six months later, in October, that a man walking his dog in fields nearby found her skeletal remains and her clothes scattered nearby. The killer hadn't bothered trying to disguise the body in any way and it had been exposed to the elements. It took two days for dental records and jewellery to confirm it was Gale. Although her mother persisted in ensuring that the police kept the investigation open, there were no real leads, and until McGray's surprise confession, it seemed as if it would be filed as one of Canada's many unsolved homicides.

Michael McGray claimed that he was responsible for over a dozen more killings than those for which he eventually stood trial, but didn't provide sufficient evidence for cases to be properly identified. He talked of drifting from Vancouver on the west coast to Halifax on the east, and hanging around red-light and gay districts where he could find easy targets. There's no certainty, therefore, whether his next definite killing, in 1987, was simply the next of many or if there was a gap of two years between events.

In Saint John, New Brunswick, McGray teamed up with two other men – Mark Daniel Gibbons and Norm Warren – both of whom also had arrest records. On 14 November 1987, the three of them concocted a plan to rob a taxi driver. When the cab arrived, Gibbons sat himself next to the driver in the front, with the other two behind. When they reached their destination, they told the driver it was a robbery. The driver reached into his pocket for a weapon and Gibbons stabbed him in the hand; the trio then ran away.

The driver called the police, who started searching the area. Gibbons's dead body was found in the Market Square mall by a janitor – he had been stabbed a single time just below the heart. Rather to the surprise of the investigating officers, Gibbons's friends called the police the next day to find out if the officers knew where Gibbons was. The call was traced back to an apartment where they found McGray and Warren, who ran from the back door but were quickly arrested.

Warren had a history of violent crime, including the murder of a cab driver for which he had served seventeen years behind bars, while McGray was primarily known for robbery and theft. McGray said Warren had killed Gibbons; the girlfriends of all three of them confirmed enough elements of his story for the police to charge Warren with the homicide. However, to the surprise of the local police, Warren was found not guilty of homicide, although he was sent away for attempted robbery. McGray received a five-year sentence for his part in the crime.

Contrary to the police view, however, the jury had got it right. Warren wasn't responsible for Gibbons's death; McGray was. In 1999, Saint John's police inspector William Reid was contacted by the investigators who had arrested McGray. He had admitted to the homicide of Mark Gibbons. Reid and his team went to see McGray in the maximum security prison where he was being held; there he gave a very detailed confession of the crime.

When the three men abandoned the robbery, Warren ran slower than the other two, and was left behind. Near the city's YMCA building, they stopped and McGray stabbed Gibbons with a homemade knife, just below the heart. He was annoyed about the robbery going wrong but he explained that he had already decided that he was going to do something to Gibbons, as he hadn't liked him since he met him. He and Warren returned separately to their apartment building, where he passed over the knife for the trio's girlfriends to clean up. He then framed Warren for the murder, and intimidated the girls into telling as much of the story as they could without implicating McGray. Two of the girls were re-interviewed and confirmed the story.

During McGray's time in prison, he was also able to commit at least two more murders, apparently having the perfect alibi – police even discounted him from suspicion because he was behind bars in Quebec when the killings took place. However, as he later admitted, the prison system was rather more porous than those on the outside of it might care to believe, and over the Easter weekend in 1991, Michael McGray was given a three-day weekend pass. (To be fair to the authorities, at that point there was no suggestion that he was a killer, simply a robber whose crime had been foiled.) That meant that he was in Montreal at a time when to all intents and purposes no one thought he could be. For five months an urge to kill had been boiling inside him, he later told Detective Sergeant Roger Agnessi of the Montreal police; now he could let it loose.

During the 1990s, there was a wave of murders among the gay community in Montreal. According to a report in the *Globe and Mail* in November 1993, since 1989 there had been at least fourteen sex slayings of homosexual men, and the gay community was demanding a coroner's inquest into the situation. 'Many of the men killed were known to be "closet" gays who sought partners in Montreal's Gay Village,' the paper noted, adding that 'four people have been convicted in connection with the killings, while nine of the crimes remain unsolved.' Near the end of the list of fourteen victims come two names – 'Robert Assaly, 59: a retired teacher beaten to death in his Nun's Island condominium on April 7, 1991; unresolved. Gaetan Ethier, 45: the labourer was fatally stabbed in his downtown apartment April 2, 1991; unresolved.' There were ten before them, two afterwards – but these two were those for which McGray would acknowledge responsibility. By 1996 the total hit twenty-one, but by the autumn of 1997 only six of them were unsolved, including McGray's pair.

McGray had arrived in Montreal and checked in, as mandated, at the halfway house in the city's North End district on Good Friday, 29 March 1991. The next day he went to the Gay Village and started chatting with Robert Assaly. The two got on well, and Robert invited McGray back to his apartment, where they drank some more until McGray fell asleep on the couch. He woke around six the next morning to hear Robert getting dressed. McGray took a knife from the kitchen and told Robert to lie on the floor. Robert, completely misreading the situation, laughed at him, and McGray lost his temper, smashing him to the ground using a table lamp, and then stabbed him in the throat and chest multiple times. He didn't bother taking Robert's wallet, just a bottle of alcohol.

A day later, when he should have been heading back to prison, McGray returned to the Gay Village and met the unemployed Gaetan Ethier. Gaetan also invited McGray back to his apartment, to watch a movie and have a bottle of wine. He made a pass at McGray, who turned him down, and Gaetan then passed out. McGray sat and watched him through the night, then in the morning smashed a beer bottle onto his head. Gaetan was younger and stronger than Robert and fought back, trying to get to the telephone, but McGray cut through the line before stabbing him repeatedly. Once he was dead, McGray took the wine and left. He had already decided not to return to Quebec, but only stayed at liberty for a few days before being rearrested and sent back to jail.

The murders for which McGray was originally arrested, which led to his multiple confessions, were of mother and daughter Joan and Nina Hicks in Moncton in 1998. Originally from Musgrave Harbour in Newfoundland, the pair had only moved to Moncton, New Brunswick, in late 1997, after Joan – who had been involved with helping prisoners in Newfoundland – had started a communication with convict Aubrey Sparks, imprisoned for murdering his wife. The letters had become more intimate and Joan decided to move to Moncton to be closer to Sparks's prison despite her family's pleas to her not to travel that distance with an eleven-year-old girl when she had not even met Sparks in person yet.

When they arrived in Moncton, the Hickses moved into a shelter where Joan became friends with twenty-two-year-old Tammy McClain, who had problems with her boyfriend, Mike. The Hickses found an apartment and Nina settled into school. Tammy and Mike often came round to the apartment, staying for a game of cards or a coffee. On the evening of 28 February 1998, Joan got a call from Tammy, who said she needed to get away from her boyfriend. Joan naturally invited her over. Around 5 a.m., Tammy left Joan's apartment in a cab.

A few hours later, Glen Bennett went to the Moncton police station and reported that he had been present at a horrific murder but had been unable to do anything about it – as soon as he had got away from the killer, he had come to the police. Officers went to the scene he had indicated: Joan Hicks's apartment. There, they found Joan lying on the floor near the bathroom in a pool of blood, her pink nightgown pushed up around her head. She had been beaten, strangled and her throat cut with a serrated knife. Nina's bed had been slept in, but she had been choked with a belt and hung up in the closet in her underwear by a piece of rope.

Mike – or Michael McGray, to give him his full name – had followed Tammy to the Hickses apartment, along with his friend Glen Bennett, with whom he had been mainlining cocaine. McGray went to use the bathroom and called to Joan for some toilet paper. When she came to get it, he grabbed her by the throat, slammed her against the wall and strangled her. According to his own evidence, McGray wasn't sure if she was dead or not, so he went into the kitchen for a knife. He then dragged Joan, who was indeed still alive, into her bedroom and slit her throat. Bennett did nothing throughout.

He did give the police McGray's address, however, and they were quick to arrest McGray. During his various interviews, he admitted to the deaths of the two men in Montreal as well as the murder of Mark Gibbons in Saint John. He then surprised everyone on 20 March 2000 by pleading guilty to the murder of Joan Hicks – according to his lawyer, Wendell Maxwell, he only made the decision that morning – and avoided a jury trial for the murders of mother and daughter. As a result, the second murder charge, relating to Nina, was stayed pending further investigation, McGray claiming that Bennett was responsible. He was given a life sentence with no chance of parole for twenty-five years for Joan's murder.

On his way to the federal penitentiary in New Brunswick, McGray told the accompanying officers that he would confess to a whole string of crimes across Canada and down into the Seattle area of Washington state, if he got immunity from prosecution and some medical help for his mental illness. When the police turned him down, McGray contacted the media and gave the Canadian Press wire service a fifteen-minute interview. '[Killing is] just something that I really love doing,' McGray said. 'And I mean, when it comes out, I mean, some of these murders were just horrendous, right? . . . Everybody asks me "Do I have any remorse for the victims?" and I'm not going to bullshit you, I don't regret it and I don't have any remorse. The only thing that I regret really is that it ended.'

Over the next months, McGray pled guilty to the deaths of Robert Assaly and Gaetan Ethier in Montreal, and Mark Gibbons in Saint John. In 2001, the Crown filed charges related to Nina's murder, and in May, he pled guilty to that death too, and then days later to Gale Tucker's death. For all the crimes, he was given further life sentences.

McGray maintained that he would kill again – he was found with a homemade knife at the end of one conference with his defence attorney, and calmly told officers that he had thought of killing his own lawyer. For some reason, in 2010, he was transferred from maximum security Kent Institution to the medium security facility, Mountain Federal Penitentiary in Agassiz, British Columbia, where he was given a cellmate, Jeremy Phillips, who was serving a six-year sentence for aggravated assault. The other man feared for his life but his concerns weren't taken seriously.

The pair devised a plan – at least, so McGray explained – which was designed to get McGray sent back to a maximum security facility where he felt he belonged. Phillips agreed to play the part of a hostage. McGray bound him with ripped bedsheets and gagged him with a sock. It was at that point that Phillips probably realised that McGray wasn't faking: McGray strangled him with a ligature for more than five minutes, then punched him to make sure he was dead. Phillips's dead body wasn't found for about twelve hours. In the end guards only realised they were one prisoner short when McGray told them. He received yet another life term.

The inquest jury recommended that 'the Correctional Service consider single accommodation for multiple murderers'. Michael Wayne McGray is so housed now, and will remain so for the rest of his life.

CHAPTER 4

Colombia & Ecuador:
Pedro Alonso López

....

'I am the worst of the worst . . . the lowest of the low – perhaps even a complete animal,' Pedro Alonso López claimed in a police interview after he had admitted to killing over 300 girls between the ages of eight and twelve. 'Perhaps I took it too far because of my ignorance.'

In March 1980, on the day that one of his last victims was being buried, López was caught in a market place in Ecuador. Over the coming months, he would lead police to the graves of dozens of his victims, sometimes having to be restrained from trying to pose for the cameras with one of the uncovered skulls, and on others being saved from the murderous intent of the young girls' families.

López apparently only gave one interview to an English-speaking writer, renowned Canadian photojournalist Ron Laytner, while he was serving part of his sentence in Ambato. However, this was by no means the only time that he talked on record – his police interrogations were made available to the A&E *Biography* crew preparing a documentary in 2004, and that programme included excerpts from many other occasions on which he spoke to the South American press over the years. Talking to Laytner, he was keen to present a certain side to himself, and the story that he gave at that point contradicted the testimony of others, particularly with regard to his upbringing and his relationship with his mother. Laytner's article also presents a dramatic account of López's subsequent release – the prison van slipping through the gates of the jail 'in the dead of night', and López 'bundled out of the back door on to the soil of Colombia' – that doesn't tally with the news footage that shows López being taken, in daylight, to a van to shouts of 'Killer!' Laytner's story has to be assessed accordingly.

Certain facts aren't disputed. Pedro Alonso López was born on 8 October 1948 in the Colombian town of Santa Isabel, not far from the capital, Bogotá. He never knew his father: Midardo Reyes was a member of the Colombian Conservative Party during the country's civil war (known as La Violencia, which gives an idea of its nature), and was killed on 9 April 1948. His mother was Benilda López De Casteneda, and, at least according to López, she was a prostitute with whom his father had cheated. 'I am the seventh son of thirteen children,' he claimed, and certainly, speaking in 2004, his mother confirmed that he was one of a large number of siblings. Aged five, he and the family moved a hundred miles out into the country, to the town of El Espinal. As a young boy, he tried to help his brothers and sisters with their education, and even told his mother he would like to be a teacher when he grew up.

However, aged eight, López ran away to Bogotá. His version was that his mother threw him out for touching his sister's breast, and that she had been abusive to him over the years – 'it is my understanding that this woman is sick in the head,' he told police, 'because that was not the proper way to punish your children; she would punish me with such violence.' His mother claimed it was a happy home and said he simply vanished, with a fortune teller informing her that he had been taken by a neighbour. Whatever the cause, López became one of the homeless street children, known as the Gamines, who roamed the avenues of the Colombian capital in gangs, stealing where necessary to survive, fighting for his life when required, and smoking an impure form of cocaine to take away some of the pain. 'I was a very alert child, very spirited, with an innocent mind,' he said, explaining that he had become dishonest because he had been abandoned. At some point, he was raped by a man, who had offered him a bed and a hot meal but instead took him to a deserted building and attacked him. López admitted to police that while he wanted to forget what had happened, he always wanted to punish those responsible. After that, he only went out at night.

When he was ten, an elderly couple took pity on López and offered him a home. He was enrolled in a school for orphans where he started to settle down. However, two years later, López said he was molested by a male teacher at the school; he stole money from the office and ran away once more. In 1969, aged twenty-one, he was arrested for stealing a car and was gang-raped within two days of arriving behind bars. This time, he couldn't run away and was not prepared to be a victim again; instead, he made a knife, and killed them – an action deemed self-defence by the authorities, who didn't add anything to his sentence for the deaths.

He was released aged twenty-three in 1971 after serving two years, and over the next eight years he carried out hundreds of murders of young innocents, crossing between three northerly countries in South America – Peru, Colombia and Ecuador. He targeted the poorest children, ones whose absence would not be noticed so quickly – and certainly ones about whose disappearance the authorities would be less likely to be concerned. White children were rarely targeted, mainly because they were not often on their own. López told Laytner that a tourist family 'from England or Scotland' had attracted his attention, and he spent two days following them. 'I really wanted to take their beautiful blonde daughter,' he explained, 'but I never got the chance. Her parents were too watchful.'

López's hunting grounds were the market places, but his approaches would vary. Sometimes, as he told Laytner, he would search for a girl 'with a certain look on her face of innocence and beauty. She would be a good girl, always working with her mother. I followed them, sometimes for two or three days, waiting for the moment she was left alone.'

On other occasions, he would pose as a salesman and approach girls of his preferred age – between eight and twelve years old – saying he was lost, and asking for help finding the town's bus terminal. The young girls would be taken in by his charms and by his apparent helplessness and accompany him willingly; he never needed to kidnap any of them. From the market place he would take them to an area he had prepared earlier; often, he had already dug the graves. He would be solicitous of their welfare initially, and the girls would start to trust him, even if they were out overnight. 'They never screamed because they didn't expect anything would happen,' he claimed. 'They were innocent.'

However, at the first sign of daylight, López would get sexually excited. He would then force the girl into sex, and put his hands around her throat – and when the sun rose, he would strangle her. He had to commit his crimes in daylight. 'It was only good if I could see her eyes,' he admitted. 'It would have been wasted in the dark.' He said it took them between five and fifteen minutes to die, but some of his victims were strangled with such force that their eyes popped out of their sockets.

Often there would be three or four bodies placed in the same grave because, López believed, his 'little friends liked to have company', and there were times when he would interact with them even after they were dead – not in a necrophiliac way, but an almost childish manner. He would chat with them, 'like having a party', but eventually he would get bored and go looking for new girls. He particularly liked the girls in Ecuador: 'They are more gentle and trusting, more innocent.'

While in Peru, López fell foul of a local indigenous tribe, who had caught him after he had killed a number of their daughters. He was tied up and buried up to his neck in sand, then syrup was placed on his face so that the ants would come and eat him alive. Luckily for him – if not for the many more girls he would go on to kill – López was rescued by an American missionary, who promised the tribe elders she would hand López over to the police to face justice. He was placed in the back of her Jeep, still tied up, but when they reached the border with Colombia, the trusting woman simply released him.

López continued killing as he travelled through Ecuador, eventually meeting eleven-year-old Hortensia Garcés Lozada as she was selling newspapers on the streets of Ambato on 5 May 1979. He gave her 100 sucres (at the time worth about $10 US), then led her to a deserted spot beneath a bridge on the outskirts of the town where he beat, raped, then strangled her. Her body was covered with the newspapers she had been selling to help her mother. Her father, Leonidas, searched for her and reported her missing to the police, but as with all of López's victims, the authorities took no action, saying that as far as they were concerned, the girl was a runaway who had failed her school year.

One of his last victims was Ivanova Jacome, the nine-year-old daughter of a successful baker, who disappeared while taking a snack to her father on Friday, 15 February 1980. Initially he believed she might have been taken for ransom and, because of his status in the community, his pleas for help from the police were taken more seriously. He and his wife posted flyers offering rewards of 20,000 sucres – a huge sum – for any news on their daughter's whereabouts. Thanks to their efforts, national newspapers began to cover the story, with *La Verdad* giving front-page coverage to 'Kidnap of girls in Ambato'. Ambato's citizens went on high alert and tension mounted as bodies of young girls were discovered, all raped and strangled. However, the police had nothing with which to work to even begin to identify a suspect; López never left any of his victims alive, and because they went with him willingly, it wasn't as if there were witnesses to their disappearances alerted by screams or other upsets.

On 8 March, a young girl's body was found in an abandoned shack on a farm near the town – it was Ivanova Jacome. The next day, the devastated parents prepared to bury their daughter, as a stranger sold chains, padlocks and trinkets in the market place. Around 4 p.m. he approached Carlina Ramon Poveda, and asked if she would sell him food; both she and her ten-year-old daughter Alicia noticed that he seemed to be trying to get the young girl's attention. 'He would look at me strangely,' Alicia told reporters nearly a quarter of a century later, 'and gesture for me to come over. I went to my mother and told her, "You know what, Mummy? This man keeps looking at me ugly and keeps calling me to come to him."' Her mother saw the stranger leaving, and she and other stall-holders went after him, dragging him back into the market place. Poveda accused him of being the murderer, and he denied it, saying he was a humble man, not a thief. However, he was still taken to the police station for questioning.

López refused to say anything for hours, but eventually he began to converse with Captain Cordova, who started to gain the killer's trust – at which point López confessed that he had raped and murdered over 300 young girls in three countries. It seemed almost unbelievable, but soon López proved it by taking the police to the various sites, and seemed to revel in the attention he was now getting. Dubbed 'The Monster of the Andes', and more specifically 'El Monstruo de Los Mangones' (referring to Andean pastures) by *La Verdad*, he spoke freely to interviewers. 'When you die, you totally lose your emotions, your vision, your ability to see – in death you can forget who you are. Everything you did is now darkness,' he explained.

It took six weeks to track down the bodies across eleven Ecuadorian provinces, during which time López displayed no regret over his actions. The killer had a very clear memory of his crimes, able to give the police dates and times as well as descriptions of the victims. Most people didn't realise that López was with the police as they carried out the search – to avoid him being lynched, he was put in uniform – after one of the first graves that he showed them was that of Hortensia Lozada, whose bones had corroded after ten months in the wild. The clothes were still intact enough for her family to identify them, and her father Leonidas screamed for justice when he recognised López, throwing rocks at the murderer, with the police reluctantly forced to protect him. In all, fifty-seven bodies were disinterred.

Based on the detail López provided in his confession, he was charged with 110 counts of murder. Under Ecuadorian law, however, those found guilty of multiple homicide faced the same penalty as those found guilty of one – a sixteen-year prison sentence. On 31 July 1981, he pled guilty to the murders of fifty-seven girls, and received that sentence. That did not go down well with the families, many of whom thought he should have been executed, and a reform of the law was sought.

He was initially incarcerated at Ambato prison. He spoke with a local reporter, stating bluntly that he was the 'author of these acts' and 'I declare myself guilty.' He claimed that he had killed because of the abuse he had received as a child; on other occasions he said he killed the girls because they were poor and he was saving them from a terrible life – in court he even went so far as to say that he was sent by God to deliver the girls' souls to heaven.

At one point, he did try to evade responsibility, claiming that an alternate personality, 'Jorge Patino', carried out the murders. 'I did not commit [the murders], I participated in the acts and was involved in them,' he said to another local reporter. 'He [Patino] was threatening to kill me, and if I left him, he would kill me.'

Standard psychiatric evaluation was carried out, which not surprisingly showed López was a sociopath who suffered from a personality disorder, not knowing right from wrong or feeling any trace of guilt or remorse for his crimes. When asked if he felt anything while he was strangling the girls, he said he didn't and made an analogy with someone shooting another person with a gun. The person who's shot feels the pain, he explained, not the shooter.

After two years he was transferred to the García Moreno prison in Quito, Ecuador, where he was placed in Pabellón D, among other murderers and rapists – including Daniel Camargo Barbosa, who carried out a similar murderous spree (see the next chapter). He spent much of his time alone, smoking, writing in a diary and carving coins with Christ on one side and the Devil on the other. On 31 August 1994, he was released after fourteen years for good behaviour.

He spent just one hour free before being taken back into custody so he could be deported to Colombia. The next day, he was handed over at the border of the two countries, where he was processed by the Colombian security agency, Departamento Administrativo de Seguridad (DAS). He was charged with a murder from December 1979 but, in late 1995, he was declared insane and put on the psychiatric wing of a Bogotá prison. Three years later, a psychiatrist said he was now sane and he paid a mere $50 fine before being released.

After visiting his mother – and making her sell her chair and her bed to give him money – he disappeared. The last heard of him was in October 2002 when Interpol released an advisory that they were looking for López after another victim was found. Since then, nothing. Maybe his victims' families finally caught up with him . . .

CHAPTER 5

Colombia & Ecuador:
Daniel Camargo Barbosa

....

Ecuadorian parents slept easier in their beds after the conviction of Pedro Alonso López, the Monster of the Andes, who had been caught in 1980 and given the maximum permissible sentence for his multiple rapes and murders, that of sixteen years. While there was a groundswell of opinion seeking a change in the law, so that such heinous crimes could be given a proper punishment, many hoped that it would not be relevant in their lifetimes: surely there couldn't be two such people alive.

Their hopes were dashed when the crimes of Daniel Camargo Barbosa were revealed just six years later. The Colombian serial killer admitted responsibility for the deaths of seventy-two girls in Ecuador, although his final tally was likely at least double. Nobody had suspected that a man in his fifties could possibly be responsible for such carnage; police believed that the multiple bodies they had been finding over the past two years had been the work of a gang. But these murders were by no means the first that he had carried out.

Camargo was born on 22 January 1930 in Colombia, and, after the death of his mother, his father remarried. His new wife – at least, according to Camargo – did not like boys (because of some trauma in childhood), and therefore dressed young Daniel as a girl on occasions, perhaps so that she might love him. Instead, other boys simply made fun of him, and he began to hate his stepmother. Otherwise, little is known of his early years.

His first conviction, for petty theft, came when he was twenty-eight; his next was six years later for the sexual assault of a number of young girls – a major escalation in his criminal behaviour. It had been caused after he met a woman called Esperanza, whom he planned to marry. By this stage, he already had two children from another less formal relationship, but Esperanza was the love of his life. The only problem, as far as Camargo was concerned, was that she wasn't a virgin (she was twenty-eight when he learned this). This began Camargo's obsession with virgins, and Esperanza agreed to help him find some virgins with whom he could have sex, as long as he stayed with her. She would entice unsuspecting young girls to an apartment, drug them with seconal sodium sleeping pills and then, once they were unconscious, Camargo would rape them. They got away with this four times; on the fifth, the girl went to the authorities, and the pair were arrested and taken to separate prisons.

Camargo was convicted on 10 April 1964, and it seemed as if he was going to get away with the judicial equivalent of a slap on the wrist – a mere three-year sentence – for the crimes. He was duly grateful, promising that he had realised the error of his ways. However, the case was taken over by another judge who had a far more hard-line approach, and Camargo received an eight-year sentence. Camargo was furious at this, and was anything but a model prisoner throughout his term. It seems that at this point he also decided that he would not leave any future victims alive to identify him.

Released in 1972, he travelled to Brazil, where he was arrested the following year for a lack of documentation. Giving a false name to the authorities, he was deported back to Colombia and released before the Brazilians received a copy of his criminal record from their Colombian counterparts. Basing himself in Barranquilla, he got a job as a street vendor, selling television screens. In late April 1974, he kidnapped a nine-year-old girl, raped and then murdered her – and was caught before he buried her, apparently because he returned to the scene of the crime to collect the TV monitors that he had left there in his haste. This was just the most recent in a series of deaths that were attributed to 'The Sadist of Chanquito', and Camargo was likely responsible for many of them (some sources suggest up to eighty – although Pedro Alonzo López was of course also active at this time in the same area). However, he was tried and convicted of just the one, and sentenced to thirty years in prison – although this was reduced to twenty-five on appeal. On Christmas Eve 1977, he was sent to the apparently escape-proof prison on the tiny island of Gorgona, off the Pacific coast.

Camargo was an extremely well-educated man by the end of his time on Gorgona – a journalist who interviewed him a few years later noted that he could quote from Hesse, Vargas Llosa, García Márquez, Guimarães Rosa, Nietzsche, Stendhal and Freud, all authors whose works he had studied while trapped on the eleven-square-mile island – although whether he was aware of the works of Henri Charrière (aka Papillon) is unknown. What is certain is that he looked at the currents in the same way that the Devil's Island convict had prior to his escape in 1945, and worked out a way of navigating a small boat across the waters. In November 1984, he escaped.

Since the waters around the island were infested with sharks, and there was no clear evidence that he had made it to land, the authorities gave him up for dead and the Colombian press went so far as to report that the monster had been eaten by the sharks. In fact, he arrived in Quito without problem, and at the start of December 1984, he took a bus to Guayaquil, the largest city in Ecuador with over half of the population of the province within its borders. It would be his base for the next fifteen months as he carried out a series of savage attacks.

The first victim was a nine-year-old girl, who disappeared from the city of Quevedo, in Los Rios province between the mountains and the Pacific coast, on 18 December 1984; the next day a ten-year-old girl disappeared. At least fifty-four rapes and murders took place in and around Guayaquil, all down to Camargo. The police were convinced it must be the work of a gang of sadistic rapists, not the pen-seller in his mid-fifties who slept on benches, and occasionally had some small items of jewellery or children's clothing to sell.

Camargo – or Manuel Solis Bulgarin, as he called himself – had a very simple way of working. As a reporter for *El Pais* would note when interviewing him in prison a few years later, he spoke in an educated tone of voice, and could easily pass for a priest or a high-school teacher. Those he approached on the streets were poor, helpless, young lower-class girls who were easily taken in by this, to them, old man who claimed that he was looking for a Protestant priest in a church on the outskirts of the town. He would tell them that he had to give the priest a large sum of money – which he would show them – and offer them a reward for helping him find his way. No one suspected anything untoward, seeing a young girl with someone who could be her grandfather.

He would then head towards the woods, claiming he thought it might be a shortcut. If the girl demurred, he let them go back to town; if they continued trusting him, their faith was rewarded by being raped, strangled and sometimes stabbed with a knife or scissors if they resisted too much. He was stronger than he looked – one of his victims was a karate expert but he still managed to overpower her. He would then leave their bodies in the open, where the heat of the tropics would reduce the bodies to mush, and the local birds of prey would do their work, picking the bones clean of flesh.

On 26 February 1986, he was seen acting suspiciously by two policemen guarding an official's residence on Los Granados avenue – in fact, he had just killed nine-year-old Elizabeth Telpes. He was arrested and his bag checked. Inside were Telpes's clothes, and her clitoris which he had cut off, as well as a copy of Dostoevsky's *Crime and Punishment*. He was taken to Guayaquil, where he gave his name as Bulgarin initially before his true identity became known after he was identified by one of his rape victims, María Alexandra Vélez. He then admitted responsibility for the seventy-two deaths, and took police to the sites of those not yet found – news footage of one such excursion that can be seen on YouTube shows how calm and matter-of-fact he was about the whole process.

On 31 May, he confirmed that he had acted alone, and he underwent psychiatric examination during the following month. During these interviews, he admitted that he had kept 'a piece' of each of his victims, and even claimed that he had fallen in love with some of them. He had chosen virgins 'because they cried', and because women were intrinsically not what he expected them to be. Francisco Febres Cordero, a journalist on the newspaper *Hoy*, inveigled his way in with the psychiatrists – since the police didn't want to let him be interviewed, and besides, Camargo was asking for a large fee for his story – and noted that 'he had an answer for everything and was able to speak of God and the Devil equally'.

He was convicted in 1989, and given a sixteen-year sentence. He was sent initially to the local prison, not far from where he had carried out many of his murders. While there, he was housed in a former machine shop, and constantly monitored to make sure he wasn't attacked or killed. He was later moved to García Moreno prison in Quito, where he claimed he had converted to Christianity, but also told the press that he remained untouched because 'I control the convicts with subtle intelligence.' Unlike during his first spell in prison, he was a model prisoner, and by November 1994 had amassed two years off his sentence for good behaviour.

Pedro Alonzo López was another inmate at García Moreno, and was released in August 1994; three months later, Camargo also left prison – but not in the way he wanted. On 13 November 1994, fellow prisoner Giovanny Arcesius Noguera Jaramillo killed him. All that the victims' families regretted, according to the papers, was that he hadn't tortured Camargo before killing him . . .

CHAPTER 6

Colombia & Ecuador: Luis Alfredo Garavito Cubillos

....

It perhaps says something about the Colombian police system that even after the actions of both Pedro Alonzo López and Daniel Camargo Barbosa in the 1970s and 1980s, they still did not put together the facts regarding the handiwork of 'La Bestia' (The Beast) Luis Alfredo Garavito Cubillos, with each separate police department initially believing that they had their own problem to deal with. For nearly seven years between 1992 and 1999, Garavito was able to kill more than 200 children aged between eight and thirteen years old (as well as one handicapped sixteen-year-old). Only after the discovery on 24 June 1998 of the corpses of three children, who had been tortured, killed and dismembered, was a task force assembled, which eventually brought him to justice.

Although most English-language accounts imply that Garavito's murderous ways only began in 1992, it is clear from local documentation that he had raped dozens of children in the twelve years prior to that – one estimate put it at a minimum of one child per month during that time, with up to four in some months. Between 1980 and 1989, the number of reported cases of child rape increased considerably in the coffee-growing belt of Circasia, Armenia, Calarca, Pereira, Santa Rosa de Cabal and Manizales. Garavito admitted that he took pleasure in raping children, biting their nipples, mutilating their arms and burning them on the sides of the buttocks. On some occasions, he cut off the children's thumbs as souvenirs, but stopped the practice when he realised that this would allow a sniffer dog to track him.

Garavito was born on 27 January 1957 in the township of Génova, Quindío, the eldest of seven children. He was only educated to fifth grade, leaving school because he had a poor memory. He claimed that his father was a sexist, violent womaniser and alcoholic, and that he regularly saw his father attacking his mother – indeed, on occasions, his father would tie him up while he beat his mother, even when she was heavily pregnant. His father was quite happy to send him on errands, but otherwise he was a 'bastard' or an 'imbecile'. He recalled sharing a bed with his mother, and her stroking him as he played with his genitals. He maintained that he was raped a number of times by a local drugstore owner, a friend of his father, who bit his penis and buttocks, and burned him with a candle – after this, Garavito killed and tore apart two small birds. He was also raped by another man after showing his dislike of heterosexual pornography. His homosexual urges grew, and he began fondling his younger brothers while they slept.

He was fifteen years old when he attacked his first victim, near the railway station in the city of Buga. He said that all he wanted to do was caress the boy, not rape him, but the youth screamed and a policeman stopped him. He wasn't imprisoned, and as the situation at home grew worse, Garavito began working on a farm, where he found himself more popular than he expected, even making platonic friends with one of the local girls. Over the years, he would have a number of relationships with women, often a decade or so older than him, which would begin well but then descend into confrontation, violence and jealousy.

Garavito began drinking, and when he got a job working at a bakery in Armenia, he was introduced to the local chapter of Alcoholics Anonymous, which helped him deal with normal day-to-day life. The only problem was that Garavito's life was anything but normal. Beneath his respectable facade, he was still drinking and was a regular visitor to Valencia park, where children sold their bodies at night. He found it hard to live this double life, and ended up getting sacked from his job. As he had paid social insurance since 1979, he was entitled to medical help and went to the doctor. Sent to a psychiatrist, Garavito claimed that he felt suicidal because he wanted to have children; he didn't mention that he was impotent with women, or that he was sexually attracted to children. He was put on anti-depression medication.

Finding a job at a supermarket, he began a relationship with a beautician, Claudia, who had a fourteen-year-old son. Garavito didn't have sex with her but was managing to keep his other impulses under control with the aid of Alcoholics Anonymous. However, he grew increasingly attracted to the youths who came into the super-market, and eventually started to use his two-hour lunch breaks to go to the neighbouring town of Quimbaya, where he raped local youths. Towards the end of 1980 and the start of 1981, he needed more and began attacking his targets with razors, candles and light-ers. The more violence he exercised against his victim, the more intense was his orgasm. Garavito would wake up crying as he remembered his victims – but then would start to laugh as he recalled the pleasure and the orgasms he had after each torture. He maintained a list of his victims, for whom he would pray.

This led him deeper and deeper into depression and, in January 1984, he was hospitalised for thirty-three days at a psychiatric clinic and put on Sinogan and Vicilan. When he was released, he went to Pereira, where he refined his technique for attracting children: he would claim that he needed help handling some small calves, and ask the children to help him, offering to pay them 500 or 1,000 pesos. The children would trust him, and go along willingly into the coffee plantations or wooded glens, where they would be attacked. He would be hospitalised on a number of occasions during the decade, but each time he persuaded the doctors he was better and was released to fulfil his desire to rape and torture. He was imprisoned for a short time, but not for rape or torture: he stole some jewellery from a friend, who turned him in to the police. He was fascinated by the case of Campo Elías Delgado, a war veteran who carried out a massacre at a restaurant in Bogotá on 4 December 1986; his other interests included the life of Adolf Hitler and the story of Dr Jekyll and Mr Hyde.

He returned to Pereira, and there continued his own variant of Robert Louis Stevenson's tale – living with Graciela Zabaleta and her son Rodolfo, and apparently making many friends, all the while raping, and starting to kill, victim after victim. Only very occasionally did any friends get a glimpse of this other life: his acquaintances Jairo Toro and Ancizar Valencia stayed in the same block as him for a time, and recalled that he was drinking heavily and often took twelve- to fourteen-year-old boys of 'humble appearance' back to his room.

It wasn't long before he took rape and torture to the next level. A report in *Pana* in 1993 noted that the skeletal remains of a young boy had been found in Jamundí, Valle del Cauca, with some of his front teeth missing, signs of torture to the soles of the feet, and his genitals absent. This was Juan Carlos, a young lad who had the misfortune to walk past the bar where Garavito was drinking. Garavito spotted him, paid his bar bill and followed the boy. When Juan stopped, Garavito nipped into a shop and bought a butcher's knife and a bottle of the cheapest gut-rot alcohol. He spun his normal tale to the boy, who followed him unsuspectingly, crossing over a railway line into the woods. Garavito recalled that when he saw the reflection of the full moon in water nearby, he was transported back to his childhood. That reignited his hatred and he felt an urge to kill Juan Carlos, to which he gave in.

Six days later he killed again while on the way to see his sister Esther, the only one of his siblings with whom he had stayed in touch. It was a hot day, and he started drinking at 10 a.m.; by mid-afternoon he was drunk, and killed twelve-year-old Jhon Alexander Peñaranda. His next eight victims were in Bogotá, where he took pleasure in mutilating the corpses even further, sometimes cutting the children's intestines out and placing them on the body. Three of the children were never identified. Towards the end of the year, he carried out multiple killings on the same day – all carefully written down in his diary, along with receipts for his various bus journeys between killing grounds. Occasionally, a child would fight back – one managed to cut the tendons in Garavito's hand – but it made little difference to the final outcome.

In February 1994, he killed thirteen-year-old Jaime Andrés González near Tuluá, but afterwards he got a guilty conscience, and believed that someone was telling him that he was worthless. He therefore went and buried the knife and stopped killing for a time, seeking refuge in the Bible – and also in forms of witchcraft. He came to believe that he was doing the Devil's work.

There were more killings in the Valle region in 1995 – four children between the ages of eight and ten. Two of them were cousins, and all came from a poor background. Each disappeared shortly before midday, and all were found on the slope of a hill, where high-growing plants hid everything from view; Garavito hadn't bothered burying them. In the summer of 1996, he was active around the town of Boyacá: on 8 June, a boy went missing after being seen in a local shop with a stranger who had bought him and his friends some sweets. The boy had followed the man on his own bike; five days later, his decapitated corpse was found with his severed penis inserted in the mouth. Garavito was questioned, but said he had just bought the sweets and not seen the boy afterwards. Only three or four days later, he killed another boy in Pereira. In January 1997, he was active once more in Bogotá, this time disguised as a Franciscan monk. Eight-year-old Jimmy was the first of three victims that time.

The discovery of three corpses two years later in Génova, once again on the slope of a hill, was the catalyst for more action by the authorities than previously. One of the three bodies had been there for some time, but they were clearly the work of the same person: they were all tied at the hands, the necks had been deeply cut, the genitalia severed off. There were bite marks and signs of anal penetration, as well as a bottle of lubricant. The investigators soon learned that one of the boys had told his mother he was helping a man with a cattle transport; all of them had disappeared mid-morning.

A special committee of investigators from the Attorney General's office was created to look into the case. When the number of such unsolved murders became clear, the investigators pondered various motives – child prostitution, Satanism (thanks to the traces of wax found at the crime scenes), organ trafficking and paedophilia. In November 1998, a mass grave was found in Nacaderos, containing the skeletons of fourteen boys aged between eight and fourteen. Forensic reconstructions had to be made after other avenues failed – and this case marked the first time that the technique was used for identifying children. Study of the bones from assorted sites suggested that in fact there might only be one person responsible for such a plethora of cases.

The investigators began to build a profile of the killer, as more bodies were found on 6 February 1999 in Palmira. Garavito had left various pieces of evidence at the scene including shoes, eyeglasses and money, which led prosecutors to believe that he had been running from something. The state of the shoes also suggested that the killer had a limp and would rotate his foot as he walked, the various physical items gave a height range of 1.63 to 1.67 metres, and the prescription in the glasses dealt with a particular condition that only afflicted people of a certain age. Trace evidence on the notes showed that the killer travelled extensively around the country.

Officers were sent undercover into the homeless community, seeking clues to the man's identity.

Using the forensic clues, a list of twenty-five suspects was drawn up, which included Garavito: he had been a suspect in the 1996 murder of twelve-year-old Renald Delgado in Tunja. Garavito had been seen with the boy by the owner of a store and several local prostitutes; he had been interrogated but released because of insufficient evidence. In his statement, he mentioned he had been to various places in which bodies had been found.

The investigation didn't go smoothly. In Pereira, Pedro Pablo Ramírez García was a suspect in the rapes and murders of boys over the same period as Garavito had been active. Ramírez was arrested and denied the murders – and while he was in jail, four more boys were killed. After premature celebrations were put on hold, the search intensified. Garavito's sister Esther was questioned and she handed over a box that Garavito had given to her for safe keeping – which included pictures of the children and his list of victims. One receipt in the bag was for money transferred to a woman in Pereira – and at the address, they found another bag, chronicling Garavito's travels from 1994 to 1997, as well as assorted other items that matched those found at the crime scenes.

The state of the glasses and other evidence found in Palmira suggested that the killer had been burned, and investigators discovered he had travelled to Pereira to get help from a pharmacist before disappearing. However, now they knew he had burns on his arm, his left side and his leg.

On 22 April 1999, Garavito tried to rape Ivan Sabogal, a boy in Villavicencio, Meta; a homeless man disturbed them and the boy escaped, getting a storeowner to call the police. Garavito had followed Ivan and the homeless man but then vanished when they found the storeowner. It seemed as if Garavito had escaped but as the police drove Ivan back to headquarters, he saw Garavito. When he was asked where he was going, he gave an obviously false reply, and was arrested. At the police station, he said he had lost his identity papers, and claimed he was Bonifacio Morera Lizcano. He had used many different aliases or nicknames – Alfredo Salazar and Goofy (after the Disney character) primary among them – during his travels.

In July 1999, the prosecutors and scientific and research teams from all the different departments across the country that had suffered such crimes came together. It became evident that there were many common links between the murders: the positions of the bodies, while synthetic fibre ties, plastic bags, bottles and caps from bottles of alcoholic drinks were found at each.

One of Garavito's friends, Umbar Toro, agreed to help investigators and was fitted with an electronic wire before meeting Garavito in prison. Eventually Garavito told her about another bag of mementos that was held by the wife of another prisoner. When that was retrieved, it gave the police more solid evidence.

Garavito wasn't going to admit to his crimes freely, however. He used every trick he could to disguise who he was – changing the way he signed documents from paper to paper, for example – but the scientists were able to get hairs from his cells for DNA tests against the bottles found at the crime scenes, and carried out eye exams on every prisoner (not just him, in case he realised what they were trying to do) to match the prescription of the discarded glasses. Despite all this, Garavito denied everything for over eight hours.

Then one of the lead detectives, Aldemar Duran, was brought in to interrogate him. He talked through all of Garavito's ways of attracting boys, and what he did to them once he had them. It took eighteen hours but on 28 October 1999 Garavito broke, and told Duran and his team everything that he had done, although he claimed that he had been possessed by an evil spirit at the time.

'Luis Alfredo Garavito has admitted the murder of about 140 children, of which we have so far found 114 skeletons, and we're still investigating the disappearance of other children,' Colombia's chief prosecutor, Alfonso Gómez, told the press on 30 October.

Because of his various confessions, no trial was required under Colombian law and effectively he was sentenced to 1,853 years in prison . . . although under the 2000 reform of the Colombian Penal Code, no prisoner can stay imprisoned for more than forty years. There were concerns that he was given a thirty-year sentence for only one of his crimes, and, since he had cooperated with the authorities, he might be released early. He even made a public apology for his crimes: 'I ask the Colombian people to forgive me,' he said, 'to give me the opportunity which maybe I deprived many people of.' Not just the Colombians, but the neighbouring Ecuadorians found this unpalatable – Garavito had crossed the border occasionally and there are outstanding charges against him there. The Colombian judiciary clarified in 2011 that there was no question of him getting out of prison any time in the near future – at the very earliest he was ten years away from a potential release after serving the sentence for one charge, and there are forty-eight others he still faces.

CHAPTER 7

Great Britain: Jack the Ripper – The Whitechapel Murders

Few serial killers have excited so much interest – both at the time of their murderous sprees and in the years that have followed – as Jack the Ripper, the killer of (at least) five women in Whitechapel in London in 1888. Perhaps it's because he (and on this occasion, it's 99 per cent certain it was a man) has never been positively identified – despite a cottage industry of books from criminologists, crime-fiction authors and plenty of gifted amateurs all claiming that they have found the defining piece of evidence that nails Montague John Druitt or the Queen's surgeon Sir William Withey Gull or painter Walter Sickert or one of the dozens of other suspects once and for all. Great fictional detectives – from Sherlock Holmes (on multiple occasions) to 1970s stalwarts Charlie Barlow and John Watt – have pitted their wits against him. But no one knows the truth – and nearly 130 years later, it seems highly unlikely that, bar the invention of a time machine or some other way of seeing the past, we ever will know. Accordingly, this entry will be rather different from others in this volume as it's impossible to chart the route that led the killer to begin his crimes.

According to the Metropolitan Police, eleven murders were collectively referred to as 'The Whitechapel Murders': Emma Elizabeth Smith, Martha Tabram, Mary Ann (Polly) Nichols, Annie Chapman, Elizabeth Stride, Catherine Eddowes, Mary Jane Kelly,

Rose Mylett, Alice McKenzie, Frances Coles and an unidentified woman whose torso was found under a railway arch in Pinchin Street. Nichols, Chapman, Stride, Eddowes and Kelly are generally regarded as the work of Jack the Ripper, but all of the others have been linked at various times.

Emma Elizabeth Smith was certainly believed to be the very first victim of Jack the Ripper by some of the detectives who worked on the case at the time, including Detective Constable Walter Dew, later to gain fame as the man who caught Dr Henry Crippen. Smith was a prostitute who was working in Whitechapel on the night of the Easter Monday bank holiday in 1888; early in the hours of Tuesday, 3 April, she was assaulted and robbed at the corner of Osborn Street and Brick Lane, but managed to get back to her lodging house in Spitalfields. She told the deputy keeper, Mary Russell, that two or three men had attacked her, and Russell took her to the London Hospital. One of her assailants had inserted a blunt object into her vagina, which had ruptured her peritoneum. This led to acute peritonitis, from which she died at 9 a.m. on 4 April. Before Emma died, she gave no description of her attackers, who could have been working for the gang to whom she paid from her takings. The case was investigated by Inspector Edmund Reid (the real-life basis for the character at the heart of the TV series *Ripper Street*), who had recently taken over as Local Inspector and Head of the CID at H Division in Whitechapel from Inspector Fred Abberline. However, with no real evidence to go on, he was unable to bring anyone to trial.

The day after the next bank holiday, which came at the beginning of August, saw another death that was definitely seen as the start of the Ripper's work by no less than Inspector Abberline, who was in charge of the hunt for the maniac, and Assistant Commissioner Robert Anderson, as well as Dew. Late on 6 August, streetwalker Martha Tabram and fellow prostitute Mary Ann

Connelly were drinking in the Angel and Crown with a pair of soldiers. Mary went with her client to Angel Alley for sex, Martha and hers went to George Yard, a parallel street. Around 2 a.m., Police Constable Thomas Barrett asked a grenadier who was loitering in the vicinity of George Yard what he was doing there, and he said he was waiting for a friend. Around 3.30, Albert George Crow walked up the stairs in George Yard Buildings and passed a figure apparently asleep on the first floor. Ninety minutes later, dockworker John Saunders Reeves came down on his way to work and realised the figure was dead. He raised the alarm, and PC Barrett sent for Dr Timothy Killeen to examine the body. The doctor estimated that Martha had been dead for around three hours: she had been stabbed thirty-nine times with a short blade around 2.30 a.m.

Reid was once again in charge, and sent Barrett to the Tower of London to see if he could identify the soldier. He was uncertain, and changed his mind; his second choice had a strong enough story that Reid had to dismiss him from the investigation. Mary Ann Connelly couldn't identify anyone at her own identity parade at the Tower of London, but her evidence suggested it might be a Coldstream Guard, so she was sent to Wellington Barracks to check the soldiers there. The two potential suspects she picked both had strong alibis. Following that, the case foundered. Deputy Coroner Collier accepted that Inspector Reid had done all he could, but 'was sorry for several reasons that the perpetrator of this crime, which was one of the most horrible crimes that had been committed for some time past, the details being so horrible that there was a refinement of brutality about some parts which was nothing less than fiendish, had not been traced'.

The first murder that is accepted by all students of the Whitechapel Murders as being carried out by Jack the Ripper was that of Polly Nichols on 31 August 1888. She was last seen alive at 2.30 that morning, on the corner of Osborn Street and Whitechapel

Road. At 3.40 a.m., her body was found by a cart driver named Charles Cross (also referred to as Charles Allen Lechmere) in front of a gated stable entrance in Buck's Row (which was later renamed Durward Street). The night she died, the alcoholic prostitute had been refused a bed at lodgings at 18 Thrawl Street because she didn't have the fourpence she needed to pay for it; she had slurred that the new bonnet that she had acquired would attract a client who would provide the money. Her last words to her roommate, Emily Holland, at 2.30 as she leaned drunkenly against a wall, were to the effect that she had already earned a shilling that evening, enough to pay for the bed three times over, but had drunk it away. Emily tried to persuade her to come back to their lodging house, but Polly refused, and headed off down East Whitechapel Road in search of another client.

Polly Nichols was found lying on the ground with her skirt around her waist. Cross and another cart driver, Robert Paul, felt her hands and face, and realised they were cold. Cross thought there might be some movement in her chest, and he and Paul went to find a constable on their way to work. Police Constable Jonas Mizen was on patrol, and Cross told him of their discovery and that 'she looks to me to be either dead or drunk, but for my part, I believe she's dead'.

The body was actually on the beat of PC John Neil, who shone his lantern on Polly's face, and saw her eyes staring into space – and the deep gashes across her throat. Fellow constable John Thain came to help, and Neil sent him to get the surgeon, Dr Llewellyn, who arrived and estimated her time of death as 3.30 or so. Neil had heard nothing around that time.

As with all the Ripper victims, the evidence at the inquest, begun on 2 September and concluded on 24 September, was clear as to the state in which the killer had left the body.

> Five teeth were missing, and there was a slight laceration of the tongue. There was a bruise running along the lower part

of the jaw on the right side of the face. That might have been caused by a blow from a fist or pressure from a thumb. There was a circular bruise on the left side of the face which also might have been inflicted by the pressure of the fingers. On the left side of the neck, about 1 in. below the jaw, there was an incision about 4 in. in length, and ran from a point immediately below the ear. On the same side, but an inch below, and commencing about 1 in. in front of it, was a circular incision, which terminated at a point about 3 in. below the right jaw. That incision completely severed all the tissues down to the vertebrae. The large vessels of the neck on both sides were severed. The incision was about 8 in. in length. The cuts must have been caused by a long-bladed knife, moderately sharp, and used with great violence.

No blood was found on the breast, either of the body or the clothes. There were no injuries about the body until just about the lower part of the abdomen. Two or three inches from the left side was a wound running in a jagged manner. The wound was a very deep one, and the tissues were cut through. There were several incisions running across the abdomen. There were three or four similar cuts running downwards, on the right side, all of which had been caused by a knife which had been used violently and downwards. The injuries were from left to right and might have been done by a left-handed person. All the injuries had been caused by the same instrument.

Although Dr Llewellyn commented at the time on the small amount of blood ('about enough to fill two wine glasses, or half a pint at the most'), the blood had soaked into her clothes and hair, and, according to PC Thain, when her body was moved there was a 'mass of congealed blood' beneath it.

The police had little evidence with which to work. Local rumour suggested that 'Leather Apron' was responsible, and Polish Jew John Pizer, who was known by that nickname and had a reputation for terrorising local prostitutes, was arrested on 10 September, but had to be freed because his alibis checked out. Police Sergeant William Thicke, who arrested Pizer, is believed to have had a grudge against him, as presumably did one H. T. Haslewood of Tottenham, who repeated the accusation in a letter to the Home Office the following year. Pizer was named by some newspapers, who had to pay him compensation. Polly Nichols was buried on 6 September 1888; by then at least one other who plied her trade had been dispatched by her killer.

At the conclusion of the inquest into Polly Nichols's death, Coroner Wynne Baxter noted that 'the similarity of the injuries' in her case and that of Annie Chapman 'is considerable'. 'I suggest to you as a possibility that these two women may have been murdered by the same man with the same object,' Baxter told the jury, 'and that in the case of Nichols the wretch was disturbed before he had accomplished his object, and having failed in the open street he tries again, within a week of his failure, in a more secluded place. If this should be correct, the audacity and daring is equal to its maniacal fanaticism and abhorrent wickedness. But this surmise may or may not be correct, the suggested motive may be the wrong one; but one thing is very clear – that a murder of a most atrocious character has been committed.' Chapman is the second of the generally accepted victims of the Ripper.

'Another murder of a character even more diabolical than that perpetrated in Back's Row [sic], on Friday week, was discovered in the same neighbourhood on Saturday morning,' was the lurid start of one of the newspaper reports under the headline 'Ghastly Murder in the East-End'. Annie Chapman had fallen on hard times after the death of her alcoholic husband, and made some money from crochet work, and some from casual prostitution. Like Polly Nichols, Annie was on the streets on the night she died because she didn't have enough money for her lodgings. She was found at 6 a.m. on 8 September 1888 by market porter John Davis on his way to work, in the back yard of 29 Hanbury Street, Spitalfields.

Annie was last seen around half an hour earlier by an Elizabeth Long (aka Mrs Durrell) standing by the back yard of number 29. She was with a man, over forty, a little taller than Annie (who was five feet tall), who had dark hair and a foreign 'shabby-genteel' appearance, wearing a deerstalker hat and dark overcoat. His back was to Mrs Long so she couldn't identify him. The man asked Annie, 'Will you?' and she replied, 'Yes,' Around the same time (although he thought it was a few minutes earlier), one of the residents of 27 Hanbury Street, Albert Cadosch, had heard a woman say 'No' and then the sound of something falling against the fence between the two yards.

When he saw the state of Annie Chapman's body – her skirts were pulled up to the groin – Davis ran for help. Inspector Chandler of H Division was quickly on the scene and sent for Dr George Phillips. He relayed to the inquest, which was opened on 10 September, what he saw at the scene, as reported by *The Times*:

The left arm was placed across the left breast. The legs were drawn up, the feet resting on the ground, and the knees turned outwards. The face was swollen and turned on the right side. The tongue protruded between the front teeth, but not beyond the lips. The tongue was evidently much swollen. The front teeth were perfect as far as the first molar, top and bottom and very fine teeth they were. The body was terribly mutilated . . . the stiffness of the limbs was not marked, but was evidently commencing. He noticed that the throat was dissevered deeply; that the incision through the skin were jagged and reached right round the neck . . . On the wooden paling between the yard in question and the next, smears of blood, corresponding to where the head of the deceased lay, were to be seen. These were about 14 inches from the ground, and immediately above the part where the blood from the neck lay that had flowed from the neck.

The body was taken to the mortuary, and – for reasons never clarified – washed before Dr Phillips carried out his post-mortem. During that he found:

> The throat had been severed as before described. The incisions into the skin indicated that they had been made from the left side of the neck. There were two distinct, clean cuts on the left side of the spine. They were parallel from each other and separated by about half an inch. The muscular structures appeared as though an attempt had been made to separate the bones of the neck. There were various other mutilations of the body, but he was of opinion that they occurred subsequent to the death of the woman, and to the large escape of blood from the division of the neck.

At that point Dr Phillips said that, as from these injuries he was satisfied as to the cause of death, he thought that he had better not go into further details of the mutilations, 'which could only be painful to the feelings of the jury and the public'. The coroner agreed, and pressed him on details that could be relevant to finding the killer.

> The instrument used at the throat and abdomen was the same. It must have been a very sharp knife with a thin narrow blade, and must have been at least 6 to 8 inches in

length, probably longer. He should say that the injuries could not have been inflicted by a bayonet or a sword bayonet. They could have been done by such an instrument as a medical man used for post-mortem purposes, but the ordinary surgical cases might not contain such an instrument. Those used by the slaughtermen, well ground down, might have caused them. He thought the knives used by those in the leather trade would not be long enough in the blade. There were indications of anatomical knowledge . . . he should say that the deceased had been dead at least two hours, and probably more, when he first saw her; but it was right to mention that it was a fairly cool morning, and that the body would be more apt to cool rapidly from its having lost a great quantity of blood. There was no evidence . . . of a struggle having taken place. He was positive the deceased entered the yard alive . . .

A handkerchief was round the throat of the deceased when he saw it early in the morning. He should say it was not tied on after the throat was cut.

Phillips's full autopsy report as relayed to the inquest fills in the details.

The abdomen had been entirely laid open: the intestines, severed from their mesenteric attachments, had been lifted out of the body and placed on the shoulder of the corpse; whilst from the pelvis, the uterus and its appendages with the upper portion of the vagina and the posterior two thirds of the bladder, had been entirely removed. No trace of these parts could be found and the incisions were cleanly cut, avoiding the rectum, and dividing the vagina low enough to avoid injury to the cervix uteri. Obviously the work was that of an expert – of one, at least, who had such knowledge of anatomical or pathological examinations as to be enabled to secure the pelvic organs with one sweep of the knife, which must therefore have been at least 5 or 6 inches in length, probably more. The appearance of the cuts confirmed him in the opinion that the instrument, like the one which divided the neck, had been of a very sharp character. The mode in which the knife had been used seemed to indicate great anatomical knowledge.

Phillips told the inquest that he thought he himself could not have performed all the injuries he described, even without a struggle, in less than a quarter of an hour. If the surgery had been performed properly, it would have taken more like an hour.

The doctor saw the body at 6.30 a.m.; his estimate of the time of death would be badly out if the witnesses' testimony concerning events around 5.30 were correct. Certainly, one of the residents of number 29, John Richardson, said he had been in the yard around 5 a.m., and he hadn't seen the body; this, of course, made him a potential suspect.

The police carefully examined everything they could find on and around the body: two pills, which Annie took for a lung condition; part of a torn envelope – in which Annie had kept the pills – that had the crest of the Sussex Regiment; a piece of muslin; and a comb. Allegedly there were two farthings as well, but surviving contemporary records don't show them; that hasn't stopped various theories being built up round medical students, who would polish the farthings and try to pass them off as sovereign coins. The police checked to no avail for anyone who might have arrived locally 'with blood on his hands or clothes'.

Various suspects were questioned: ship's cook William Henry Piggott was found with a bloodstained shirt, but had an alibi. Swiss butcher Jacob Isenschmid was confined to a mental asylum after a local public-house landlady saw him bloodstained and acting strangely. On 18 September, German hairdresser Charles Ludwig tried to stab a man not long after attacking a prostitute; he too was arrested – but, like Isenschmid, was cleared of involvement in Annie's death when the next murders took place while they were in custody.

Annie Chapman was buried on 14 September 1888. The funeral was held in secret because, by then, the public was starting to panic. There were anti-Semitic demonstrations after rumours spread that the state of the bodies fitted Jewish rituals; the Whitechapel MP, Samuel Montagu, offered a £100 reward. On the day of the inquest, 10 September, the Whitechapel Vigilance Committee was set up, led by builder George Lusk, to patrol the streets; it would also offer a reward. Sir Charles Warren, the Chief Commissioner, appointed Chief Inspector Donald Swanson to head the investigation into Polly Nichols and Annie Chapman's deaths.

On 27 September, a letter was sent to and received by the Central News Agency. Written in red ink, it was probably the single item that ensured that the Whitechapel murders would not be quickly forgotten. (The spelling and grammatical errors are reproduced.)

Dear Boss,

I keep on hearing the police have caught me but they wont fix me just yet. I have laughed when they look so clever and talk about being on the right track. That joke about Leather Apron gave me real fits. I am down on whores and I shant quit ripping them till I do get buckled. Grand work the last job was. I gave the lady no time to squeal. How can they catch me now. I love my work and want to start again. You will soon hear of me with my funny little games. I saved some of the proper red stuff in a ginger beer bottle over the last job to write with but it went thick like glue and I cant use it. Red ink is fit enough I hope ha. ha. The next job I do I shall clip the ladys ears off and send to the police officers just for jolly wouldn't you. Keep this letter back till I do a bit more work, then give it out straight. My knife's so nice and sharp I want to get to work right away if I get a chance. Good Luck.

Yours truly

Jack the Ripper

Dont mind me giving the trade name

PS Wasnt good enough to post this before I got all the red ink off my hands curse it No luck yet. They say I'm a doctor now <u>ha ha</u>

The letter was forwarded to Scotland Yard on 29 September and believed to be a hoax, written by a local journalist concerned that after nearly three weeks without a murder, public interest was waning (indeed there are many who still maintain this is the case). However, within twenty-four hours, they had to reconsider . . .

On 30 September, the Ripper struck again in the so-called 'double event', this time killing two women within the space of an hour – Elizabeth 'Long Liz' Stride and Catherine Eddowes, whose earlobe was severed, just as the letter writer had promised.

Around 1 a.m., the steward of the International Working Men's Educational Club, Louis Diemschutz, came out from a party that had followed a meeting on the subject of 'Why Jews Should be Socialists'. The club, mainly formed of expatriate Russian and Polish Jews, met at 40 Berner Street (now renamed Henriques Street), off Commercial Road in Whitechapel. There was a passageway between number 40 and number 42 that led out to Dutfield's Yard, and when Diemschutz took his pony and two-wheeled cart down it, the pony shied away, almost knocking into the passageway wall. Diemschutz dismounted and found the body of a woman; the blood was still flowing from a gash in her neck, clotting into a pool near her face.

PC Henry Lamb was patrolling Commercial Road and was brought to the scene by two members of the Socialist Club. He sent for Dr Frederick Blackwell, whose assistant Edward Johnston got there before him and found that the woman was 'all warm except the hands'. Blackwell arrived shortly afterwards, as did Dr George Phillips.

'The body was lying on the near side, with the face turned toward the wall, the head up the yard and the feet toward the street,' Phillips later testified. 'The left arm was extended and there was a packet of cachous in the left hand. The right arm was over the belly; the back of the hand and wrist had on it clotted blood. The legs were drawn up with the feet close to the wall. The body and face were warm and the hand cold. The legs were quite warm.

'Deceased had a silk handkerchief round her neck, and it appeared to be slightly torn. I have since ascertained it was cut. This corresponded with the right angle of the jaw. The throat was deeply gashed, and there was an abrasion of the skin about one and a half inches in diameter, apparently stained with blood, under her right brow.'

Less than a mile away from where the police and public were gathering, in Mitre Square, the Ripper was busy. At 1.44 a.m., PC Edward Watkins was on routine patrol; he had passed by Mitre Square at 1.30 and all was quiet. However, now there was a woman lying on her back, with her skirts up to her waist. Next to her face were her innards; she had been disembowelled. Watkins called for help, and at 2 a.m. Dr Frederick Brown arrived.

'The body was on its back, the head turned to left shoulder,' he noted and later relayed in court. 'The arms by the side of the body as if they had fallen there. Both palms upwards, the fingers slightly bent. A thimble was lying off the finger on the right side. The clothes drawn up above the abdomen. The thighs were naked. Left leg extended in a line with the body. The abdomen was exposed. Right leg bent at the thigh and knee.

'The bonnet was at the back of the head – great disfigurement of the face. The throat cut. Across below the throat was a neckerchief . . . The intestines were drawn out to a large extent and placed over the right shoulder – they were smeared over with some feculent matter. A piece of about two feet was quite detached from the body and placed between the body and the left arm, apparently by design. The lobe and auricle of the right ear were cut obliquely through. There was a quantity of clotted blood on the pavement on the left side of the neck round the shoulder and upper part of the arm, and fluid blood-coloured serum which had flowed under the neck to the right shoulder, the pavement sloping in that direction.

'Body was quite warm. No death stiffening had taken place. She must have been dead most likely within the half hour. We looked for superficial bruises and saw none. No blood on the skin of the abdomen or secretion of any kind on the thighs. No spurting of blood on the bricks or pavement around. No marks of blood below the middle of the body. Several buttons were found in the clotted blood after the body was removed. There was no blood on the front of the clothes. There were no traces of recent connection.'

Brown carried out the post-mortem that day. 'After washing the left hand carefully, a bruise the size of a sixpence, recent and red, was discovered on the back of the left hand between the thumb and first finger. A few small bruises on right shin of older date. The hands and arms were bronzed. No bruises on the scalp, the back of the body, or the elbows . . . The cause of death was haemorrhage from the left common carotid artery. The death was immediate and the mutilations were inflicted after death . . . There would not be much blood on the murderer. The cut was made by someone on the right side of the body, kneeling below the middle of the body . . . The peritoneal lining was cut through on the left side and the left kidney carefully taken out and removed . . . I believe the perpetrator of the act must have had considerable knowledge of the position of the organs in the abdominal cavity and the way of removing them. The parts removed would be of no use for any professional purpose. It required a great deal of knowledge to have removed the kidney and to know where it was placed. Such a knowledge might be possessed by one in the habit of cutting up animals. I think the perpetrator of this act had sufficient time ... It would take at least five minutes ... I believe it was the act of one person.'

On 1 October, Phillips and Blackwell carried out the autopsy of the Ripper's first victim of 30 September. 'Rigor mortis was still thoroughly marked,' the court heard. 'There was mud on the left side of the face and it was matted in the head. The body was fairly nourished. Over both shoulders, especially the right, and under the collarbone and in front of the chest there was a blueish discolouration, which I have watched and have seen on two occasions since.

'There was a clear-cut incision on the neck. It was six inches in length and commenced two and a half inches in a straight line below the angle of the jaw, one half inch over an undivided muscle, and then, becoming deeper, dividing the sheath. The cut was very clean and deviated a little downwards. The arteries and other vessels contained in the sheath were all cut through. The cut through the tissues on the right side was more superficial, and tailed off to about two inches below the right angle of the jaw. The deep vessels on that side were uninjured. From this it was evident that the haemorrhage was caused through the partial severance of the left carotid artery.

'Decomposition had commenced in the skin. Dark brown spots were on the anterior surface of the left chin. There was a deformity in the bones of the right leg, which was not straight, but bowed forwards. There was no recent external injury save to the neck.'

They recorded the state of the organs and noted that 'the stomach was large and the mucous membrane only congested. It contained partly digested food, apparently consisting of cheese, potato, and farinaceous powder. All the teeth on the lower left jaw were absent.' This would become relevant later.

This first victim was 'Long Liz' Stride, the daughter of a Swedish farmer; she had come to London in 1866 aged twenty-three after a conviction for prostitution in her native land. She was working the streets of Whitechapel when she died: on 29 September, she was seen around 11 p.m. with a client near Berner Street, and with another one three-quarters of an hour later. At 12.35 on the morning she died, PC William Smith saw her with a third man opposite the International Working Men's Educational Club; the man was carrying a package about a foot-and-a-half long. No one saw anyone enter the yard, and members of the club leaving between 12.35 and 12.50 a.m. didn't see anything untoward. One witness – whose statement wasn't found in the case files until Stephen Knight's investigation in the 1970s – was Hungarian Israel Schwartz, who said he saw Liz attacked and thrown to the ground outside the yard at 12.45 a.m. The man who did it apparently said 'Lipski' to a second man nearby.

Little was found around her body, and many, including Diemschutz himself, believe that the Ripper was interrupted by Diemschutz's arrival. A story circulated that she and her murderer had bought some grapes from grocer Matthew Packer; he only told this version of events to the Whitechapel Vigilance Committee's private detectives, and Superintendent Donald Swanson dismissed the story as 'valueless'.

The other victim was Catherine 'Kate' Eddowes, another casual prostitute who also had a drink problem. Five hours or so before her death, at 8.30 p.m. on 29 September, she was found drunk in the middle of Aldgate High Street and held at Bishopsgate Police Station until she sobered up. At 1 a.m., she was judged fit to leave and released. Instead of taking the direct route back to her lodging, she headed back towards Aldgate, and at 1.35 was passed by three men who had just left the Imperial Club. She was talking to a man at the entrance to Church Passage, which went from Duke Street to Mitre Square, along the wall of the Great Synagogue of London. Two of the witnesses – furniture dealer Harry Harris and butcher Joseph Levy – took little or no notice of them. The third, commercial traveller Joseph Lawende, said the man was around thirty, five-foot seven-inches tall, with a moustache, wearing a loose-fitting jacket and a red handkerchief around his neck.

The immediate area was searched by the City of London Police, in whose jurisdiction Mitre Square fell, in the aftermath of the body's discovery. On Kate's body were two pawn tickets, but no money. A bloodstained piece of material was found in the passage of a doorway leading to Flats 108 and 119, Model Dwellings, Goulston Street, Whitechapel, around 3 a.m. Above it was a piece of graffito in chalk that read, 'The Juwes are the men that Will not be Blamed for nothing' (according to Constable Alfred Long's inquest evidence) or 'The Juwes are not the men who Will be Blamed for nothing' (according to Detective Constable Daniel Halse). Petrified at the thought that this could lead to further anti-Semitic behaviour – and, apparently, unsure that it was really connected with the case – the Metropolitan Police Commissioner Sir Charles Warren demanded that it was washed away. As many conspiracy theories have been triggered by that action as by the death of President John F. Kennedy in Dealey Plaza in Texas seventy-five years later.

On 1 October, the Central News Agency received another communication, apparently from the Ripper. This time it was a postcard:

> I was not codding dear old Boss when I gave you the tip, you'll hear about Saucy Jacky's work tomorrow double event this time number one squealed a bit couldn't finish straight off. Had not got time to get ears off for police thanks for keeping last letter back till I got to work again.
>
> Jack the Ripper

Journalist Fred Best claimed in later life that he and a colleague were responsible for both the letter and the postcard. Certainly by the time the latter was sent, details of the 'double event' were public knowledge.

Little progress was made by the police through October. According to a report Inspector Swanson made to the Home Office on 19 October, more than 2,000 people were interviewed, upwards of 300 people warranted further investigation and 80 were detained.

A final communication allegedly from the Ripper was received on 16 October by George Lusk, the head of the Whitechapel Vigilance Committee.

From hell
Mr Lusk
Sor
I send you half the
Kidne I took from one women
prasarved it for you tother piece
I fried and ate it was very nise I
may send you the bloody knif that
took it out if you only wate a whil
longer.
signed Catch me when
you Can
Mishter Lusk.

The handwriting and the style of the letter were very different from those in the previous two messages, but it was taken seriously enough at the time (bearing in mind that the police were receiving hundreds of obviously fake letters). It came accompanied by 'proof' – a preserved part of a human kidney. Lusk himself wasn't convinced, believing that this was a hoax, but eventually passed it over to the police. It was confirmed that it was a left kidney, but whether it belonged to Kate Eddowes was beyond science at the time. The day before the letter was received, a man in a long black overcoat, with a dark beard and moustache, asked locally for Lusk's address; it could, of course, be pure coincidence that this Irishman was making his enquiries at that point.

On Thursday 8 November, Sir Charles Warren resigned as Commissioner of the Metropolitan Police. On the next morning, the Ripper's next victim was found. Thomas Bowyer was sent to collect six weeks' rent from Mary Jane Kelly by her landlord, John McCarthy. Bowyer got no reply when he knocked on the door, so reached through the broken window, and pushed aside the coat that acted as a makeshift curtain. All he could see was a mutilated body.

Mary Jane Kelly was around twenty-five at the time she died, and, according to Walter Dew, was a 'pretty, buxom girl'. She was believed to have come originally from Limerick in Ireland, but she told Joseph Barnett, with whom she lived in London, that her family had moved to Wales when she was young, and she was fluent in Welsh. In 1884, she had come to London, and worked in a brothel in the West End before going to France with a client but returning quickly. She ended up in the East End, and moved in with Barnett in April 1887 to 13 Miller's Court at the back of 26 Dorset Street, Spitalfields. The pair argued and he moved out of their shared lodgings a week before she died. They stayed in touch: Barnett went to see her on the evening of 8 November, and left her to go back to his own lodgings.

Mary went out after Barnett left, and was seen returning home, drunk, along with a stout ginger-haired man, around 11.45 p.m. She sang a lot when drunk, and was heard singing at midnight, and again at 1 a.m. However, by 1.30, she had stopped – presumably because she had gone out again. Around 2 a.m., acquaintance George Hutchinson was asked for a loan of sixpence; he refused, then saw Mary approached by a rich-looking man of 'Jewish appearance'. Although it was dark, Hutchinson was able to remember every detail about the man when he went to the police; although Fred Abberline sent Hutchinson out to look for the man later, nothing further appears to have come of it. However, around 2.30 a.m., laundress Sarah Lewis saw a man around the entrance to Miller's Court. Mary Ann Cox, who saw Mary Jane Kelly at 11.45 p.m., returned home at 3 a.m. and didn't remember seeing a light in the other woman's room. Around 4 a.m. two other residents thought they heard a faint cry of 'Murder!' but ignored it; it was hardly an uncommon plea in that part of London.

Bowyer found Mary's body at around 10.45 a.m. and went straight to the police. Inspector Walter Beck went to the scene, joined by Superintendent Thomas Arnold, Inspector Reid, Fred Abberline and Robert Anderson, and the room was broken into at 1.30 p.m. – there was a delay because there was consideration of using bloodhounds to track the murderer from the room, and any other presence would confuse the dogs. A huge fire had been burned in the grate, using Mary's clothing – possibly to give the Ripper light to carry out his grisly tasks.

Doctors Thomas Bond and George Phillips examined the body, both giving the time of death as around twelve hours previously. The mutilations would have taken around two hours to carry out, and rigor mortis was beginning to set in. Thomas Bond's notes were comprehensive:

The body was lying naked in the middle of the bed, the shoulders flat but the axis of the body inclined to the left side of the bed. The head was turned on the left cheek. The left arm was close to the body with the forearm flexed at a right angle and lying across the abdomen. The right arm was slightly abducted from the body and rested on the mattress. The elbow was bent, the forearm supine with the fingers clenched. The legs were wide apart, the left thigh at right angles to the trunk and the right forming an obtuse angle with the pubis.

The whole of the surface of the abdomen and thighs was removed and the abdominal cavity emptied of its viscera. The breasts were cut off, the arms mutilated by several jagged wounds and the face hacked beyond recognition of the features. The tissues of the neck were severed all round down to the bone.

The viscera were found in various parts viz: the uterus and kidneys with one breast under the head, the other breast by the right foot, the liver between the feet, the intestines by the right side and the spleen by the left side of the body. The flaps removed from the abdomen and thighs were on a table.

The bed clothing at the right corner was saturated with blood, and on the floor beneath was a pool of blood covering about two feet square. The wall by the right side of the bed and in a line with the neck was marked by blood which had struck it in several places.

The face was gashed in all directions, the nose, cheeks, eyebrows, and ears being partly removed. The lips were blanched and cut by several incisions running obliquely down to the chin. There were also numerous cuts extending irregularly across all the features.

The neck was cut through the skin and other tissues right down to the vertebrae, the fifth and sixth being deeply notched. The skin cuts in the front of the neck showed distinct ecchymosis. The air passage was cut at the lower part of the larynx through the cricoid cartilage.

Both breasts were more or less removed by circular incisions, the muscle down to the ribs being attached to the breasts. The intercostals between the fourth, fifth, and sixth ribs were cut through and the contents of the thorax visible through the openings.

The skin and tissues of the abdomen from the costal arch to the pubes were removed in three large flaps. The right thigh was denuded in front to the bone, the flap of skin, including the external organs of generation, and part of the right buttock. The left thigh was stripped of skin fascia, and muscles as far as the knee.

The left calf showed a long gash through skin and tissues to the deep muscles and reaching from the knee to five inches above the ankle. Both arms and forearms had extensive jagged wounds.

The right thumb showed a small superficial incision about one inch long, with extravasation of blood in the skin, and there were several abrasions on the back of the hand moreover showing the same condition.

On opening the thorax it was found that the right lung was minimally adherent by old firm adhesions. The lower part of the lung was broken and torn away. The left lung was intact. It was adherent at the apex and there were a few adhesions over the side. In the substances of the lung there were several nodules of consolidation.

The pericardium was open below and the heart absent. In the abdominal cavity there was some partly digested food of fish and potatoes, and similar food was found in the remains of the stomach attached to the intestines.

You would think from that that the Ripper knew what he was doing, but Bond did not think so. 'In each case the mutilation was inflicted by a person who had no scientific nor anatomical knowledge,' he wrote. 'In my opinion he does not even possess the technical knowledge of a butcher or horse slaughterer or a person accustomed to cut up dead animals.' The inquest was handled with remarkable speed, on 12 November, in front of Dr Roderick Macdonald rather than Wynne Baxter, and Mary Jane Kelly was buried a week later, on 19 November.

Dr Bond was convinced that the five murders were 'no doubt committed by the same hand', and a pardon was offered to anyone who could provide information that led to the conviction of the murderer, even if they were an accomplice. One hundred and forty-three extra police officers were deployed in Whitechapel in the aftermath of Mary's killing, and maybe that was enough to prevent the Ripper from striking again.

Fears were raised when prostitute Rose Mylett was found dead on 20 December in Clarke's Yard off Poplar High Street. She had been strangled; four doctors believed she had been murdered – and the inquest jury agreed, returning a verdict of 'wilful murder against some person or persons unknown'. However, both Thomas Bond and coroner Wynne Baxter disagreed with the majority, siding with Robert Anderson who thought Rose had accidentally hanged herself on the collar of her dress while she was drunk.

The next case that was linked to the Ripper was the death on 17 July 1889 – eight months after Mary Jane Kelly's murder – of Alice McKenzie in Castle Alley, Whitechapel. Around 12.45 a.m. PC Walter Andrews entered the alley and discovered the body of a woman lying on the pavement. Her head was angled toward the kerb, her feet pointed towards the wall. Blood was flowing from two stabs in the left side of her neck and her skirts had been lifted, revealing blood across her abdomen, which had been mutilated. The pavement beneath the body of Alice McKenzie was still dry, which helped confirm her time of death as being between 12.25 and 12.45 a.m., when it began to rain.

There was more cause for believing her murder, rather than that of Rose Mylett, was connected to the earlier murders, and even

Coroner Baxter acknowledged the Ripper links. 'There is great similarity between this and the other class of cases, which have happened in this neighbourhood, and if the same person has not committed this crime, it is clearly an imitation of the other cases,' he said at the inquest. Alice died from severance of the left carotid artery; the two stabs in the left side of the neck 'carried forward in the same skin wound', and there was some bruising on her chest, and five bruises or marks on the left side of her abdomen. A cut was made from left to right, apparently while Alice was on the ground, and a long (seven-inch) 'but not unduly deep' wound ran from the bottom of the left breast to the navel. Seven or eight scratches began at the navel and pointed towards the genitalia, and there was a small cut across the mons Veneris.

Thomas Bond believed that the Ripper had returned: 'I see in this murder evidence of similar design to the former Whitechapel murders, viz. sudden onslaught on the prostrate woman, the throat skilfully and resolutely cut with subsequent mutilation, each mutilation indicating sexual thoughts and a desire to mutilate the abdomen and sexual organs. I am of opinion that the murder was performed by the same person who committed the former series of Whitechapel murder.' The information in this chapter about the states of the bodies was given at the inquests; it is entirely possible that a copycat killer took advantage of that knowledge. Inspector Fred Abberline certainly didn't think the Ripper was involved.

The penultimate case to be linked was that of an unknown woman, whose torso was found at 5.15 a.m. on 10 September 1889 beneath a railway arch in Pinchin Street, Whitechapel. No other body parts were found; the woman was never positively identified. Other dismembered bodies had been found in Rainham and Chelsea, as had human remains during the construction of Scotland Yard. Sir Melville Macnaghten noted, 'The stomach was split up by a cut, and the head and legs had been severed in a manner identical with that of the woman whose remains were discovered in the Thames, in Battersea Park, & on the Chelsea Embankment on 4th June of the same year; and these murders had no connection whatever with the Whitechapel horrors.'

The 'final' victim was prostitute Frances Coles, found by PC Ernest Thompson at Swallow Gardens – a passageway under a railway arch between Royal Mint Street and Chamber Street in Whitechapel. She had been first thrown violently to the ground, as revealed by a few wounds on the back of the head. Her throat was cut, with her body tilted at the moment the wound was inflicted so that the killer would avoid becoming bloodstained. Her clothes were in order, and there were no abdominal mutilations. The doctors who checked the body weren't sure how many times her throat was cut – Dr Phillips said three, Dr Oxley just two. A verdict of 'Wilful Murder against some person or persons unknown' was once again given; the only suspect, a sailor named James Sadler, was released for lack of evidence.

There are countless volumes setting out the case against various suspects in the Jack the Ripper killings and the Whitechapel Murders in general. None of them has made a conclusive case.

CHAPTER 8

Great Britain: John Christie

'I do not know whether any jury before in this country or perhaps in the world has seen and heard a man charged with murder go into the witness box and say, "Yes I did kill this victim, I killed six others as well over a period of ten years,"' Mr Justice Finnemore said during his summing up at the conclusion of the trial of John Christie in 1953. The case would become even more notorious following the publication of Ludovic Kennedy's investigative book *Ten Rillington Place* (1961) and the subsequent feature film starring Richard Attenborough as Christie (1971), both of which confirmed many people's suspicion that Christie had claimed more victims than just those he had killed directly – he was responsible for an innocent man being hanged.

John Reginald Halliday Christie was the sixth child of Ernest John Christie and his wife Mary Hannah, born in Northowram in the West Riding of Yorkshire on 8 April 1899. Christie's father was very strict, whipping his children as he saw fit, and his older sisters bullied him. Aged eight, he saw his grandfather in an open coffin, and this led to an interest in playing in the local graveyard – particularly around the vault that contained the coffins of children. He was disturbed by the sight of one of his adult sisters' bare legs when he was ten, something Kennedy saw as exacerbating an already tense situation in the family, and leading to a hatred of women.

He won a scholarship to Halifax Secondary School, leaving there aged fifteen to become an assistant movie projectionist. He enlisted for service in the Great War in 1916, and joined the 52nd

Nottinghamshire and Derbyshire Regiment. He served in France in 1918 as a signalman, and was injured in a mustard-gas attack that June. He claimed that this left him blind for a time and mute for three and a half years, leading to him whispering in later life – although since he was discharged as fit for duty, he may have been exaggerating considerably. He was already suffering from the sexual dysfunction that characterised his life: he had been known as 'Reggie No Dick' and 'Can't Do It Christie' as a teen, and he was only able to perform sexually with prostitutes.

He married Ethel Simpson in Sheffield on 10 May 1920, but they separated after four years. During that period, Christie spent time as a postman, but was imprisoned on 12 April 1921 for three months for stealing postal orders. In January 1923, he received twelve months' probation for obtaining money under false pretences and violent conduct, and in September 1924 was sentenced to consecutive three- and six-month terms for larceny. He decided to move to London.

Christie continued to go in and out of prison over the decade. In London, he was convicted in May 1929 for assaulting the prostitute with whom he was living with a cricket bat and served six months' hard labour. His last stretch inside was for three months after stealing a car from a priest who had tried to help him in late 1933. When he got out, he contacted his estranged wife Ethel and they resumed their life together, eventually moving into the top-floor flat at 10 Rillington Place in Ladbroke Grove in late 1937, and then taking over the ground floor in December 1938.

After the Second World War broke out in September 1939, Christie applied to join the War Reserve Police and was assigned to Harrow Road Police Station; his criminal record wasn't checked. He served there until 1943, becoming involved in an extra-marital relationship with a female colleague whose husband was serving in the military. This came to an abrupt end in the summer of 1943 when the man returned from service and found Christie with his wife; he beat Christie severely.

Not long after that, John Christie killed for the first time. His victim was a twenty-one-year-old Austrian munitions worker and part-time prostitute, Ruth Fuerst, who he picked up in a snack bar in Ladbroke Grove in August 1943 and took back to Rillington Place. 'I got her on the bed and had intercourse with her and strangled her with a rope,' he explained later. 'She was completely naked. I tried to put her clothes back on her. She had a leopard-skin coat and I wrapped this around her. I took her to the bedroom and put her under the floorboards.' (Christie's contradictory statements about the bedroom weren't challenged.) Ethel was away visiting relatives in Sheffield; before her return, Christie moved Ruth's body and buried it in the garden.

Christie resigned as a special constable at the end of 1943, and started working as a clerk at the Ultra Radio Works factory in Acton. There he met thirty-two-year-old Muriel Eady, who suffered badly from bronchitis, and in October 1944, when Ethel was once again in the north, Christie invited Muriel back to Rillington Place where, he said, he had created a special mixture that would help her breathing. He had even concocted a device for her to use: a square glass jar, with a screw top. In the top were two holes, one of which had a rubber tube protruding from it. Inside the jar was some Friar's Balsam, a very strongly scented compound that would indeed clear her sinuses – but as she was inhaling this and her eyes were watering, Christie connected a second tube to the jar. The other end of this was connected to the coal gas tap in the wall, and when Christie opened the tap, Muriel was rendered unconscious by the high carbon monoxide content. He then took her to the bedroom and raped her while pulling on a rope to strangle her. 'Once again I experienced that quiet, peaceful thrill,' he remembered. Muriel was buried, fully clothed, next to Ruth Fuerst in the Rillington Place garden.

There was some time before Christie killed again. On Easter Monday 1948, he and Ethel got new upstairs neighbours at 10 Rillington Place – Timothy Evans and his wife Beryl. Evans was born in 1924, and was slow both physically and mentally (he was judged to have a mental age of around nine when he was hanged). He had moved up from his birthplace in Wales to Ladbroke Grove where he met Beryl, and they married in September 1947, with Beryl falling pregnant early in the new year. Geraldine was born on 10 October.

It wasn't a happy marriage: the Evanses had considerable money problems, and Timothy exacerbated the situation by drinking heavily. They frequently rowed, with a number of physical altercations witnessed by the neighbours, and Timothy even having a brief one-night stand with one of Beryl's friends. However, they reconciled, and when Beryl became pregnant a second time in late 1949, Timothy reluctantly agreed to her having an abortion – something that was both illegal and highly risky.

John Christie offered his services as the abortionist, and although Timothy Evans wasn't at all happy about the idea, Beryl was willing to let her fifty-year-old neighbour carry out the operation. On the morning of 8 November 1949, Timothy got up for work, leaving his wife expecting to have the abortion that day. That evening, when he got home, he was told by Christie that the operation had gone wrong, and that Beryl had died. 'I could see that she was dead and that she had been bleeding from the mouth and nose and that she had been bleeding from the bottom part,' Evans later told police. Christie said he would dispose of the body, and he would make arrangements for Geraldine to be looked after.

Unfortunately for him, that wasn't the story that Timothy Evans originally told the police. On 30 November, he walked into Merthyr Vale Police Station back in Wales and said that he had 'disposed of' his wife, and put her down the drain. In a statement, he said his wife had had a miscarriage after she 'drank some liquid which [Evans] obtained from a lorry driver some time previous at a café between Chelmsford and Ipswich'. Metropolitan Police officers duly went to Rillington Place, where it took three of them to remove the cover of the drain – and there was nothing there. When Evans heard that he refuted his first statement, saying he had been trying to 'protect a man named Christie'.

Evans had gone back to Wales, at Christie's suggestion, on 14 November, after disposing of Beryl's possessions, and handing Geraldine to Christie along with her pram and highchair. Christie told Beryl's friend Joan Vincent that Beryl and Geraldine had gone to Bristol, but Joan was suspicious after seeing Geraldine's things in Christie's apartment. Meanwhile, Evans told his relatives that his wife and daughter had gone to Brighton. However, when the lies began to catch up with him, Evans went to the police.

'At no time have I assisted or attempted to abort Mrs Evans or any other woman,' Christie said when questioned on 1 December at Notting Hill Police Station. 'I cannot understand why Evans should make such accusations against me, as I've been very good to him in a lot of ways.' Later that night, the police carried out a further search of Rillington Place, finding an object wrapped in cloth in the wash house in the back garden. When it was dragged out into the back garden, the officers realised the package was in a green tablecloth, bound by rope. When that was undone, Beryl Evans's body was discovered. Worse was to come: when they went back into the wash house, they found the body of baby Geraldine, a man's tie around her neck. Both had been strangled; both had been dead about three weeks.

Evans was brought back to London ostensibly over a stolen brief-case that police had found in his flat. There, he was told of Geraldine's death and DCI Jennings told him that he thought Evans had killed both Beryl and Geraldine. 'Yes, yes,' Evans apparently replied. He then allegedly gave statements, which most objective observers believe were not verbatim – and may even have been completely falsified. (The vocabulary used was far too erudite for Evans.) In these he confessed to killing Beryl on 8 November, and Geraldine two days later. He was charged with their murders, but in the end police decided only to prosecute Geraldine's death.

Timothy Evans's trial began on 11 January 1950, with the defendant maintaining throughout that Christie was responsible for the deaths of Beryl and Geraldine. Christie gave evidence against Evans, and despite the defence bringing up Christie's past record of violence, Evans's fate was sealed. The trial lasted just three days, and the jury took only forty minutes to find him guilty. He was hanged on 9 March.

Christie had got away with it. According to his various confessions before his own execution, he strangled Beryl while having intercourse with her, possibly because she wanted to commit suicide (he said she had tried to gas herself – but no trace of gas was found in her body at the second post-mortem after his arrest). He denied agreeing to carry out an abortion. He said he had kept the bodies in the empty first-floor flat before they were moved to the wash house – although he maintained that he hadn't moved them. (Workmen who had been employed at Rillington Place knew that there were no bodies in the wash house at the time that Evans would have moved them there; their evidence was altered after they were interviewed by police to make it seem that this wasn't the case.) However, at no stage did Christie ever admit to killing Geraldine. Timothy Evans's mother wrote to him in the condemned cell, noting, 'You are where my boy was three years ago . . . You did say half the truth last week when you told the judge you killed poor Beryl but only the whole truth will save you from the wrath of God.' Christie never replied to her but wrote in a piece for the *Sunday Pictorial*, 'I did not – most emphatically I say this – harm the baby.'

He lost his job at the Post Office Savings Bank after his criminal record was brought up in Evans's trial – which was a cause célèbre and covered by all the newspapers in great detail – and was not happy when his landlord at Rillington Place sold the property to Jamaican immigrant Charles Brown, who found new tenants from his home country for the middle and upper storeys. The Christies and their new neighbours did not get on at all well, with Ethel prosecuting one of them for assault; however, they did agree that the Christies could have exclusive use of the back garden, much to John Christie's relief. The bodies of his two earlier victims were still buried there – the police search had ended when Beryl and Geraldine Evans's corpses were located.

Christie's health deteriorated. He had always been a hypochondriac, but now the stress of his quadruple murders – and the constant fear of discovery of the other bodies – meant that he sought help. He was unable to perform sexually with Edith after the hanging of Timothy Evans, and in the end he decided he needed to be rid of her.

On 6 December 1952, Christie resigned from his job at British Road Services, claiming that he was going to get work in Sheffield near his wife's family. Four days later, Ethel wrote to her sister and asked Christie to post the letter; instead, he hung on to it. On 12 December, Ethel left Rillington Place to take clothing to the laundry; it was the last time she was seen alive. Two days later, on the morning of 14 December, Christie strangled her with a stocking while she slept. He later tried to make out that she had suffered a convulsive fit and his was an act of mercy. In fact, it seems likely that Ethel did wake briefly before the end but was unable to stop her husband from killing her.

Christie left the body in bed for two days while he laid the groundwork for her disappearance. He re-dated her letter to her sister to the 15th, and a few days afterwards wrote to her sister himself claiming Ethel's rheumatism was so bad she couldn't write. By then he had wrapped Ethel in a blanket, secured with a safety pin, with a pillowcase over her head, and placed her under the floorboards in the living room. He sold her wedding ring and items of furniture at the start of January 1953.

Around the time of Ethel's murder, Christie had visited two young women in a room, where one had stripped and allowed him to photograph her, in exchange for cash. Christie became fascinated by the other woman, who had remained dressed throughout, and this girl, Kathleen Maloney, would become his second victim of 1953. Prior to that, he killed twenty-six-year-old Rita Nelson, who was from Northern Ireland. She was around six months pregnant and Christie agreed to help her get rid of the child – as he had Beryl Evans. Rita was drugged with Christie's special gas machine, and strangled. (Christie later tried to claim he had simply opened the gas tap in the kitchen, but this would have incapacitated him as well.) Christie then raped her as she died, ejaculating inside her. He wrapped her in a woollen blanket and tied her feet with plastic wire. He then hid her in an alcove in the kitchen. Her date of death isn't certain but she was last seen on 12 January, and was reported missing a week later.

Kathleen Maloney ran into Christie not long after that and agreed to come back to Rillington Place. She was drunk and easy prey. She was strangled and raped; this time Christie put a nappy (diaper) between her legs before he began his assault. The next day she was put in a blanket and placed next to Rita Nelson in the cupboard. On 26 January, Christie forged Ethel's signature on a letter to her bank in Sheffield, who sent him over £10 – money he desperately needed as he was still unemployed.

John Christie's final victim was twenty-six-year-old Hectorina MacLennan. The young Scots woman had stayed on in London in February 1953 with her brother after her parents returned to

Scotland, taking her young daughters with them. Hectorina's boyfriend, lorry driver Alex Baker, and she met with Christie on the evening of 3 March when they discussed a flat that Christie said he was going to let. Christie hadn't expected Alex to be there, so instead of trying anything with Hectorina, he showed them around the flat. He said he was being transferred for work and had sent his furniture on; in passing he mentioned that his wife was 'asleep' next door. The young couple stayed with Christie for three nights, as they had nowhere to sleep after being evicted from their original flat.

On 6 March, Christie tracked Hectorina down at the local labour exchange where her boyfriend was looking for work. She agreed to come back to Rillington Place, and told Alex she would see him later. Christie attacked her on their return, and was able to strangle her. She never got as far as the bedroom; he raped and killed her in the kitchen, then dragged her and put her in the alcove with his previous two victims.

That evening Alex Baker arrived looking for Hectorina, as she hadn't kept their rendezvous. Christie told him that she hadn't come back with him in the end, even opening the doors of the flat to show Alex she wasn't there, and offered to help him look for her. The lorry driver noticed a nasty smell, which Christie blamed on the drains. The next week, Christie ran into Alex and asked if there was any news.

A week after he killed Hectorina, Christie showed two more prospective sub-letters around his flat – even though it wasn't his to rent out – and despite the odd odour, the Reillys agreed to move in. Christie wallpapered over the alcove in the week before moving out, and the Reillys took possession on 21 March. That afternoon, the landlord, Charles Brown, came round searching for the three weeks' back rent Christie owed, and was amazed to find the Reillys there. He allowed them to stay overnight but told them they needed to chase Christie to get back the twelve weeks' advance rent they had paid him. The Reillys didn't think they stood much chance of success – Christie had told them he was going to Birmingham.

He hadn't. He was staying at a lodging house in King's Cross, and wandering the streets. He met Margaret Wilson in a café, and when she confided she was pregnant, he offered to assist her – even though he no longer had any of his equipment.

Charles Brown had agreed that the upstairs tenant at Rillington Place, Beresford Brown, could use Christie's kitchen, so long as he tidied it up. On 24 March, Beresford was trying to put a bracket up on the wall when he realised there was nothing behind a strip of wallpaper. He peeled it off – and saw the decaying corpses Christie had secreted there.

The police responded immediately – 10 Rillington Place wasn't an address they would forget any time soon after the Evans murders – and a full search of the property was instigated. Early the next morning, Ethel's body was found under the floorboards. The newspaper headlines about the grisly discoveries prompted Christie to move out of the lodging house, particularly as he had given his real name when registering.

Alex Baker was able to confirm that the clothing worn by one of the bodies matched that of Hectorina; Kathleen Maloney was identified from her fingerprints, as was Rita Nelson. The search continued, and on 28 March, the skeletal remains of Christie's first two victims were unearthed in the garden – and alongside Ruth Fuest's was a newspaper dated 19 July 1943. (Why that was there was never explained.)

By 29 March, Christie was desperate, and rang the *News of the World*, agreeing to trade his story for a hot meal, a cigarette and somewhere to stay for the night, even though he knew they would have to tell the police. He arranged to meet reporter Jock Rae early the next morning, but in the end he was spooked by the arrival of a policeman and ran off.

Just over a day later it was all over. Around 9.10 a.m. on 31 March, Police Constable Thomas Ledger saw Christie leaning over the embankment wall at Putney, in south-west London. Christie tried to give a false name, but Ledger recognised him and arrested him. In his pocket was a newspaper cutting from Jock Rae's *News of the World* report on the trial of Timothy Evans.

Under questioning about his wife's death, Christie claimed he was woken at 8.15 by his wife's convulsions and did what he could to help her, to no avail. Accordingly, he 'put her to sleep'. He also claimed that she had taken a load of phenobarbitone tablets; there was no trace of them in her system. He said that Rita Nelson had been abusive to him, and she hit him with a frying pan before he 'must have gone haywire' and used rope to strangle her. He maintained that Kathleen Maloney had made a pass at him, and that Hectorina had got angry with him, her clothing had 'got torn' and she had 'fallen limp'. He did not mention the use of gas or his sexual assaults of the three women. A few weeks later, while he was being observed in prison, he also admitted to killing Beryl Evans: 'I feel really bad about that, sir,' he told Dr Jack Hobson. 'I must have been intimate with her then strangled her.'

Christie's legal team made him aware that they would be going for a defence of insanity; otherwise he would hang. On 5 June, he admitted the murders of Ruth Fuest and Muriel Eady; three days later he formally confessed to Beryl's murder.

His trial began on 22 June 1953, with much mention of Timothy Evans's court case and the police adamant that they had got the right man for baby Geraldine's murder. Christie was only on trial for the murder of Ethel, and the Attorney General pointed out that 'There is every possible proof that he knew he had done wrong and was making every effort to conceal it. There is even some evidence it was premeditated . . . The state of mind of Christie when he killed his wife is the only relevant state of mind.' That didn't mean that evidence relating to the other murders couldn't be heard, and there was no question of his defence team trying for a 'not guilty' verdict. As Christie's counsel, Derek Curtis-Bennett QC, explained in his opening speech, 'My submission is that the evidence is such that there is no other conclusion to be found than that Christie is as mad as a March hare when he kills people.' However, when the Attorney General asked Christie on the stand if he would have killed Ethel had there been a policeman present, he replied, 'I do not suppose so.' The judge didn't think this was categorical proof of Christie's sanity, and said so specifically in his summing up on 25 June.

It didn't matter. The jury took only eighty-five minutes to decide Christie was guilty and sane. He was sentenced to death. In the condemned cell, he wrote pieces for the *Sunday Pictorial*, giving a twisted version of events, and pointing out that he already had his eyes on someone else – a woman he had seen in Ladbroke Grove. 'She would have been my next victim had I not been arrested.' The piece was published posthumously; the woman has never been identified.

John Christie was hanged on 15 July 1953 at 9 a.m. According to Albert Pierrepoint's account, Christie complained that his nose was itching after his hands were pinioned. The hangman told him, 'It won't bother you for long.'

The question of Timothy Evans's guilt hung over Christie's trial, with the judge warning the jury clearly to put it 'entirely' out of their minds when they were deciding Christie's sanity or otherwise when he killed Ethel. The jury may have obeyed that edict, but the general public were not so constrained. Even before Christie was hanged, an inquiry was announced: the Scott Henderson Inquiry was empowered by Parliament on 6 July to investigate whether Evans had killed Geraldine. Was it really likely that there were two killers living at 10 Rillington Place?

'I want to know the truth about it as much as you do,' Christie told Scott Henderson, when the barrister in charge of the inquiry visited him in the condemned cell on 9 July, but was deliberately vague in his answers, now hinting that he might not have killed Beryl after all, despite his admissions. Scott Henderson interviewed twenty witnesses in total, and reported his findings to the House of Commons on 13 July – an incredible speed that raised many suspicions that he had been seen as a 'safe pair of hands' to absolve the Establishment of guilt. 'In my opinion there is no ground for thinking there may have been any miscarriage of justice in the conviction of Evans for the murder of Geraldine Evans,' he stated categorically. A heated debate in the house on 29 July, two weeks after Christie's death, indicated that many thought otherwise; however, the Home Secretary refused to open a public inquiry.

In 1955, there was a petition to a new Home Secretary for another inquiry; his predecessor admitted that he thought a mistake had been made. Two key books – Michael Eddowes's *The Man on Your Conscience* (1955) and Kennedy's *Ten Rillington Place* – appeared but, despite prompting further debate, did not generate an inquiry. However, four years after Kennedy's book appeared, the Timothy Evans Committee was formed in 1965, with Harold Evans, later editor of *The Times*, and politician Herbert Wolfe at its forefront. This did finally achieve something, and High Court judge Sir Daniel Brabin headed an inquiry.

It was 'more probable than not' that Timothy Evans murdered his wife, Brabin found in his report, published on 12 October 1966. However, Brabin did not think Evans had murdered Geraldine – which meant that he was hanged for a crime he did not commit. A royal pardon was granted in October 1966, despite the question mark over Evans's involvement in Beryl's death (normally pardons weren't granted unless the recipient had 'clean hands' of all crimes). Nearly three decades later, on 27 January 2003, the Home Office gave Evans's half-sister Mary Westlake and his sister Eileen Ashby *ex gratia* payments for the miscarriage of justice. Lord Brennan QC, the independent assessor for the Home Office, considered that 'there is no evidence to implicate Timothy Evans in the murder of his wife. She was most probably murdered by Christie.' Mary Westlake tried to get a formal quashing of her half-brother's conviction; the case was dismissed, even though the High Court accepted that he did not murder either Geraldine or Beryl.

Of course, none of this legal manoeuvring made a difference to Timothy Evans, who had been hanged for a crime he didn't commit – although his remains were moved from the grounds of Pentonville Prison to a cemetery in Leytonstone.

CHAPTER 9

Great Britain: John George Haigh – The Acid Bath Murderer

....

'It was an effort to refrain from audible laughter when the Judge donned his black cap. He looked for all the world like a sheep with its head peering out from under a rhubarb leaf.'

So wrote John Haigh on 26 July 1949, a mere fortnight before he was hanged for the murders of William Donald McSwan, Donald and Amy McSwan, Archibald and Rosalie Henderson, and Henrietta Helen Olive Robarts Durand-Deacon. Known as the Acid Bath Murderer, after his method of disposing of the bodies of his victims, Haigh admitted to police that he was responsible for at least three other murders (although these could not be substantiated), as well as claiming in a letter to his girlfriend from prison that '[t]here were men as well as women how many I don't know probably a dozen or more . . .', although he maintained in the same letter that she herself had never been in danger from him. Perhaps if she had been wealthy, and he had been able to find a way to get hold of her assets on her death, the situation would have been very different.

John George Haigh was born in 1909 to fanatically religious parents, growing up in the small village of Outwood, not far from Wakefield, in Yorkshire. Members of the Plymouth Bethren, his parents did not want their son to be affected by the outside world, so he was confined to play within a ten-foot high wall that his father built around their garden. He was a gifted pianist (taught, unsurprisingly, at home) and, thanks to his musical talents, gained a scholarship to the local grammar school, and then to Wakefield Cathedral, where he was a choirboy and later assistant organist.

To those around him, the young Haigh seemed charm personified, but like so many of those whose actions are featured in this volume, beneath the surface he was a mass of contradictions. He would later claim that his killing spree was triggered by the return of a nightmare he had as a child:

> I saw before me a forest of crucifixes which gradually turned into trees. At first, there appeared to be dew or rain, dripping from the branches, but as I approached I realized it was blood. The whole forest began to writhe and the trees, dark and erect, to ooze blood ... A man went from each tree catching the blood ... When the cup was full, he approached me. 'Drink,' he said, but I was unable to move.

However, it wasn't as if he went from being a model citizen to a killer; his criminal career had begun a full decade before he committed his first murder.

After leaving school, Haigh was apprenticed to a firm of motor engineers before taking jobs in insurance and advertising, but, aged twenty-one, he was suspected of stealing from a cash box and fired. In July 1934, he wed Betty Hamer – Haigh was imprisoned for fraud four months later, leaving Betty pregnant with their child. (She gave the baby up for adoption, and left her husband.) Further sentences for fraud followed over the next decade but, in 1936, during one of his periods outside jail, he was hired as chauffeur/secretary to Donald McSwan, a local politician who also owned some amusement arcades. Haigh became friendly with McSwan's son William (known as Mac), who ran the arcades, and helped maintain the machines.

It was during a stint in Lincoln Prison, following conviction in 1942 for attempting to defraud his landlady, that Haigh started to be fixated on the idea of 'corpus delicti' – a legal principle which at its core states that the prosecution must prove that a crime has been actually committed. If, Haigh reasoned, there was no evidence that he had committed a crime, he could not be tried and imprisoned (or worse) for it. If he committed a murder and there was no body then, to his mind, that meant nobody could convict him. He therefore started to work out the 'perfect' murder.

Haigh carried out various experiments with acid that he obtained from the tinsmith's shop, and discovered that the corpse of a field mouse would only take half an hour to dissolve completely, leaving no evidence. It was then a simple matter of mathematics to calculate how much acid would be needed to get rid of a human body.

On his release in 1943, Haigh got a good job as a bookkeeper with Hurstlea Products Ltd, a small engineering firm in Crawley, West Sussex, and eventually was able to set up his own firm, Union Group Engineering. According to his version of events, it was in early 1944 that he suffered a head injury in a car crash, which triggered his decision to turn his theory into practice. The dream, Haigh's barrister Sir David Maxwell Fyfe said at his trial, left him 'with an overpowering desire to have blood'. The fact that he had already been experimenting with small animals was an inconvenient truth Haigh preferred to ignore.

It was Mac McSwan's bad luck that he ran into his old friend at the Goat public house in Kensington, west London, not far from Haigh's lodgings in Queen's Gate Terrace. Haigh got to know his parents Donald and Amy better, and they confided in the personable young man that they had invested in various properties. Mac also told Haigh that he was worried about being called up for war service, and Haigh promised to help. On 6 September 1944, Haigh invited the younger McSwan to the basement of 79 Gloucester Road,

Kensington, where he had set up a workshop. There he hit his victim over the head with an iron bar from behind, killing him pretty much instantly (although he hit him twice more till he felt a 'squashy' feeling) and then slit his throat. After that, he claimed, he 'withdrew a quantity of blood' and drank it from a mug; when this was revealed, Haigh became known as the 'Vampire Killer' thanks to some lurid headlines in the *Daily Mirror*. He dropped Mac's body into a forty-gallon drum of sulphuric acid (which Haigh had been able to obtain in small quantities as 'Technical Liaison Officer' for Union Group) and waited to see if his calculations had been accurate. Haigh admitted that the wait took its toll on him – the crucifixion- and communion-based dreams he had suffered as a child returned – but, after a couple of days, he was delighted to discover that he had been correct. Mac McSwan was now nothing more than an acidic sludge – which Haigh poured down the drain.

Mac's parents were naturally concerned about the disappearance of their son, but Haigh persuaded them that he had gone into hiding to avoid being called up. One of Haigh's many criminal talents was as a forger and he arranged for several postcards to be sent to the McSwans from Scotland, where Mac was apparently hiding. He was soon living in Mac's house, as well as maintaining the workshop basement in Gloucester Road and taking a room at the Onslow Court Hotel in Kensington. After the end of the war in Europe at the start of May 1945, the McSwans started to become suspicious. Why hadn't Mac come out of hiding? The final communication from their son said he was coming back to London, and invited them to meet him at Haigh's basement in Gloucester Road on the evening of 2 July 1945. Haigh suggested that they arrive separately, and when each made their way downstairs, they were murdered, and their bodies disposed of in a similar way to that of their son. (Haigh claimed that he had refined his technique, adding some hydrochloric acid to the mix, on a middle-aged woman from Hammersmith in the interim; no such victim was ever identified. He also told police that in the months after the McSwans' deaths, he killed and disposed of a young man called Max from Kensington; again, this was never proved.)

Over the next three months Haigh forged various powers of attorney so that he could use, and then liquidate, the McSwans' assets, claiming to any friends or neighbours who might enquire that the pair had emigrated to America and he was acting on their behalf. Haigh financed his gambling habit with the money – he was able to raise around £8,000 from the various sales – until it began to run out, and he started to look for more victims. He had tried returning to his fraudulent ways with a car scam in Stockport, but that hadn't panned out. He needed a more direct approach.

Behind the locked doors of a workshop in Crawley that he was renting from his former employers at Hurstlea, Haigh assembled the tools that he would require for his task, arranging for some to be brought from his Kensington basement. These included a gas mask (still easy to obtain in the years immediately after the war), a stirrup pump, an enamel bucket, a large rubber apron, rubber gloves and wader-length rubber boots, as well as an oil drum, around forty gallons in volume, in which he could place his victim ready for disposal.

During his time at the Onslow Court, Haigh had become friends with Dr Archibald Henderson and his wife Rosalie, and in February 1948, the three went for a brief holiday at the Metropole Hotel on Brighton seafront. On Friday 13 February, Archie Henderson accompanied Haigh on a visit to his workshop twenty-five miles north in Crawley. Archie had a considerable sum of cash (hundreds of pounds) on him, and Haigh was well aware of how to get hold of the rest of his assets. The unsuspecting Archie walked into the workshop – and was shot in the back of the head. Haigh stripped him and then put him in the acid before driving back to Brighton, where he told the new widow that Archie was feeling ill and she needed to come with him. Rosalie did so, and suffered an identical fate to her husband. Within two days, the bodies were dissolved and disposed of down the drain. Haigh checked out of the Metropole on the Monday, paying his and his friends' bills, pawned Rosalie's jewellery, and then drove to Edinburgh. In his diary, he made an unusual inscription for 12 February: A.H. and R.H. and a small cruciform cross.

Over the next few months, Haigh disposed of their assets as easily as he had their bodies, allaying the fears of Rosalie's brother with a series of forged letters suggesting they had gone to South Africa. He kept their dog for a while, but eventually tired of the company, preferring to spend time with young Barbara Stephens, whom he had met in Crawley in 1944 when she was just fifteen. He also began to cultivate his friendship with Henrietta Helen Olive Robarts Durand-Deacon, another resident at the Onslow Court.

Haigh had known the sixty-nine-year-old widow, known as Olive, throughout his time at the hotel, but as 1949 dawned, they were spending increasing amounts of time together. Haigh had gambled away the Hendersons' money far too quickly, and once again was being pressured to pay his rent. On Valentine's Day, Olive mooted the idea of them going into business together to develop a new kind of artificial fingernail. It was the pretext that Haigh needed to get her to his workshop. On Tuesday, 15 February, he ordered ten gallons of acid, and arranged to have it delivered to Crawley; twenty more gallons were already there. The following day, he invited Olive to visit the workshop on Friday to discuss the fingernail project further; straight afterwards, he went to Barking where he bought a forty-five gallon tank which he took down to Crawley. On Friday morning, he checked that everything was prepared, then returned to Kensington, collected Olive Durand-Deacon and brought her to his workshop.

Haigh's final victim was dispatched in the same way as her two predecessors, with a shot to the back of her head. However, this time, he had more problem with the disposal. Fat didn't dissolve as easily, and, as Haigh said in his statement, 'for this reason, Mrs Durand-Deacon was a confounded nuisance . . . [N]ext day when I had expected her body to be entirely dissolved I found a large piece of buttock floating on top of the sludge and grease that was the rest of her.' He therefore emptied off the grease, and refreshed the acid – but 'she simply would not go and there were still some parts left, though quite unrecognisable for what they were, when I emptied the sludge on to a rubbish heap outside the shed'.

He also found that he had far more questions to answer than normal. The next morning, one of the other residents, Constance Lane, revealed that she knew that Olive was planning on going with Haigh down to Crawley. Haigh had to think fast. He told Constance that Olive had failed to make their rendezvous at the Army & Navy Stores in Victoria Street after lunch, and he hadn't seen her since. Haigh spent the Saturday pawning Olive's jewellery.

On the Sunday, Constance Lane said she was going to report Olive missing, and Haigh volunteered to come to the police station with her. There, policewoman Sergeant Lambourne took down the story and began investigations, instinctively suspicious of Haigh – a suspicion that deepened when she visited Onslow Court to be told of his financial problems. After his criminal record for fraud was uncovered, Haigh was questioned on the Monday by Detective Inspectors Symes and Webb; he kept to his story. The following day, he finally was able to pour Olive's remains away, although carelessly; he simply hid her undissolved handbag under some bricks. Despite the police interest, he was sure that, without a body, nothing more could happen.

The police investigation continued, with Haigh's old employer questioned about a loan that he had made to Haigh the previous week. By Saturday, the case against him was becoming clear, and that day, Detective Sergeant Patrick Heslin, the head of Horsham CID, forced open the door of Haigh's workshop at Leopold Road, Crawley, and discovered the tools of his trade, including a gun, and a receipt from a cleaner's in the nearby town of Reigate. This was for Olive's coat – which was quickly identified by Constance Lane and others.

John George Haigh was taken to Chelsea Police Station on Monday, 28 February, ten days after Olive's murder, where he was faced with the considerable evidence the police had amassed. During a brief break, he asked DI Webb, 'Tell me frankly, what are the chances of anyone being released from Broadmoor?' – a very odd thing for anyone to ask, but the preparation for his eventual defence of insanity. He then admitted that he had killed Olive but 'no trace of her can ever be found again . . . I've destroyed her with acid . . . Every trace has gone. How can you prove murder if there's no body?'

Haigh was wrong. Firstly, corpus delicti didn't apply in cases of murder if other evidence could be found – but, more to the point, there still was evidence of Olive Durand-Deacon's presence and disposal at Leopold Road. The Home Office pathologist Dr Keith Simpson attended the site, and after finding a small 'pebble' that he realised was a gallstone, he ordered that the sludge be collected up – all 475 pounds of it. Gallstones, eighteen pieces of bone and Olive's false teeth were found in the sludge, while her hairpin remained undissolved in the acid vat. Haigh might as well not have bothered. He was charged with Olive's murder on 2 March 1949.

In his statement to police, Haigh admitted the murders – as well as three others in total that could never be proved – and claimed that, after each, he had sipped the blood of his victim. Parts of his statement were leaked to the *Daily Mirror*, which included them in a story about a 'Vampire Killer', although, because of the sub judice legislation (which prevents active court cases from being discussed in the media), Haigh was never named. That didn't prevent the newspaper from being fined £10,000 and the editor sent to prison!

Haigh's trial at Lewes Assizes began on 18 July. He had made a deal with the tabloid Sunday newspaper, the *News of the World*, for his true story, and that enabled him to hire a high-powered, and expensive, legal team to counter the Attorney General, who would be prosecuting. He was only on trial for the murder of Olive Durand-Deacon and the judge often refused to allow evidence that related to the other cases as the defence attempted to prove their client was guilty but insane. At the time the M'Naghten rules were in effect, which stated that to

establish a defence on the ground of insanity, it must be clearly proved that, at the time of the committing of the act, the party accused was labouring under such a defect of reason, from disease of mind, and not to know the nature and quality of the act he was doing; or if he did know it, that he did not know he was doing what was wrong.

Eight out of nine psychiatrists who observed Haigh in prison thought he was sane; the ninth, Dr Henry Yellowlees, admitted in court that while he believed the defendant was insane, he thought Haigh had been aware that his actions were legally wrong.

It took the jury seventeen minutes to find him guilty. Haigh maintained his claims of insanity in the *News of the World* articles that followed, as well as in his letters from prison to his parents and others, knowing that the only thing that could save him from the gallows was a reprieve from the Home Secretary – and that would only be given if he could be proved insane. 'After all, did they not accuse Christ of being mad too?' he wrote to his solicitor. 'Was I not burned at the stake as a Warlock in Salem?'

Despite such efforts, no reprieve was forthcoming. John George Haigh was hanged by Albert Pierrepoint at Wandsworth Prison on Monday, 10 August 1949. He left his green suit and red tie to Madam Tussauds waxworks to adorn the figure that was placed in the Chamber of Horrors.

CHAPTER 10

Great Britain: Ian Brady and Myra Hindley – The Moors Murderers

·············

'At some stage of this trial, you will have to suffer the burden of listening to a tape recording being played and hearing a little girl's screams and protests,' Attorney General Sir Elwyn Jones told the jurors and court officials at the start of a triple-murder trial at Chester Assizes in April 1966. The young girl's sobbing voice still re-echoes for any who have heard the recording, as she pleads with her captors to release her – she doesn't know why they've taken off her clothes, or why they want her to put a gag in her mouth. She doesn't know why they've not let her go to her mother. She calls the woman who's making her do these things 'mummy', the man 'daddy'. All she knows is that if she's not back home by 8 p.m., she will be in awful trouble . . .

Lesley Ann Downey was just one of the five known victims of 'two sadistic killers of the utmost depravity': Myra Hindley and Ian Brady, collectively known as the Moors Murderers, since they buried the bodies of the children they raped and murdered on Saddleworth Moor in Yorkshire. Not all the graves have yet been found, and with Hindley dead and Brady's health deteriorating (he sent early Christmas cards in October 2015 because of his concern that he wouldn't last much longer), the odds of them being found by anything other than happenstance are very low.

Brady was born Ian Duncan Stewart in a Glasgow slum on 2 January 1938, to an unmarried waitress who eventually had to give him up to a local couple, John and Mary Sloan, as she couldn't look after him. The Sloans brought up Ian as one of their own – although his birth mother saw him regularly through his childhood – but they were unable to keep him out of trouble. His behaviour at Shawlands Academy, a school for above-average pupils, grew progressively worse, and he appeared before a juvenile court on charges of house-breaking aged thirteen. He left school at fifteen, working at a Govan shipyard and then as a butcher's messenger boy. His relationships with girls his own age weren't strong; he threatened one, Evelyn Grant, with a flick knife when she went to a dance with another boy.

Stewart, as he was still known, appeared in court on nine charges shortly before his seventeenth birthday and was placed on proba-tion, on condition that he lived with his mother, who was now resi-dent in Manchester and married to an Irish fruit importer named Patrick Brady. It was his new stepfather who got the boy a job at Manchester's Smithfield Market, but this was simply seen as an opportunity by the teenager, who was caught within a year with a sack of lead seals stolen from the market. He was put into the borstal system, starting at Latchmere House in London before being sent to Hatfield borstal in Yorkshire and finally – after getting caught drunk on homemade alcohol – to a very tough Hull institution. He was finally released on 14 November 1957, and returned to Manchester where, after an abortive attempt to get a job, he decided to 'better himself' and studied bookkeeping, as well as German (which allowed him to read Hitler's *Mein Kampf* in the original language). This led to employment in January 1959 at wholesale chemical distribution company Millward's Merchandising in Gorton.

Most colleagues of Ian Brady – as he now called himself – thought of him as a quiet, punctual, if short-tempered man, who liked to ride his Tiger Cub motorbike round the Pennines. One new arrival in 1961 thought far more of him. Eighteen-year-old Myra Hindley found him fascinating.

Hindley was born on 23 July 1942 in the Manchester suburb of Crumpsall, and brought up in Gorton. She had a hard childhood: her father was an alcoholic who, when he returned from service in the war, not only subjected her to corporal punishment, but also insisted that she stand up for herself with others, getting her to beat up another eight-year-old 'because if you don't, I'll leather you', after the boy scratched her cheeks in the street. Hindley spent much of her time with her grandmother, particularly after the birth of her sister Maureen in August 1946.

Her life was turned upside down by the death of her friend, thirteen-year-old Michael Higgins, who had invited her to join a group of friends going swimming at the local reservoir. Hindley refused, and Higgins drowned. Hindley blamed herself for the death; she turned to the Roman Catholic Church for support (she had been baptised, but not brought up in the Church) and she also started to bleach her hair. Hindley started working as a junior clerk at a local engineering firm, and went through various jobs before joining Millward's. She'd also had a relationship with a local lad, Ronnie Sinclair, but broke off their engagement when she realised that he didn't share her ambitions.

While Hindley was infatuated with Brady, it seems that he didn't take too much notice of her across the latter half of 1961, until he finally asked her out on a date on 22 December. They went to the cinema – Hindley recalled they saw the biblical epic *King of Kings*, although many sources claim that it was the eerily appropriate *Judgement at Nuremberg*. The two dated for some time, going to X-rated films (the contemporary equivalent of today's 18 classification in the UK), then going back to Hindley's house to drink and talk. They shared an interest in Nazi atrocities, crime and torture, and would spend their lunchbreaks discussing such topics – as well as classical music and English literature.

According to Hindley, she was completely under Brady's spell. Whatever he wanted, she would do. 'He could have told me that the earth was flat, the moon was made of green cheese and the sun rose in the west,' she wrote to the then Home Secretary in 1978, Merlyn Rees, when applying for parole. 'I would have believed him, such was his power of persuasion.' The two spent more and more time together until, in June 1963, Brady moved in with Hindley at her grandmother's house in Bannock Street.

During their eighteen-month courtship prior to then, they had considered various criminal acts, including bank robberies, although these came to nothing. Hindley tried to learn to shoot, buying a .22 rifle from a Manchester gun merchant, and two pistols – a Webley .45 and a Smith & Wesson .38 – from members of the Cheadle Rifle Club, which she joined. Hindley became more outré in her appearance, adopting short skirts, high boots and leather jackets, and becoming increasingly distant from her other colleagues. The pair also began to develop an interest in photography, taking of each other photos of an explicit nature.

Brady was fascinated by the works of the Marquis de Sade (his copy of *Justine* was kept as evidence against him), and penned his own thoughts on the subject in his notebooks: 'Perversion is the way a man thinks, the way he feels, the way he lives. People are like maggots. Small, blind worthless fish bait ... You are your own master. You live for one thing, supreme pleasure in everything you do. Sadism is the supreme pleasure!!!'

He also began to consider the idea of the perfect murder. This was inspired, according to Hindley, by Meyer Levin's book *Compulsion*, a thinly fictionalised version of the Leopold and Loeb case – in which two students kidnapped and murdered a fourteen-year-old, and escaped the death penalty thanks to the brilliant oratory of their lawyer, Clarence Darrow – which was published in 1956 and filmed three years later. Brady would put his ideas into effect within a month of moving in with Hindley.

On 12 July 1963, Pauline Reade was kidnapped and killed. She was just sixteen at the time, and lived not far from Hindley. Although their accounts differed as to exactly what happened once they were on Saddleworth Moor, both Brady and Hindley agreed that he had decided to commit the perfect murder that evening. Brady told her to drive a van she had borrowed from the local greengrocer around the nearby streets, and he would follow on his motorbike; if he saw a likely target, he would flash his headlight. Hindley was then to stop the van, and offer the person a lift.

Brady's first choice of target as they drove in tandem down Gorton Lane was a young girl. He signalled, but Hindley ignored him, pulling over a little further down the road. She explained that she knew the young girl Brady had indicated; Marie Ruck lived near Hindley's mother. She was concerned that taking a child of seven or eight would gain far more attention than someone older. They therefore continued their quest, and on Froxmer Street, just after eight o'clock, Brady saw a girl in a pale-blue coat, pink and gold dress, cardigan and white high-heeled shoes. Hindley also recognised this teenager – Pauline Reade, who was a friend of her sister Maureen, heading to a dance for the first time on her own. The sixteen-year-old was happy to help Hindley try to find an expensive glove that she said she had lost on Saddleworth Moor, thirteen miles away.

Hindley drove to the moor, where they were joined by Brady. It's at this point that the serial killers' stories differ. Hindley maintained that she stayed in the van while Brady and Pauline went to look for the glove, and after half an hour or so, Brady returned on his own. He took her to the place where Pauline was lying, her life blood draining away through the two cuts in her throat that Brady had inflicted. Brady fetched a spade, and Hindley guessed from the state of Pauline's coat and the disarray of her clothes that Brady had sexually assaulted her. Brady's version of events implicated Hindley far more heavily. He stated that she was there throughout, and aided in the sexual assault on Pauline. Whichever was true, the pair buried the body (using a spade that Brady had previously placed on the moor), put Brady's motorbike in the back of the van, and then drove home, passing Pauline's mother and brother looking for her – but ironically, all they found was her glove.

Pauline Reade's body was not located until 1987, after Myra Hindley provided fresh information. According to Home Office pathologist Dr Geoffrey Garrett, the cause of death was haemorrhage following the 'homicidal' throat-cutting. The larger, gaping wound was four inches long and 'inflicted with considerable force', and Pauline had also been dealt a blow to the head with either a fist or a blunt instrument. The killers had forced a throat chain and the collar of the girl's coat into the wound; 'it may have been carried out in an attempt to reduce the amount of bleeding,' Dr Garrett suggested.

Pauline's disappearance was investigated by the police who were unable to find anyone who had seen her on the night of her death. Fifteen-year-old local boy David Smith – who would go on to play a critical part in the capture of the Moors Murderers – briefly came under suspicion, as he had been in a relationship with Pauline for a short time and had a conviction for wounding with intent, but he was cleared of any involvement in her disappearance.

The pair's next victim was killed on 23 November 1963, when the eyes of the world were focused on the assassination of US President John F. Kennedy the previous day. This time their target was a twelve-year-old boy, John Kilbride, who was out on the Saturday evening at a market at Ashton-under-Lyne in Lancashire. He had left his home in Smallshaw Lane, Ashton, at 1 p.m. to go with a friend to the local cinema. His friend left him at the market at 5.30 p.m.

Hindley was driving a two-door white Ford Anglia van she had hired for twenty-four hours (eventually returning it in 'a very dirty condition'), and offered the boy a lift home, as his parents would be bound to be worried he was out so late. She also said that she had a bottle of sherry at home, which they would need to pick up on the way. Brady was a passenger in the van and suggested that young John could help them look for a glove that Hindley had lost on the moor. On reaching Saddleworth Moor, Hindley waited in the car, while Brady took him off to search. John was 'subjected to sexual indignities' – his trousers were pulled down to about mid-thigh level, and the underpants were rolled down to above thigh level and appeared to be knotted at the back, according to the Attorney General at the trial – before Brady tried to cut his throat with a six-inch serrated blade, without success. He then strangled the boy, using either a piece of string or a shoelace.

A police search for John turned up no clues. The boy's clothed body was eventually discovered on 21 October 1965; his mother was able to identify it from the unusual buttons on his coat, which were plastic in the shape of a soccer ball. Brady and Hindley returned to the spot where John was buried on more than one occasion, with Brady taking photographs of his partner in crime with her dog on top of the grave. Brady would try to claim these were just snapshots and the position was mere coincidence.

Seven months elapsed before the pair killed again. Keith Bennett disappeared while heading to his grandmother's house in Longsight during the early evening of 16 June 1964, a mere four days after his twelfth birthday. Hindley asked for Keith's help to load some boxes into her car, and offered him a lift home. When they reached a layby on the A635 road across Saddleworth Moor, Brady once again used the excuse of looking for a missing glove to entice Bennett from the car, and he and the young boy disappeared onto the moor. Brady returned after half an hour, and told Hindley he had sexually assaulted Keith before strangling him with a piece of string. Despite multiple searches of the moor, his body has never been found. Keith Bennett's stepfather, Jimmy Johnson, was considered a serious suspect in the disappearance, and was interrogated on four occasions in the two years before Brady and Hindley were arrested.

The next death wasn't for a further six months, but during that time there were considerable changes to Brady and Hindley's living arrangements. Hindley's sister Maureen married David Smith – Pauline Reade's former boyfriend – on 15 August 1964, when he was just sixteen and she was eighteen. Maureen was seven months pregnant at the time of the wedding, and they moved into the house of Smith's father. The two sisters and their partners went out on a day trip to Windermere in the Lake District the next day, and according to David Smith's second wife, Mary, he thought that 'being with them was a party'. He was impressed by Brady's apparent sophistication, and the fact he had paid for all of Smith's food and drink during their outing; Brady was equally impressed by the young man, who wasn't put off by talk of robbing a bank. The Smiths, Brady and Hindley went out frequently as a foursome.

Hindley and Brady – along with Hindley's grandmother – moved to 16 Wardle Brook Avenue in Hattersley, a new home on a freshly built council estate, in September 1964, and the pair frequently travelled to Saddleworth Moor to collect peat to use in the garden. During that time they were helped by eleven-year-old Patricia Hodges, who would often come round to their house and drink wine and whisky with them after Hindley befriended her. Hindley later said they had taken pity on her because she was one of seven children in a relatively poor family and she did not have a television set. She denied that there was ever anything sexual about their interest.

'On two occasions I went for walks on the moor with Ian and Myra,' Patricia Hodges told police. One of these was on Christmas

Eve 1964, when her mother gave her permission to go on a late outing with Hindley; they went out at 11.30 p.m. and Hindley suggested that they spend the night there, but in the end took her home at 1.30 on Christmas morning.

Patricia Hodges was lucky. Myra Hindley had known Pauline Reade, and that hadn't stopped her from being involved in her rape and murder. And it was clear that Brady was ready to kill again because on Boxing Day 1964, Lesley Ann Downey disappeared.

This time, the killers' modus operandi was very different from previously. Their other victims had been found, taken to the moor, raped, strangled and buried. This one, they were going to bring home. On Boxing Day morning, Hindley took her grandmother to visit her uncle. She and Brady went to the fairground at Ancoats in search of their new victim. Ten-year-old Lesley Ann Downey was standing by one of the rides, clearly not there with anyone else (her friends had already gone home). The pair enticed her into the car by asking for help with some packages they were carrying, and took her home. There she was undressed and gagged with a scarf despite her protests. She was then made to pose for pornographic photos before she was raped and killed. Brady claimed Hindley killed the young girl; Hindley said she left the room to fill a bath for the girl, and when she came back, Lesley Ann was dead. The pair recorded the torture; the thirteen-minute tape was one of the most telling pieces of evidence against them at their trial, with Hindley clearly being brusque and hard with the young girl. No matter what she might claim later, the tape shows she was present throughout. Hindley then went to her uncle's and said she couldn't bring her grandmother home as 'the roads are too bad' and was adamant that she could not return until the next day.

Another recording would form part of the evidence, one in which Patricia Hodges can be heard reading out details from newspaper stories about the police hunt for Lesley Ann Downey. It wouldn't be long before Brady would warn her to stay away: 'Don't let me cop you in here again' were the last words he spoke to her in the spring of 1965. Brady and Hindley had taken Patricia up to the moor, near the shallow grave where, on the morning of 27 December 1964, they had buried Lesley Ann's body, naked, with her clothes in a heap at her feet. It was unearthed on 16 October the following year.

Brady, Hindley and the Smiths spent more time together as 1965 unfolded. David and Maureen lost their baby daughter in April and, three months later, they moved to Underwood Court, an apartment block not far from where Brady and Hindley were living. Smith became a regular visitor at Wardle Brook Avenue.

Towards the end of September, Brady and Smith were chatting in the small hours of the morning at the Smiths' home, and discussing a potential armed robbery. Brady insisted that their weapons would need to be loaded with live bullets, and asked Smith if he was capable of murder. Smith looked at him blankly, and Brady told him, 'I have done it.' He then admitted to Smith that he had 'done three or four murders': he would 'pick people between 16 and 20 years of age, because they would not be reported missing to the police' (so the Attorney General told the court at Brady and Hindley's trial). Brady also told Smith that he took a drug before committing the murders. On 2 October, the subject came up again, and Brady repeated he had committed three or four murders, and that 'he was not due for another one for about three months' and that 'this one would not count'. Three days later, Brady got Smith to help him take two large suitcases from the house at Wardle Brook Avenue.

On 6 October 1965, Brady got chatting with a stranger outside the buffet at Manchester Central railway station; Hindley had dropped him off there with a view to finding their next victim. Seventeen-year-old apprentice engineer Edward Evans enjoyed his conversation with the older man, and agreed to come back to Wardle Brook Avenue for a drink with Brady and his 'sister', Myra Hindley.

They shared a bottle of wine, then Brady told Hindley to fetch her brother-in-law, David Smith. Hindley did so, and told Smith to wait outside the door for her signal, which would be a flashing light.

Smith did as he was told, and when the signal came, he knocked on the door. Brady opened it and, in what Smith described in his police statement as 'a very loud voice for him', asked: 'Do you want these miniatures?' Smith nodded and followed Brady into the kitchen, past the closed living-room door. Brady then asked if he wanted the rest, and left him there. 'Ian went into the living room . . . I waited about a minute or two then suddenly I heard a hell of a scream; it sounded like a woman, really high-pitched. Then the screams carried on, one after another really loud.'

At that point Hindley called Smith in. He raced into the living room, where he saw Brady with what he later realized was Edward Evans. 'My first thought was that Ian had hold of a life-size rag doll and was just waving it about,' Smith told the court, having earlier said in his statement that Edward was

lying with his head and shoulders on the couch and his legs were on the floor. He was facing upwards. Ian was standing over him, facing him, with his legs on either side of the young lad's legs. The lad was still screaming . . . Ian had a hatchet in his hand . . . and he hit the lad on the left side of his head with the hatchet. I heard the blow, it was a terrible hard blow, it sounded horrible.

After he had incapacitated Edward with the axe, Brady placed a cushion over the teenager's battered head, then throttled him with a length of electrical cord, all the while saying, 'You [expletive deleted by the newspapers], you dirty bastard', over and over again. Once it was done, Brady looked up at Hindley. 'That's it. It's the messiest yet.' Normally, he added, it only took one blow.

'He was very calm, very calm indeed,' Smith told the trial. 'I have seen butchers working in the shops show as much emotion as he did when they are cutting up a sheep's ribs.'

The plan was to dispose of Edward in the same way as Lesley Ann and the others, up on Saddleworth Moor, but Brady had sprained his ankle and couldn't help Smith take the body out to Hindley's car. They cleaned up the walls, linoleum and carpet, then they wrapped the body in a blanket and a big sheet of Polythene, and put it in the upstairs spare room. Smith agreed that he would come back the next evening with a pram he would borrow from his grandfather, and under the cover of darkness help Brady dispose of the corpse.

But Brady had overestimated the power he had over Smith. He wasn't the pliant apprentice-cum-partner that Myra Hindley had proved to be. Instead, Smith went home and told his wife Maureen what had happened. It was Myra's sister who insisted that they should call the police, and at 6.07 a.m., the Smiths went to a public phonebox (very few houses had their own telephone lines at that point in time) and rang 999. They took a screwdriver and carving knife with them, just in case they encountered Brady; Smith was well aware that he was taking his life in his hands by informing on Brady to the police. The police collected them from the phonebox as soon as they heard the allegations Smith was making.

Superintendent Bob Talbot of the Cheshire Police was passed the information that Smith gave the officer on duty, and early on the morning of 7 October, he and twenty-five other officers went to 16 Wardle Brook Avenue, the majority forming a ring around the property, there in case Smith's report that Brady had a firearm were true. Talbot had a baker's overall over his uniform when he knocked on the door to allay suspicion, and when Hindley answered, Talbot said he needed to speak to her boyfriend. Brady was on a divan in the living room, writing a sick note to his employer following his ankle injury. Talbot said there had been a report of 'an act of violence involving guns', and while Hindley denied any such thing had happened, she allowed the police to search the house. The upstairs room was locked, and Hindley said the key was at work; Talbot offered to have a police officer drive her to the office to collect it, at which point Brady seemed to have realised that the game was up, and told Hindley to give them the key. In the room, Talbot saw a large bundle wrapped in a blanket. 'I went to it and saw the shape of a human foot sticking out of the blanket,' Talbot told the trial. A hatchet and a stick were in a carrier bag beside it.

They had found the body of Edward Evans. The examination by Dr Charles Arthur St Hill, the Home Office pathologist for the Liverpool area, would reveal there were fourteen lacerations in the scalp and the side of the head – both the blade side and the head of the hatchet were used. Edward died of cerebral contusion and haemorrhage, resulting from fractures of the skull, accelerated by strangulation by ligature. Even if the ligature had not been applied, Edward could not have survived his injuries; St Hill agreed in court that he might have died just before the electrical cable was used.

'Eddie and I had a row and the situation got out of hand,' Brady said when he was arrested on suspicion of murder. Hindley wasn't arrested at the same time, but she and her dog came along to the police station with Brady. She was questioned about her involvement, but she simply maintained that Edward's death was an accident; she wasn't arrested until 11 October, which gave her time to dispose of some papers of Brady's (which she said were related to planned bank robberies), and asked to be dismissed from her job so she could claim the dole.

Aware of who had shopped him to the police, Brady took revenge in the only way he could, by claiming in interviews that David Smith had been an active participant in the murder of Edward Evans (and that Hindley wasn't). Despite clear evidence to the contrary over the years, rumours surrounded Smith until his premature death over thirty years later, not helped by the revelation at the trial that he and Maureen had accepted payments from a newspaper. Smith, of course, denied he was an active participant, but did tell police that he knew Brady had 'a thing about railway stations'. He also told them that Brady had packed suitcases with 'dodgy books'. The police requested a search of all the left luggage offices in the area, and on 15 October, the British Transport Police found a load of suitcases belonging to Brady at Manchester Central railway station. Inside was the evidence that the police needed: nine photographs of a naked Lesley Ann Downey, and the tape-recording of her torture.

Searches at Brady and Hindley's home had already turned up an exercise book with the name 'John Kilbride' written inside, as well as many of the photographs taken on Saddleworth Moor. Patricia Hodges helped the police to identify the spots where she had been taken by the murderers – and was later adamant in court that she had been the one to tell the police where to stop, not responding to their suggestions of locations. The day after the discovery of the suitcases, a body was found on the moor by the 150 officers who had been tasked with finding where the photos had been shot. It was Lesley Ann Downey. Her mother identified her the next day. Four days after that, John Kilbride's 'badly decomposed' body was found on the opposite side of the A635. Brady and Hindley had already been charged with the murder of Edward Evans; now Lesley Ann Downey's name was added to the charge sheet. Both were separately brought before a court and remanded in custody.

Brady could hardly deny that he had been involved in Lesley Ann's disappearance, given the tape recording and photographic evidence, but he said that he hadn't killed her – instead two other men had brought her to Wardle Brook Avenue, and then taken her away again when Brady had finished photographing her. 'I was told later she had been dropped at Belle Vue,' he told Detective Chief

Superintendent Arthur Benfield. At a committal hearing on 6 December, he was additionally charged with John Kilbride's murder; Hindley was charged with harbouring Brady, knowing he had killed the boy.

The proceedings took eleven days to hear, with both saying they were not guilty. Hindley's barrister, Philip Curtis, tried hard to get the accessory charge dropped, without joy, and said that the photograph of Hindley by John Kilbride's grave was of no significance. The prosecutor, William Mars-Jones, suggested otherwise. 'This is a spot which is 70 yards away from the road in the middle of nowhere, in the middle of many square miles of desolate moorland. There we have a snapshot taken in the middle of nowhere, of the accused, Myra Hindley, in an unusual pose. Does it not remind your Worships of a bereaved relative standing alongside the grave of a dearly departed, looking at the grave with downcast eyes? Or do you think that the explanation by Myra Hindley is the reasonable one – "No, it's just a normal snap. I was looking at the dog."' Hindley had also said it was a 'coincidence' in her police interview on 28 October that she was photographed near Lesley Ann's grave.

The pair were remanded to Cardiff Assizes for trial in January 1966, although it was actually 19 April before it began at Chester Assizes, with the two accused behind bulletproof screens because of the depth of hatred against them. By now, Hindley was accused of John Kilbride's murder as well, although the accessory charge remained part of the indictment. The defence made much of Smith's contract with a newspaper, which was apparently dependent on conviction, and Brady's claims that Smith was an active participant in the crimes, but the playing of the tape of Lesley Ann Downey's torture on the sixth day, 26 April, affected everyone present. 'Three women in the public gallery covered their ears with their hands and two of them bent forward, dropping their hands on to their chests,' the *Glasgow Herald* reported. Everyone, that is, bar the defendants, who 'sat quietly in the dock, looking straight in front of them towards the judge'.

Giving evidence on the eighth day, Brady admitted hitting Edward Evans but 'the axe just bounced on his head, and it did not seem to have any effect'. He said that he had decided to 'roll a queer' and met Edward, whom he knew was homosexual, at Manchester station. 'I decided that he was the one who would do for what Smith and I had been talking about earlier that night.' He had brought Edward back to the house and told him to give him his money, as the 'bloke at the door . . . does not like queers'. Smith was the one who had dealt the fatal blows with his stick and treated the death lightly: Brady said his demeanour was 'theatrical, jocular. He was trying to crack jokes.' He denied all knowledge of the deaths of the other two victims. In her evidence, Hindley said that it was Smith who had procured Lesley Ann Downey for Brady to photograph, and that the girl had left the house with Smith.

Summing up, the Attorney General pointed out that there was 'a mass of evidence in this case from other quarters, other sources, than the mouth of David Smith, pointing inescapably to the guilt of these two accused on these three charges of murder'. He also commented on the way Brady and Hindley presented themselves in the witness box: 'Did you see the slightest flicker of emotion when the most poignant and harrowing details were being discussed by them?' The judge summed up the case: 'If – and I underline the word "if" – what the prosecution says is right, you are dealing here, are you not, with two sadistic killers of the utmost depravity?'

The jury took two hours and fourteen minutes on 6 May 1966 to reach their verdicts. Brady was found guilty of three murders, Hindley of two, but also of assisting Brady to cover up John Kilbride's death. Both were sentenced to life imprisonment. The death penalty was abolished in the United Kingdom on 9 November 1965 – a month after they had been arrested.

However, there were still missing children, but it was twenty years before either Brady or Hindley made any form of admission. In 1985, Brady apparently told *Sunday People* journalist Fred Harrison that he had killed Pauline Reade and Keith Bennett, and the investigations into their deaths were reopened, headed by Detective Chief Superintendent Peter Topping. Brady denied having said anything when Topping questioned him at Gartree Prison; however, Hindley did start to cooperate in November 1986 after she received a letter from Keith Bennett's mother, Winnie Johnson, wanting to know what happened to her son. Hindley and David Smith both made visits to the moor without success.

Hindley finally confessed to her role in all five murders on 10 February 1987 (or, as Topping would note, 'told me just as much as she wanted me to know, and no more'). Faced with Hindley's words, Brady agreed to confess, on condition he could commit suicide afterwards – which the authorities couldn't allow. All the same, he provided information, and after Hindley made a further visit to the moor, a new area was identified for search. On 1 July 1987, Pauline Reade's body was found, and Brady formally confessed. He made two trips to the moor – one in July, one in December – but couldn't find Keith Bennett's body. It remains somewhere out there.

Brady was diagnosed as a psychopath in November 1985 and moved to Park Lane Hospital (now known as Ashworth Hospital). He has refused any suggestion of being released, although he did apply to be moved to prison so he could starve himself to death.

Hindley tried to escape from prison, and had numerous relationships with fellow inmates and staff. In 2002, it seemed as if her release was possible because of various legal rulings affecting 'lifelong' prisoners such as her; however, on 15 November of that year, she died from bronchial pneumonia caused by heart disease. According to contemporary reports, twenty local undertakers refused to handle her cremation ceremony; as one, Nick Armstrong, told the *Guardian*: 'Everyone who has asked me this, I have put the question to them: how would they feel if it was their mother or their grandfather in the same chapel of rest or in the same hearse as Myra Hindley?'

CHAPTER 11

Great Britain: Fred and Rosemary West

....

Those who investigate serial killers have to try to maintain their own sanity when all around them they are seeing evidence of humanity at its worst. Bernard Knight, the Home Office forensic pathologist assigned to the case of the Cromwell Street murders, is a case in point. 'I scrabbled about a bit in the muck and the mud, 'cos it was filling up with water all the time; it was being pumped out,' he recalled of his investigations at the scene after the first human thighbone had been found. 'And I always remember picking up a couple more bones and looking up at Superintendent Bennett, rather mischievously perhaps, and saying, "Well, I've seen one thighbone, so either this lady's got three legs or you've got more than one body."'

They certainly had got more than one body. Fred West was responsible for the deaths of at least twelve people; his wife Rose was convicted of killing nine, although it is believed that both of their tallies were higher. (Not all the bodies were found at Cromwell Street, it should be noted.) Fred West escaped justice, hanging himself on New Year's Day, 1995, while on remand. Rose West was given a whole-life tariff – although she pleaded innocence for a long time. 'They'll never get a confession out of me for something I haven't done,' she said in a conversation that the police had bugged. 'If they think I've got fuck-all to do with this, then the best thing they can do is put me in the cells, and fucking throw the key away. Because I shall always protest my fucking innocence, no matter if I do spend the rest of my life in fucking nick.'

Perhaps more than in any other case related in this volume, the exact sequence of events is unclear: Fred West told multiple different stories to the police during his questioning, and Rose has been consistently uncooperative. What follows therefore cannot be definitive, but is drawn from police reports, contemporary interviews with the Wests, and with the survivors of their attacks.

Frederick Walter Stephen West was born in the village of Much Marcle in Herefordshire on 29 September 1941. The second of six children, he seemed to some to be 'such a nice boy' growing up, 'a bit cheeky, a bit mouthy, but that was the way these kids were'. However, according to West's own accounts, his childhood was blighted by the removal of innocence at an early age. His father had incestuous sexual relations with Fred's sisters when they were young, and also taught young Fred to have sex with sheep. 'Do what you want, just don't get caught doing it' was the apparent code he was told to live by, and Fred admitted to police that 'I wanted to be Dad. I admired all he stood for.' There were rumours that his mother abused him from when he was twelve, while West himself claimed that he slit the throat of a family pig when he was young. (It's worth noting that West's brother Doug – six years younger than him – said that much of this was not true. 'As far as Mum and Fred, and Dad and animals, that was just fantasy by somebody,' he said in 2014. '[Fred] never killed a pig in his life. The bloke who used to kill the pigs worked with Dad on the farms and he used to do that. None of us touched any of that.')

Fred West wasn't a particularly academic child, having some talent in woodwork and art, and left school in December 1956 to work on the farm. Whether he behaved oddly prior to turning seventeen is therefore perhaps questionable, but what is certain is that a motorbike accident in November 1958 had long-ranging side effects. He suffered a fractured skull, requiring the insertion of a metal plate, and broke his arm and leg. He was in a coma for a week, and thereafter his personality seemed to change: according to his family, he became boastful, a liar who began stealing. He received another head injury a couple of years later, after falling from a fire escape at the local youth club.

He definitely began to display aberrant sexual behaviour from this point onwards. In 1961, he was accused of getting a thirteen-year-old girl pregnant – most sources say this was his sister, others that it was a family friend – and was thrown out by his parents and sent to live with his aunt. When the case came before the Assizes in November, the girl refused to say anything in the witness box; the judge had to dismiss the case. His family doctor gave evidence that the blows to his head might mean he was an epileptic, prone to 'blackouts'. Fred used this as an excuse 'not to remember' raping a fifteen-year-old girlfriend a few weeks later.

In 1962, West and his brother John ran into Scottish runaway Catherine Bernadette Costello, known as Rena, in a milk bar in Ledbury. The eighteen-year-old hitched a lift from West, and as she was telling him her life story (she was on the run and pregnant), they were stopped by a police officer. To help her, West maintained that he was the father of the baby, and after a failed attempt by Fred to abort the foetus (and possibly to annoy his mother), Fred agreed to marry Rena on 17 November 1962. They moved up to Coatbridge, near Glasgow in Scotland, where West discovered his new bride was in fact a stripper, who worked in a brothel for a Pakistani pimp, the father of her baby. Charmaine Carol was born on 22 February 1963, and the Wests claimed they had adopted the mixed-race child.

West became Rena's 'minder/chauffeur', and the Pakistani pimp provided plenty of women for West to sleep with – since it was made very clear to him that Rena was off-limits. However, West and Rena had a one-off liaison, which resulted in the birth of their daughter Anne-Marie (despite Rena's best efforts to abort her). West eventually took a job in 1964 driving an ice-cream van around the Gorbals and Castlemilk area. He took his first life at this time: in November 1965, he ran over and killed four-year-old Hugh Feeney, but was never charged. Instead, his other offences caught up with him.

Not content with making money from the ice-cream sales, West started to use his van as a way of enticing young girls. According to Gorbals historian Colin MacFarlane, West was regarded as a 'comical-looking character as he handed out cones to the young girls' but 'we soon heard he . . . was abusing some of them'.

It seems that West chose the wrong girl to approach – the twelve-year-old sister of the leader of the Cumbie gang, 'Malky Frazer'. Her brother 'vowed to slash West's throat "like a pig" ', and lay in wait for the ice-cream van to arrive. After two fruitless days, West turned up. 'Mad Malky and the rest of his gang all ran towards the van with knives, razors, bricks and hatchets. West got hit on the head with a large stone but he still managed to get to his steering wheel and speed off.'

That marked the end of Fred West's ice-cream run in Glasgow – indeed the end of his time in Scotland. He had made one key friend during this time, however: Annie McFall, a young girl that he'd seen 'crying her pissing eyes out' on the streets. West's story was that he had learned that Annie's alcoholic mother was making her work as a prostitute to fund her drinking habit. He therefore took her home, where Rena agreed she could become the children's nanny.

The sequence of events over the next couple of years is not certain: West's own statements don't always tally with the official police 'sequence of events' which they released as part of their media briefing. After the death of Hugh Feeney, West went back to Much Marcle, leaving Rena behind, but taking the children. Rena came to visit periodically, and in March 1966, they moved into a caravan on the Willows Caravan Site at Sandhurst. However, West had to pass Charmaine and Anne-Marie to social services until, to his surprise,

Annie arrived, having surreptitiously got hold of West's address from Rena. (Certainly the children were in care throughout July 1966.) Within a short time, they were lovers, and Annie became pregnant with his child in early 1967.

Annie McFall was last seen alive at the Gloucester Carnival in July 1967. West was accused of her murder but denied it consistently. According to him, he had told Annie to move away from the Willows site to keep her away from Rena, who, West said, wanted Annie to be a prostitute. He then claimed that he came back to his caravan late one night and found Rena and her pimp, Ralph. The pair told him that Rena had stabbed Annie by mistake. Ralph wanted to dump Annie's body on the tip but West refused, and said she should be buried in their 'special place' on the hill at Marcle. Ralph agreed and he and West dug a hole together before burying Annie. What West couldn't explain was why Annie's body was mutilated in the same way as other corpses for which he did accept responsibility. It's believed that Annie was pressurising West to dump Rena and marry her.

Six months or so later, on the evening of Saturday 6 January 1968, fifteen-year-old Mary Jane Bastholm disappeared from a bus stop in Gloucester while on the way to meet her boyfriend for an evening playing Monopoly – game pieces were found in the snow nearby. Detective Chief Superintendent William Marchand of the Metropolitan Police Scotland Yard Murder Squad was brought in to investigate after ten days, but the teenager's body was never located. She was a waitress at the Pop In Café where West both ate and had done some building work, and witness Vincent Oakes saw her sitting in West's car on four or five occasions. No clear evidence was ever found to link West to her disappearance, but West's son Stephen said his father maintained 'I will never tell anyone where she is.' Rose has consistently refused to pass on any information her husband might have told her. In their media pack, Gloucester Police noted, 'During the course of the investigation into Mary's disappearance over 250 different lines of enquiry were pursued . . . Despite these enquiries no evidence was found to support arresting Frederick West for any offence whatsoever in connection with Mary Bastholm, although he was questioned but denied any involvement.'

Mary was by no means the only girl whom West approached (if indeed he did do so) during this time. At the trial at Winchester Crown Court in November 1995, 'Mrs C' recalled hitchhiking in Cheltenham in 1966. 'He pulled into a lane. He grabbed my body. I can't remember the precise details but it was a sexual and physical attack . . . I managed to get halfway out of the car and he had his arm around my throat dragging me back into the car.' West masturbated in front of the fully clothed girl then took her back to Cheltenham. In 1968, thirteen-year-old Alison Clinton was grabbed by West, but she got free and ran to the nearest house.

On 29 November 1968, West met his soulmate, the woman with whom he was able to indulge his perverted desires to his heart's content. It was Rosemary Letts's fifteenth birthday.

Rose Letts was born in Northam, Devon after a difficult pregnancy, during which her mother underwent considerable amounts of electroconvulsive therapy (ECT). She was a difficult child but that may have had a lot to do with the highly unusual situation at home: her father was violent to his wife and children; her mother suffered badly from depression. She was the youngest of the four daughters; she had three brothers. Rose had regular sexual contact with her younger brothers, and, it's believed, with her father from when she was thirteen years old – certainly, they would have sex in later years. Her parents separated when she was a teenager, and Rose initially lived with her mother before moving in with her father. On her sixteenth birthday in November 1969, she moved in properly with West, despite her father's fury and threats – he even went to social services to no avail. Rose lived with West at the Lake House Hotel

Caravan Park in Bishop's Cleeve, looking after Charmaine (who briefly went to Bishop's Cleeve County Primary School) and Anne-Marie. There was no sign of Rena – supposedly she had gone back to Scotland.

This wasn't the case. It seems likely that by that point Rena was dead at Fred West's hand. According to one of West's versions of events, she and West had gone out to their 'favourite spot' out in a field, where they had drunkenly had sex before 'I lost me 'ead with her a bit and we had a right set-to and a right row there. And that was when she ended up getting killed against the gate.' Because it was too difficult to dig a hole large enough for the whole torso, West cut off her head and legs – leaving her arms attached – and then buried her. It was never established exactly when this was; Gloucester Police state that she was last heard of 'in about 1971' but it would seem possible that she died some time before then: Rose gave birth to West's daughter, Heather Ann on 17 October 1970; they moved to Midland Road, Gloucester, during the pregnancy. (An alternate version West told was that he had asked Rena to keep an eye on Rose as he worried about how she was treating the children; he didn't know exactly what had happened, but 'Rena got killed'. When they were moving from Midland Road to Cromwell Road, Rose came clean, and West then buried Rena's body. This was a typical West ploy, however; he was always the one who was helping others, never quite directly involved in the killing himself.)

Fred West served a three-day prison sentence in 1969 for non-payment of fines. He was then imprisoned for nine months on 4 December 1970 for motoring offences (stealing a road tax disc) and theft from his employer – an earlier suspended sentence was brought into force after he had breached it by stealing fence panels from his employer. His absence put considerable pressure on Rose, who had just turned seventeen: she was looking after her own six-week-old baby, as well as both nearly eight-year-old Charmaine and six-year-old Anne-Marie. Rose was a stern stepmother – the eight-year-old daughter of the Wests' upstairs neighbour saw Rose about to attack Charmaine with a wooden spoon while her wrists were tied behind her back with a leather belt – and couldn't really cope. Both Charmaine and Anne-Marie ended up attending casualty at the local hospital after incidents involving Rose. 'I think she likes to be handled rough,' Rose wrote to West in prison. 'But darling, why do I have to be the one to do it. I would keep her for own sake, if it wasn't for the rest of the children.' And eventually, she lost her temper. 'She grabbed her, or summat by the throat or summat and killed her,' was the only description Fred West gave.

During his questioning, West told officers that Rose had only told him that Charmaine was dead – rather than returned to Scotland with her mother, as he claimed he believed – after the police had arrived to dig up his patio. 'Charmaine's buried in the coal cellar in Midland Road,' Rose told him. 'She's not cut up ... She's fully clothed, wrapped in blankets and buried.' There were dental pictures of Charmaine from 14 April 1971, which enabled forensic dentist Dr David Whittaker to both identify the remains when they were dug up from the cellar at Midland Road, and to confirm the date of death – which was while Fred West was still serving time in prison.

Fred and Rose married on 29 January 1972 at Gloucester Registry Office. There was no reference to West's first wife, Rena: he described himself as a bachelor. Rose was pregnant again, with their second daughter, Mae, who would be born on 1 June. By that point, they had moved to 25 Cromwell Street. West converted the upper floor of the building into bedsits, as well as creating 'Rose's room' – from where she worked as a prostitute – and a torture chamber in the cellar. West created an intricate net of peepholes and spy cameras throughout the house so he could record Rose with her clients, as well as the other depredations. Rose advertised her services looking for a 'West Indian W. E. male. Age 50–60 for sex with young housewife with view to living in.' For the first decade or so, she didn't charge; however around 1985, 'Mandy' decided that her clients should pay. Writer Martin Amis's cousin Lucy Partington was to become one of the Wests' victims, and after the trial, he noted that the average day at 25 Cromwell Street was 'a scarcely credible inventory of troglodytic squalor, including theft, violence, incest, rape, sexual torture, whoredom, pimpdom, peeping-tomdom, pornography, child prostitution and paedophilia'.

Seventeen-year-old Caroline Roberts was hired in September 1972 to act as the children's nanny: the Wests had met her when she was hitchhiking on a secluded country road. She found life at Cromwell Street strange: the Wests constantly asked about her sex life, and encouraged her and her boyfriend to use their bed. Fred West told her that he could sort her out if she needed an abortion at any stage – and others he had helped in this way had thanked him sexually. She decided to leave the house, and with the help of Roy Morgan, a visitor to the house, she went back to her mother.

However, on 6 December, the Wests picked her up again on the same stretch of road, and apologised for their actions. She agreed to come back for a cup of tea, but then was attacked. When she regained consciousness, her hands were tied, and parcel tape was being wrapped around her head. Fred raped her (which Caroline recalled, only 'took a few seconds') but then so did Rose. ('She gave me oral sex – which I had never participated in – and it made me feel utterly degraded.') Fred threatened to keep her in the cellar and let some of Rose's black clients 'use' her, and then 'bury me under the paving stones of Gloucester' with the 'hundreds of girls' who were already there. Caroline let them do what they wanted, and promised to return as their nanny – but when she went to the launderette with Rose, she saw a chance to get away. She went to the police.

On 12 January 1973, the Wests were convicted of indecent assault and fined £50 each – Caroline said she hadn't pressed a rape charge because the Wests knew she'd had an affair with one of the lodgers and had told the police. She was concerned about that getting out, and her stepfather didn't want her to go to court in case the neighbours gossiped. Caroline admitted feeling guilty for a long time for not pursuing the case, particularly as she thought that the Wests progressed to murder to avoid the possibility of another victim going to the police. Unfortunately, it meant that, in Gloucester Police's own words, 'The sexual offence for which the Wests were convicted – indecent assault – was not considered a serious sexual offence' and therefore they did not automatically come under suspicion in the months and years to come.

Rose gave birth to their son, Stephen, in August 1973. In all, she would have eight children, but at least three of these were fathered by people other than her husband. It was even suspected that her father continued his incestuous affair with her, leading to the birth of one of her children.

Over the next six years, the Wests killed at least eight young women, whose bodies were found at Cromwell Street during the investigations in 1994. Lynda Gough was killed sometime shortly after 19 April 1973, not long before her twentieth birthday. She had left home at the start of April, leaving a note for her parents telling them not to worry because she had got a flat, and would come and see them. She had previously been collected from there to go for a drink with Rose West. Her mother managed to persuade her friends to tell her where Lynda was. She accordingly turned up at 25 Cromwell Street, where Rose West opened the door in Lynda's cardigan and slippers – and behind Rose, Lynda's mother could see her daughter's clothes on the washing line. Rose brazened it out, saying Lynda had left for Weston-super-Mare, and had left her stuff behind. Lynda's parents searched Weston but had no luck; however, they didn't report her missing to the police.

In fact, by the time that Lynda's mother arrived, the girl was already dead. She had lodged at Cromwell Street, and apparently shared lovers with Rose West. She acted as a nanny for the children as well as doing some seamstress work at the local Co-op, and partook in the Wests' sadistic games, allowing Fred to take her down to the cellar and suspend her from the ceiling. She was then gagged with masking tape and beaten mercilessly by the pair, raped and eventually strangled. It was a pattern that the Wests could follow for the next six years – at the trial, the pathologists recounted all that they could reconstruct, and noted that at least one victim had had hollow plastic tubes stuffed into her nostrils so that the masking tape wouldn't suffocate her. (Fred claimed Rose had killed Lynda after an argument and buried her.) Trophies of small bones were kept by the killers.

Carol Ann 'Caz' Cooper died in November 1973 at the Wests' hands. She was fifteen and a half, and living in The Pines Children's Home in Worcester, but had been given permission to go and spend the weekend with her grandmother. On the afternoon of 10 November, she went to the cinema with friends, and around 9.10 p.m. was seen getting on to a bus in Warndon, where her grandmother lived. That was the last time anyone outside Cromwell Street saw her alive. According to Fred, she either came willingly as a nanny or was a prostitute he had picked up. She was subjected to severe sexual torture before she died; forty-nine of her bones were missing from the skeleton discovered in 1994.

Exeter University student Lucy Katherine Partington was staying with her mother in Gloucestershire over the Christmas holidays in 1973. On the evening of 27 December, she was driven by her brother to see an old friend, Helen Render, in Cheltenham with whom she spent a few hours, working on a letter of application to the Courtauld Institute of Art in London. She left Helen at 10.15 p.m. to make the three-minute walk to the bus stop. She never got on the bus, or posted the letter. She ended up at Cromwell Street, where the Wests decapitated and dismembered her body after torturing her for some time. A knife, a rope, some masking tape and two hairgrips were buried with her corpse. Fred maintained that he had met Lucy for sex in Pittville Park (near the bus stop from where she disappeared) on a number of occasions; he also said she had asked him for money for an abortion because she was pregnant by him – and also that he had killed her because she wanted him 'to see her parents, he wanted me to do bloody everything'. Her family denied she had ever had anything to do with West previously. As with Caz Cooper, there was a major police investigation into her disappearance; it turned up nothing. On 3 January 1974, Fred West went to the casualty unit at Gloucester Royal Hospital with a laceration to the right hand; at Rose's trial, it was the prosecution's contention that West had sustained the injury when cutting up the body – and there was no reason not to suppose that she had been kept alive until then 'for whatever hideous purpose'.

Swiss student Therese Siegenthaler was the next confirmed victim. The twenty-one-year-old had been living in Lewisham, south London, studying sociology at Woolwich College of Further Education. On 15 April 1974, she left her accommodation, planning to hitchhike via Holyhead to Eire. Her friend Edward Simmons warned her against it, but she was confident she could look after herself – after all, as she told him, she was a judo expert. She never got there, and when she didn't return, she was reported missing on 26 April. The next time Therese was seen was when the police uncovered her remains; her brother had made several trips to England and Eire trying to find her. Her body had been decapitated and the hips disarticulated. At the burial site was a knotted cloth loop adjacent to the skull, used to secure the victim's mouth. There were no clothes found nearby.

Shirley Hubbard disappeared in the autumn of 1974. The prosecution at Rose West's trial explained Shirley had been placed with foster parents aged six, but had run away from them in October

1974 and was found camping in a field near Worcester; the following month she ran away again. According to contemporary newspaper reports, the fifteen-year-old had been doing work experience at Debenhams department store in Droitwich but failed to return home on 14 November. She had certainly taken her clothes and possessions with her into work. She spent some of her time with her boyfriend, who put her on a bus around 9 p.m.

Somehow, she found her way to Cromwell Street, where her head, according to the prosecution in court, was 'encased in a mask made of consecutive windings of brown adhesive tape passing around the skull from below the chin to above eye-level. Inserted into the front of this mask was narrow plastic tube in the nostril position with about 3 inches of tube internally bent upwards in the position which would enter the nostril. There was a short length of tube protruding from the mask. The breathing tube or tubes demonstrate that Shirley must have been alive when the mask was applied. Its purpose can only have been to keep her wholly under control, unable to see, unable to cry out, just to breathe.'

Juanita Mott was just eighteen when she disappeared. Described by the prosecution as a 'very rebellious and self-willed girl', Juanita was the daughter of an American serviceman. She had left school and home aged fifteen, and lodged with the Wests at Cromwell Street for a time – she had met Fred at the Pop In Café and lived with him from the summer of 1974 to March 1975 when she moved out to live with a family friend. On 11 April 1975, she set off to hitch-hike to Gloucester, promising to be back the next day to babysit for a friend who was getting married. She never returned.

When her body was found nineteen years later, it transpired she had suffered a severe depressed fracture of the skull caused by a heavy impact, probably with a circular or dome-shaped object such as a ball-headed hammer. A plastic-covered rope, such as a clothes-line, had been wrapped around the top end of her upper arm and attached to the right leg, where it was wrapped around the thigh-bone. The only conclusion the prosecution could draw was that, when she was buried, dismembered as she was, her bindings were still in place. Around the top of the skull a band of fabric passed beneath the jaw and around the back of the head – formed of two long nylon socks, a bra and two pairs of tights, one inside the other. She had been kept immobilised for her torturers' sexual gratifica-tion, the prosecution said. 'She died while she was being degraded either as part of what for her attackers was doubtless fun or because she could not be released afterwards,' Brian Leveson QC said in his opening speech. By a horrible irony, Juanita's sister Belinda would be a regular visitor to 25 Cromwell Street a few years later when she was dating one of the lodgers.

For reasons that have never been clear, Juanita appears to have been the last victim for some time. This might have been because the Wests' own children were growing up; certainly they became the targets of their parents' perverted desires. The next confirmed victim was eighteen-year-old Shirley Anne Robinson, who had been having sex with Fred – with Rose's full knowledge – and working as a pros-titute at Cromwell Street. However, when Shirley became pregnant, things changed. 'I am expecting a child from Freddy,' she wrote excitedly to her father. 'We are in love.' (Fred, true to form, claimed to police that he wasn't the father – he was only saying that for Shirley's sake.)

She was eight-months pregnant when she disappeared some point shortly after 9 May 1978. The foetus of West's child was found next to her body. The right thighbone had been chopped through, there was evidence of decapitation, and numerous bones of the hands and feet were missing. It was clear that the dismemberment had been done hurriedly. The prosecution suggested strongly that it was more likely that Rose rather than Fred was responsible for her death.

The final confirmed victim was Alison Chambers, who was murdered in August 1979, shortly before her seventeenth birthday. Another rebellious child, she had been taken into care a couple of years before she died, and was living at the Jordan's Brook care home. She worked at a solicitors' office in Gloucester. During the summer of 1979, Fred was working as a builder next door to the care home, and would chat up the girls there, persuading them to come to Cromwell Street where they could earn some easy cash – working as prostitutes. Alison went there along with her friend Sharon Compton, and became caught up in the Wests' sexual games, giving Fred blowjobs while tied to a bed before the 'games' became even more vicious with Rose participating sexually, and telling Fred what to do. Although Sharon managed to avoid the ultimate punishment, Alison was tortured to death – a purple coat belt was found wrapped round her jaw and the top of her head to stop her screaming.

There were no recorded deaths during the first half of the 1980s, but the Wests' perverse behaviour certainly continued – with Fred's brother John a frequent participant, as well as Rosemary's father, according to Anne-Marie. (John hanged himself on 28 November 1996, the night before the jury was expected to return verdicts against him on rape charges.) Son Stephen ran away, aged thirteen, but when he returned, he was beaten and told it would soon be time for him to have sex with his mother – something his father regarded as normal. Anne-Marie was the target of her father and uncle's lust – raped from the age of eight after having her hymen broken forcefully with a vibrator, and later made pregnant by her father (the foetus was aborted in hospital) – but when she left home aged fifteen, they turned to Heather and Mae, who tried their hardest to resist the attentions. (Stephen maintains that Mae has been in denial over this, and that Fred did have full intercourse with her.) Fred called Heather a lesbian for not letting him have his rights as a father, and eventually Heather had enough. She told a friend about the abuse, and news of this got back to her parents. She had to go, and on 19 June 1987, she did.

There are multiple different accounts of what happened to Heather, but what is certainly not true was Rose's comment to one of Heather's workmates, 'There was a hell of a row here a couple of nights ago. We found out that she was going with a lesbian from Wales and she has gone to Wales with her.' Heather's brother Barry was seven at the time, and said that 'Mum stamped on her head five times and Heather didn't move again.'

She was killed, and her body was dismembered. The head was decapitated using a knife or sharp-edged instrument. Both thighs were chopped with a sharp heavy instrument – an axe or spade. When her body was discovered, bones were missing mainly from the feet and hands, although some detached fingernails were discovered. Two lengths of rope that had perhaps been used to tie her hands and feet together were also found. Fred and his children built a patio over the spot where she was buried.

Fred and Rose West were heavily into pornography, and made many movies featuring Rose and her various visitors of both sexes. Rose took a lesbian lover, Kathryn Halliday, in October 1988, but the relationship only lasted five months because of Rose's brutality.

In August 1992, Fred was arrested for raping one of his daughters (who cannot be named). He had vaginal and anal intercourse with her, and eventually she had told one of her friends. This friend mentioned it to a policeman – which led to a knock on the door of 25 Cromwell Street. The Wests were known to the police: there had been multiple arrests of lodgers over the years for assorted offences and allegations (strongly denied) that policemen had been among Rose and the other girls' clients, while Anne-Marie's behaviour had attracted the attention of the law many times. This time, though, things were rather more serious: the police had a warrant and were looking for pornographic material following an accusation of child abuse. They found plenty. The Wests were arrested, and the children put in the care of social services.

Rose was released the next day – Friday, 7 August 1992 – and phoned Anne-Marie telling her not to say anything. However, this was the opportunity Anne-Marie wanted, and she told Detective Constable Hazel Savage – who had known the West family since 1966 – everything that had happened to her at her father and step-mother's hands. Fred tried to persuade Stephen to take responsibility, but the police didn't believe him.

Unfortunately, the case didn't go according to plan. Mae and her raped sister thought if they said nothing had happened, everything would go back to normal. Anne-Marie, worried at what Fred and Rose might do to her own children, also retracted her statement. Fred was kept at a bail hostel in Birmingham, but allowed to see Rose. Slowly but surely he began returning to Cromwell Street, as did the younger children, who had been brought up to mistrust authority, particularly one that kept them from their parents. By the time the case was heard on 7 June 1993, none of the children would give evidence against them. Fred and Rose walked free.

Not for long. Detective Constable Savage had not been satisfied with the answers she was given about the whereabouts of Heather – her input regarding her father was regarded as vital, but no one could satisfactorily explain where she was. Savage was unable to find any trace of Heather, but was informed of comments that the younger children had been making while in care about Heather being 'under the patio'. Fred had also joked about it. By the end of 1993, these were taken seriously enough for DCI Terry Moore to be placed in charge of the investigation. In January 1994, social workers were questioned about what the children had said. On 23 February, a search warrant was issued for 25 Cromwell Street, which was served the next day.

During the afternoon of 24 February, paving slabs were lifted ready for the digger to start work. That evening, Rose was questioned at Cromwell Street while Fred voluntarily went to the police station. Both maintained the story that Heather was alive. The next day, however, DC Savage and DC Darren Law came to the house, and Fred was asked to accompany them. As they sat in the car, Fred admitted he had killed Heather. He was arrested, as was Rose, and taken back to Cromwell Street to show the police where the body was.

The next morning, 26 February, Fred denied everything, but the physical evidence was starting to appear. Around 4 p.m., a human thighbone was found – and then a second and a third. There was obviously more than one body; the other bone belonged to Alison Chambers – although Fred's initial reaction was that it was that of Shirley Robinson. Rose was taken with the children to a safe house – bugged by the police – but never incriminated herself.

On 28 February, Alison Chambers and Shirley Robinson's bodies were found in the back garden. On 5 March, Therese Siegenthaler's remains were unearthed in the cellar; Shirley Hubbard's body was found the same day. Lucy Partington and Juanita Mott's graves in the cellar were located on 6 March. Lynda Gough's body was dug up from beneath the bathroom floor the next day, and finally Carol Cooper's remains were located in the back of the cellar on 8 March.

Rose was arrested on 23 April for the murder of Lynda Gough. During her questioning the next evening, she simply replied 'no comment' and, when charged, she said she was innocent. She said exactly the same throughout every interview between then and her trial in October 1995.

Fred was considerably more garrulous, telling many contradictory stories about the murders, sometimes taking responsibility, other times blaming Rose. On 4 March, he signed a note, 'I,

Frederick West, authorise my solicitor, Howard Ogden, to advise Superintendent Bennett that I wish to admit to a further (approx) nine killings expressly Charmaine, Rena, Lynda Gough and others to be identified' to Detective Superintendent John Bennett, now in charge of the case. He was cooperative, showing the police not only the burial sites at Cromwell Street, but also elsewhere. On 10 April, Rena Costello's remains were found in a field near Kempley, where West had indicated. Charmaine's skeleton was found at Midland Road on 4 May. Annie McFall's remains were dug up on 7 June. However, during his last interview at Gloucester Police Station on 13 May 1994, Frederick West denied he had anything to do with Heather's murder and said that he had lied throughout.

The Wests appeared periodically at Gloucester Magistrates' Court and the committal hearing was set for 6 February. However, while being held at Winson Green prison in Birmingham, Fred West accumulated the items he needed to create a noose and hanged himself on New Year's Day 1995. Rose West's trial ended on 22 November 1995, when she was unanimously found guilty of ten murders. Mr Justice Charles Mantell sentenced her to life imprisonment, and in July 1997 the Home Secretary gave her a whole-life tariff. In 2001, she decided not to appeal. She is currently held at maximum security prison Low Newton in County Durham.

CHAPTER 12

Great Britain: Dr Harold Shipman

....

On 13 January 2004, the day before his fifty-eighth birthday, Dr Harold Shipman hanged himself in his cell at Wakefield Prison. 'Ship Ship Hooray!' ran the headline in tabloid newspaper the *Sun* the next day, and then Home Secretary David Blunkett recalled being given the news: 'You wake up and you receive a call telling you Shipman has topped himself and you think, is it too early to open a bottle? And then you discover that everybody's very upset that he's done it.'

At the time of his suicide, Shipman was serving fifteen concurrent life sentences for the murders of Marie West, Irene Turner, Lizzie Adams, Jean Lilley, Ivy Lomas, Muriel Grimshaw, Marie Quinn, Kathleen Wagstaff, Bianka Pomfret, Norah Nuttall, Pamela Hillier, Maureen Ward, Winifred Mellor, Joan Melia and Kathleen Grundy, all of whom had been under his care. He never admitted responsibility for administering the diamorphine found in their systems, nor did he take any part in the 'Shipman Inquiry' set up by the Home Office under Dame Janet Smith in the wake of his conviction.

What is indisputable, though, is that on far more than the fifteen occasions for which he was found guilty – according to Dame Janet, well over two hundred times more – he administered drugs that assisted his patients to an early grave. 'None of your victims realised that yours was not a healing touch. None of them knew that in truth you had brought her death, death which was disguised as the caring attention of a good doctor,' Mr Justice Forbes said as he passed sentence. Doctor Shipman was a very different sort of serial killer.

Harold Frederick Shipman was born on 14 January 1946; he was the much-loved middle of three children, who grew up on the Bestwood council estate in Nottingham and attended High Pavement grammar school. On 21 June 1963, his mother died of cancer; during the latter days of her life, she was given shots of morphine at home by a doctor – nowadays, patients often have access to painkillers that they can administer themselves, but in 1963, that wasn't the case. Shipman took note of the release that the morphine gave his mother.

In September 1965 – on his second attempt at entry – Shipman started studying medicine at the University of Leeds School of Medicine where he would spend five years, leaving in 1970 with an MB ChB. He married Primrose May Oxtoby on 5 November 1966 – she was seventeen, and five months pregnant with their first child. He spent a year as a pre-registration house officer at Pontefract General Infirmary, and was registered with the General Medical Council in August 1971; he then became a senior house officer at Pontefract, and gained diplomas in child health and obstetrics and gynaecology.

Initially, although one death at Pontefract hospital during his time there was reported to the Shipman Inquiry in its early stages and investigated, there were no grounds for believing anything untoward had happened this early in Shipman's career. However, once the Inquiry delivered its First Report stating this, evidence was produced that suggested there could have been up to 137 deaths at his hands. 'It seemed not unreasonable to think that Shipman's criminal career began later than this, and I did feel quite comfortable with that conclusion,' Dame Janet explained, but after nurse Susan Whitehead – who had been training at Pontefract at the same time as Shipman – came forward, the inquiry interviewed sixty-three staff. 'I felt I just knew he had been killing patients on that ward and it explained for me why there had been such a high death rate,' Whitehead explained. After examining the evidence, the Inquiry found that 'Shipman was interfering with the ordinary processes of death and was hastening the deaths of patients who would have died quite soon in any event.'

'There are 14 deaths about which I entertain some suspicion that Shipman might have been involved in causing the death, although, in these cases, my suspicions are not grave,' Dame Janet reported. There were at least three deaths at Pontefract that the Inquiry unequivocally laid at his door – Thomas Cullumbine, John Brewster, James Rhodes – and there were four others that were deemed highly suspicious, including that of four-year-old cerebral palsy sufferer Susan Garfitt. In what could be seen as establishing a pattern he would use later, Shipman sent Susan's mother away while he treated her, although he had said that any further medication would just prolong Susan's suffering; when she returned, her child was dead. The quartet of suspicious deaths also included Shipman's probable first victim, Margaret Thompson, in 1972.

'I estimate that while at Pontefract General Infirmary Shipman probably caused the deaths of between 10 and 15 patients . . . In those early years, I think Shipman killed by the reckless administration of drugs rather than with the calculated intention to kill that he displayed later,' Dame Janet noted.

Shipman left Pontefract hospital on 1 March 1974 when he was appointed as an assistant general practitioner at the Abraham Ormerod Medical Centre in Todmorden, in the Pennines, quickly becoming a junior partner. He was liked by his colleagues, particularly since he took on some onerous work categorising the data in patient records, and overseeing the disposal of out-of-date controlled drugs that were at the surgery.

However, drugs were a problem for Harold Shipman. Almost immediately after he started work at Todmorden, he started to get extra quantities of pethidine (and sometimes pethilorfan) for 'practice use' from pharmacies – in total around 30,000 mg – and also forged the signatures of patients who might be prescribed the drugs. It seems probable that he started abusing the drug during his time on the obstetrics unit at Pontefract. He started getting hold of drugs illicitly very early – the first recorded instance is 8 April 1974, five weeks after he arrived at Todmorden. His high level of requisitioning did attract attention: the Home Office Drugs Inspectorate and the West Yorkshire Police Drugs Squad spoke with the pharmacists involved (although not Shipman himself) and concluded 'It would seem . . . that there is no drug abuse by Dr Shipman' but that they would keep an eye on the situation. In June 1975, when the pattern continued, Shipman was interviewed and denied abusing the drugs. However, it was hard to confirm exactly what was happening because there weren't proper written records. A Home Office drugs inspector visited the practice two months later, and insisted that proper procedures were followed – he would check up in six months.

Things came to a head long before that six months was up. Shipman had been suffering from 'blackouts' for some time, and on 18 August, he was diagnosed with idiopathic epilepsy. In fact, the condition was caused by his drug use, and on 29 September 1975, Shipman was confronted by his partners, who had become aware of his illegal activities. He tried to persuade them to help him continue to get supplies, but when they refused, he resigned from the practice. He tried to rescind the resignation, but his partners were able to dismiss him. He was admitted to the Halifax Royal Infirmary, and then to a private psychiatric hospital, the Retreat in York. He was discharged on 30 December.

While there, Shipman was questioned by the Home Office Drugs Inspectorate and the West Yorkshire Police Drugs Squad. He admitted his deceptions, and said he took the drugs because he was depressed about his working conditions. According to one of those who interviewed him, 'all his veins had collapsed, something I would have expected to see on an addict of at least five years standing'. It made them suspect he had been an addict much longer than the few months he admitted. He also told his interviewers that 'I have no future intention to return to General Practice or work in a situation where I could obtain supplies of pethidine.' On 13 February 1976, he pleaded guilty at the magistrates' court to eight specimen charges, and asked for seventy-four others to be taken into consideration. He was fined £600 plus costs.

He may have been using the majority of the drugs for himself but, after his conviction, there were those who were convinced that even this early in his career, Harold Shipman was killing – or trying to kill – his patients. Professor Elaine Oswald believed that on 21 August 1974, Shipman injected her with pethidine in an attempt to kill her; while Dame Janet found that Shipman had certainly illegally used the drug on her ('possibly because he wanted to involve her in some sexual activity'), he simply miscalculated the dose or failed to take into account its reaction with other drugs the professor was taking.

However, in the case of Mrs Eva Lyons, Dame Janet is clear: 'I think he probably gave a dose of opiate, which was not assessed in good faith with the primary intention to relieve pain, but was intended to end life.' Mrs Lyons had terminal cancer, and on the night of 17 March 1975, Shipman gave her an intravenous injection into the back of her hand, then stayed chatting with her husband until she passed away. Even he believed that Shipman had helped his wife 'on her way'.

There were six other deaths that, in hindsight, were suspicious – although they probably wouldn't even have been thought twice about had Shipman not been the attending physician. Three of them occurred on the same day (21 January 1975) and it seems possible that Shipman was present when they died. However, there is not enough evidence to be clear either way.

Shipman steered clear of drug usage himself after his experiences at Todmorden. He stuck to his word, and applied for a job with the Durham Area Health Authority as a clinical medical officer at the Newton Aycliffe Health Centre, starting work there eleven days before his trial for the illegal use of drugs. He was offered the post on condition that he had follow-up care from a psychiatrist, and he would have no access to controlled drugs. As a result of his conviction, his case was automatically reviewed by the General Medical Council, and its Penal Cases Committee wrote to him advising that 'if information relating to any further conviction of a similar nature should be received by the Council, a charge would then be formulated against you on the basis of both the earlier and the later convictions'.

In 1977, Shipman replied to an advert for a doctor at a practice in Hyde, Greater Manchester. He explained his pethidine abuse and his conviction to his potential colleagues, and after the other doctors consulted with one of Shipman's psychiatrists, and the Home Office confirmed that there were no restrictions against him, he was invited to join the practice. He started there on 1 October and would remain there for fourteen years, during which time he became a serial killer.

To begin with, Shipman did not have anything to do with controlled drugs, wary of the consequences of being caught. However, he began to build up a stash of opiates, often collecting them from the families of those who had died while in the middle of taking the drugs in the pretence of disposing of them on their behalf. These he used to kill four victims in the latter half of 1978.

In the decades after the Second World War, it was very common for general practitioners to visit their patients at home, particularly the elderly or infirm, as much on a social basis as a medical one. Harold Shipman was seen as a relic of those days by the elderly patients in his care, so 'cold calls' by him were not viewed as unusual – and there were occasions when he would provide those patients with more pain relief than their systems could handle. On at least one occasion in 1978 – the death of Sarah Marsland on 7 August – Shipman was found over the dead body by a family member, and was able to provide what, to a lay person, seemed a satisfactory explanation.

He was likely responsible for a couple of deaths in the summer of 1979, and definitely for the death of Jack Leslie Shelmerdine in November of that year. Shipman gave the chronic bronchial patient some opiate – he admitted to administering 10 mg but it was probably more – which would depress his respiration. However, Jack took thirty hours to die, and it's probable that this delay in the death frightened Shipman; certainly, his next confirmed murder wasn't for nearly eighteen months.

Shipman was able to get hold of opiates after attending natural deaths in January and March 1981, and on 18 April, he used them to kill May Slater at the sheltered accommodation at Bradley Green Old People's Centre. Although it was the warden's normal practice to accompany doctors when they visited patients, Shipman persuaded her to look after May's family, who had been called after she had been taken ill. He then took the opportunity to kill her. In August Shipman gave Emma Smith an injection using drugs he had obtained from another patient who had died naturally, and she died shortly afterwards.

Two patients were apparently over-sedated in the period before their demise in the autumn of 1981, which led to their deaths; Shipman may not have had access to opiates at the time, or it's feasible that he may have done it simply to keep the patients comfortable. These aside, he did not kill again until January 1983, when he gave ninety-year-old, terminally ill Percy Ward an injection that led to his death – one of the occasions on which Shipman could have reasonably be said to have simply provided a pain-free end for some-one who was suffering. However, that wasn't the case in his next killing, that of Moira Fox, who had been in 'quite good condition for her age', according to the caretaker, Ralph Unsworth, at her shel-tered accommodation at Chartist House.

Shipman kept a detailed diary of his appointments, and on 27 June, noted, 'Miss Fox, 104 Chartist House blood tomorrow'. However, on June 28, Ralph Unsworth was summoned by Shipman who told him that he'd had a phone call from Moira Fox and when he had got there, he had found the door ajar and his patient lying dead on the floor. That seemed odd to Unsworth, since Moira's clothes hadn't been disturbed. Shipman made a fuss about getting Unsworth to check the body and confirm she was dead. In fact, Moira Fox was the first of a number of patients whom Shipman killed with an injection under pretence of taking a blood sample, playing on the fact that most people don't really look carefully when such a procedure is taking place, and will often deliberately turn their head away.

There was a six-month gap before Shipman murdered again, but over the next five years he would kill between eight and twelve times a year. His first victim in 1984 was the overweight Mary Tucker, to whom he gave an injection around 2 p.m. on 7 January; she was found dead in the early evening. Shipman had deliberately set the gas fire on high to keep the room warm, quite possibly to obscure the time of death by speeding up the onset of rigor mortis and lowering the rate of drop in body temperature. (Since Shipman, unlike most serial killers in this book, never admitted to his crimes, either verbally to investigating officers, in court, or in any form of diary or writing, deductions have to be made about some of his odder pieces of behaviour.)

More of Shipman's regular modus operandi came to light with his second confirmed killing of 1984, Gladys Roberts. Gladys was expecting the doctor to visit her to look at her ulcerated leg, and told her daughter-in-law around 12.40 p.m. that she would phone her after he had been. When she had heard nothing after three hours, Enid Roberts called her mother-in-law. Shipman answered the phone and said that Gladys was dead – he had been with her and was in the middle of calling the hospital for an ambulance when he turned round and saw she had died from a pulmonary embolism. Although it can't be categorically stated that he was lying on this occasion, on many subsequent times when Shipman told relatives he had called for an ambulance, phone records showed he had not done so – or, as in the case of Hilda Hibbert, he hadn't called it as an emergency, so it took an hour to arrive.

The death of Joseph Bardsley on 15 April also added to the pattern – Shipman claimed that he had not been able to get into Joseph's flat so had an alibi when the eighty-three-year-old widower was found dead. Mary Winterbottom's murder on 21 September (his fourth of 1984) also demonstrated a couple more of his regular habits: the seventy-six-year-old widow was still in her day clothes, lying on the bed when she died, but Shipman claimed that he had tried to resuscitate her when he found her – although he had neither called an ambulance nor placed her on a hard surface. He had also removed her dentures; one of the doctors advising the Inquiry suggested this might be to avoid the dentures slipping down the patient's throat as the opiates took effect, causing them to struggle. Shipman seemed keen that his victims had a painless and smooth progress towards death.

Shipman grew more confident, apparently sure that no one would query his claims regarding his victims' times of death, killing eleven patients during 1985. After he murdered May Brookes on 1 February, he said that he had lifted her onto her chair; Mrs Brookes weighed over 13 stone (over 180 lbs). He changed the times of his visits to Margaret Conway, who he killed a fortnight later. He offered to arrange for a post-mortem examination for Selina Mackenzie, whom he killed on 17 December, if her relatives wished, but pointed out the disadvantages; they decided not to proceed. He was always keen on such misdirection: on a later occasion, following the death of Alice Prestwich in October 1988, he said to the warden of the home, 'We'll go back and check her if you like. I wouldn't want her waking up in the Chapel of Rest.'

Eight people died while under his care in 1986; the same number were murdered the following year. Jane Rostron's death on 8 May 1987 added a new excuse to Shipman's arsenal of reasons for his patients passing on: he claimed that he had urged the seventy-eight-year-old to go to hospital after he had found her following a slight stroke, but she refused. It was therefore not a surprise that she had died 'after' he had left.

Shipman escalated his activities early in 1988, killing two people in January and then four within the space of a week in February, including his oldest victim, ninety-three-year-old Ann Cooper. He then didn't kill again for another seven months, and Dame Janet Smith hypothesises that four deaths in a week may have led to comment at the practice about the high mortality rate, and Shipman had been scared of discovery. His next victim, in September, was terminally ill Rose Adshead, who was in great pain; thereafter he returned to killing those who were not in immediate danger of death (no matter what Shipman might have claimed to the families). His total for the year was eleven; he murdered twelve the following year, including his first in the surgery itself, when he administered drugs to kill eighty-one-year-old Mary Hamer. It seems likely that he was nearly caught over the body of his final victim of the year, Joseph Wilcockson: the district nurse arrived to dress his leg and found his body still warm. Once again, there was a large gap between this murder, on 6 November 1989, and the death of Dorothy Rowarth on 18 September 1990 – and once again, Shipman's first victim was someone who was already terminally ill. Dorothy was one of only two deaths attributable to Shipman that year; sixty-nine-year-old Mary Dudley died on 30 December – Shipman falsified her records to suggest she had been suffering from chest pain for two weeks prior to her 'fatal heart attack'.

During 1991, Harold Shipman did not murder anyone – at least, so far as the Shipman Inquiry could ascertain. This is probably because he was preparing to move into practice on his own. He told his colleagues that he was leaving the practice because he disliked the new computer system and was against the fundholding scheme being proposed. These may well have been simply excuses, particularly given he became an avid proponent of computerisation a few years later, and in 1995 joined a consortium specifically for fundholding! Certainly, it's true that relations with his colleagues were not strong: he disliked being confronted by other doctors or staff members, and it would be considerably easier for him to continue assisting his patients on their way if he was on his own.

From 1 January 1992, Shipman ran a single-handed practice; initially, this was from within Donneybrook House, alongside his old colleagues. On 24 August, he moved to his new premises at Market Street, Hyde, taking with him several members of staff and his patient list, leading to recriminations and lengthy financial negotiations. Over the next six years, Shipman gained a reputation in the community as an attentive, caring doctor who was more than happy to go out to visit his elderly patients at home; it reached the point that he was regarded by many as 'the best doctor in Hyde'.

Some of his patients may have thought that they had won the lottery when they were accepted on to his list, but at least 143 of them were murdered during the time that Shipman was at Market Street. He refined the methods and the excuses that he had used while at Donneybrook, and found new ways of obtaining diamorphine to kill his patients without throwing suspicion on himself – at least initially.

After murdering seventy-two-year-old Monica Sparkes on 7 October 1992, he returned to his old ways at the start of February 1993. He obtained the diamorphine by prescribing low doses of the drug for various patients; some of these were his victims, and the prescriptions were dispensed either on the date of death or within a few days. He then used the drugs to kill his next victims. Other prescriptions were issued to unsuspecting people on his patient list, who knew nothing of it and never received the drugs. Once again, he was nearly caught, this time on 31 August while trying to kill Mary Smith; he was interrupted by the unexpected arrival of her stepdaughters.

He didn't kill again for four months, and by then had worked out a new way to get the drugs. Raymond Jones was the first of Shipman's patients to be issued with a syringe driver for self-administration of diamorphine. After Raymond's death on 27 November, Shipman kept the boxes of diamorphine that remained at the cancer sufferer's home, instead of disposing of them. This gave him a ready supply of opiates, and his murder rate increased. Three patients were killed in December 1993, making sixteen in all that year.

He killed Joan Harding and Elsie Platt during the first five weeks of 1994, but his efforts to murder Renate Overton on 18 February went wrong. Shipman was left alone with her and gave her the diamorphine injection, then called Renate's daughter down because, he claimed, her mother had suffered a heart attack. The daughter called an ambulance and the paramedics were able to restart Renate's heart. She never regained consciousness and was in a persistent vegetative state for fourteen months before dying on 21 April 1995. Although the staff at Tameside General Hospital realised that Shipman had erred in giving an asthmatic the dose of diamorphine to which he had admitted, there was no follow-up to this apparent negligence. After Renate's eventual death, Shipman was questioned by the coroner, at which point he failed to mention giving any drugs. The coroner decided not to hold an inquest, which saved Shipman from some very difficult questions – and possibly even a trial for attempted murder. (Since Renate had survived more than a year and a day, at the time he couldn't be tried for murder; that law was changed in 1996.)

Once again, he refrained from killing until he was certain he was in the clear, and his next victim was Mary Smith, whose murder had been interrupted in August 1993. She died on 17 May 1994, and he killed again four more times before the end of July. Three further victims followed in November and December, and one in January 1995. In March he killed nine people, and in April three more; perhaps because of the coroner's interest in Renate Overton's death, there were none in May. In June he restarted, killing Bertha Moss at his surgery – and claiming to her distraught daughters that he even had an electrocardiograph reading showing that she had suffered a heart attack. (Of course, he didn't; nor had he called for help from staff or summoned an ambulance.) In all thirty patients were murdered in 1995, including Dora Ashton who was also killed at the surgery. No one seemed to think that this high mortality rate was unusual.

He killed thirty more patients in 1996, two per month for the first four months of the year, and then four in May, including seventy-two-year-old Edith Brady, yet another death at the surgery. He continued to obtain diamorphine from the syringe drivers of those who had died – some of the supplies were found at his home after his arrest – and was getting increasingly sophisticated in his techniques for deflecting attention from himself. On the cremation form, the doctor had to note who was present at the death, and if he had to admit that he was, then Shipman would claim others were with him, such as practice staff for the deaths at the surgery, or a neighbour. Otherwise, he would make out that others had seen his victim between his last visit and the time of death, even if on occasion his own diary entries contradicted what he put on the official paperwork, and he would give highly precise times of death, something which a general practitioner simply does not have the information or ability to do (despite what television series may suggest).

In the eight months from 30 August 1996, Shipman killed four next-door neighbours – Sidney Smith first; Thomas Cheetham on 4 December; Kenneth Smith, Sidney's brother, on 17 December, and then finally Elsie Cheetham, Thomas's wife, on 25 April 1997. Elsie was one of thirty-seven deaths Shipman caused in 1997, nine of them in January and February. Ivy Lomas's murder on 29 May was the last that he carried out at his surgery before his arrest – he claimed that he had been trying to use the ECG machine on her, but realised she had died. In court, however, he claimed that she had collapsed as she climbed onto the couch, and he had tried to revive her. When her body was exhumed, there was morphine in the tissue.

Shipman continued his lethal practices during 1998, murdering fifteen patients in the first three months of the year. Three of his patients had died naturally, meaning that he had certified eighteen deaths; of these, sixteen were cremated. The Form C required for cremation had to be signed by another doctor, and Shipman would cross the road to the Brooke Surgery, whose doctors became accustomed to Shipman arriving, bearing the medical file for the deceased in his hand (although not actually letting them examine it), and giving a full account of their history. For the most part, they knew Shipman had a high proportion of elderly patients on his list, with the corresponding increase in potential mortality, and accepted this as normal.

Dr Linda Reynolds, one of the doctors at the Brooke Surgery, wasn't convinced. She thought that Shipman's death rate was too high – something that had been brought to her attention by undertaker Deborah Massey – and on 24 March 1998, she registered her concerns with John Pollard, the coroner for the South Manchester District. The Brooke Surgery had 9,500 patients and they had 14 patient deaths during the first quarter of the year – but Shipman had more than that from a patient list around a third the size. Dr Reynolds was also concerned that many of the deaths seemed to be of elderly women, who had been found dead at home, apparently alone, fully dressed, who had not appeared to be ill previously. (The undertakers were used to collecting people from home who were in their night clothes; Shipman's were nearly all dressed.) Reynolds was not sure if Shipman was simply a caring doctor, who looked after his patients in their own homes and visited them frequently when they were ill – or if he was killing them.

Pollard briefed Chief Superintendent David Sykes and Detective Inspector David Smith of Greater Manchester Police. DI Smith spoke with Dr Reynolds who told him that the bodies of a couple of Shipman's patients (Lily Higgins and Ada Warburton) were still at funeral directors, and that she suspected that Shipman was killing them with a drug – as indeed he was. DI Smith didn't suggest to the coroner that one or both should be autopsied, and both ladies were cremated before the end of March 1998. In her Second Report, Dame Janet Smith criticised DI Smith's inaction and failure to ask pertinent questions. DI Smith wasn't able to access the medical records at the West Pennine Health Authority directly, so Dr Alan Banks did so on his behalf, and found that there were some cases that he himself would have referred to the coroner. However, Dr Banks didn't spot a lot of the correlations between the deaths – perhaps, according to Dame Janet, because he was 'simply unable to open his mind to the possibility that Shipman might have harmed a patient', after not being given all the pertinent information by DI Smith. Dr Banks therefore reassured DI Smith that all seemed in order, and this 'effectively marked the end of this investigation' on 1 April.

The next day, Alan Massey – father of the undertaker who had spoken with Dr Reynolds – went to see Shipman at his surgery to tell him that people were talking about the high death rate, although he himself did not think that there was anything unusual. Shipman showed Massey his book of Medical Certificate of Cause of Death counterfoils, and said that it was open to inspection by anyone who was concerned. Massey left, reassured. DI Smith visited the Masseys around 15 April, and 'gave the impression that he had made a thorough investigation and found nothing untoward'. DI Smith then spoke with CS Sykes, and the investigation was effectively closed. At no point had DI Smith checked the Police National Computer, where he would have found details of Shipman's drug conviction from two decades earlier. DI Smith visited Dr Reynolds on 16 April, and said he had found no evidence to confirm her suspicions; he said similar to John Pollard the next day, who accepted his reassurances.

'Although I cannot be certain of this,' Dame Janet wrote, 'I think that, if the police and the Coroner had moved with reasonable expedition, the lives of Shipman's last three victims would probably have been saved.' Although Shipman appeared relaxed and confident when he spoke with Alan Massey, he was clearly rattled by the gossip, and didn't kill again until 11 May. This victim, Winifred Mellor, was Roman Catholic and Shipman knew she wanted to be buried – so he wouldn't need to get a form signed by anyone from the Brooke Surgery. His penultimate victim was Joan Melia, on 12 June – also buried – and his last was Kathleen Grundy, buried after her death from 'old age' on 24 June. He was visited by Dr Banks in July to discuss prescribing practice and volunteered information about the high death rate.

By this point, however, more questions were being asked as the result of a will apparently made by Kathleen Grundy, dated 9 June, just over a fortnight before her death. It had been drawn up on a pro forma template. 'All my estate, money and house to my doctor,' it read in typed capitals. 'My family are not in need and I want to reward him for all the care he has given to me and the people of Hyde. He is sensible enough to handle any problems this may give him.'

This had been sent to a firm of solicitors in Hyde for registration, and it named Harold Shipman as the sole beneficiary. This rang serious alarm bells for Kathleen Grundy's daughter, Angela Woodruff, who was a practising solicitor. She had drawn up her mother's will in 1986 and had handled all her legal affairs. Angela spoke with the 'witnesses' to the will – two of Shipman's patients – and on 24 July, she went to her local police in Warwickshire. They passed the matter to the Greater Manchester force, who quickly realised that this was the same doctor whom DI Smith had 'cleared' just three months earlier.

Kathleen Grundy's body was exhumed on 1 August, and Shipman's home and surgery were searched; his typewriter was taken away, along with Kathleen's medical notes. (Shipman claimed that Kathleen had borrowed the typewriter periodically, but could never explain how it came to be back in his possession.) At Shipman's home, police found around 150 sets of case notes in his garage; some of these had the word 'Dead' written on them in red ink. A quantity of jewellery was found in the garage, one piece of which was definitely taken from a patient. Most importantly, a quantity of drugs, which testing proved to be diamorphine, was also found. Two days later, Detective Superintendent Bernard Postles was appointed senior investigating officer into what was now deemed a major incident. After the post-mortem failed to establish Kathleen's cause of death, toxicology tests were run, and on 14 August the lab confirmed the presence of an opiate, probably morphine. The same day, Shipman was interviewed by the Home Office Drugs Inspectorate and a chemist inspector from the police; four days earlier, they had been informed of Shipman's prior drug offences. The other cases that DI Smith had briefly looked into were reopened, as well as nine others.

Around the same time, in August 1998, taxi driver John Shaw went to police and reported his suspicions of Shipman. He had become friends with some of Shipman's long-term patients and was surprised at their deaths. 'I was asking who was their doctor?' he told the BBC later. 'The thing that made me suspicious was that they had all been in good health prior to their deaths.'

Kathleen Grundy's will was confirmed as a forgery on 26 August; the police were told that the body showed signs of a morphine overdose two days later. Harold Shipman was arrested on suspicion of murder, attempting to obtain property by deception and forgery on 7 September. Three more bodies were exhumed during September, and Shipman was charged with those murders on 7 October. Two more underwent post-mortem in October; Shipman was charged on 11 November. The same pattern happened in November: two more exhumations, two more charges of murder. On 22 February 1999, Shipman was charged with one more murder following an exhumation, and with the murder of six others whose bodies had been cremated.

Over a hundred witnesses gave evidence at Shipman's trial, which began on 5 October 1999 and lasted until 31 January 2000. The defence tried to claim that the morphine found in the bodies could have come from slow-releasing tablets and that one of the victims may have committed suicide. On the witness stand, Shipman claimed he thought Kathleen Grundy was abusing drugs and later broke down in tears when describing the death of Kathleen Wagstaff, claiming 'This was one of the few times I was possibly more upset than the relatives.' His defence barrister, Nicola Davies QC, tried to attack the scientific evidence, and told the jury it was 'unsafe and unreliable ... In the absence of such evidence, the inferences to be drawn from it relating to the behaviour of the doctor by the Crown also fail – and with it so does the entirety of it.'

The jury of seven men and five women took thirty-three hours and five minutes to find him unanimously guilty of all charges. Even then, Shipman never gave any explanation as to why he killed – although prosecuting barrister Richard Henriques QC did suggest he was 'exercising the ultimate power of controlling life and death'. He continued to do the same with his own life, killing himself, according to one report, to secure his wife's financial security. She refused to accept his guilt.

A memorial garden for Shipman's victims, known as the Garden of Tranquillity, was opened in Hyde on 30 July 2005. 'It'll enable us to draw a line under the events in Hyde over the past few years and move on,' Hyde Councillor Joe Kitchen said at the dedication ceremony. 'But most importantly we can say goodbye to our relatives, which unfortunately we weren't able to do at the time.'

CHAPTER 13

Great Britain: Peter Sutcliffe – The Yorkshire Ripper

....

'We'll go on and on until we catch this swine,' swore Assistant Chief Constable George Oldfield in January 1980 after he returned to work following hospitalisation for exhaustion. 'I know that everything possible is being done and I am certain we will get him.' Almost exactly a year later, Peter William Sutcliffe was arrested with a prostitute and admitted to being the Yorkshire Ripper, the man responsible for at least thirteen deaths between 1975 and 1980. Held in Broadmoor for many years, Sutcliffe was returned to Frankland Prison in Durham in August 2016 – judged, after over thirty years, to no longer be mentally ill enough to warrant being kept in the secure psychiatric hospital. He will never be released into the wider community. 'This was a campaign of murder which terrorised the population of a large part of Yorkshire for several years,' Mr Justice Mitting stated. 'The only explanation for it, on the jury's verdict, was anger, hatred and obsession. Apart from a terrorist outrage, it is difficult to conceive of circumstances in which one man could account for so many victims. Those circumstances alone make it appropriate to set a whole-life term.'

Peter Sutcliffe was born on 2 June 1946 to John and Kathleen Sutcliffe in Bingley, Yorkshire. Brought up a Catholic, he wasn't a strong youngster, and preferred his own company or that of his mother. He didn't fit in with his classmates at primary school or in the early years at secondary school, often being bullied. However, he eventually took up bodybuilding and started to be less of a loner. He left school at fifteen, and through the 1960s had various jobs – including at the local mill alongside his father, as an engineering apprentice and as a gravedigger at Bingley Cemetery. In February 1967, he met Sonia Szurma, the daughter of immigrants from Czechoslovakia, and they married on her twenty-fourth birthday, 10 August 1974, after a long courtship. By then, Sutcliffe was working at the Britannia Works of Anderton International. He had also started using and attacking prostitutes.

According to Sutcliffe's story at his trial, in 1967, while working as a gravedigger, he started to hear a voice, which he took to be divine. In 1969, the voice told him that it was his mission in life to kill or eradicate prostitutes. However, during his police interviews, he told a different story: a prostitute had humiliated him in 1969, and his anger from that had built over the years. Sutcliffe had heard that Sonia was two-timing him, so decided to get his revenge by going with a prostitute. The woman didn't give him the £5 change he was owed, and her pimps suggested Sutcliffe forget about it; when he saw the same girl three weeks later, he asked her for his money back, but she went round the pub they were in, telling everyone the tale, and making the customers laugh at him.

Sutcliffe certainly knew his way around the red-light districts of Yorkshire – his brother-in-law, Robin Holland, went drinking with him, and Sutcliffe would boast of his times with the working girls. Another friend, Trevor Birdsall – who later reported his suspicions of Sutcliffe to the police – spent hours with Sutcliffe cruising the streets. Birdsall was with Sutcliffe when he committed his first assault on a prostitute, between a week and a month after his humiliation. Sutcliffe followed an 'old cow' to her house near Manningham Park, Bradford, and hit her on the back of her head with a stone in a sock. The next day he was visited by two police officers; the woman had taken down the number of Birdsall's van. Sutcliffe admitted hitting the woman, but only with his hand;

however, the woman didn't want to press charges, and Sutcliffe was advised that he had been 'very lucky'.

He wasn't so lucky with his next run-in with the police: he was arrested on 29 September 1969, hiding behind a garden hedge, clutching a hammer. He claimed that he was trying to find his hubcap and needed the hammer to put it back on; the court disbelieved him and he was fined £25 for 'going equipped for theft'. At his later trial, he claimed, 'I were driving me old Morris Minor and I were looking for a prostitute. I knew this were the mission I had to carry out. The voices told me it wasn't good enough just to attack them. I had to do it properly. I had to kill.'

There is no confirmed evidence that Sutcliffe carried out any more attacks over the next half decade, although, in recent years, he has been linked to multiple other cases, some of which fell during that time. However, in July 1975 came the first of the assaults that would become known as the work of the Yorkshire Ripper. In February of that year, Sutcliffe was made redundant, and used the money from that to learn how to drive large trucks. On 4 June 1975, he passed his HGV Class 1 test, and to celebrate bought a white Ford Corsair car, which he kept with his lime-green Ford Capri GT; both cars would be spotted at Ripper attack sites over the coming years. He looked for prostitutes and, when searching around the Keighley area, spotted an attractive blonde in her mid-thirties, and tried unsuccessfully to follow her home. He approached the same woman at Wild's coffee bar a few weeks later but vanished when she started to cause a scene. Early on the morning of 5 July, the woman, Anna Rogulskyj, was walking to her boyfriend's home after going drinking in Bradford following a row between them. As she went, a voice asked her if she 'fancied it'. 'Not on your life,' she replied and hurried onwards. However, when she got to her boyfriend's place, there was no reply so she took off her shoe and threw it through the window.

Anna started to head home, but as she passed an alleyway near the Ritz cinema, the same voice she had heard earlier asked her again if she 'fancied' it. She declined – and Peter Sutcliffe followed her and then hit her with his ball-peen hammer three times on the head. She fell, unconscious, to the ground. Sutcliffe uncovered her abdomen – raising her blouse, and pulling down her skirt and knickers – and started to slash her. However, a neighbour was alerted by the noise and shouted out, asking what was happening. 'I intended to kill her but I was disturbed,' Sutcliffe told police. In court, his story was 'I was certain she was a prostitute – scum. I was being given instructions on what was the best moment to attack . . . It was all over in less than ten seconds. I didn't mean her to suffer. I meant her to die.'

Found at 2.20 a.m., Anna was rushed to Airedale General Hospital and then Leeds General Infirmary. She needed a twelve-hour operation to remove splinters of bone from her brain, and was given last rites. However, she survived with a steel plate in her skull; she died in April 2008. The crime was investigated by Detective Superintendent Perry of West Yorkshire's Western Crime Area, but wasn't linked to any of Sutcliffe's other attacks until June 1978. The neighbour was able to give a vague description of the attacker, but otherwise there were no real clues.

Sutcliffe started looking for work using his HGV licence, as Sonia decided to complete her teacher training; the pair had been told that following a series of miscarriages, they could not have children, so Sonia elected to continue the course she had given up some years earlier. On the night of 15 August 1975, Sutcliffe went out drinking with Trevor Birdsall and in the Royal Oak pub in Halifax town centre he spotted forty-six-year-old office cleaner Olive Smelt. 'I bet she's on the game,' Sutcliffe told Birdsall, but when he made a similar comment to Olive, she gave him short shrift. Olive was given a lift home from the pub, and was dropped off not far from her front door.

Unfortunately for her, Peter Sutcliffe saw her. According to Birdsall's trial evidence, Sutcliffe stopped the car, and 'seemed to put his hand down the side of the seat . . . Peter went round the back of the car and disappeared.' Birdsall didn't think he had followed the woman, but in fact Sutcliffe went down a parallel alley to Olive, and when he caught up with her, 'said summat about the weather'. Olive wasn't frightened by the man until he hit her twice on the head with his hammer. He then disarranged her clothing and 'scratched her buttocks with a piece of hacksaw blade or maybe a knife. My intention was to kill her but I was disturbed by a car coming down the road.' At trial, once again, he claimed the 'voices' had told him to do so. Sutcliffe went back to join Birdsall, who noticed that he was 'unusually quiet'. Olive was found some yards down the road, moaning and calling for help; she was taken to hospital with severe injuries: she described her skull as 'like a crushed coconut shell'. 'She never got over that night,' her daughter Julie said after Olive died in 2011. 'She did well to survive and had to learn to accept what happened mentally. But physically her mobility was never the same. She has been through hell and suffered in silence. She never complained.'

The next evening, Birdsall read the report about the 'brutal attack . . . It crossed my mind that Peter might be connected with it.' Once again, West Yorkshire's Western Crime Area investigated, but there was no correlation with other cases – and according to Olive, they didn't believe her when she said her attacker had a Yorkshire accent.

Twice, Peter Sutcliffe had been interrupted when he had been about to take a life. Luckily for fourteen-year-old Caroline Tracy Browne (known as Tracy), it would happen again when Sutcliffe attacked her on the night of 27 August 1975. The schoolgirl and her sister had been out in Silsden, near Keighley, but her sister Mandy headed home early. Tracy was walking back along a country lane around 10.30 p.m. when Sutcliffe started to chat with her. When they reached the gateway to her home, he attacked her from behind, hitting her five times, grunting, she later said, 'like [tennis player] Jimmy Connors serving each time he struck'. Tracy pleaded for her life, but Sutcliffe seemed implacable until a car started to approach. He threw the girl over a fence, but she managed to crawl to a caravan whose occupants called for help. She needed four hours of neurosurgery.

Tracy was able to give a clear description of Peter Sutcliffe, but even once Sutcliffe had started killing, Detective Chief Superintendent James Hobson didn't believe there were any links to other attacks. 'Tracy was not a prostitute [like those the Ripper killed]; we thought at the time she was hit with a piece of wood; and all of the other attacks were in city areas,' he claimed, despite the medical evidence showing she had been hit with a hammer.

Tracy's description was clear. She told an interviewer, 'I remembered his taupe-coloured V-neck jumper over a light blue open-necked shirt and dark brown trousers which had slit pockets at the front, rather than the side. I told the policeman he was 5ft 8in, had very dark, almost black Afro-type wrinkly hair and a full beard. I even mentioned the gap between his teeth and his insipid voice – a little man with a high-pitched voice,' she recalled twenty-four years later. She was treated for two fractures to her skull and given fourteen stitches. She was left with a permanent three-inch crescent-shaped dent on the top of her head and a smaller one at the rear. Sutcliffe was never charged with attacking Tracy, but he did eventually admit to the assault in 1992.

Two months after the attack on Tracy, Peter Sutcliffe killed for the first time. On 29 September 1975, he had started working as a delivery driver for Common Road Tyre Services at Oakenshaw. Exactly one month after that, on the night of 29 October, he was flagged down by twenty-eight-year-old Scottish mother of four, Wilomena 'Wilma' McCann. Wilma had been out on the town that evening as usual, leaving her children at home, and drinking at four different pubs before going to a drinking club. She had consumed between twelve and fourteen measures of spirits, and was reeling around. She tried to get a lorry driver to give her a lift home; seeing her state, he refused. She thumbed a lift from a driver in a Ford Capri GT, and he stopped. They chatted as he drove her the short distance to her home, and just before they reached her home, Wilma asked Sutcliffe if he wanted 'business'. Sutcliffe was a little slow on the uptake, but realised Wilma was a prostitute when she said 'it' would cost £5. He pulled the car off the road where she suggested but he had problems getting aroused when she was too business-like. 'I suddenly felt myself seething with rage,' he told police officers in 1981. 'I got out of the car wanting to hit her to pay her back for the insult.' He followed her up into a field, and when she had laid down on his coat and unfastened her trousers, she told him to get it over with.

Peter Sutcliffe hit Wilma twice over the head with the hammer that he had concealed under his coat as they walked. He was going to leave her there, but realised he had to silence her. He fetched a seven-inch knife from the toolbox he kept on the back seat of the car, pulled off her blouse and bra 'so I could see where I was stabbing her'. After ensuring she was dead, he collected his coat, and drove back to his mother-in-law's home where he and Sonia were living. According to his initial confession, 'that was the turning point. I realise I'd overreacted at the time, nothing I have done since then affected me like this . . . After that first time, I developed and built up a hatred for prostitutes in order to justify within myself why I had attacked and killed Wilma McCann.' (He corrected himself in a later statement to detectives, saying he had the hammer and the knife with him all the time and that he had never intended to have sex with her.)

Wilma McCann was stabbed fifteen times in the neck, chest and abdomen and there was semen around the back of her trousers and her underwear, pathologist Professor Gee found. Detective Chief Superintendent Dennis Hoban of West Yorkshire's Eastern Crime Area was put in charge of this enquiry; once again, it was not linked to the other hammer attacks. Seven hundred and fifty police officers were involved with the murder investigation, with 7,000 house-holders and 6,000 lorry drivers all questioned. Peter Sutcliffe was not among them.

Although police for a time believed that the death of twenty-six-year-old Joan Harrison on 20 November 1975 was linked to Sutcliffe (thanks to letters that were sent to them purportedly from the Ripper), his next confirmed victim was actually forty-two-year-old Emily Monica Jackson, who was murdered on the night of 20 January 1976. Emily and her husband Sydney had experienced financial problems over Christmas, and Emily had started taking money for sexual favours. Sydney would wait in the pub while Emily scouted the streets for clients, then use their blue Commer van (which she, but not he, could drive) to earn the cash. That night, they parked in the car park of the Gaiety pub on Roundhay Road, Leeds. After a quick drink together, Sydney stayed inside while Emily went out. When she hadn't returned at closing time, Sydney wasn't overly concerned – the van was still there, so she was either in a different pub or with a client. He took a taxi home.

By that point, Emily Jackson had been dead some hours. Peter Sutcliffe had seen her, agreed to pay her £5, and followed her direc-tions to a deserted spot behind a cul de sac. 'I remember when she got in there was an overpowering smell of cheap perfume and sweat,' Sutcliffe told detectives. 'This served all the more for me to hate this woman even though I didn't even know her.' Sutcliffe didn't want to go through the pretence of intercourse, so faked a problem with the car engine and asked for her help. After surrepti-tiously picking up his tools, he lifted the bonnet and Emily offered to use her cigarette lighter so he could see inside. 'I took a couple of steps back and I hit her over the head with the hammer,' Sutcliffe recalled. He then dragged her into a yard, pulled up her clothes, then 'stabbed her frenziedly without thought with a Phillips [cross-head] screwdriver' and pushed a large piece of wood up against her vagina. He also stamped on her. As he got to his car, he was startled by headlights, and drove home.

Emily's body was found at 8.10 the next morning, and this time the police did link it to a previous case, given the similarities with Wilma McCann's murder. A footprint was identified as between size 7 and 8 from a Dunlop Warwick wellington boot. A week later, another prostitute told police that Emily had been seen with a client in a Land Rover, and a detailed description of car and driver were circulated; they were never traced.

Peter Sutcliffe lost his job at the tyre company on 5 March 1976; it would be some time before he found employment. That didn't stop him from his attacks. Around four in the morning on 9 May, twenty-year-old Marcella Claxton was walking back to her home off Roundhay Road in Leeds from drinks with friends. Marcella often worked as a prostitute, but she was off duty that evening. Peter Sutcliffe had been trawling the streets of Chapeltown and pulled up beside her in his white Corsair. Both Sutcliffe and Marcella had differing accounts of what happened next: she said that she asked him for a lift and he drove to Soldiers Field. He then offered her a fiver to have sex on the grass beside the car. She said she didn't want to, and went to urinate behind a nearby tree. Sutcliffe's version is that he never wanted sex with her, 'and certainly not that one' and used a racially offensive description of Marcella (echoing one made by Leeds police later).

Either way round, she left the car to have a pee, and Sutcliffe followed. Marcella claimed he dropped something and she said she hoped it wasn't a knife; he said it was his wallet. If it was his hammer, he quickly picked it up and dealt her eight or nine blows to the head.

Marcella claimed that he then masturbated as he watched her writhing on the ground; Sutcliffe has denied doing that. He then drove off. Marcella managed to stagger to a phone box and called for help. She saw Sutcliffe return to the spot where he had left her, and believed 'he must have come back to finish me off'. Sutcliffe told police in 1981 that 'I went back to the car in a stupefied state of mind, I just had a feeling of morbid depression, I didn't care whether she told anybody or not.'

Like Sutcliffe's three previous living victims, Marcella required brain surgery. She continued to suffer from blackouts and headaches. She was able to furnish police with a description that, like Tracy Browne's, was fairly accurate. The case was investigated by Detective Chief Inspector Bradley but not linked to the Ripper case – at least initially. However, when twenty-eight-year-old Irene Richardson's body was found on 6 February 1977 at almost exactly the same place as Marcella was attacked, more consideration was given to her story.

Sutcliffe had finally found a new job in October 1976: he was hired as a lorry driver for T. & W. H. Clark (Holdings) Ltd on the Canal Road Industrial Estate, between Bradford and Shipley. On the night of 5 February 1977, he 'drove to Leeds after the pubs shut. It was my intention to find a prostitute to make it one more less.' Irene Richardson was in the wrong place at the wrong time: she had gone into the centre of Leeds late in the evening to drown her many sorrows, and was spotted by Sutcliffe not far from the Gaiety pub. Sutcliffe stopped, she got in, and was obviously desperate to make money: 'I'll show you a good time,' she told him. 'You are not going to send me away, are you?'

Soldiers Field was their final destination, and Irene tried the toilets so she could urinate before they had sex, but found they were locked. As she squatted in the field, Sutcliffe 'hit her on the head from behind, at least twice, maybe three times. She fell down. I then lifted up her clothes and slashed her in the lower abdomen and also slashed her throat. I felt her lying face down and I covered her up with her coat. I put her knee boots on top of her before I covered her up.' It was the first time that Sutcliffe had posed the bodies of his victims.

Irene's skull was fractured and one blow had sent a piece of her skull into her brain. The slashes he inflicted had caused her intestines to spill out. There was semen in her vagina, but the police pathologist considered this was not from her killer. More important evidence was found near the corpse: tyre tracks indicated the killer had a medium-sized car or van, and the specific make of tyre looked like it might help narrow the suspect field. Unfortunately, as Detective Chief Superintendent Hobson discovered, there were 53,000 registered owners of the potential fifty-one makes of car in the West Yorkshire Metropolitan area and the Harrogate area. Thirty-three thousand cars were checked; 20,000 remained to be seen when the exercise was stopped in July 1977. Peter Sutcliffe's white Ford Corsair – which he had bought the previous year – was one of those not seen at that point.

'By this time, after Richardson killing [sic], prostitutes became an obsession with me and I couldn't stop myself, it was like some sort of a drug,' Sutcliffe said in his first confession. On the night of 23 April 1977, he killed again. Patricia 'Tina' Atkinson worked as a prostitute in Bradford, but because she worked from her flat in Oak Avenue, she thought she was safe from the depredations of the murderer, who only killed outside. That had been true – until then.

That night, Tina had gone out drinking, knocking back around twenty measures of spirits across the evening. Eventually she was thrown out of the Carlisle pub, and stood in the street screaming 'fuck off' at the driver of another car. Peter Sutcliffe had been driving around the area, and pulled up next to her. She jumped in and told him they could go back to her flat. 'I parked up outside her flat, and she got out and went in,' Sutcliffe explained. 'I picked up a hammer as I got out of the car. I remember this was a claw hammer that I had bought at the Clayton hardware shop.'

Tina sat on the bed, undressing for sex, and Sutcliffe 'hit her on the back of the head with the hammer'. She fell off the bed and Sutcliffe continued his attack. He then put her back on the bed, and 'hit her several times on her stomach and back with the claw part of the hammer'. He left her alive: 'She was still making a gurgling noise when I left, but I knew she would not be in a state to tell anybody.' He also left another wellington-boot print.

The murder was linked quickly with the other murders, and 'special notices' were released by the police on 9 and 30 May 1977, which also mentioned an attack on prostitute Barbara Miller in March 1975 – not, as it transpired, one for which Sutcliffe was responsible. However, with his next crime, Sutcliffe showed that no one was safe – and gave the lie to his claim that he was only after prostitutes.

Peter and Sonia Sutcliffe went to look at a potential new home on the afternoon of 25 June 1977; he then went out for the evening in Bradford drinking with friends. Sixteen-year-old Jayne MacDonald was also out that night, dancing with friends before missing the last bus home. She started to walk home with a new friend, Mark Jones, who was going to sort a lift out for her with his sister, but his sister wasn't home. Mark and Jayne carried on walking towards Jayne's home in Chapeltown (just six doors from where Wilma McCann had lived), but around 1.30 a.m., Mark went back to his own place after agreeing to meet Jayne for a date later in the week. Jayne found a phone box near Dock Green pub, and tried to call a taxi, but there was no reply. She carried on walking up the road.

Sutcliffe was lying in wait. He had dropped his friends home then driven to Chapeltown, and had spotted Jayne, walking through the red-light district. He claimed, 'I believed at the time that I did it she was a prostitute . . . The urge to kill prostitutes was very strong and I had gone out of my mind.' Taking his hammer and a knife with him, he walked up behind Jayne and hit her on the back of the head. He then pulled her by the arms face down into what he called a yard, but was in fact an adventure playground. 'I hit her another once at least, maybe twice, on the head. I pulled her clothes up exposing her breasts, and I stabbed her several times with the knife in the chest. Before this I stabbed her in the back.' He left the body lying in the corner of the playground, where it was found the next morning by two children. Her father Wilfred was broken by his daughter's death, and died two years later. 'I read recently about her father dying of a broken heart,' Sutcliffe told police in January 1981, 'and it brought it all back to me. I realised what sort of monster I had become.' He failed to mention initially that he had embedded a broken bottle with the screw top still attached into Jayne's chest; he later claimed this must have happened when he dragged her body.

Jayne's murder brought considerable attention onto the police forces investigating the Ripper. 'An innocent young woman has been slaughtered,' was the tenor of the news reports, and far more help came from the public. Her death was immediately linked with those of Wilma McCann, Emily Jackson, Tina Atkinson and Irene Richardson, with Assistant Chief Constable George Oldfield stepping in to take over the enquiry personally. Car numbers were taken down of those kerb-crawling in the Chapeltown area in case of future attacks.

Aware of the scrutiny, Sutcliffe switched killing grounds again. His next victim was Maureen Long, whom he attacked less than a fortnight after killing Jayne. In the early hours of 10 July 1977, he offered Maureen a lift home. She had spent the evening drinking in pubs in Bradford, and agreed to spend the night at her estranged husband's home. She was walking down the road around 2 a.m. when Sutcliffe stopped, and she accepted his offer. He had once again been out drinking with friends in Bradford, and had dropped them home; this time, however, he stayed locally rather than heading to Leeds.

Maureen told Sutcliffe she lived in Bowling, and asked him not to stop at the house. If there was no one home, she explained, they could go in – if, that is, Sutcliffe fancied her. 'I told her that I did, just to please her.' She knocked on the door, but then came back to the car and suggested they went round the corner. Sutcliffe followed her directions, stopping near some waste land. When she went to urinate, he got his hammer and knife out. 'As she was crouching down, I hit her on the head with the hammer.' He then pulled her over to the waste land, 'pulled up her clothes and I stabbed her three or four times with the knife in her chest and back.' He wasn't put off by a caravan with its light on, and once 'I thought I had stabbed her enough', he went back to the car and drove off.

At 8.30 that morning, a pair of women were walking near the waste ground and heard cries that they originally thought were coming from a baby. Maureen had survived. She was rushed to hospital, and ACC Oldfield persuaded doctors to let her talk to the police before the operation – she gave a description of Sutcliffe and his car, but, as Oldfield had feared, remembered nothing post-operation. 'I got a nasty shock and thought it was the end of the line there and then,' Sutcliffe recalled. 'A few days after, I read that Long was suffering from loss of memory and this made me less worried about being caught.'

It wasn't Maureen's memory he needed to worry about. The night-watchman at the site had registered the presence of what he believed was a Ford Cortina, and while this meant that the police stopped looking for Sutcliffe's Corsair, it was still a liability. After not managing to sell it, he stripped it for parts, buying a red Corsair in its place. Ten thousand vehicles were checked as a direct result of this attempted murder, with 3,000 owners interviewed. Three hundred and four police officers were working full-time on the case, interviewing over 175,000 people and taking over 12,500 statements. Given that Ford Cortinas were regularly used by taxi drivers, people in that job were given closer scrutiny, with one in particular, Terry Hawkshaw, brought in for intensive questioning; eventually, police realised he had an airtight alibi for one of the later killings.

The Sutcliffes moved into their new home on 26 August; a week later, Sonia started teaching at Holmfield First School. On 1 October, Sutcliffe killed again, this time much further afield, in Manchester. 'I realised things were hotting up a bit in Leeds and Bradford. People had dubbed me the Ripper. I decided to go to Manchester to kill a prostitute.' Jean Jordan (aka Jean Royle) lived with her common-law husband Alan Royle and their two children on Moss Side, and that evening had gone out to meet other prostitutes for a drink. Sutcliffe saw Jean with a group of friends, and she agreed to go with him; 'the biggest mistake she ever made,' Sutcliffe himself said – Jean had been about to go with another punter. He paid her £5, and drove her to a place on Princess Road, Chorlton, near the Southern Cemetery.

Jean agreed to climb over a fence so they would be in privacy, and as she did so, Sutcliffe hit her over the head with a hammer. When he was worried that Maureen Long would remember details about him, he had disposed of his previous murder weapon; this new one he had found in the garage at his new home. 'I hit her again and again on the head until the moaning stopped.' He was disturbed by the arrival of another car, so pulled Jean into the bushes, and threw her bag away. It was only while driving home that he remembered that he had paid Jean with a brand new fiver taken from his wage packet. He didn't dare go back – at least not immediately.

Rather to Sutcliffe's surprise, Jean's body wasn't discovered immediately, as his other victims had been. That meant he had a chance to rectify his error so, about a week later, he returned to the allotments where he had left her, stripped the body and searched for the £5 note. He couldn't find it, nor could he locate her bag. He decided to try to 'create a mystery about the body'. 'I gave vent to my frustrations by picking up a piece of broken pane of glass and slashing it across her stomach,' he explained, noting that he had brought a hacksaw from his car, 'intending to remove her head. I started sawing through her neck, the blade might have been blunt because I was getting nowhere at all, so I gave it up.' Sutcliffe kicked her, and rolled her over before departing.

He was right to be concerned about the fiver. As Sir Lawrence Byford later wrote in his report about the failings of the police's Ripper inquiry, 'The recovery of this note some two weeks after the death marked a significant new stage in the series inquiry'. It brought the police to Peter Sutcliffe's door on 2 November – but the two detective constables who questioned him were moderately satisfied with his story that he had not been to Manchester except for work in the past year, and that he had been with his wife on the night of Jean's murder as well as the time of the mutilation of the body. He was questioned again on 8 November; Sutcliffe's mother confirmed that her son and daughter-in-law had been at a housewarming party on the night of the mutilation. Sutcliffe had in fact carried it out after dropping his family back to Bingley after the party; Jean's body was found the next morning where he had dumped it.

His next victim was twenty-five-year-old prostitute Marilyn Moore, on 14 December 1977, who was working in Chapeltown when she was picked up by Sutcliffe, calling himself 'Dave'. She realised he was obviously familiar with the girls in the area, and he took her to some waste ground behind a mill – not far from the site of Wilma McCann's murder. When they stopped, Sutcliffe suggested she get into the back of the car, and as she went to do so, took his hammer and hit her. However, the area was, in his words 'an oasis of mud', and Sutcliffe slipped. 'I only caught her a glancing blow on the head.' He tried to hit her again, but Marilyn continued to scream, attracting attention. Sutcliffe got in the car, and after the tyres spun in the mud for a few moments, managed to drive away.

In fact, Sutcliffe had hit her eight times, leaving her with a depressed fracture of the skull and defensive injuries to her hands. Marilyn was able to give a very good description of her attacker, but the police failed to give it sufficient credence. However, tyre tracks did match those found at Irene Richardson's murder. The case was eventually linked to the Ripper inquiry the following May.

The next victim, Yvonne Pearson, was killed on 21 January 1978 but not found until March. She was picked up by Sutcliffe in Lumb Lane, Bradford, and taken to an open space near Silvio's Bakery. As she went to get in the rear of the car, Sutcliffe hit her twice and dragged her next to an old settee. To his horror, another car pulled up and parked next to his, with a man and a woman in it. Yvonne was moaning, so Sutcliffe shoved some of the filling from the settee into her mouth and down her throat as he held her nose. The car finally left, leaving Sutcliffe 'seething with rage'. He kicked Yvonne hard – but then, he claimed, apologised to her before realising she was dead. He placed her under the settee and drove home.

Yvonne was reported missing a couple of days later – she had left her children with a sixteen-year-old babysitter – but since she was due in court and was likely to be sent to prison, some believed she had simply disappeared. Her body was found on Easter Sunday, 26 March, but there were oddities about the discovery: her arm was sticking out, which would have meant she should have been seen a lot earlier, and there was a newspaper from February beneath her body. Sutcliffe always denied returning to the scene. It also seemed as if she might have been hit with a boulder rather than a hammer, so it was a while until it was accepted as a Ripper killing.

Only ten days elapsed between Yvonne's death and Sutcliffe's next killing. On 31 January, he murdered Helen Rytka, a prostitute who worked with her twin sister in Huddersfield. The two tried to watch each other's backs, making a note of the registration number of their sister's client, and agreeing to meet after a certain time. That night, Helen arrived at the agreed rendezvous a few minutes before her sister Rita, and took the opportunity to grab a quickie with a further client. Unfortunately for her, it was Peter Sutcliffe with whom she went to Garrards timber yard.

Rather than get in the back of the car, Helen started to undress in the front but then decided the back would be better after all. As was his habit, Sutcliffe took his hammer and hit her as she went through the rear door – but he caught the edge of the door sill, and 'diminished the impact with her skull to a mere tap. She jumped back in alarm out of the car . . . and she exclaimed, "What was that?" To which I replied, "Just a small sample of one of these" and I hit a furious blow to her head which knocked her down.' As she lay there Sutcliffe hit her again.

However, there were taxi drivers nearby so Sutcliffe pulled Helen up to the end of the wood yard and then had sex with her 'as the only means . . . of persuading her to keep quiet'. (The police found this hard to believe, given everything else he had said about prostitutes; 'there is no conclusive forensic evidence to support his claim,' Sir Lawrence Byford wrote.) She was still moaning, and moving, so Sutcliffe stabbed her through the ribs into her heart five or six times. He then pulled her out of sight, and covered her with an asbestos sheet. Helen's sister Rita didn't report her missing for three days, but after she did so, a police dog took only ten minutes to find her body at the yard.

On 10 March, ACC Oldfield received a letter purporting to be from 'Jack the Ripper'. It wasn't the first such communication, and like another that had been taken seriously earlier, it was postmarked

Sunderland. A letter was also sent to the editor of the *Daily Mirror* at the Manchester office three days later. No immediate action was taken. Two days after that, DCS Hoban died unexpectedly; in part this led to a reconsideration of the many different killings and attacks, with Detective Chief Superintendent John Domaille in charge of the review.

Sutcliffe's final victim in 1978 – and indeed, his last for nearly a year – was forty-year-old Vera Millward, whom he picked up in Manchester on 16 May and drove to the grounds of the city's Royal Infirmary. By now, Sutcliffe was in a routine: as Vera went to the back of the car, he hit her, dragged her away and slashed at her stomach, causing her intestines to spill out. Her cries for help were ignored. She was found the next morning with her shoes neatly on her body. The tyre tracks found nearby were the same as those at the Irene Richardson and Marilyn Moore crime scenes.

The Police National Computer staff and Police Scientific Development Branch spent some time computerising the results of the 'observations' of car registration numbers in the red-light areas, and when Peter Sutcliffe's name came up as a result of his Corsair being seen in both Chapeltown and Bradford, he was interviewed again but once more was able to provide a credible reason for his car being seen. He denied ever having used prostitutes. However, Detective Constable Peter Smith was not convinced by his answers, and questioned Sutcliffe again in November; DC Smith also tracked down Sutcliffe's Corsair, which he had sold in August, and which now had new tyres.

All this attention may explain why Peter Sutcliffe did not strike again for some time. Although it was never officially linked to his list of crimes, twenty-two-year-old student Ann Rooney was hit on the head with a hammer on 2 March 1979. The description she gave of her attacker matched Sutcliffe; the car he drove also matched Sutcliffe's, but the police were not aware that his current vehicle, a

Sunbeam Rapier (which he had bought in May 1978, getting rid of his red Corsair three months later), had been spotted three times in the red-light areas. According to then Cleveland Chief Constable Keith Hellawell, Sutcliffe confessed in 1992 to attacking a young Irish student in Bradford, with the details matching the attack on Ann.

It wasn't long before he struck again. His murder of Josephine Whitaker on the night of 4 April 1979 came a fortnight after ACC Oldfield received yet another 'Ripper' letter from Sunderland – and erroneous conclusions were drawn from its contents by the police. The letter writer included the attack on Joan Harrison in the Ripper's crimes, and the police drew on the forensic evidence from that as part of their profile. The letter also said the next victim would be an 'old slut'.

Josephine Whitaker was not. She was a building-society clerk who had no connection with prostitution. Just nineteen years old, she had been visiting her grandparents before walking home late at night. As he had done with Tracy Browne a few years earlier, Sutcliffe walked up beside Josephine and started chatting with her, his hammer and sharpened Phillips screwdriver in his pocket. 'I said you don't know who you can trust these days,' Sutcliffe recalled. After a few minutes, he distracted her attention and then hit her with the hammer. He dragged her into bushes, then stripped off her clothing and stabbed her in the chest and stomach 'in a frenzy'. To police at the time of his arrest, he said, 'I realised she was not a prostitute but at the time I wasn't bothered, I just wanted to kill a woman.' In court, he maintained the voice had told him, 'This is a likely tale. She is really trying to play tricks on me. She is very clever, this one. You are not going to fall for this.'

Her body was found at 6.30 the next morning. In Josephine's wounds, police found evidence of milling oil, used in engineering shops, which had also been found on the Sunderland letter. Small pieces of metal, from where Sutcliffe had sharpened the screwdriver, were also in the wound, leading police to suspect an electrical or mechanical engineer of some sort. The boot prints found nearby also suggested that the wearer might be a lorry driver. (When Sutcliffe was interviewed the following year, he was actually wearing the same boots; he said the police officers didn't notice.)

The police were further put off Sutcliffe's scent by a cassette recording that was sent to ACC Oldfield on 18 June from Sunderland, by someone who 'had lived within 5 miles of Sunderland for much of his life'. 'I'm Jack,' the voice said. 'I see you're having no luck catching me. I have the greatest respect for you, George, but, Lord, you're no nearer catching me now than four years ago when I started.' Forensic examination of the envelope linked it to the previous letters and the Harrison murder, and at a press conference on 26 June, details were released to the public.

Those vehicle owners whose cars were seen in three separate observation areas were prioritised for interview. Peter Sutcliffe had been seen in all three – Leeds, Bradford and Manchester – so was interviewed on 29 July 1979. However, those questioning him didn't know that he had previously been interviewed, and although the officers weren't happy with Sutcliffe's answers, his handwriting didn't match that of the Ripper letter writer – so he was eliminated from the inquiry. Less than six weeks later, on 2 September, Sutcliffe killed again.

His victim was twenty-year-old university student Barbara Leach, who had decided to go for a walk after leaving the Mannville Arms, where she had been drinking with friends. Peter Sutcliffe had got rid of his Sunbeam Rapier and was now driving a Rover 3.5. He had gone 'to look for a victim' and saw Barbara (to whom he referred as Miss Leach in his confession – for his earlier victims, he used their first names). She walked past his car, he got out, followed her, hit her over the head with the hammer and dragged her behind a house. He then stabbed her eight times and hid her behind the dustbins. She was found the next afternoon after her roommate called the police.

Ten days after Barbara's body was found, a 'Special Notice' was issued by West Yorkshire police to all forces around the country, linking sixteen attacks, as well as the tyre tracks and the letters and tape. Quite surprisingly, none of the descriptions or photofit impressions were included. It also stated:

A person can be eliminated from these inquiries if:-
(a) Not born between 1924 and 1959
(b) He is an obvious coloured person
(c) His shoe size is 9 or above
(d) His blood group is other than B
(e) His accent is dissimilar to a North Eastern (Geordie) accent.

Peter Sutcliffe was interviewed yet again on 23 October, thanks to DC Smith who was concerned that his alibi for Jean Jordan's murder was inadequate. The officers involved didn't know of Sutcliffe's subsequent interviews. Sonia alibied him for the night of 2 September, and his handwriting again helped dismiss him.

(In 2005, nearly thirty years after the fake communications were sent to the Ripper team, the hoaxer responsible was caught when DNA from one of the letters was matched to John Samuel Humble. His DNA was in the system from an arrest in 2000, and he was charged with perverting the course of justice. He was sentenced to eight years' prison in 2006 and released on licence in 2010. The murder that Humble had added to the Ripper's tally – that of Joan Harrison – was eventually proved to have been carried out by sex offender Christopher Smith.)

Conspiracy theories have grown up around the police's seeming inability to coordinate their investigations and to realise that Peter

Sutcliffe's name was constantly coming up. By the end of 1979, police knew that there were probably only 241 people who might have had the £5 note; Sutcliffe was number 76 on that list, 44th of the 49 employees at Clark's. Somehow when that list was correlated with those who had been previously questioned, officers believed that Sutcliffe had not been seen before.

On 13 January 1980, Sutcliffe was interviewed by two detectives, unaware of his previous history. He volunteered that he had been questioned about the cars, and the officers' suspicions were increased. His footwear and tools were checked, but the detectives failed to find the pair of wellington boots in the wardrobe that Sutcliffe had worn when he killed Emily Jackson. They suggested Sutcliffe be questioned by another team, which took place at Kirkstall Forge Engineering on 30 January – the time when he was wearing the boots. A third team questioned him on 7 February. Although the officers were all suspicious, his alibi for the night that Jean Jordan's body was mutilated seemed to clear him. He was arrested for drink driving on 25 June in a red-light district, but the arresting officers were told that he had been eliminated from the inquiry.

Since September 1979, Sutcliffe hadn't given in to his urges to kill. From the spring of 1979, he had been having an affair with Theresa Douglas, who lived near Glasgow. He claimed to be Peter Logan from Yorkshire, and created a whole fictitious identity. Theresa's family found it hard to equate 'Peter Logan' with 'Peter Sutcliffe' when the truth came out.

While awaiting trial for the motor offence, Sutcliffe started to kill again. Forty-seven-year-old Marguerite Walls – a civil servant, although Sutcliffe maintained he believed she was a 'filthy prostitute' – was walking home late from work in Leeds on the night of 20 August 1980. He hit her over the head then dragged her with a rope around her neck into a driveway. Then, most unusually, he strangled rather than stabbed her, before stripping her and covering the body with grass cuttings and leaves. The police didn't think this was a Ripper killing – until Sutcliffe confessed. 'Because the press and the media had attached a stigma to me, I had been known for some time as the Yorkshire Ripper,' he said in his second set of interviews three weeks after his arrest. 'Which to my mind didn't ring true at all. It was just my way of killing them, but actually I found the method of strangulation was even more horrible and took longer.' (In court, of course, he claimed that it was the 'voice' that was responsible.)

He used strangulation once more when he attacked thirty-five-year-old Singaporean doctor Uphadya Bandara on 24 September. She was walking home from visiting friends in Headingley in Leeds when she moved aside to let the person walking up behind her pass. He didn't stop, but instead hit her over the head. Peter Sutcliffe thought she was 'walking slow like a prostitute' but he 'didn't have any tools on me to finish her, so I used that rope to strangle her'. According to the serial killer, 'I was overcome with remorse, so I didn't finish her off.' It's more likely that because her shoes had been scraping against the ground when he dragged her by the blue and pink cord he had placed around her neck, the sound alerted one of the local residents, Mrs Valerie Nicholas, who called the police. They arrived just after Sutcliffe had fled. Because of the similarities to the attack on Marguerite Walls, the police thought they were dealing with a second attacker, not the Ripper.

On 5 November, Sutcliffe attacked sixteen-year-old Theresa Sykes in Huddersfield around 8 p.m. She was simply in the wrong place at the wrong time: 'She was the first person I saw that night,' Sutcliffe said. 'I saw her walking along the road and followed her down this footpath and hit her a couple of times and knocked her down. But someone started shouting and I ran away and hid in a garden.' Theresa tried to grab at the weapon and was able to confirm it was metal. Her boyfriend Jim Furey, who was at home looking after their baby, heard her screams and raced out of their house, chasing after Sutcliffe as he fled. The police didn't officially link this to the Ripper inquiry, even if a large number of officers believed that it was his handiwork.

Peter Sutcliffe's final victim was twenty-year-old Jacqueline Hill, murdered on 17 November 1980, not far from where he had attacked Uphadya Bandara. He followed his usual pattern, creeping up on Jacqueline from behind, hitting her over the head and dragging her out of sight. He waited until a girl walked past the entrance to the drive where he was hiding, then pulled Jacqueline's clothes off, and stabbed her with a screwdriver in her lungs and her eye. He didn't realise he had left her handbag and glasses in the street where he had first attacked her. This was found by a student, whose flatmates – one a former Chief Inspector from Hong Kong – called the police. Jacqueline's body wasn't found, however, that night; it was discovered the next morning.

The reward for information was increased following this attack, reaching £50,000, and over 8,000 letters were received by Leeds police – 7,000 anonymous. One such was from Sutcliffe's friend Trevor Birdsall, who also visited Bradford police station to air his suspicions. However, nothing appears to have been done with his information.

On 2 January 1981, Peter Sutcliffe prepared to strike again. He left home in Bradford around 4 p.m. and picked up some number plates that he could put on his Rover so it wouldn't be recognised. Nineteen-year-old prostitute Denise Hall nearly got in the car with him, but something about his eyes scared her, and she declined to go. Olivia Reivers was five years older and had fewer reservations. Sutcliffe stopped and asked if she was doing business. They drove to the Light Trades House where they wouldn't be disturbed. Olivia was happy to have sex in the front of the car, but Sutcliffe failed to get an erection so said he just wanted to chat. He was waiting for her to get out of the car so he could get on with his real business.

On patrol, Probationary Constable Robert Hydes and Sergeant Robert Ring saw the car, and approached it. While Ring checked the number plates with the police computer, Hydes was informed by Sutcliffe that his name was Williams and Olivia was his girlfriend. Hydes didn't believe the story, and when Ring confirmed that the plates were registered to a Skoda, not a Rover, it was clear something was up. The police officers took Olivia to their patrol car, while Sutcliffe claimed he needed to urinate. He went out of their sight, and hid the knife and hammer that had been concealed in the car near an oil storage tank. At the police station, he managed to get rid of the other knife he had been carrying in his pocket. He still had the rope he had used on Marguerite and Uphadya in his pocket.

Sutcliffe probably thought he could get away with the theft of the number plates, but hadn't reckoned on the directive given that anyone found with prostitutes in suspicious circumstances should be dealt with by the Ripper squad. He was transferred to Dewsbury Police Station, where Detective Sergeant Desmond O'Boyle from the Ripper team arrived to interview him around midday on 3 January. Sutcliffe was cooperative although initially resistant to giving a blood sample. He claimed he hadn't wanted sex from Olivia, just someone to talk to about problems at home.

Sergeant Ring came back on duty at 10 p.m. that evening and, when he learned Sutcliffe was being questioned by the Ripper team, recalled that the suspect had disappeared to urinate. Going back to the yard, an hour later, he found Sutcliffe's weapons. This was what the police had been waiting for and, the next day, the Sutcliffes' home was searched, and Sonia Sutcliffe questioned. Detective Sergeant Peter Smith (promoted from Constable) was one of those who interrogated her husband during that day. The answers both gave differed on a key point – what time Peter Sutcliffe got home on the night Theresa Sykes was attacked. He said it was no later than eight; Sonia clearly recalled him coming in two hours later.

Detective Inspector John Boyle kept on at Sutcliffe, telling him he was sure that the reason he had been in Sheffield the night he was arrested was to kill a prostitute. 'I think you are in trouble, serious trouble,' he said. 'I think you have been leading up to it,' Sutcliffe replied and then admitted he was the Ripper.

At which point, he confessed in detail. 'I just want to tell you what I've done. I'm glad it's all over. I would have killed that girl in Sheffield if I hadn't been caught.' It took nearly sixteen hours for him to give his initial statement. He was charged on 5 January 1981, and on 20 February he appeared at Dewsbury Magistrates' Court where he was committed to trial – which was moved to the Old Bailey, as neither prosecution nor defence thought he had a chance of a fair trial in Yorkshire. On 29 April, he pleaded guilty to seven charges of attempted murder, but guilty only on manslaughter for thirteen murders on the grounds of diminished responsibility because he had been told to carry out the killings by a voice coming from the headstone of Bronislaw Zapolski back when he was digging graves at Bingley cemetery. However, Mr Justice Boreham wouldn't accept the plea, since the medical evidence was 'based simply on what this defendant has told the doctors, nothing more. Moreover what he has told the doctors conflicts substantially with what he told the police on the morning of arrest.'

Peter Sutcliffe's trial began on 5 May 1981, with the Attorney General, Sir Michael Havers, prosecuting, and James Chadwin QC and Sidney Levine for the defence. Mr Justice Boreham noted in his summing up that Sutcliffe was alleged to have told his wife that 'he would only serve ten years in a loony bin if he could convince people that he was mad . . . If you think that this is an indication that he had made up his mind to be deliberately deceitful and try to prove he was mad, then it could be very significant.' It came to one thing: did

Sutcliffe lie to the police in order to divert them from his mission? Or did he lie to the doctors in order to persuade them he was mad?'

The jury deliberated for five minutes short of six hours, and returned with a majority verdict of ten to two. 'It is difficult to find words that are adequate in my judgement to describe the brutality and gravity of these offences,' Mr Justice Boreham said, sentencing him to twenty life-imprisonment sentences, adding, 'I express my hope that when I have said life imprisonment, it will precisely mean that.'

Sutcliffe changed his name to his mother's maiden name, Coonan, and was diagnosed with paranoid schizophrenia. He went to Broadmoor in 1984. He was attacked both in Parkhurst before his transfer and in Broadmoor on two occasions, losing the sight in one eye. He will never be released.

CHAPTER 14

Great Britain: Dennis Nilsen – The Coleherne I

....

As Ian Fleming wrote in *Goldfinger*, 'Once is happenstance. Twice is coincidence. Three times, it's enemy action.' The Coleherne Arms public house in London was definitely the scene of enemy action in serial killer history: three notorious killers are believed to have used the gay meeting place as a hunting ground. Located at 261 Old Brompton Road, Earls Court, it was a pub Dennis Nilsen, Michael Lupo and Colin Ireland all frequented between 1978 and 1993, searching for victims. (No point heading there now, hoping to find that ambience: in 2008, the Coleherne was acquired by new owners, renovated and reopened as the Pembroke.)

Nilsen – nicknamed 'Britain's Jeffrey Dahmer' – was responsible for the deaths of up to fifteen young men between 1978 and 1983, all of whom he met in bars in London, brought back to his flat, drank and/or had sex with, and then, while they were sleeping, strangled. Once they were dead, he would carry on having conversations with them before disposing of their bodies – often down the toilet. In fact, it was this that led to his arrest on 9 February 1983, when a Dyno-Rod engineer concluded that pieces of flesh and bone were blocking the drains and called the police. When the pathologist confirmed that the pieces were human, and it became clear that they had come from the upstairs flat at Cranley Gardens, the police were very keen to chat to the tenant, who was due home from his work at the Job Centre . . .

Dennis Andrew Nilsen was born on 23 November 1945 in the Scottish town of Fraserburgh, Aberdeenshire; his Norwegian father was a soldier who had been stationed in Scotland during the Second World War and married a local girl. Nilsen was the middle child of three, and his parents separated and divorced in 1948 – they had hardly lived together during the marriage, as his father was more interested in his soldiering than in bringing up a family. Nilsen was raised by his mother and grandparents, and was very close to his grandfather, a fisherman, until he died of a heart attack in 1951. His mother took the nearly six-year-old boy in to see the corpse, telling him that his grandfather was 'sleeping'; Nilsen recalled his heart beating faster on seeing the body.

Nilsen withdrew into himself after his grandfather's death, resenting both his siblings, and then his mother, who remarried in 1955 – she would have four further children quickly by her new husband. The ten-year-old Nilsen didn't get on with his stepfather initially, but gradually came to respect him. Nilsen himself nearly drowned around this time, but felt confident his grandfather would somehow save him. (He was actually rescued by another boy.)

As puberty hit, Nilsen realised that he was homosexual, although he never acted on the attraction that he felt for his contemporaries. He did claim that many of those he fancied reminded him of his sister, and on one occasion he did fondle her; he also said that he was himself sexually caressed by an older boy. He made the mistake of fondling his older brother, Olav, as he was sleeping, leading to his sibling guessing his sexuality and making humiliating remarks about him in public.

Aged fourteen, he joined the Army Cadet Force, and when he left school – after a very brief interlude working in a canning factory – he signed up for the British Army, intending to train as a chef. He carried out basic training at St Omer Barracks in Aldershot, and passed his first catering exam at the end of the three-year period. He tended to stay out of the way of his fellow recruits when he showered in case he got an erection when he saw them – homosexuality was illegal in those days and a cause for disciplinary proceedings in the Army.

He was posted to the 1st Battalion, the Royal Fusiliers in Osnabrück, West Germany, where he started to drink heavily and fantasise about being molested by some of his comrades. He also found himself on one occasion waking on the floor of the flat of a German youth with whom he had been drinking the night before; nothing had happened, much to his chagrin, but he started to think about partners who were either unconscious or dead.

Nilsen spent two years in Osnabrück, returning to Aldershot in the summer of 1966; he passed his official catering exam, and was sent to a posting in Norway. In 1967, he was transferred to Al-Mansoura prison, in Aden, South Yemen, during the Aden Emergency: the National Liberation Front were battling the Front for the Liberation of South Yemen, with the British Army trying to keep the peace in the middle. It was a hazardous time for British military personnel, who regularly came under attack as they travelled around. Nilsen himself was kidnapped by an Arab taxi driver; the man beat him up and put him in the boot of his taxi. When he reached his destination and pulled Nilsen out, the young soldier grabbed a jack handle and proceeded to beat the living daylights out of his kidnapper, locking him in his own taxi. (Nilsen told a psychiatrist before his trial that he had actually killed the man.)

This frightening experience fuelled Nilsen's fantasies; he had his own room, where he could masturbate how and when he chose. He recalled that he used a mirror to create the effect of there being a second, unconscious, person there with him, and he could be both dominant and passive partner in the sexual experience. He was influenced by the Théodore Géricault painting *The Raft of the Medusa*, a depiction of the starvation, dehydration and eventual descent into cannibalism of the crew of the French naval frigate the *Méduse*, who set out after their shipwreck on a raft. In its centre is an old man holding the limp, naked body of a youth, as he sits on the dismembered body of another young man. In his mind, Nilsen changed this to a fantasy about a slender, attractive, young blond soldier, recently killed in battle, who was dominated by an anonymous 'dirty, grey-haired old man' who washed the body before having sex with the corpse. Nilsen did have a sexual partner during this time, a young Arab boy.

Nilsen left Aden in January 1968, joining the Argyll and Sutherland Highlanders during their postings to Plymouth, England; Cyprus; Berlin; and then Inverness, Scotland. In Germany he had his first heterosexual experience with a prostitute; he was cocky about this with his comrades in arms, but privately found it 'over-rated' and 'depressing'. Corporal Dennis Nilsen ended his military career stationed on the Shetland Islands, off the north coast of Scotland, in October 1972.

He moved back to his family home in Strichen once he was demobbed, but fell out with his relations after his older brother informed his mother that Dennis was gay. In December 1972, he moved to London to join the Metropolitan Police. He trained with them until April 1973, when he was posted as a junior constable to Willesden Green police station. The police wasn't a comfortable fit for Nilsen, who enjoyed the camaraderie of the Army, and, although homosexuality had been decriminalised, he thought that his lifestyle was incompatible with his work: he was spending his evenings drinking and indulging in casual pickups in gay bars. When his father died and left him £1,000, he took that as a sign, and resigned in December at the end of his first year, taking a room at 80 Teignmouth Road in Cricklewood.

After five months working as a security guard, he joined the civil service in May 1974, where he was employed at a Job Centre in Denmark Street, central London. He was not a particularly remarkable worker, often volunteering for overtime, and he was appointed

Acting Executive Officer in 1979, receiving the post properly in June 1982, when he was transferred to Kentish Town. It was from there that police were waiting for him to return in February 1983.

In November 1975, eighteen months after starting work at the Denmark Street Job Centre, Nilsen met twenty-year-old David Gallichan, after helping him when he was being threatened outside a pub. The young gay man came back to Nilsen's flat, where the two men chatted and drank for hours, establishing a friendship. Nilsen had found the company he wanted – even if Gallichan later noted that they rarely had sex, and that he was 'uninterested' in Nilsen sexually, even if the older man was attracted to him. They decided to rent a place together, and found a ground-floor flat at 195 Melrose Avenue, Cricklewood; Nilsen negotiated sole use for them of the rear garden. Over the next few months, Gallichan redecorated the place while Nilsen went to work.

The relationship started to deteriorate, with each bringing back casual partners for sex, and by the start of 1977, they were arguing frequently. In May, Gallichan moved out, and Nilsen lived on his own from then on, despite having three brief relationships over the next year and a half, believing that he was not someone with whom anyone else would choose to live. Not if they were alive, anyway. He would have company; he was going to have what he described in 1983 as 'a new kind of flatmate'.

In December 1978, Nilsen took his first life. The victim was fourteen-year-old Stephen Holmes, who had been trying to buy an alcoholic drink at the Cricklewood Arms pub. According to the version that Nilsen gave to London's *Evening Standard*, he had been drinking all day on 29 December and was 'bingeing' in the pub. He invited Stephen to come back to Melrose Avenue to drink (believing the teenager to be about seventeen years old), and the pair drank heavily into the night. They fell asleep, and when Nilsen woke the next morning, he found Stephen asleep on his bed. 'Afraid to wake him in case he left me,' Nilsen wrote, he caressed the boy, and then decided that Stephen was going to 'stay with me over the New Year whether he wanted to or not'. He straddled Stephen and strangled him into unconsciousness with a necktie, then drowned him in a bucket of water.

Nilsen masturbated over the body at least twice before he placed Stephen under the floorboards ('I eased him into his new bed,' was his euphemistic description of the act). A week later, he wondered about the state of the body, so disinterred him, and found that his skin was very dirty. He stripped himself naked, and carried the corpse into the bathroom, where he washed it before replacing it. Holmes remained as Nilsen's reluctant flatmate for eight months until, on 11 August 1979, Nilsen took advantage of the privacy of his back garden to burn the body in a bonfire.

Two months to the day after that, Nilsen tried to get a replacement lodger, picking up a young student from Hong Kong in a pub in St Martin's Lane, central London. Andrew Ho managed to escape from Nilsen's flat, to which he had gone back on the promise of sex, and reported the incident to the police. Eventually, however, although Nilsen was questioned, Andrew decided not to press charges.

Another seven weeks elapsed before Nilsen tried again. On 3 December 1979, Nilsen murdered twenty-three-year-old Canadian student Kenneth Ockenden, using the cord from a pair of headphones. The pair had met in the West End; Kenneth was visiting the UK to meet relatives, and Nilsen offered to show him various London landmarks – and while he was at it, Kenneth could come back for something to eat and drink at Nilsen's apartment nearby. Kenneth agreed, and they bought whisky, rum and beer at an off-licence on the way back, splitting the bill. While the young student was listening to music, Nilsen wrapped the cord of his own set of headphones around Kenneth's neck, and started to strangle him, dragging him across the floor with the wire as he killed the boy. Once Kenneth was dead, Nilsen poured a glass of rum, untangled the headphones from around the Canadian's neck, and used them to listen to some music. The next day, he bought a Polaroid camera and took various shots of the body in suggestive poses. He then put the corpse spread-eagled over him on his bed as he watched TV for some hours, before wrapping it in plastic bags and placing it, like Holmes's body previously, beneath the floorboards. At least four times over the next two weeks, Nilsen brought Kenneth from his resting place to sit beside him on an armchair as he watched television.

There was some while before Nilsen found his next victim. Sixteen-year-old catering student Martyn Duffey was murdered on 17 May 1980 after accepting the offer of a meal and a bed for the night from the man who took pity on him outside Euston railway station. Nilsen was returning from a union conference in Southport, and saw the boy sleeping rough as he passed through: Martyn had run away from home four days earlier, after being questioned by police over failing to pay a train fare. Nilsen fed him, and the exhausted youngster fell asleep in Nilsen's bed. Nilsen then tied a ligature around his neck, sat on the boy's chest, and tightened the ligature with a 'great force' until he became unconscious. He then dragged the boy into the kitchen and drowned him in the sink. He then took a bath with the corpse, and washed it.

Initially, Nilsen placed Martyn's body on a kitchen chair, and then on the bed, where Nilsen kissed, caressed and complimented 'the youngest-looking I had ever seen'. He sat on the boy's stomach and masturbated, before placing the body in a cupboard. After a couple of days, however, the corpse began to bloat, and Nilsen put him 'straight under the floorboards'.

It is believed that Nilsen killed five more victims – only one of whom has been identified – before the end of 1980. Occasional male prostitute Billy Sutherland was murdered around 20 August: the twenty-six-year-old Scot met Nilsen in a pub near Piccadilly Circus and came back to Melrose Avenue. Nilsen wasn't sure exactly how he killed Billy, although he did remember that he had strangled the man as he was standing or kneeling in front of his new flatmate.

According to the confession he gave early in his imprisonment, Nilsen killed an Irish labourer with rough hands at some point in September. The man wore an old suit and jacket, and was between twenty-seven and thirty years old; they met in the Cricklewood Arms. He would later claim that none of this happened. He never denied the next victim, a slender male prostitute in his twenties, who had 'gypsy-like features' and was either of Filipino or Thai descent. The pair met in the Salisbury Arms in October.

A tramp in his twenties whom Nilsen found sleeping in a doorway in Charing Cross Road was the next to die, at some point in November. Nilsen recalled the Englishman was in his twenties and emaciated from living on the street, with a pale complexion and missing teeth. Like Martyn Duffey, the vagrant was strangled in his sleep – Nilsen remembered that the man had made a cycling motion with his legs as he died. This was a murder that Nilsen thought relieved the man of a life 'of long suffering', and had been 'as easy as taking candy from a baby'.

Nilsen tried to keep the smell from beneath his floorboards from getting too overpowering: when he looked at the bodies, he could see the putrefaction, with maggots crawling out of the eye sockets and mouths. He put deodorants under the floorboards, and sprayed insecticide twice daily. However, he realised that they could not stay there much longer and, late in 1980, he disinterred the bodies, dissecting them, and taking them out to a bonfire that he built on waste ground behind the flat. In an attempt to disguise the very distinctive smell of burning human flesh, he put an old car tyre in with them – and watched them burn. Three local children stood and watched too, but weren't there to see Nilsen rake through the ashes and smash into pieces a skull that had remained intact.

On 10 November, Nilsen invited Scottish barman Douglas Stewart to come back to the flat; they met at the Golden Lion in Dean Street, Soho. Nilsen tried to strangle him once he had fallen asleep, but Douglas woke up and fought him off. He reported the attack immediately to the police, but apparently they dismissed it as a 'domestic' disagreement.

A 'long-haired hippy' was Nilsen's last victim in 1980, some point in November or December. The man in his late twenties met Nilsen after the pubs had closed (i.e. after 11 p.m. or so) in the West End, came back to his flat, and was killed. Nilsen buried the remains under the floorboards. Again, Nilsen later denied this happened.

The serial killer began 1981 as he meant to go on, challenging an eighteen-year-old, blue-eyed young Scot he met in the first few days of the new year at the Golden Lion pub to a drinking contest back at his flat. All that stuck in Nilsen's mind about this murder, which took place in the usual way (getting his victim drunk and then strangling him with a necktie), was that the man wore a green tracksuit top and trainers. 'End of the day, end of the drink, end of a person . . . floorboards back, carpet replaced, and back to work at Denmark Street,' Nilsen later commented. Around a week later, on 12 January, he took a day sick from work, and spent the time dissecting this and the hippy's bodies (trisecting the latter corpse) before replacing them under the floorboards. A month later, a man in his early twenties from Belfast was next to die; once again, they met in the West End, Nilsen brought him back to Melrose Avenue and the inevitable followed.

His target in April 1981 was rather more of a challenge (although it was yet another one that Nilsen would later retract his confession to killing). This was a muscular young English skinhead, aged around twenty, whom he met at a food stall in Leicester Square. Nilsen promised him better food and drink, and recalled that the youth was full of bravado about how tough he was and how much he enjoyed getting in a brawl. He had tattoos, with one around his neck that read 'Cut here'. Nilsen strangled him, and then obeyed the instruction. He hung the naked torso in his bedroom for a full day before sending him beneath the floorboards.

There was a gap before Nilsen killed again. This may have been in part because his landlord had informed him during the summer that he wanted to renovate the property. After what Nilsen suspected were shock tactics to get him to move failed (his flat was completely vandalised), the pair began negotiations and Nilsen eventually agreed to move out on payment of £1,000 by the landlord. He moved into an attic flat, 23D Cranley Gardens, Muswell Hill, on 5 October 1981.

However, before he moved out, he added to his tally, murdering twenty-three-year-old Malcolm Barlow on 18 September. Nilsen had found Malcolm collapsed outside his house twenty-four hours earlier, after his epilepsy medicine had affected his legs. Nilsen called an ambulance for the man, and Barlow was taken to hospital; released the following morning, he came back to say thanks to Nilsen. After they ate together and drank rum and coke, Malcolm fell asleep. Nilsen promptly strangled him – but there was no more room beneath the floorboards, so he put Malcolm's body under the kitchen sink.

One of Nilsen's last actions at Melrose Avenue was to have another bonfire, to dispose of the remains of his most recent victims. He had dissected the corpses of the Northern Irishman and the skinhead in August, and now completed the job on Malcolm Barlow before burning the five bodies on 4 October. When police searched the property after his arrest, they recovered over a thousand items of bone.

Nilsen realised he had some serious logistical problems with his new flat, as it was on the top floor of the building and he no longer had the use of a back garden to dispose of the remains. He tried to strangle nineteen-year-old student Paul Nobbs on 23 November 1981 (Nilsen's thirty-sixth birthday) after meeting him at the Golden Lion pub in Soho, but for some reason failed to see it through; Paul woke the next day remembering little about what had happened the previous night. He found bruising on his neck, and his doctor told him that it seemed as if he had been strangled. However, Nobbs, afraid of revealing his sexuality, did not go to the police. Toshimitsu Ozawa had a similar close encounter on New Year's Eve 1981, but managed to escape: he told police that Nilsen had come towards him with a tie stretched between his hands. However, there was no follow-up by the authorities; when questioned about Toshimitsu's claim, Nilsen said, 'I find that frightening.' Nilsen then restrained himself for nearly three months until March 1982, when he badly underestimated the resilience of his next target.

Twenty-three-year-old John Howlett met Nilsen in a pub near Leicester Square and returned with him to Cranley Gardens to continue drinking. They did so as they watched a movie, and then John went into the front room, which Nilsen was using as a bedroom, and fell asleep. About an hour later, Nilsen tried to wake him up, without success, then sat on the edge of the bed, staring at the sleeping man, drinking a rum. 'It's about time you went,' he decided in the end, and started to strangle him. But John wasn't going to go quietly: he fought back, leaving marks on Nilsen's own neck that took over a week to fade. However, Nilsen used an upholstery strap to render him unconscious, and then retreated to the living room, shaking from what he called the 'stress of the struggle'. He then tried on three occasions to throttle John, but the man kept on breathing. Finally, Nilsen filled the bathtub with water, and held John's head under water for five minutes until he drowned. Once the man was definitely dead, Nilsen dismembered the body, and flushed some of his internal organs and flesh down the toilet; the larger bones, he put out with the rubbish.

Two months later, Nilsen tried again, but once again, things didn't go according to plan. His target was twenty-one-year-old Carl Stottor, with whom he got drinking at the renowned gay pub, the Black Cap in Camden, where Carl performed as Khara Le Fox. As ever, he persuaded the younger man to accompany him back to his flat, where they had more to drink. Carl passed out on top of an open sleeping bag. He woke a bit later to find Nilsen strangling him, and telling him to 'stay still'. Carl thought that Nilsen was trying to free him from the zip of the sleeping bag, but then realised what was happening. 'I woke up feeling something round my neck,' Carl said at Nilsen's trial. 'I couldn't breathe properly. I felt his hands pulling at the zip at the back of my neck. I passed out.'

Learning from his troubles with John Howlett, Nilsen proceeded to try to drown Carl. 'The pressure was increasing, my head was hurting and I couldn't breathe,' Carl testified. 'I knew I was in water. He was trying to drown me. He kept pushing me into the water. One time, when I was out of the water, I said, "No more, please – no more" and he pushed me back in again.'

'I had strangled him unconscious,' Nilsen recalled in a statement, read out at his trial after Carl had given his evidence. 'I thought he was dead. I stripped him, carried him into the back room and put him down. I took a very large drink after the effort, and put on headphones to listen to music.'

But Carl wasn't dead – as Nilsen's mongrel dog (called Bleep, but misreported in various contemporary documents) recognised. 'Blip appeared and pawed at my arm,' Nilsen's statement continued. 'She went over to the man and starting whining and licking what I thought was a dead body. Then I noticed the corpse had started breathing and shivering with cold. I pulled him over to the fire and rubbed his arms and legs to get the circulation going. After ten more minutes he started to breathe more normally. I was desperate he should live. I put him to bed and got in myself holding him, to transfer as much of my own body heat as I could to him.'

Carl recalled waking up at one point with the dog licking his face, and then that Nilsen told him he had become caught in the zip following a nightmare, and Nilsen had put him in cold water because he had been in shock. Carl took two days fully to regain consciousness, after which Nilsen took him to a train station, hoping they might meet again! (Nilsen's dog was a regular witness to the crimes: 'I think she knew what was to happen,' he wrote later. 'Even she became resigned to it. If there was a violent struggle, she would always become excited and start barking.')

In September 1982, Nilsen met twenty-seven-year-old Scot Graham Allen in Shaftesbury Avenue when Allen was trying to hail a cab. He came back for a meal at Cranley Gardens and as he was eating the omelette that Nilsen had prepared, his host strangled him. He kept Graham's corpse in the bathtub for three days before dissecting him on the kitchen floor. He flushed some of Graham's flesh and small bones down the toilet, hoping to lose them in the vast London sewerage system, but they became caught in the drains and started to clog them.

'Here I go again,' Nilsen muttered to himself, just before he strangled what turned out to be his final victim, twenty-year-old heroin addict Stephen Sinclair. They had met in Oxford Street on 26 January 1983, where Stephen was living rough; his wrists were bandaged concealing deep slash marks from recent suicide attempts. Nilsen bought him a burger and invited him back to Cranley Gardens. There Stephen drank some alcohol and shot up with heroin before passing out. Nilsen listened to the Who's rock opera *Tommy* for a time (one of his accounts suggests it was the Clannad theme from the IRA thriller *Harry's Game*) before kneeling in front of Stephen and strangling him with a ligature formed from a neck-tie and a rope. He then bathed the body, and took it to his bedroom.

There he put three mirrors around the bed, so he could see from all angles, undressed, and lay down beside the corpse. A few hours later, he turned Stephen's head towards him, kissed him on the forehead and wished him goodnight, before falling asleep himself.

He then dissected the body and distributed the parts around the flat in plastic bags: some were in a wardrobe, some in a tea chest and others in a drawer under the bathtub. He used the bandages from Stephen's wrists to seal them. As he had done with the other 'flatmates' at Cranley Gardens, he boiled the heads, hands and feet on the stove to remove the flesh – the saucepan became a particularly grisly exhibit at the trial and is now part of Scotland Yard's display at the Crime Museum – although he didn't have time to complete the job.

On 5 February 1983, Nilsen wrote to the property managing estate agents, complaining that the drains were blocked and that something needed to be done. He wasn't the only one to do so – other residents had already registered their distaste, and Dyno-Rod employee Michael Cattran attended site on 8 February. He opened a drain cover and found small bones and a flesh-like substance. Having no reason not to do so, Cattran chatted with a couple of the residents, including Nilsen, who said that 'It looks to me like someone has been flushing down their Kentucky Fried Chicken.' Once everyone was gone for the night, Nilsen opened the manhole and removed the flesh. He debated buying some chicken to put down the drain to put the police off his trail but, he claimed, 'I was sickened by the past, the present, and a doubtful future. I had found the whole mad burden of guilt intolerable.'

Despite the lack of the fleshy substance in the drain, the next morning Cattran found some that Nilsen had missed. He and his supervisor called in the police; Professor David Bowen confirmed the remains were human; and Detective Chief Inspector Peter Jay and two colleagues were waiting for Nilsen when he got home from work. They told him they were there about the blockage in the drains from his flat, which led Nilsen to enquire why the police would be involved in this. They asked him to let them into his flat. Nilsen had known this was coming: earlier in the day he had told a colleague at the Job Centre that 'If I'm not in tomorrow, I'll either be ill, dead or in jail.'

Nilsen agreed, and immediately the police officers smelled rotting flesh. They told Nilsen the drain was blocked by human remains, and when Nilsen tried to pretend he was shocked, DCI Jay said, 'Don't mess about – where's the rest of the body?' Nilsen didn't feign further: he told them the rest of the body was in the wardrobe. They asked if there were any other body parts there, and Nilsen replied, 'It's a long story; it goes back a long time. I'll tell you every-thing. I want to get it off my chest. Not here – at the police station.' He was arrested on suspicion of murder and taken to Hornsey Police Station.

While he was being held there, the flat was searched properly, and Professor Bowen took the plastic bags from the wardrobe to the mortuary. One had two dissected torsos in it (one vertically dissected), and a shopping bag with internal organs. The other had two heads, one that was almost entirely absent of flesh, the other more intact, along with a torso with arms attached but no hands. Both heads showed evidence of moist heat (i.e. it appeared that they had been boiled – something Nilsen admitted to when questioned).

Nilsen was interviewed on 10 February and confessed to the murders, and mentioned that he had killed twelve or thirteen men at his previous home. He also said he had been unsuccessful in kill-ing a further seven people, some of whom had escaped, others whom he had allowed to leave. He gave the police the locations of further remains at Cranley Gardens, allowing body parts to be located in a bag in the bathroom and in a tea chest, and then accompanied them to Melrose Avenue, and showed where he had set the fires.

Professor Bowen began the macabre jigsaw puzzle of remains, and was able to find fingerprints for Stephen Sinclair, which matched the young man's police record. That enabled police to charge Nilsen on 11 February, and formal interviews began. Thirty hours of questioning followed in sixteen separate sessions over the next few days; Nilsen accepted a lawyer, Ronald T. Moss, who sat and listened as Nilsen matter-of-factly described the many killings and attempted murders that he had carried out over the preceding half decade. He pointed out that he hadn't killed everyone who came back with him. 'Only a tiny percentage came to grief.' Police were able to locate fourteen men who visited Nilsen in one or other of his flats and had come to no harm, including some from the Coleherne.

Asked if he felt any remorse, Nilsen replied, 'I wished that I could stop, but I couldn't . . . I felt I was taking on a quasi-God role.' He hadn't enjoyed killing itself, but he 'worshipped the art and the act of death'. 'I have no tears for my victims,' he added, 'I have no tears for myself, nor those bereaved by my actions.'

Nilsen was held on remand at Brixton Prison, and on 26 May 1983 committed to stand trial at the Old Bailey on five counts of murder and two of attempted murder. Initially, Nilsen was going to plead not guilty, but five weeks before his trial began on 24 October 1983, he dismissed Moss (not for the first time, but he had consistently rehired him on other occasions), and was represented by Ralph Haeems. His new solicitor's advice was to plead not guilty by diminished responsibility.

The trial lasted until 4 November. He was charged with six counts of murder; despite intensive inquiries, the police had been unable to identify the other victims. There was no doubt that Nilsen had killed the six men he was accused of murdering, prosecutor Allan Green told the jury. The only issue was whether the diminished responsibility plea held water. The Crown's argument was that 'even if there was mental abnormality, that was not sufficient to diminish substantially his responsibility for these killings'. Douglas Stewart, Paul Nobbs and Carl Stottor all testified about their memories of being attacked by Nilsen, and then DCI Jay recounted Nilsen's arrest and subsequent confession, with Detective Superintendent Chambers reading out Nilsen's formal confession to the court. As the gory details of the entrapment, murders, dissection and disposal were recited, the jury and the judge looked queasy, while Nilsen remained impassive in the dock.

The defence team was led by barrister Ivan Lawrence, who explained that their case was that Nilsen was suffering from an abnormality of mind at the time of each killing that stopped him from forming the specific intention of murder. Various psychiatrists gave evidence – two for the defence, one in rebuttal – but the case still came down to a simple matter, as Allan Green noted at the beginning of his closing statement: 'The defence says he couldn't really help it. The Crown says, oh yes he could.' The judge summed up, noting 'there are evil people who do evil things. Committing murder is one of them ... A mind can be evil without being abnormal.'

While most people expected the jury to be back quickly, they weren't; they retired to deliberate on the morning of 3 November, and by the end of the day were no nearer making a decision. The following morning the judge said he would accept a majority verdict (up until then, as is normal for a jury trial, a unanimous verdict was required). Five hours later, the jury returned. There was a unanimous guilty verdict on the attempted murder of Paul Nobbs and majorities of ten to two on the other attempted murder count (Stewart) and all six murders. Nilsen swayed slightly in the dock when the first guilty verdict came back, but otherwise remained unemotional.

The judge passed sentence: life imprisonment with a recommendation that he serve at least twenty-five years. 'It may well be that even if the verdicts had been guilty of manslaughter it would have been impossible to pass any other sentence, which is one of life imprisonment,' Mr Justice Croom-Johnson said. 'This is one case in which life should mean life,' wrote the editor of the *Glasgow Herald*. 'In the case of Nilsen his lack of remorse, his pride in being the "killer of the century" and his twisted humour should disqualify him from release for ever.'

Nilsen started his sentence at Wormwood Scrubs; he did not appeal against the sentence. After he was attacked in December 1983, he was transferred to Wakefield Prison (after a brief stay at Parkhurst). He went from there to a vulnerable prisoner unit at HMP Full Sutton until 1993, thence to HMP Whitemoor. The following year, he was given a whole-life tariff by the then Home Secretary, Michael Howard; he was returned to Full Sutton in 2003. His first victim, Stephen Holmes, wasn't identified until 2005; the Crown Prosecution Service concluded that 'there is sufficient evidence from which a jury could be satisfied that Stephen was Nilsen's first victim' but that it wasn't in the public interest to prosecute. If convicted, his sentence couldn't be increased; the evidence of the unidentified victims had already played a part in his 1983 trial; and Rene Barclay, Director of Serious Casework in London, noted that 'I have also taken into consideration the clear views of Stephen Holmes' family.'

Nilsen has had various run-ins with authority during his time in prison – notably over whether he could publish his autobiography, 'The History of a Drowning Boy' – but has not attempted to apply for any form of parole or challenge his conviction. He remains in Full Sutton. His epitaph may well be his own line after he was sentenced: 'He has committed fifteen homicides, and it is other people who think him important.'

CHAPTER 15

Great Britain: Michael Lupo – The Coleherne II

....

Two weeks after learning that he was HIV positive, it seems as if Michele de Marco Lupo decided that the world would pay. Over the next eight weeks, he was responsible for strangling four gay men, and only because a fifth, who had survived, was willing to act as live bait was he arrested and imprisoned. He didn't care – he allegedly laughed about the victims – because he was sure that he would be dead soon. The link between his diagnosis and his crimes was jumped on by the newspapers at a time when the AIDS virus was just starting to become public knowledge – *The Times* headline from his trial read: 'Aids sufferer haunted bar in war against homosexuals'.

Born in 1953, Lupo was a choirboy in his native Italy before joining an elite Italian commando unit. He was openly gay and had multiple relationships in the areas where the unit was posted, developing a taste for sadomasochism, in which he took the dominant role. He moved to Britain in 1975, where he became known as Michael Lupo, and started working as a hairdresser at the Yves Saint Laurent boutique in west London. He eventually became successful enough to open his own 'styling boutique', which attracted attention from the rich and famous – and 'the Wolf Man' (*lupo* means wolf in Italian) kept very detailed notes on all those with whom he had slept. His address book started to fill with important names, including what was described in court as 'a leading television comedian', later revealed to be Kenny Everett. (Everett was questioned by police, and couldn't remember anything about him.)

Over the next decade, Lupo claimed that he slept with around 4,000 men, finding them in pubs such as the Coleherne, and bringing many back to a house in Roland Gardens, South Kensington, where he had designed and built his very own underground torture chamber. His overnight guests would leave with bruises, incisions and multiple other markings after they had spent time subjected to Lupo's manacles and whips. He also travelled the world, visiting Amsterdam, Berlin, Hamburg, Los Angeles and New York, frequenting bars that specialised in sadomasochism and coprophilia (sexual arousal from faeces).

In early March 1986, his world came crashing down around him when he tested positive for HIV. He no longer took pleasure purely in inflicting pain: he needed to take it further, and on 15 March, he picked up his first victim, Alex Kasson, at the Coleherne. (Some sources name Kasson as James Burns.) The thirty-seven-year-old railway worker was cruising the bars looking for a partner, despite his own AIDS diagnosis a few days earlier, and he found one in Lupo. Exactly what happened isn't known, but Alex's body was found in a derelict flat in Kensington by tramps. His body had been mutilated – the scrotum opened, and the chest cavity slashed open and smeared with excrement. He had been strangled with a silk sock. Since there were no obvious links between Lupo and Alex, police were unable to process the case very rapidly.

Lupo's next victim was found on 6 April. This time he had left the body of twenty-four-year-old Anthony Connolly on a railway embankment in Brixton, south London, where it was found by a group of children. He had been mutilated in the same way as Alex Kasson, and strangled with the same silk sock. However, there were some serious delays over the prosecution of the case: Anthony's flatmate was HIV positive, and the coroner delayed the autopsy because he was concerned that Anthony himself might be. This led to some tension between the gay community and the police when it was revealed: it was suggested that the other deaths and attacks that followed might have been prevented had the post-mortem been carried out earlier, and that – as was often believed to be the case at the time – the police didn't care that much about another dead gay man. Of course, it also didn't help that officers investigating Anthony's death would not necessarily have known about Alex Kasson's murder in those pre-computerised days.

Less than two weeks later, on the night of 18 April, Lupo found another target after leaving a gay bar. He was on Hungerford Bridge, which crosses the Thames from Charing Cross on the north to the Southbank complex, when he saw a tramp, aged about sixty. (He was never identified.) According to Lupo's own testimony, something inside him 'screamed out at the world', and he attacked the man. After kicking him in the groin, he strangled him and threw his body into the river.

The following day, Lupo's anger had not worn off when he met Mark Leyland at Charing Cross. They headed for a public toilet to have sex, where Mark changed his mind. Lupo attacked him with an iron bar; however, Mark was able to escape. He reported the incident to the police, but only as a mugging, rather than attempted murder; after Lupo's arrest he amplified his story.

Hospital worker Damian McClusky was Lupo's final confirmed murder; he was last seen alive on 24 April, five days after the attack on Leyland, in a pub in Kensington. His body – also strangled, raped and mutilated with a razor before being excreted on – was found in a basement flat.

On 7 May, Lupo picked up David Cole, a British Rail worker, at the Copacabana gay club in Earls Court and took him to a south London lorry park for sex. Lupo tried to strangle him with a black nylon stocking, but David was able to escape and went to the police. Detective Superintendent John Schumacher was heading the investigation, and was able to persuade David to act as bait to try to identify Lupo. Backed up by undercover police officers, David returned to various haunts, and, on the night of 15 May, within five hours of setting off, he had spotted and identified Lupo on the dance floor of the Prince of Wales pub in Brixton.

Lupo's home was searched, and the torture chamber confirmed police suspicions. Lupo was arrested and charged with the murder of Anthony Connolly and Alex Kasson on 18 May; three days later, charges referring to Damian McClusky and the tramp were added. He was also charged with the attempted murders of Mark Leyland and David Cole. During his interrogation, he told police he had an 'urge to kill' and that learning he had acquired the AIDS virus had created a 'callous rationale' and a burning hatred for other gay men.

At his trial at the Old Bailey in July 1987, Lupo pled guilty to all six charges, and was given four life sentences (with the judge pointing out, 'life meant life') plus fourteen years. However, within a year of being sent to Frankland Prison, County Durham, he became a regular inhabitant of the hospital wing, with various AIDS-related illnesses, and he died on 12 February 1995. Although police worldwide investigated his travels, no other murders were laid at his door.

CHAPTER 16

Great Britain: Colin Ireland – The Coleherne III

....

'To take one human life is an outrage; to take five is carnage.' So said the judge at the trial in December 1993 of Colin Ireland, the third serial killer to use the Coleherne pub as his hunting ground. Like Michael Lupo, his reign of terror in London didn't last that long, and it was brought to an end thanks to assistance from the gay community – who held a party at the Coleherne to celebrate his arrest. Ireland had decided at the start of 1993 that he was going to become a serial killer – and that's exactly what he did from March to June.

Colin Ireland was born in a former workhouse on 16 March 1954, in Dartford, Kent, to Patricia Ireland, an unmarried seventeen-year-old girl who was abandoned by his teen father soon after the birth; she never told Colin who he was. His mother moved in with her parents for five years, then went back to Kent for the next six years, which saw Ireland and his mother move home nine times. This meant his education was severely disrupted – he went to six different schools in the important primary-school years – and his mother had various partners. One of their residences, Ireland would later recall, was a house for homeless women and children which he described as 'degradation personified'.

Eventually Ireland's mother settled in Dartford with a new partner, an electrician whom she married, and Colin took his new stepfather's surname, Saker. In 1964, Patricia fell pregnant, and then they were evicted from their house. Unable to cope with the expense of a ten-year-old and a new baby, his mother opted to place Colin into care; when she and Saker found a new home, they invited him back, but Saker left shortly after. In 1966, when Ireland was twelve, his mother remarried but rather than change his surname yet again, Colin reverted to Ireland.

Ireland would later state that around this age he was propositioned by older men while living in Sheerness, Kent. The first was when he was helping out at a local fairground: a man offered him a necklace he could give his mother in return for a sexual act. The next came in a public toilet, when a man peered over the cubicle wall at him. The third was when he was at the cinema and his optician recognised him and asked for sexual favours. The final was at a second-hand shop. On each occasion, Ireland didn't do as they asked, but became increasingly angry.

Four years later, he stole £4 so he could run away to London; unfortunately he was caught, and sent to Finchton Manor School, a 'free expression' school – with fees partly paid by the county council. However, as he had been throughout his school career, Ireland was bullied and, in reply, he set fire to one of his bully's belongings. This resulted in him being thrown out of Finchton Manor, and he ran away to London.

It wasn't the panacea that he might have been hoping for. He was still broke and without a roof over his head, so he was quickly caught up in criminal activity. Arrested for robbery when aged seventeen, he was sent to Hollesley Bay borstal; he ran away from there, was recaptured, and sent to Borstal Prison, the original borstal now renamed HMP Rochester, and from there to HMP Grendon.

He spent much of the 1970s in what he described as his 'lost period, common to those who suffer from psychopathy', where the years went by in a blur. He tried to join the French Foreign Legion, but was rejected. He spent eleven months (of an eighteen-month sentence) in prison from December 1975 for burglary, stealing a car and damage to property, and when he came out, he moved to

Swindon. There he fell for an older West Indian woman, and they planned to marry – until he was convicted of demanding money with menaces in 1977 and sent back inside for eighteen months. He was then imprisoned for robbery, and later for attempted deception.

In 1981, he met Virginia Zammit at a lecture on 'survivalism'. Nine years older than him, Zammit was paralysed from the waist down as the result of a car accident and confined to a wheelchair. She and Ireland fell in love, and he became a stepfather to her five-year-old daughter. Ireland had filled out after adolescence, losing the weak, lanky frame that had made him so susceptible to bullying: at six foot two, he became known as 'the gentle giant' to locals, and held down various jobs, including as a bouncer at a gay nightclub.

However, this idyllic period came to an end in 1985 when Ireland was sentenced to six months inside for 'going equipped to cheat'. Zammit divorced him in 1987 on the grounds of adultery. His interest in survivalism intensified: he would periodically go down to Dartmoor and try to live off the land, usually unsuccessfully, but became obsessive about eating only fresh food and drinking bottled water – not something that was that common a fad in the UK in the 1980s.

Ireland didn't stay single for long: he met Devon pub landlady Janet Young in 1989, and within three months they were married and he became stepfather to two more children. The relationship didn't last that long, at least amicably. Ireland became a control freak, throwing Young out of the bedroom, and stalking her around a darkened room. At Easter 1990, four months after the wedding, he cleared out her house and her bank account, and she was forced to move to a homeless hostel with her children.

He crossed country for his next job, working at Southend-on-Sea in Essex at a homeless shelter, where he ended up as deputy manager. He had another girlfriend by this point, but she was wary of his mood swings, and eventually left him when he broke the fingers of one of her former boyfriends. At the shelter, Ireland was popular with the homeless, but was known to make homophobic comments, and, on at least one occasion, entertained fantasies of killing one of the difficult clients – forcing snooker balls down the man's throat. In December 1992, he was pushed into resigning: some sources say it was after he had touched female colleagues; former FBI profiler Robert K. Ressler, who was invited to advise by Scotland Yard during Ireland's killing spree, noted it was because he had manhandled a client.

Ireland went on to work at an adult training centre where, far from the responsible tasks he had been given at the shelter, his job was to break up wooden pallets. As the manager of the shelter recalled, at this point Ireland was troubled and frustrated, and didn't know what to do with his life.

So, on 1 January 1993, he decided to become a serial killer. He knew enough about the subject to try to avoid some of the obvious pitfalls: for a start, he wouldn't kill in his own immediate area. Instead, he would pick his targets in London. Ireland put together a murder kit that included everything he might need to commit the crimes and avoid detection: handcuffs, plastic bags, rope, a change of clothes and a pair of gloves. He was self-aware enough to know that masochistic men were the sort of people that would trigger his desire to kill, so he investigated possible meeting points. And at that time, the Coleherne was known as the 'destination venue for gay leather men in London', according to *Queens' Country* author Paul Burston, a place where casual pickups were common and different coloured handkerchiefs were placed to denote sexual preference.

On Monday, 8 March 1993, Ireland chose his first victim. Forty-five-year-old Peter Walker was a theatre director and choreographer who had just been hired as an assistant director on the West End musical *City of Angels*. He drank in the Coleherne, displaying signs that he was a submissive; Ireland was posing as a dominant. After Peter spilt his drink on Ireland, the pair started chatting and it wasn't long before they left the pub together, taking a cab across the river to Peter's flat in Battersea, south London. Ireland put on his gloves before they entered the apartment and, once there, Peter happily allowed Ireland to strip him naked, tie him to his four-poster bed, and gag him with knotted condoms. However, at some point he must have realised that Ireland was taking things too far, as the other man beat him with a belt and his fists, and then got a plastic bag from the kitchen and pulled it over his head. Walker nearly suffocated before Ireland removed the bag, allowing him to gasp in some much-needed oxygen – but then Ireland replaced the bag. He repeated this process over and over – at some point, persuading the director to give him his bank PIN – until eventually he didn't take the bag off, and Peter suffocated.

Once he was dead, Ireland posed his body with a condom on his nose, trailed across his cheek, and another condom in his mouth. Two teddy bears were nestled in a '69' position against him. (Ireland had done this to humiliate Peter, after he discovered evidence in the flat that showed that the man hadn't told him he was HIV positive.) He cleaned up the apartment, changed his clothes and then waited for 7 a.m., when he simply left and mingled with the crowds heading to work. 'I remember walking down the road and I thought they must see in my face that I have just murdered someone else. I remember losing my virginity, and it was like the same feeling then,' Ireland later recalled. He took money out of Peter's account, then threw the cash card and the keys he had taken into the Thames from Battersea Bridge. He caught a train back to Southend, getting rid of his soiled clothes, gloves and shoes by dropping them out of the window into a canal.

Ireland was concerned about one thing – Peter Walker's two dogs, a white Alsatian named Sammy and black Labrador Bessie, which he had left locked in the flat. He therefore rang the Samaritans and said they needed to be let out, and then an hour later rang the *Sun* newspaper anonymously, calmly telling night news editor Brandon Malinsky, 'It was my New Year's resolution to kill a homosexual. He was a homosexual and into that kinky sex. You're into all that stuff, aren't you?'

However, the police already knew. On 10 March, called in by a caretaker who had found Peter's dead body, they went to his flat and found his corpse, but very little in the way of evidence. The place had been almost forensically cleaned; even the handcuffs that were used were easily obtainable. Detective Martin Finnegan tried a TV appeal on the BBC show *Crimewatch* but with no success. All the investigating officers could do was wait and see if the killer contacted them or struck again.

He did so on 28 May. Christopher Dunn also liked to be dominated, and the thirty-seven-year-old librarian was picked up at the Coleherne and taken back to his Victorian cottage in Wealdstone, north London. The pair watched S & M videos before Christopher put on a black leather harness and a studded belt. Ireland then tied him up and handcuffed him, before using a cigarette lighter to burn him until he revealed his PIN number. Ireland then strangled him. Once again, he cleaned up, removing any evidence that he had been there (even wiping the fingerprints from the batteries in his torch before throwing them away), and waited for morning before leaving. He took Christopher's bank cards with him and visited an ATM on his way to the station – as far as he was concerned, this was reimbursement for his costs.

This time, there were no dogs to release, so Ireland wasn't as concerned about letting anyone know what he had done, and it was two days before Christopher Dunn's body was discovered. Ireland was surprised that the two cases didn't seem to be linked, and rang the police directly, wondering why they hadn't connected Peter

Walker and Christopher Dunn's deaths: if they looked carefully, they would see that the latter had been strangled. The pathologist had suggested that Christopher might be the victim of a sexual game that had gone wrong, and police discovered that he frequented the Coleherne. However, in light of Ireland's anonymous call, the case was passed to Detective Chief Superintendent Ken John. He didn't have long to wait until Ireland added to his tally.

Less than a week after Dunn's murder, on 4 June 1993, Ireland killed American Perry Bradley III, another regular at the Coleherne, although he had kept his homosexuality hidden from most friends and family – the Texan businessman, the international sales director for adhesives manufacturer J-B Weld, was the son of a former US congressman. Perry lived in Kensington, not far from the Coleherne. On this occasion, Ireland took time to make himself a sandwich after killing the American. This murder had been harder for him than the previous two – Perry hadn't wanted to be tied up, but eventually agreed when Ireland maintained that he couldn't get aroused without that. Ireland had considered letting this third victim go after he had fallen asleep, he later told police. 'Then I thought, "It's easier to kill him." I walked round and just pulled the noose.' The crime scene only differed in one important way: Ireland placed a doll on top of the corpse. Partly to protect Perry's family, no mention was made of the gay elements of his death in newspaper reports – or later, crucially, to other detectives.

There were only three days between Perry Bradley's death and Ireland's next murder. His fourth victim was thirty-three-year-old Andrew Collier, a live-in caretaker at some sheltered housing for the elderly. Ireland wasn't aware that Andrew, like his first two victims, was HIV positive, something he discovered when rifling through Andrew's possessions while the younger man was tied up on the bed. Once again, Ireland had had problems getting his victim to cooperate, and he admitted to police that he had got angry with

Andrew: there were signs of a struggle, as well as cigarette-burn marks, and police found the mutilated body of Andrew's cat posed on top of his genitals – Ireland killed the animal in front of him. Andrew been suffocated and then a condom shoved down his throat. Ireland carried out his usual cleaning routine, then waited for morning.

However, on that early morning of 8 June, Ireland had made his first real mistake. Not long after they arrived at the flat, at around one in the morning, he and Andrew heard a fight going on in the street outside. Ireland leaned against the window to look, and forgot that he was not wearing gloves. Between the glass panes, on the rail, there was a fingerprint facing downwards.

A different team of detectives were investigating Andrew Collier's case, and started to see connections to previous crimes – although they were told that Perry Bradley's case didn't fit their profile, it was clear that Peter Walker's did. Nothing was made public about the connection, and Ireland rang Kensington Police on three occasions five days after the murder of Andrew to find out why they hadn't linked everything together and caught him yet. Detective Gareth Barlow asked why he was doing this, and Ireland explained, 'Because I set out to, see, cos I've read several books on serial killers and you see, you know, I wondered if it could be possibly done and got away with.' However, he was not going to give himself up. The clues were there, he explained, and he had read the FBI manual on serial killers. He would be in touch about the fifth murder.

And he was. On 15 June, he rang them and said that he had killed another man, and provided the address for what would turn out to be his final victim. 'I will go on killing,' Ireland warned. 'You can't catch me. I'll kill one a week.'

The fifth victim was Emanuel Spiteri, a forty-two-year-old Maltese catering assistant. Ireland met him on the night of 12 June in the Coleherne – the same day on which he had taunted the police on the phone – and went back to Emanuel's flat in Catford. The usual routine played out: Ireland bound the other man to the bed, handcuffed him and put a noose around his neck. He then asked for Emanuel's PIN number, but the Maltese wouldn't play ball. Ireland therefore strangled him, and watched television while he waited to leave. He also started a fire in the centre of Emanuel's bedroom – for no apparent reason, he agreed – but it went out before it achieved Ireland's aim of burning down the building.

Detective Chief Superintendent John felt he had little option but to go public with the information, particularly with the annual Lesbian and Gay Pride Parade taking place on 19 June. 'We feel we owe this to the gay community,' DCS John explained at a press conference as details were revealed of Ireland's five victims. 'When you get five victims who are all more or less at this social level, somebody somewhere must have seen something,' Robert Ressler told reporters. 'I think this guy is going to get caught.'

The problem was that there had been a recent court ruling upholding a prison sentence for sadomasochistic acts between consenting adults, so any potential witnesses were concerned that police might take action against them if they revealed that they frequented the Coleherne or took part in such acts. Police handed out 10,000 leaflets at the parade, but got very few tips. A 2007 report by the Independent Lesbian Gay Bisexual Transgender Advisory Group found that the police inquiry was 'hampered by a lack of knowledge of the gay scene in London and the special culture of S&M bondage. In particular, valuable time was lost before the police managed to recognise two common threads to the crimes. These links were established only after the death of the fourth victim.'

That changed a week later. Detectives worked out Emanuel Spiteri and his killer's most likely route from the Coleherne back to Catford, and went to Charing Cross train station to see if there was any sign of Emanuel on the footage from the closed circuit TV cameras that had recently been installed. There was. And next to him was a large man, clearly travelling with him.

On 24 June, the police issued a description of the man they wanted to interview: a white male, aged thirty to forty, over six feet tall, clean-shaven with a full to fattish face, short dark-brown hair and dirty, discoloured teeth, based on the evidence of a man who had been on the train with them going down to Hither Green station. On 2 July, they were able to release a photo taken from the CCTV footage. They received over forty calls, many of which placed the man at the Coleherne.

Colin Ireland went to his solicitor on 19 July, saying that he was indeed the man in the CCTV footage, and he had gone to Emanuel Spiteri's flat with him – but when he got there, he found another man there. Ireland said he wasn't interested in a threesome with Emanuel and this stranger, so left, and stayed the night in a garden nearby. The Metropolitan Police came down to Southend and arrested him on suspicion of murder – and on the way back, the driver recognized Ireland's voice: he had been one of the detectives to whom Ireland had spoken in his anonymous calls.

Ireland didn't cooperate at all with the detectives, but with the fingerprint evidence from Andrew Collier's flat, they were able to charge him with two murders – not the multiple that Ireland wanted to prove he was a serial killer. After a magistrates' court hearing remanding him in custody a month after his arrest, Ireland told officers that he wanted to confess to being the gay serial killer.

He gave police a full confession on 19 August 1993. 'He was very factual about his acts, as if he was describing someone else's activities,' Martin Finnegan recalled. 'Absolutely no compassion at all . . . it was just very matter of fact.' Ireland made four points clear: he had not been under the influence of drugs or alcohol when he committed the murders; despite being a bouncer at a gay night club, he was not homosexual or bisexual; he himself had not undressed at the time of the murders, nor was he turned on in any way by them; and the only reason he had targeted gay men was because they were easy targets – it could easily have been women that he killed, although he did not deny that extreme male deviancy did trigger his anger. Ken John said after Ireland's conviction that 'he told us, "I wanted to burn down the world" and that he hated people'. Ireland also blamed the TV cop show *The Bill* for providing him with all the useful information on cleaning up the scenes, suggesting it should be banned.

Colin Ireland was charged with the other three murders on 20 August; a full trial wasn't required because of his confession, and the case was heard on 20 December. Mr Justice Sachs said he had killed in 'a grotesque and cruel fashion' and that he was 'exceptionally frightening and dangerous'. Ireland himself agreed; 'I think I should be placed in a position where I can no longer inflict harm upon others,' he had told police during his confession.

'You expressed the desire to be regarded as a serial killer,' Judge Sachs said. 'That must be matched by your detention for life.'

Colin Ireland boasted in prison that there were other deaths for which he was responsible, and detectives believed that another habitué of the Coleherne, who died in January 1993, might have been down to him – the man's dogs had eaten the body through starvation, possibly prompting Ireland's call to the Samaritans after Peter Walker's death. Nothing was ever proved, nor was he charged. Ireland fractured his hip in mid-February 2012, and was found dead from pulmonary fibrosis and the hip injury ten days later on 21 February 2012 at Wakefield Prison.

CHAPTER 17

Great Britain: Steve Wright

Serial killers have inspired many fictional representations, from Thomas Harris's infamous Dr Hannibal Lecter to Stephen King's examination of the 'BTK Killer' Dennis Rader. Perhaps one of the most unusual – and to many minds, apparently the most tasteless – was the National Theatre in London's 2011 presentation *London Road*, in which Alecky Blythe and Adam Cook took verbatim accounts, overheard dialogue and newsreel footage about the effects of the murders of five prostitutes in Ipswich in 2006 and set them to music. While the creators were at pains to emphasise the positives that came out of the tragedy, there's no hiding from the fact that its existence is owed to the actions of Steven Wright between 30 October and 10 December 2006.

Born in Erpingham, Norfolk, on 24 April 1958, Steven Gerald James Wright was the second of four children of military policeman Conrad Wright and his veterinary-nurse wife Patricia, living on bases in Malta and Singapore before returning to RAF West Beckham when Wright was around eight. Not long after, his mother walked out (she claimed because of her husband's propensity for violence); his father divorced her in 1977 and remarried. The children were brought up in Felixstowe where their father worked for the Port of Felixstowe police, and Wright joined the merchant navy as a teenager. He wed for the first time aged twenty, and had three children from the eight-year marriage.

During his travels, Wright developed a taste for prostitutes, visiting massage parlours in various ports when he got what he described as 'the urge' – he was even filmed in Thailand during the 1980s by documentary series *Whicker's World* while talking to prostitutes in a bar in Pattaya's red-light district.

Wright was employed on the *QE2* as a steward, and met Diane Cassell, who worked in the on-board shop. They married in Braintree, Essex, in August 1987, but he was controlling during their time together. 'The marriage was a nightmare,' Diane recalled after his arrest. 'Steve used to strangle Diane right in front of us,' their neighbour Elizabeth Roche told the *Daily Telegraph*. 'He would pin her up against the wall and put both hands around her throat . . . It would end when either my ex-husband or I would pull him off or he would come to his senses.' Wright was looking for work as a pub manager and the brewers insisted that he and Diane had to be married. He spent some time as the manager of the Ferry Boat Inn in Norwich, and after leaving there (and deserting his wife), Wright moved to Chislehurst, in south-east London, where he ran the White Horse pub. He had a daughter with Sarah Whiteley, a barmaid there, and they moved to Plumstead to run the Rose and Crown. That job didn't last long – according to Sarah, it was because of Wright's excessive drinking and gambling.

Steve Wright continued to use prostitutes: he was well known in Norwich's red-light district, sometimes cruising the streets in high heels, PVC skirt and a wig, other times refusing to take no for an answer from a girl: 'If you didn't get in the car he would get naked and just sit there with the headlights on,' one Norwich prostitute told the *Daily Telegraph* following his conviction. He moved back in with his father, but was spending all his money on prostitutes, even buying a car on hire purchase then selling it to raise cash. He tried to commit suicide in 1994, but the police pulled him out of the car in which he was attempting to gas himself.

After running up nearly £40,000 worth of debt, Wright returned to Thailand and became heavily involved with a local girl there, but she was simply after his money, and once he had none left to give, he returned home penniless, where his father and stepmother took him back in. He tried suicide once again, this time with an overdose of pills. He then worked at a fruit-machine arcade for a time but was caught stealing money so took a job at the Brook Hotel in Felixstowe. Again he stole from the till, and was convicted of theft; he had to carry out a hundred hours community service. As part of his arrest procedure, a DNA sample was taken.

In 2002, he moved to Ipswich and met Pamela Goodman (who later took his name – it wasn't the coincidence that is sometimes suggested in reports). He apparently started to get his life in order, becoming well known in the area as part of a 'lovely couple'. He became a member of the Hintlesham Hall golf club and won trophies, and signed on for driving and labouring jobs with Gateway Recruitment Agency, firstly in Levington, and then Nacton. His sex life with Pamela was good enough that he stopped using prostitutes for a short time, but six months after they moved to Bell Close in Ipswich in 2004, he started up again, going to Cleopatra's and Oasis massage parlours after golf games or when he 'got the urge' once more. However, he soon started to go downmarket and use street-walkers who might charge as little as £20 for sex, either bringing them to his home or having sex with them in his car. 'You get two girls for the price of one,' he explained to the court during his trial – a comment that had resonance given later discoveries.

On the morning of 2 December 2006, volunteer fisheries warden Trevor Saunders was carrying out his patrol checking for blockages along Burstall Brook, near Hintlesham in Suffolk, about seven miles west of Ipswich. 'I noticed two round, smooth surfaces sticking out of the water, which I later found was the woman's bottom,' he explained. He investigated, and discovered a naked female body. By the next day, police had confirmed that it was twenty-five-year-old prostitute Gemma Adams. She had been reported missing on 15 November, last seen the previous night near a BMW dealership in Ipswich. She had developed a heroin addiction as a teenager and had turned to prostitution to fund her habit (something her parents were not aware of until after her death). The post-mortem established that Gemma had not been sexually assaulted, and although her handbag had been found near the crime scene, her clothing had not.

On 5 December, police were starting to have 'grave concerns' for another prostitute, nineteen-year-old Tania Adams, who also had drifted into street prostitution to fund her drug habit, although she was still living at home with her mother and younger brother. She had vanished on 30 October, and was reported missing on November 1; CCTV footage from the red-light district showed her around 11 p.m. on 30 October on the London Road. On 8 December, during the search for Gemma's clothing about a mile-and-a-half from where her body was dumped, police found Tania's body, also submerged in water. She too was naked and had not been sexually assaulted.

The links between the two crimes seemed clear, and the national press started to focus attention on the inquiry. 'New Vice Girl Victim of Ripper' ran the *Sun*'s headline on 9 December. 'We're all afraid there's a maniac on the loose,' an anonymous prostitute told the paper. 'People feared the worst when Gemma and Tania went missing. Now another body's been found, that fear has turned to panic.'

During the afternoon of 10 December, that panic was set to increase. The body of Anneli Alderton was found in an area of woodland, near the village of Nacton, seven miles south-east of Ipswich. Three days earlier a motorist had spotted something near the road, but had assumed it was a shop dummy and not thought more of it – until the news of Anneli's body hit the papers. The twenty-four-year-old had also worked as a prostitute, and had a 'chaotic' lifestyle, according to the police. She had started using crack cocaine in her mid-teens, and some of the other working girls referred to her as 'Crackhead Annie', but after the birth of her daughter in 2002, she had tried to clean up, albeit unsuccessfully – she was still addicted to heroin. Anneli was last spotted on the 5.53 p.m. train from Harwich to Colchester on the evening of Sunday, 3 December. Later that evening, it's believed she went to Ipswich to work. The autopsy revealed that Anneli was three months pregnant at the time of her murder – which had been caused by asphyxiation. There were no defensive wounds on her body, which had surprised detectives at first, given that Anneli was renowned for being feisty. Like the earlier two girls, Anneli had not been sexually assaulted.

Police were not just investigating the murders of the three girls; they were concerned about two other prostitutes who had gone missing – twenty-five-year-old Annette Nicholls and Paula Clennell, who was twenty-four. On the afternoon of 12 December – the day after Anneli had been identified – yet another body was found, this time by a member of the public who had seen it just over a mile south-east of Nacton. A helicopter was flown to the scene, and as it hovered overhead, the crew aboard spotted another body, just 200 metres away from the first. 'We can only fear the worst,' Detective Chief Superintendent Stewart Gull told the media immediately. 'The natural assumption is that these are the bodies of the two missing women.'

Gull's pessimism was justified: Paula was identified on 14 December; Annette the next day. Paula had been interviewed by Anglia Television on 5 December following the discovery of the first body, and admitted it would be 'safer to get a flat and work from there but it's getting a flat that's the problem'. She had no option about continuing to ply her trade: she 'needed the money'. She too was a heroin user, whose three children had been taken away by social services; she was last seen on 10 December. Annette was only reported missing on 11 December, the day before her body was found, but she hadn't been seen since 5 December. She had trained as a beautician, but started to use heroin and descended into prostitution. Like Paula, she was frightened of the serial killer, and had decided only to see her regular clients. She was seen getting into a dark blue BMW – just as Anneli had.

On 15 December, DCS Gull confirmed what everyone knew: there was a serial killer in Ipswich. Women were frightened to go out after dark, and preferred to celebrate their birthdays at home rather than hit the nightclubs. Only those who absolutely had to go out did so – the prostitutes who had to work to pay the rent. Over 5,500 calls had been received by the incident room and 1,000 emails; and officers were drafted in from other forces to assist. Post-mortems showed that Paula had died from compression to the neck; no definitive cause could be determined in Annette's case.

On the morning of 18 December, police arrested thirty-seven-year-old supermarket team leader Tom Stephens at his home in Trimley St Martin, Suffolk. Stephens also worked as a taxi driver and had been questioned on four occasions during the hunt for the missing girls, once in a police car shortly after Tania Nicol's disappearance, and then under caution at different Ipswich police stations. His house had been searched by both forensic officers and detectives on 22 November, and his garden scanned with a metal detector. He was under police surveillance on 9–10 November, and then again from 11 December.

Stephens's name wasn't released by police, but he was named by the media (and he had given his story to the *Sunday Mirror* for a feature that appeared the day before his arrest). He was brought up near Norwich, and worked as a special constable for five years, patrolling the red-light district of the town. He was married for five years but by now was living alone in Trimley St Martin. He spent some of his time driving Ipswich prostitutes around, having started visiting them in the middle of 2004 (about a year after his divorce), and befriended them. The girls saw him as a 'sad lonely bloke' who 'liked working girls because he could get closer to them than other women,' according to Ipswich prostitute 'Katie' in the *Sun*. Even when the girls were getting increasingly worried by the disappearances, they saw Stephens as a friend, someone they could call if they needed an errand run – which meant that he had the numbers of many of them on his mobile phone – even if, at the end of the day, he was a punter, really only interested in them for sex. He had gone to the police on 16 November, saying that prostitutes he knew 'had such an overwhelming addiction to drugs that they would take irrational risks'; five days later, he had told them that he 'did not want to be seen as another Ian Huntley and wanted to help police' (referring to the recent case in which Soham caretaker Huntley had been apparently helping the police search for two missing girls when he himself was responsible for their deaths).

The story in the *Sunday Mirror* almost seemed to build the detectives' case for them: Stephens admitted that he knew all five girls, and had no alibis for the times when they disappeared. He called Gemma and Tania 'the best-looking girls who do this in Ipswich', and said that Annette regarded him as her boyfriend. He admitted the girls trusted him so much it would have been easy for him to get them to do whatever he wanted. The bodies were found near his home. But he was adamant that he was innocent. 'I am certain it won't go as far as me being charged,' he maintained. 'I am completely confident of that. It's not unusual for someone to be arrested, released without charge and then someone else be arrested and charged.'

Stephens had also spoken with the BBC's Radio 5 Live, which had passed the information to the task force. The story he gave the radio station was at odds with that in the *Sunday Mirror* – he was Tania rather than Annette's boyfriend – and that he had only come to know Anneli since Gemma and Tania's disappearance.

He wasn't the focus of media attention for long. At 4.45 on the morning of 19 December, Steven Wright was arrested at his flat in

London Road, and the property was forensically searched. His Ford Mondeo was taken away for tests. He and Pamela had moved there in September, apparently because Wright wanted a garden. After working as a forklift-truck driver, he had become foundry supervisor at Cerro Manganese Bronze (Alloys) in west Ipswich. Some reports suggested that he ceased being employed around the same time that he and Pamela moved home, but evidence was given in court that he was at Cerro until his arrest. Pamela had a job working nights at a call centre, which allowed Wright to continue his pursuit of prostitutes. He was well known to the local working girls, picking them up and taking them back to his house for ordinary 'vanilla' sex, often on consecutive nights. This, according to a police source quoted by the media, was 'a far more significant arrest' than that of Tom Stephens.

'I'll never forget 7 p.m. on 17 December 2006 when I got a phone call telling me there was a DNA match,' DCS Gull later said. Wright wasn't really on their radar prior to that, Gull admitted, but the DNA evidence tied him to the scenes of the latter three murders – because Gemma and Tania were found in water, forensic traces were negligible, and it made the police believe that the killer had some awareness of the dangers of leaving a DNA trace. They couldn't understand why the latter three bodies had been left on land. Wright's DNA was on Anneli's breast – the odds of such a match by chance were, according to the prosecution, 'in the order of one in a billion'.

Wright was questioned extensively during the next two days but simply replied 'no comment' to everything. It wasn't the first time he had been asked about his habits: early on the morning of 1 December, he had been stopped by police in the red-light district, and claimed he couldn't sleep so had gone out for a drive. He claimed he didn't realise where he was. Late on the evening of 21 December, DCS Gull told media that Tom Stephens (who remained officially unnamed) 'was this evening released on police bail, pending further enquiries ... The second man, Steven Wright from Ipswich, has been charged with the murder of all five women.' After his initial court appearance, he was held in a suicide-prevention cell at Belmarsh Prison in south-east London until his trial began on 14 January 2008.

The prosecution made clear that they believed it was possible that Wright wasn't the sole killer – more than one person had been seen in the car that approached Tania Nicol, and Anneli Alderton's body had been carried, not dragged to its final resting place – but were focusing on Wright's guilt. 'Mr Wright was a user of prostitutes,' prosecutor Peter Wright (no relation) explained, 'a local resident of Ipswich, a man with transport and also the wherewithal not only to pick up prostitutes in the red-light area of Ipswich but also to transport and dispose of their bodies after killing them.'

By this point, the prosecution had further forensic evidence, including fibres from the victims found in the footwell of Wright's car, on the sofa at his flat, and on various pieces of clothing. Although the prosecution accepted that there were no fingerprints from any of the girls in Wright's home or car, there were bloodstains on the clothing of two of the women that had been found, while a pair of semen-stained gloves taken from Wright's car had DNA samples that could have come from Annette and Anneli (the forensic scientist said there was 'very strong support' for a theory that Wright had worn them while with the two girls). Another pair of gloves had Paula Clennell's DNA on them. Why would he have needed gloves if he was only having ordinary consensual sex? The defence accepted that Wright had indeed had sex with the girls, bar Tania, with whom he had decided not to. The question of Tom Stephens's involvement was raised frequently, but the DNA evidence didn't link him to the scenes.

Steve Wright gave evidence in his own defence, admitting that he had sex with Gemma Adams 'some time in the middle of

November', and with Anneli Alderton on the day she was last seen. He said it was quite possibly him who was seen in the CCTV footage of Tania just before she disappeared because he had seen her that night, but decided not to have sex with her because of her acne. He used a glove to remove his condom after sex 'because I found it distasteful', and he would either take them back to his place or have sex in the car. Under cross-examination, he said that the presence of the fibres must have been coincidence – as were so many other aspects of the case – and he denied the murders.

The jury didn't believe his version of events. On 21 February 2008, Steve Wright was found guilty on all counts. He was sentenced to whole-life terms. There is speculation that he was involved with a number of other cases, including the disappearance of estate agent Suzy Lamplugh, with whom Wright worked on the *QE2*. He lodged an appeal on 19 March 2008 but this was rejected four months later. He then renewed the appeal on 15 July, which would have led to a hearing at the Royal Courts of Justice on 24 February 2009, but three weeks beforehand, he dropped the bid. His brother David hoped to get the Criminal Cases Review Commission to examine the evidence. A third appeal was mooted in 2012 but, as of the time of writing, Wright has not taken it further. He will die in prison.

CHAPTER 18

Indonesia: Ahmad Suradji

....

'If he wants to get powerful magic, he has to kill seventy women.' That was the explanation most commonly given for the crimes of Ahmad Suradji, also known as Datuk and Dukun AS, an Indonesian sorcerer who admitted to killing forty-two girls and women, but who may well have been responsible for many more.

Say you're a sorcerer in Western cultures, and chances are that somebody will make a comment about Harry Potter and his ilk. But in the Indonesian islands, particularly in small communities like Aman Damai, in North Sumatra, the 'dukuns' are revered. Suradji was one such, respected as the 'datuk', a healer with great powers who villagers believed had telekinetic powers that enabled him to move the clouds. He would give out advice on everything from financial and marital problems to physical ailments. However, he was also a master of darker arts. To gain even more power, he believed that he needed the saliva of a dying woman, and he had to swallow it as they passed away.

Suradji was born on 12 December 1952, in Pasar Rangkat; his father was a farmer who was also a practising sorcerer, his mother a housewife. He was given the name Nasib (which means 'fate' in Javanese). He was a petty criminal as a boy, getting into fights and carrying out thefts. Aged nineteen, he was jailed for theft and violent behaviour; shortly after his release from that sentence, aged thirty-one, he was convicted again, this time for cattle theft. Once he had served his time for that, he headed into the jungles and began practising sorcery, based on what he remembered his father doing. He seemed to settle down to the life of a farmer, marrying three sisters (against the tenets of Islam), who between them gave him a total of nine children, and offering his sorcerous services to others in his village.

Everything changed in 1986. According to Suradji, it was at this point that he had an almost ghostly vision and recalled something his father had told him when he was just ten years old: drink the saliva of seventy dead young women to attain invincibility. 'My father did not specifically advise me to kill people,' Suradji admitted shortly after his arrest. 'So I was thinking it would take ages if I have to wait to get seventy women. Because I was trying to get to it as fast as possible, I took my own initiative to kill.'

At least forty-two women disappeared over the next eleven years. There didn't seem to be a connection to Suradji – most of his 'clients' didn't tell their families that they had sought his help, so nobody realised that he was a common denominator in their disappearances. Some were prostitutes who wanted help getting more clients, others wives who were having marital problems: all wanted a quick fix from the dukun. He would talk with them, assess what their spiritual needs were and tell them his fee. Once he was paid, they would follow him into the sugar-cane fields to carry out the ritual that he said was required. There, the victims were ordered to get inside a hole that Suradji had often dug already – or they would give him a hand doing so. Trusting the dukun, they agreed to have their wrists and feet bound, and then were placed in the hole with their legs outstretched, expecting to be buried up to their waists; at that point they were strangled, and then Suradji would twist their necks so he could suck their saliva. Often, one of his wives would come to help strip the body, and then the naked corpse was buried with her head facing Suradji's home so the spirit would head straight to him. Not all his victims were his clients; on occasion, Suradji would hire prostitutes for his ritual, and then kill them.

His last victim was twenty-one-year-old Sri Kemala Dewi, who came to visit him on 24 April 1997 because she wanted to get back with her husband. Suradji recalled that she had been scared because they had to walk through a cemetery to get to the plantation, and asked if Suradji's wife would accompany them. Dewi was bound, placed in the hole and then strangled, taking ten to fifteen minutes to die. He then sucked her saliva, and stripped her ('if I bury her without any lining,' he explained, 'her body would decompose faster'), then put the clothes in plastic bags he had brought with him. Although many disbelieved him, Suradji always maintained that he did not rape or have other sexual interest in his victims, and the forensic evidence, such as it was, backed that up. He would later claim that robbery was the motive, but again, this wasn't really believed.

Three days later, a young man found an oddly shaped mound of dirt in the sugar-cane fields, revealed after rain had washed away the topsoil. He ran to get his uncle, the village elder, Sugito, and they proceeded to investigate the pile, which smelled of decay. They contacted the military, who told them to carry on digging but to stop if they found human remains. It took six men some hours to move the dirt aside, but beneath, they did indeed find a woman's corpse. It was Dewi, identified by her mother Arsanah purely from her legs.

A rickshaw driver, Andreas Suwito, told police Dewi had wanted to visit Suradji, but had been very secretive about why. The police immediately went to Suradji's house and found Dewi's handbag, her dress and a charm bracelet. Suradji denied killing Dewi, and said that he was grieving with the family. Three days after the discovery of Dewi's body, he was arrested.

Suradji didn't cooperate with the police, who had found evidence, including twenty watches and clothing buried in his goat pen, connecting him to other crimes when they carried out a full search. However, eventually he admitted to forty-two killings stretching back over a decade to 1986 (not without first trying to say there were just nine, then thirteen, eighteen and finally twenty-three). 'We are all human beings,' he said. 'We have our own strengths and weaknesses. If I remember correctly, I've murdered forty-two women. I didn't suspect I was going to get caught. I did not try to run away when I saw the police because I was resigned to my fate.' It took four days of interrogation for him to reveal all the details, and the police made him re-enact his gruesome killings, using mannequins. The subsequent footage was then deemed suitable to be shown on the television news!

The nearby sugar-cane field was bulldozed up and the police and Army worked together to sift through the mud. Suradji's victims were located, four of them so decayed that they were past identification, the rest skeletons. Forensic work at the laboratory at Medan concluded that there were forty-two victims, all women between the ages of seventeen and forty. Suradji was charged with each of these murders, and sent to trial in December 1997. His wives were all arrested and questioned, and it transpired that it was his first wife, Tumini, who went with the victims to the fields or joined Suradji after the murder. The other two knew that the victims had come to their home to see their husband.

When the case began, Suradji retracted his confession, making a blanket denial. This posed a major problem for the prosecution: they were unable to identify any of the victims with the exception of Sri Kemala Dewi. However, over the next four months they built their case, and on 27 April 1998, Suradji was convicted for the murder of forty-two women. 'From various witnesses' statements as well as other examination results, the judges stated that there was no mitigation factor which could lighten the sentence,' the local news channel reported. 'Ahmad Suradji was declared to be legally violating article 340 of the Criminal Code. Watched by hundreds of visitors, Ahmad Suradji came to the court and followed the sentencing with a calm face.' The sentence was death – and a fine of 7,500 rupiah. His wife Tumini was also sentenced to death but this was later commuted to life imprisonment.

By the time various appeals had been heard and dismissed – including a final plea for clemency rejected by President Susilo Bambang Yudhoyono – ten years had passed before Suradji faced his sentence. On 10 July 2008, he was shot by firing squad; he took three minutes to die. His body was taken home for burial, but the villagers didn't want it and blocked the police vehicle. It was eventually buried at Keling Garuda public cemetery, several miles away.

CHAPTER 19

Iran: Ali Asghar Borujerdi

....

'Never in my life have I seen a person who perpetrated such homi-cides and carnage. It is clear that such crimes have a bad influence on the thoughts and minds of the people. Basically, if his deeds remain unpunished, it is possible that everybody will perpetrate murders out of personal whim, and will be sure that they will not be punished.'

So said the public prosecutor at the trial of Ali Asghar Borujerdi, nicknamed Asghar-e Ghatel (Ashgar the Murderer), the first known Iranian serial killer of the twentieth century, who was responsible for the rapes and deaths of thirty-three young adults between 1907 (when he was just fourteen years old) and January 1934 when he was arrested for the first time. At his trial his defence counsel, Mirza Ahmad Khan Shari'atzadeh, tried to argue that he was a 'natural-born criminal' and that he could not be held responsible for his crimes – or, at the very least, be executed for them. It was to no avail – Borujerdi was executed on 26 June 1934, and his nickname entered Iranian lore, where Asghar-e Ghatel became a mythical figure used as the bogeyman to scare children.

Borujerdi was born in 1893 in the western Iranian town of Borujerd, a city established as early as AD 900. His father, Ali Mirza, was renowned for attacking caravans on the roads around the area and leaving the owners for dead – something Borujerdi's counsel would suggest meant that his client had a natural disposition towards illegal and immoral behaviour – and at the age of eight, Ali Asghar left Borujerd with his mother and siblings to go and live in the Iraqi town of Karbala. Six years after that, he moved to Baghdad, living with his brothers who owned a coffee shop (regarded as a place of dubious morality).

Aged just fourteen, he began to sexually abuse adolescents. He spent some time in prison, and thereafter his brothers and mother stymied any attempts by him to marry. This upset him, and although he claimed to police after his capture that he only started to kill his targets in order to trick the police who were observing him, he also admitted that he became 'used' to his 'terrifying practice . . . step by step'. In his confession, his indifference to his victims' suffering was clear: 'With two additional hits into the stomach [of a boy], I knocked him unconscious, and [began] to cut off his head with a knife. As I was cutting his head off, he became conscious again and implored me [to save his life] and cried.' Such pleas fell on deaf ears.

He amassed a total of twenty-five victims in Baghdad, creating an atmosphere of tension between the Sunni and Shi'a communities, which police had to try to curb, and was lucky to escape without being arrested. He moved to Tehran, and worked as a vegetable-seller and porter, living in the poor Bagh-e-Ferdows neighbourhood while continuing his murderous ways, killing eight boys, most of them homeless beggars, and decapitating them. The first bodies were found on New Year's Eve 1933, and Borujerdi was arrested in January. However, he was released for lack of evidence. It only took the police a couple of months to put the pieces together, and he was rearrested in March. At this point, he confessed, and was sent to trial – which lasted just one day. In court, he claimed that he was acting for the good of Iran, since those that he killed 'had bad morals and were using corruption, and that their existence was harmful for the country'. He saw himself as a national martyr, who was saving the future generation from pain.

An unsuccessful appeal followed and he was hanged in front of a huge crowd in Tehran's Sepah Square – although given the depth of feeling against him, he might have counted himself lucky to receive such a swift end. 'If I would be the state, I would heat a long nail in a fire and drive it through the length of his back in Sepah Square,' one Tehranian citizen was reported as saying, while another suggested, 'His body should be cut, in one day, into 33 pieces in Sepah Square, and each one of the 33 pieces should be sent to one of the [provincial] towns of Iran, so that will serve as a lesson to others.' A huge police presence was deemed necessary at his public execution.

CHAPTER 20

Morocco: Hadj Mohammed Mesfewi

....

Some serial killers stand out in the annals because of their modus operandi – the way in which they chose their victims, or the way in which they disposed of them. Occasionally, one deserves to be remembered for the way in which he or she was brought to justice, or the way in which that justice was executed. Hadj Mohammed Mesfewi was one such, put to death in a way that summons up memories of the best of Edgar Allan Poe.

Mesfewi was a cobbler and 'public letter-writer' in Marrakesh in the early twentieth century – for the vast majority of the population who were uneducated, he would prepare documents as required. His exact age isn't recorded, but accounts of his demise regularly note that he was an 'old man', and certainly his accomplice's age was given as seventy. Western newspapers described his deeds as a 'a series of murders probably unexampled in the annals of crime' for Mesfewi was one of the most prolific serial killers of all time.

He and his female accomplice, variously named as Annah and Rahali in the newspaper reports, were responsible for the disappearance of many young girls in Marrakesh in 1906. The parents of one young girl traced her to the cobbler's shop, where Annah was arrested. Under torture, she admitted that the girls had come to dictate letters to Mesfewi, who invited them to stay for dinner. The victims were then administered a narcotic in their wine, and were then murdered in their sleep, apparently purely with the object of robbing them of whatever jewels and other valuables they had on them at the time.

In a pit beneath the cobbler's shop, the authorities found twenty decapitated bodies, and a further sixteen buried in the garden. All of the corpses had been mutilated with dagger cuts to make it seem as if they were the victims of attacks by fanatics.

As Mesfewi and Annah were being taken to jail, the crowd tried to lynch them, and one report suggested that they were driven round the city on donkeys, in a 'half-naked state', and were then publicly flogged, during which they confessed to their crimes. Annah died under the torture. Mesfewi survived but was condemned to be crucified, as laid down in the Koran.

When this was reported in the Western press, via a cable to the *New York American* on 29 April 1906, there was something of an outcry. It would be the first crucifixion carried out in Morocco in living memory, and it was condemned as barbaric. There was some speculation that Mesfewi might be burned alive, according to an old Moorish custom which permitted this method of execution if there was a strong enough public demand. However, on 2 May, a further cable arrived in New York saying that the execution by crucifixion would not take place, and it was announced that Mesfewi would be beheaded. The attention of the outside world turned elsewhere.

Mesfewi was kept in the jail in Marrakesh for a fortnight, and then his sentence began. It was quite clear that the Moroccan authorities waited for foreign eyes to be turned away from his case before implementing what many might think was a very suitable end for the serial killer. Nothing so quick as beheading for Mesfewi; nothing so merciful as crucifixion.

On 15 May, and daily thereafter, he was led out into the market place and whipped with switches of thorny acacia. Stripped to the waist, his arms held outstretched, Mesfewi was given ten lashes each day by the city executioner, with each stroke drawing blood.

The decision to restrict the number of lashes wasn't out of any sense of leniency or respect towards Mesfewi's age; it was simply because the authorities – and the people – didn't want him to die too quickly. After each beating, his back was cleaned with vinegar and oil to toughen the skin so he was ready for the next day's punishment.

And so it went on. Each day Mesfewi would be brought out; each day he received ten lashes; each day his back was treated – and still he survived. It was therefore decided that a 'supreme' sentence should be carried out: he was to be walled up alive in the public market place. Such a decision required the agreement of the Sultan, which was duly given, and the date of execution set: Mesfewi would be immured on 11 June if he had not succumbed before then.

Although nobody told Mesfewi his fate, the news spread far and wide, and on the appointed morning, the market place was filled with thousands of Moroccans, eager to watch a form of execution that had not been seen in Marrakesh for many years. Older members of the crowd with long memories recalled that some victims had survived for up to a week.

The chief bazaar stood just outside the jail where Mesfewi was being held, and it was within its very thick walls that he would be permanently placed. Two masons dug a hole six feet high, two feet wide and two feet deep. Since Mesfewi was by now painfully thin, this would allow him some space and air – after all, they didn't want him to be smothered too quickly. About halfway up the recess, staples with chains were fixed to the back wall so that Mesfewi would be kept upright; he couldn't avoid the crowd's gaze while he was being bricked in.

Mesfewi was brought out as normal, anticipating that he was going to receive his daily whipping – but while each day's flogging had attracted a crowd filled with the relatives of his victims, he realised from the size of the mob and their howls of hatred directed at him that his final day had come. But it was only when he saw the hole dug in the wall that he realised what was intended.

According to witnesses, Mesfewi had handled his whipping with 'fatalistic fortitude', hoping to die as a result of the beating, but he lost all control when he saw his true fate. He struggled desperately with his jailers as he was dragged towards the bazaar wall, screaming for mercy. He received as much as he gave his young victims.

Still screaming, he was pushed into the recess, and chained up. The masons weren't quick to set to work, and he was left there at the mercy of the people, who struggled and fought to get to the front of the crowd where they could scoff in derision at him, and pelt him with 'the frightful filth and offal of the market place'.

After a time, the crowd was pushed back and the masons came forward, and laid the first courses of the new wall. When the masonry reached Mesfewi's knees, the chief jailer gave the condemned man some bread and water. The masons took a break from the sweltering sun, allowing the crowd to harangue and jeer Mesfewi once more.

The very deliberate and slow execution took some time to carry out. Courses of masonry were laid, Mesfewi was given more bread and water, the crowd pelted him, until only his head could be seen, still screaming. It's reasonable to assume that Mesfewi had lost his reason by this stage but he continued begging and screaming for mercy, even though he must have known that there was absolutely no chance of success. And every time that he screamed, the crowd yelled. He was finally fully encased in the late afternoon.

By dusk, Mesfewi was still alive, so braziers were lit and coffee made. Mesfewi screamed continuously through the night – and throughout the whole of the next day. By that night, though, the screams were getting fainter, and by dawn on Wednesday, all that could be heard was the occasional moan.

Those who had hoped that he might last the week were to be disappointed, and they cursed Mesfewi when he was finally declared dead after no moans were heard for a time. The marketplace resumed normal activity. In the words of the dispatch to the Western papers, Mesfewi had expiated his sins.

CHAPTER 21

Russia: Vasili Komaroff

'Well it's my turn to be put in the sack now,' fifty-two-year-old serial killer Vasili Komaroff said as he was led away to his cell after sentence of death was passed on him by a court in Moscow, Russia, on 8 June 1923. The signature of the horse trader's crimes had been his disposal of the bodies of his victims – each had been 'trussed like chickens for roasting', according to the police reports, placed within sacks and dumped on waste ground. In all, Komaroff reckoned that he had killed thirty-three people – although only twenty-one corpses were found – and said that he had been prepared to kill up to sixty more. He was the first serial killer apprehended in the newly formed Union of Soviet Socialist Republics.

Komaroff was born Vasili Petrov in the Vitebsk region of Russia in 1871, one of many children in a working-class family, all of whom drank heavily. He served his requisite four years in the Russian Army, and aged twenty-eight he married for the first time. During the Russian–Japanese War of 1904–5, he served in the Far East, and was able to set aside a good amount of savings. Once he was discharged, Petrov and his wife travelled extensively, but when the money ran out, he began working for an Army store. However, he was caught stealing from there and sent to prison for a year, during which time his wife died of cholera.

After his release, Petrov moved to Riga, where he married a Polish widow, Sofia, who was bringing up two children. Petrov was by now a heavy drinker and often beat his wife and stepchildren. When the German Army occupied the Baltic region at the start of the First World War, Petrov moved with his family into the Volga region. After the October Revolution in 1917, he joined the Red Army where he was taught how to read and write. He was captured by General Anton Denikin's Volunteer Army, but he somehow managed to escape. To cover his tracks, he changed his name to Vasili Ivanovich Komaroff, and after the civil war was over in 1920, he and his family moved to Moscow, where he settled at 26 Shabolovka Street. He found a job as a cab driver, but his main income was derived from a series of robberies, the spoils of which he disposed of on the black market. (There were some theories that he might have been sent to Moscow as a spy for Denikin, but there appears to be little evidence for this.)

After Lenin introduced the New Economic Policy in 1921, which allowed workers effectively to become self-employed, Komaroff became a horse dealer, keeping a stable at his home. No one connected this apparently friendly, smiling family man with the spate of murders that began towards the end of that year. Bodies were found dumped on various waste grounds, initially in the Shabolovki neighbourhood but then further afield. Despite police investigations, the corpses continued mounting up throughout 1922, with at least another dozen attributable to the same killer, and into the start of the following year. The killer gained the nickname 'The Wolf of Moscow', and even Lenin himself apparently took an interest in his capture after rumours started circulating that this new Communist government wasn't able to catch a killer. Expert criminologists and former members of the Tsarist police were brought in to help.

A pattern began to emerge. The bodies were clearly the work of the same killer, given the way in which they were found, and oats were found in the sacks used for the body dumps. Couple this with the wide area over which bodies were being discovered, and the police deduced that a cab driver could well be the culprit. The problem was – there were thousands of cab drivers in Moscow. They needed to narrow down the search.

The bodies were nearly always found on either a Thursday or a Saturday; detectives soon learned that horses were nearly always taken to the Shabolovki market on Wednesdays and Fridays. It seemed logical that the victims were selected from those who went to the market, particularly as they all seemed to be visitors to the area rather than locals – but there didn't seem to be any immediate suspects. Once the detectives started to question the traders, they learned of the rather odd behaviour displayed by Vasili Komaroff: he would often turn up at the market on his own, unaccompanied by any of his horses, but would be seen leaving with customers. Since his stables weren't that far from the market, it was obviously easier for him to take his customers there rather than go through the palaver of transporting his animals only a few yards, but in a murder investigation, every assumption needs to be challenged.

The detectives began to look into Komaroff and discovered that, far from being an upstanding pillar of the community, he had a cruel and violent streak. According to one neighbour, he had tried to kill his eldest son, then eight years old, by hanging him, but his wife had cut the boy down. Another piece of evidence pointed towards him: in one of the bags, police had found a used nappy; Komaroff and his wife's baby boy had been born in the summer of 1922.

On 17 March 1923, on the pretext of searching for bootleg liquor, the police raided Komaroff's stable – and found his latest victim, trussed up in his bag ready for disposal, hidden beneath a pile of hay. Komaroff, however, had become nervous when it was clear that the detectives were looking for evidence of blood in the stable, and jumped out of a window, somehow evading the police who were waiting outside for exactly such a move. He was on the run for twenty-four hours before being arrested in the nearby village of Nikolskoye.

Komaroff didn't bother hiding what he had done once he was captured. He admitted that he was responsible for the bodies that had been found, and said that he had disposed of half a dozen more in the Mockba river. (These were never found.) His method was very simple: he would introduce himself to a potential client at the market, offering to sell horses at a bargain rate, and invite him to come back to the stables. There he would serve the potential buyer vodka, and once he was inebriated, Komaroff would usually kill him by knocking him on the head with a hammer (although some victims were strangled), then place him in the bag and hide the body. His motive seemed to be simple robbery – although it appears that he managed to accrue the grand total of US \$30 for all of his work. However, his killing spree, he claimed, began after he became angered by one of the horse traders admitting that he was planning to buy Komaroff's horses at a cheap rate so he could sell them outside Moscow for grain, and make a good profit. Class hatred at such rampant speculation angered him so much that he killed the man.

The killer took the investigators to other dumping grounds that they hadn't previously discovered, where they found five more corpses. The police found it hard to prevent Moscovites from taking the law into their own hands when Komaroff was showing off his handiwork – *Izvestia* sent their best journalist Mikhail Bulgakov, the future novelist, to cover the case and he reported that the women in the house where he was staying wanted Komaroff to be boiled alive or fed into a meat grinder.

Komaroff himself tried to commit suicide three times before his trial, but eventually stopped trying, relying on the court to grant him a speedy trial and death. He was very happy to talk about what he had done, telling the press that murder was 'an awfully easy job'. As he explained, 'I am fifty-two, I have had a good time, and don't want to live any longer.' He only recalled one occasion when he had a problem: 'I killed a man who tried to beat me in a horse trade. He was the only one who ever resisted.'

His wife Sonia was arrested and put on trial alongside him. Some sources state that this was because the authorities didn't believe that she could have been unaware of her husband's activities, although contemporary accounts suggest that she was an active participant in his crimes from the end of 1922 onwards, helping to mop up the blood from the stables, and then spending the night praying for the 'innocent victims'. Their trial was held at Moscow's huge Polytechnic Museum, since there was such a public interest in the crimes, with the case heard on 7 June 1923. Bulgakov attended, and noted that Komaroff initially appeared to be an 'old, ordinary' person – 'unpleasant but not brutal' with 'no signs of degeneration' obvious to the naked eye – until he started to giggle and divulge that he looked at people as no more important than caterpillars. Three leading psychiatrists had declared him sane, and in the early hours of the next morning, the couple were sentenced to be executed by firing squad within three days.

Komaroff's desire for death seemed to desert him at this point, and there were unsuccessful attempts to appeal against the sentence. The children were sent to state orphanages, and he and his wife were shot on 18 June. Bulgakov concluded his report on the case hoping that the harsh laws of heredity didn't affect the children, and that they wouldn't grow up like their parents. Some, unconfirmed, reports suggest that at least one of them, however, did, and was responsible for atrocities against the Red Army during the Second World War . . .

CHAPTER 22

South Africa: Moses Sithole

....

'I fully hate black women and even if I came back to earth as a black man I could never want a black women . . . I would rather masturbate.' So said Moses Sithole, known as the ABC Killer or the South African Strangler, who was responsible for a minimum of thirty-eight deaths in 1994 and 1995 in Atteridgeville, Boksburg and Cleveland (hence the ABC nickname). All his victims were aged between nineteen and forty-three; like him, all were black; and all had been strangled with articles of clothing – the killer used sticks to wind a stocking or another item of clothing around their necks. And, as it transpired, nearly all were looking for work and were very happy to go along with someone who could help them find it . . .

Moses Sithole was born on 17 November 1964, the fourth of five children of Simon and Sophie Sithole, in Vosloorus, near Boksburg, which at that point was part of the Transvaal Province in South Africa. His father died when he was about five, and his mother, an alcoholic who was unable to cope, dumped the children at the local police station. They were placed in a local orphanage, where, Sithole claims, they were mistreated. 'You had to be strong to survive,' Sithole told fellow prisoners when he was confessing his crimes. Sithole ran away to try to find his mother but she sent him back; in his teens, he hitchhiked 300 miles to live with his older brother, Patrick, but when that didn't work out, he found employment in the Johannesburg gold mines. Records of the period are sparse, but Sithole himself admitted that he was arrested for rape in his teens, and spent seven years in prison.

Sithole didn't kill his earliest victims. He was certainly again raping women by 1987 when he attacked twenty-nine-year-old Patricia Khumalo (who testified against Sithole nine years later at his trial). She had been looking for a job, and on 14 September, the day before her daughter's birthday, she was introduced to a man named 'Martin' (whom she identified as Sithole), who said he could provide her with work in Cleveland. She happily caught the train with him to Geldenhuis station, where 'Martin' said he knew a short cut through the veldt. Once out of sight, Sithole grabbed Patricia by the blouse and ordered her to lie on the ground, where he raped her repeatedly. She asked him not to kill her, and he said he wouldn't because she had 'the kind of eyes that makes him feel sorry,' she told the court. He tied her hands with her bra, pulled her dress over her head and told her to wait while he escaped. Scared of Sithole, she didn't go to the police.

Dorcas Kedibone Khobane was similarly raped a year later; accompanying Sithole for a job, she was taken through the veldt and raped. Oddly, after he had ejaculated, he started to chat with her, saying he wanted Dorcas to go and look for his girlfriend who had stolen items from him. He asked Dorcas if they could have sex again; Dorcas refused so he raped her again.

The girlfriend he mentioned, Sibongile Nkosi, did exist, and also knew Sithole as Martin. She was seventeen at the time and petrified of Sithole, she testified in 1996; outwardly charming if there was anyone else around, on their own he would beat her and threaten her family's lives if she made any move to leave him. Her fifteen-year-old sister Lindiwe was raped by Sithole in October 1988 in the same way as Patricia and Dorcas; in her case, though, she was beaten, raped and then strangled into unconsciousness. When she revived, Sithole threatened to kill her and her family if she said anything.

Sithole dropped the Martin pseudonym for his next confirmed victim, Buyiswa Doris Swakamisa, this time calling himself 'Lloyd

Thomas' when he offered Buyiswa a computer job in February 1989. Once again, he made his attack when they were walking through the veldt, producing a panga, which he had kept hidden in a newspaper under his arm. (A panga is a large weapon around sixteen to eighteen inches long, with a sharpened blade; such weapons were used regularly during the conflict between the African National Congress and the Inkatha Freedom Party in Natal during the 1980s and 1990s.) He told Buyiswa they were going to have sex, but if she didn't want to do so, she could run away – but she would need to make sure he didn't catch up with her or he would kill her. Buyiswa stood her ground and refused to strip when he told her to. Sithole couldn't get an erection until Buyiswa (believing he would kill her if he didn't get to have intercourse with her) put her fingers in his ears and kissed his neck – whereupon he raped her. He claimed that he had once had a child with a woman in Alexandra, who had poisoned the child, and that's why he hated women.

Buyiswa reported the rape to the police, and a few months later she spotted 'Lloyd' in the street near where she worked. She told the police, who arrested Sithole – and then insisted that Buyiswa ride alongside him back to the police station. Sithole said he should have killed her when he had the chance, although when the rape case came to trial, he denied that he was responsible. The judge disbelieved him and he was sentenced to six years in Boksburg prison. Sithole would later maintain that he selected his later victims because they resembled Buyiswa, since she had falsely accused him. During his time in prison, Sithole was sodomised by other inmates, and otherwise attacked for being a rapist.

Sithole was released in November 1993 for good behaviour. Like other killers before him, he realised that leaving his victims alive simply meant that they could give evidence against him. Those he attacked from July 1994 onwards never had the chance to survive.

In prison, he met Martha Nbolo, the sister of another inmate, and he moved in with her after his release, treating her as his common-law wife. He worked on cars with Martha's brother, and it seemed as if he was turning his life around at the same time as South Africa's future was changing with the end of apartheid. After a few months, he stopped working on cars, and claimed that he was going out looking for work. In July 1994, he met eighteen-year-old Maria Monene Monama on the streets of Pretoria, and charmed both her and her family, so much so that they weren't concerned when she went off with 'Sylvester'. But when they reached the veldt, Sithole strangled her. Once she was dead, Sithole wrote an odd note on her leg: 'I am not fighting with you,' it read. 'We will stay here until you understand.'

Maria was the first of six women that Sithole assaulted and strangled over the next four months. There were a number of other murders in the latter half of 1994 in the same region; not all of these can be laid at Sithole's door, and police believed for a long time that self-employed businessman David Abraham Selepe was responsible for the crimes. He was arrested in Mozambique on 15 December while trying to flee his creditors, and verbally confessed to fifteen murders, although he refused to sign a written confession. He took police to some of the dump sites on 17 December, and the next day he showed them where Amanda Thethe's body was dumped. He claimed he had hidden her underwear in a plastic bag in the bushes; the police removed his handcuffs so he could search but – according to the officers – he hit one of the detectives over the head with a branch, and made a run for it. He was fired at and received a head wound, dying in hospital that evening. Two days afterwards, under intense pressure, the police had to admit that all Selepe had said were 'things which strengthened our suspicion' of him. (Amanda Thethe was one of those who Sithole was later charged with killing, making the police actions over Selepe's death even more unusual.)

Much to the embarrassment of the police, the killings didn't stop, despite Selepe's death. Another woman was killed near Cleveland at the end of January 1995, but police claimed it was a copycat murder. However, around this time bodies started to appear around Atteridgeville, near Pretoria. This was by no means the first time that a serial killer had plagued the area: six boys had been killed in a five-month period by the so-called Atteridgeville Mutilator back in 1956; Elias Xitavhudzi murdered sixteen women in the 1960s and was nicknamed Pangaman – like Sithole, he favoured the large machete for his crimes; and an 'Ironman' had attacked residents late at night during the 1970s. The local people could be excused for believing that past sins had come back to haunt them when a half-naked female corpse was found on 4 January 1995; the woman was never identified but the body was severely decomposed, so she had been killed at some point in December.

She was just the first. On 9 February, the naked body of twenty-seven-year-old Beauty Nuku Soko was discovered; her clothes were on her chest, with rocks keeping them held down. Four weeks later, on 6 March, the body of twenty-five-year-old Sara Matlakala Mokono was located – she had last been seen three days earlier, on her way to see about a new job. Her killer had left her breasts visible through the surface of the soil. Nikiwe Diko went to meet a new employer on 7 April; she wasn't found until 24 June, by which time wild dogs had torn apart her body and her husband could only identify her from her wedding ring. Letta Nomthandazo Ndlangamandla's body was found near a shooting range on 12 April; her hands were tied behind her back with her bra. Worse, shortly afterwards, the body of her two-year-old son Sibusiso was discovered, abandoned there by his mother's killer. Letta had taken her son with her to the new job. Seven miles from there, near Hercules, Esther Moshibudi Mainetja was killed in a cornfield on 12 May; her body was found the next day.

Sithole killed five more women over a four-week period from 23 May to 22 June; Francina Nomsa Sithebe was located first, on 13 June, apparently sitting by a tree. Sithole used the strap from her own handbag to kill her, tying it on the low branch of a tree so the woman was standing there until she tired, at which point she slumped, and effectively strangled herself. Nineteen-year-old Elizabeth Granny Mathetsa vanished on 25 May; she was found on 16 June. Six days later, Ernestina Mohadi Mosebo was found in Rosherville, near Johannesburg. Granny Dimakatso Ramela was murdered on 23 May but not found until 18 July; unusually, she was still fully clothed. Eight days later, Mildred Ntiya Lepule was found in a canal; in her case, her husband had taken her to Pretoria to see about a job at the end of May.

On 17 July, Sithole murdered Josephine Mantsali Mlangeni but didn't realise he was being witnessed. He and Josephine were seen walking into the veldt, and then Sithole came out alone, acting suspiciously. Local resident Absalom Sangweni went to investigate and found Josephine, who had been assaulted, and ran for help. It arrived too late to save her – and Absalom was unable to give much of a physical description of the killer. Shortly after that, Sithole killed Elsie Khoti Masango, but her body wasn't found for nearly a month. Near her corpse was another body, who was never identified.

Throughout, Sithole continued using the same technique – he would approach a woman and earn her trust, chatting about day-to-day matters, and then on maybe the third or fourth meeting, he would offer to take her where he could get her work. He would then hire one of the minibuses that acted as taxis in the townships and get the driver to drop them off near an opening in the veldt – supposedly a shortcut to wherever the office was meant to be. Once out of sight, he would reveal his knife and tell his victim to strip, then rape and strangle her, sometimes allowing her to revive for a time before strangling her again. He would force the women to look at the ground while he raped them, and masturbated as they died. With one of his later victims – thirty-one-year-old Monica Gabisile Vilakazi, who was murdered on 12 September 1995 – he even rang the woman's grandmother and told her she was walking over her granddaughter's grave. He gave some of his victims a small chance: one woman, Amelia Rapodile, was a karate expert, and he said that they could have a fight. If she lost, she died. She lost. 'It's sort of a masterpiece of a thing,' he explained later, 'that happens during the day and no one can see . . . It's so quick; it takes a split of a second to put everything under control.'

In the summer of 1995, he started to refine his entrapment technique, creating a charity called Youth Against Human Abuse – allegedly trying to reunite orphans with their families. This meant that he would need staff, and he began distributing job application forms. These were to prove his downfall.

Sithole was an intelligent man: he borrowed books from the library in Pretoria when living there, and listened to classical CDs. When he read in the papers that the police were hunting a serial killer, he switched his dumping grounds. Later, to discover what the police knew about the murderer, he left an anonymous message suggesting his brother-in-law was responsible – and then found out from him, once he had been released, what line of questioning had been taken.

In August 1995 Sithole contacted photographer Peter Magubane, who helped Sithole rehome two children at a charity home, Kids Haven. There, Sithole met single mother Makoba Tryphina Mogotsi, and offered her a job at Youth Against Human Abuse. She was delighted at the idea, and the next day, Sithole suggested he should take her to her new place of work – they could travel together on the train. She was never seen alive again after she went with him on 15 August. She was not Sithole's only victim that month: Oscarina Vuyokazi Jakalase vanished on 8 August, and was found on 23

August. Two more bodies were discovered a few days later; neither of these has ever been identified.

On 16 September, a police reservist found that a field close to the Van Dyk Mine near Boksburg was littered with ten bodies, in varying states of decay. Tryphina was one of them and it was clear to the police and profiler Dr Micki Pistorius that some of the later victims had been led past the rotting corpses before they were murdered. This crime scene provided the best evidence yet for the police, and there was considerable public interest in the discovery – even President Nelson Mandela came to view the site. Three of those found there have never been identified; additionally, one of Sithole's victims had travelled to South Africa from Lesotho, so it took nearly a year to discern her identity.

Police were still unsure if there were multiple killers at work. Police Commissioner John George Fivaz was adamant that the 1994 Cleveland murders were not done by the same person – they couldn't be because David Selepe had committed them, and he was now dead. FBI profiler Robert Ressler lent his assistance, but suggested that Selepe was at least involved in the killings, if not the perpetrator.

Investigating the backgrounds of those whose bodies could be identified, the police quickly learned that both Tryphina and Amelia Rapodile had made appointments with a Moses Sithole. When they showed the staff at Kids Haven a photograph of Sithole from his arrest for rape in 1989, they recognised him. Newspapers – who had been berating the police for their apparent total inability to stop the serial killer's crime spree – ran Sithole's picture on the front page.

Sithole wasn't intending to stop, despite the publicity. On 24 September, he killed Agnes Sibongile Mbuli, and on the day her body was found, he rang the Johannesburg *Star* newspaper to find out what was happening, telling Tamsin DeBeer, the reporter who answered, that he was 'Joseph', the man everyone was looking for, i.e. 'the Gauteng serial killer'. They had three long conversations over the next couple of weeks, with Sithole stating he was killing out of revenge after his wrongful conviction for rape, and that the murders were to draw attention to that injustice. He gave details of the killings that only the real serial killer would know – including the location of a body that the police had yet to find. He had returned to the scene and moved the metal that had hidden the corpse from view. On 11 October, he told DeBeer about his most recent victim, Beauty Ntombi Ndabeni, whom he had killed just the day before. But he denied being responsible for the Cleveland murders ascribed to Selepe or the deaths of Letta Ndlangamandla and her son.

At the end of the fourth call, Sithole ran out of money, and DeBeer offered to call him back. Sithole gave her the number and the police traced it to a nearby train station. DeBeer kept him talking but by the time police got there, he was gone, abandoning the call mid-sentence. The reporter was concerned that police might have killed Sithole, particularly given the controversy over David Selepe's death while in their custody.

On the evening of 13 October, Sithole called DeBeer again and castigated her for breaking the trust they had been building. That didn't stop him from continuing to kill: an unidentified woman was found not far from the Village Main Reef Mine near Johannesburg. A few days afterwards, he rang his brother-in-law, Maxwell Makabene, and asked for help in getting hold of a gun, and arranged to meet at Maxwell's work. Makabene then told the police, who set a trap – but Sithole sensed something was wrong and made a run for it. An undercover police officer chased after him, and when Sithole turned on him with an axe, Inspector Francis Mulovhedzi fired at Sithole, hitting him in the leg and abdomen. Commissioner Fivaz defended the inspector's action: 'This was a person who has been sought for many weeks for the killings of many persons and up to now we can't determine how he may react,' he pointed out.

Rushed to hospital, Sithole was initially uncooperative when questioned, but when a female detective was sent in, he became excited, and masturbated in front of her while boasting about his rapes and murders. Sithole recovered from his wounds and was transferred into prison, where his conversations with fellow prisoners (ex-cops) were videotaped – something that was to cause problems during his trial, as this was illegal in South African prisons. The plan was for the ex-cops to write Sithole's story and sell it, and Sithole's portion of the money would be given to the daughter he and Martha had the previous December. In his conversations, Sithole confessed to twenty-nine murders. 'I don't know where the other nine come from,' he noted. 'If there was blood or injuries, they weren't my women.'

A year after his arrest he stood trial at the High Court in Pretoria for thirty-eight murders and forty rapes – considerably fewer than the number of victims that police were convinced he was responsible for, but all that they could prove. His case began on 21 October 1996; he pleaded not guilty, and his testimony on the witness stand was 'rambling, often incoherent', according to the Johannesburg *Star* report.

The new South Africa had abolished the death penalty, but to ensure that he would never be released, Sithole was sentenced to 2,410 years in prison – fifty years per murder, twelve years for each rape and five years for each of six counts of robbery, to be served consecutively. 'Nothing can be said in favour of Sithole,' Judge David Curlewis said. 'In this case I do not take leniency into account. What Sithole did was horrible ... I want to make it clear that Moses Sithole should stay in jail for the rest of his life.' Sithole was diagnosed with AIDS shortly after his arrest and has been receiving treatment in prison. He was moved from Sun City Prison in

Johannesburg to a private facility in Mangaung in 2012, and tried to sue the government as the move was 'inhumane, inconsiderate and unconstitutional'. He failed: 'With high-risk prisoners you can't tell them before they are transferred,' Judge Mathilda Masipa explained. 'Next thing you'll have people waiting for you along the way.' Sithole will never be released.

CHAPTER 23

United States: John Wayne Gacy

Some people are coulrophobic – they have an irrational fear of clowns, sometimes inspired by childhood experiences at the circus, or seeing Tim Curry's Pennywise in the TV version of Stephen King's *It*. But those who grew up around Cook County, Illinois, between 1972 and 1978 would have a better reason for such a fear – for it was as a clown that serial killer John Wayne Gacy disguised himself when he appeared at charitable events and children's parties. 'Pogo the Clown' was just one of the personas that Gacy would adopt during his career before he was arrested for what the FBI would later describe as 'a bizarre series of murders'.

Not that Gacy would ever dream of taking responsibility for anything that others might think. When he was arrested and sent for psychiatric reports in 1968, his inability to do so was noted: 'The most striking aspect of the test results is the patient's total denial of responsibility for everything that has happened to him,' wrote the two doctors who examined him at the psychiatric hospital of the State University of Iowa. 'He can produce an "alibi" for everything. He presents himself as a victim of circumstances and blames other people who are out to get him . . . the patient attempts to assure a sympathetic response by depicting himself as being at the mercy of a hostile environment.'

Gacy was born in Chicago, Illinois, on 17 March 1942. His parents – John Stanley Gacy, and his wife Marion Elaine, née Robinson – did not have that happy a marriage: his father was an alcoholic, who was regularly abusive to his wife, as well as to John junior and his two sisters. Young John tried to gain his father's approval, but it was rarely forthcoming: one of his first memories was being beaten after he had moved some car parts that his auto repair machinist father had assembled, and he was regularly called 'dumb and stupid', particularly in comparison to his two sisters. His father used a leather belt on him regularly – notably after the six-year-old John had stolen a toy truck from a neighbourhood store – but after his arrest, Gacy maintained that he never hated his father, and even when the beatings continued into his teens, he never struck back at his parent. His mother tried to protect John, but her husband only thought this proved the youngster was a 'mama's boy' who would 'probably grow up queer'.

In 1949, Gacy received his worst beating yet, with a leather strop, after his father was told that he and another child had been caught 'sexually fondling' a young girl. This may have been linked to the molestation that Gacy himself was receiving at the same time from a family friend, who took the boy for rides in his truck then fondled him. The young Gacy never told his father about this, as he believed he would be held responsible.

Through his teens, Gacy was overweight and unable to take part in games because of a heart condition and his tendency to suffer seizures. He was hospitalised on various occasions, and he later guessed that he probably missed a year of education between the ages of fourteen and eighteen. After he gave up on school – he failed to graduate – he worked as an assistant precinct captain for a Democratic Party candidate in the area. Again, this was a decision that didn't go down well with his father. After an argument with his father over a car that John senior had bought for his son but over which he retained control, Gacy drove the 1,800 miles to Las Vegas, Nevada, where he worked initially with the ambulance service, before being transferred to work as a mortuary attendant.

It was while in this job that Gacy had something of an epiphany. One night he climbed into the coffin of a dead teenage boy, embracing and caressing the corpse before getting a sense of shock. It was enough to persuade him that he should return home, where he enrolled in the Northwestern Business College, graduating in 1963. He seemed to be on the straight and narrow for the next few years: he took a post as a management trainee at the Nunn-Bush Shoe Company, and rose through the ranks, becoming a department manager in Springfield, Illinois. He also became engaged then married to one of his colleagues, Marlynn Myers, and joined the United States Junior Chamber (known as the 'Jaycees'), an organisation set up for those between eighteen and forty to develop their personal and leadership skills through service to others. At the time (and up until 1985), it was a male-only club, and Gacy was one of its most prominent members, becoming vice-president of the Springfield Jaycees in 1965, and named the third most outstanding Jaycee in the whole state. It was with another Jaycee, however, that Gacy had his second homosexual experience, receiving oral sex from the man after an evening of drinking.

In 1966, Gacy's father-in-law offered him the chance to manage three Kentucky Fried Chicken restaurants that he owned in Waterloo, Iowa. Gacy jumped at the chance and moved 300 miles north-west with his wife. Even Gacy would admit later that his life at this point was 'perfect': he became involved with the local Jaycees, again becoming vice-president (even if some of his colleagues thought he was a bit too full of himself); his wife gave birth to two children – Michael in February 1966, Christine in March 1967; and even his father seemed proud of him.

However, surface appearances were deceiving. Gacy was already cheating on his wife with other women, and his homosexual tendencies were also becoming more evident. He socialised with his male employees, making advances towards them that he would dismiss as a joke if he was rebuffed. In August 1967, he carried out his first confirmed sexual assault, on fifteen-year-old Donald Voorhees. The boy came back to Gacy's home believing he was going to be shown pornographic movies; Gacy got him drunk and persuaded Donald to fellate him. He was but the first of many whom Gacy would either blackmail or trick into performing oral sex on him; others were told Gacy had been commissioned to carry out experiments for 'scientific research' for which they were paid up to $50 each.

Donald Voorhees eventually told his father what Gacy had made him do; his father immediately called in the police, who arrested Gacy in March 1968 on charges of oral sodomy regarding Donald, and the attempted assault of sixteen-year-old Edward Lynch. Gacy demanded a polygraph, but the readings were ambiguous – he was clearly nervous when denying any wrongdoing with regard to Donald and Edward. He was indicted on 10 May 1968.

Gacy wasn't going to let a teenager tear down what he had accomplished, so on 30 August 1968 he persuaded one of his employees, eighteen-year-old Russell Schroeder, to attack Donald Voorhees so he wouldn't testify against Gacy. This Schroeder did, spraying Donald in the eyes with Mace and beating him up, telling him not to testify. Voorhees went straight to the police, who arrested Schroeder – who immediately implicated Gacy. He too was arrested, and was sent for psychiatric evaluation at the State University; the doctors believed he had antisocial personality disorder (ASPD), wouldn't benefit from medical treatment, was mentally competent to stand trial – and would end up in repeated conflict with society as a result of the way that he viewed himself and the world.

His trial began on 7 November 1968, and Gacy admitted one count of sodomy regarding Donald Voorhees. He disputed the rest, and in court claimed that the boy had been a willing participant. He was convicted on 3 December and sentenced to ten years at the

Anamosa State Penitentiary. The same day, his wife filed for divorce; Gacy never saw her or their two children again.

While inside Anamosa, Gacy seems to have been a model prisoner, becoming head cook, driving an increase in the inmates' Jaycee chapter, helping prisoners gain a daily pay increase and even arranging for a miniature golf course in the yard. He tried for early release at the first opportunity, in June 1969, but this was turned down, although he was allowed to apply again the following May. He worked to complete his high-school education, gaining a diploma in November 1969. However, he was devastated by the news of his father's death on Christmas Day that year, and was denied compassionate leave to attend the funeral.

Gacy was eventually released on parole on 18 June 1970 on condition that he relocated to Chicago to live with his mother and he observed a 10 p.m. curfew. He duly moved back to Illinois, and got a job as a short-order cook. Eight months later, on 12 February 1971, Gacy was charged with sexually assaulting a teenage boy, but the case was dismissed after the youth failed to turn up at court. Gacy had allegedly picked him up at the Greyhound bus station, driven him home, and tried to force him to have sex. Luckily for Gacy – if not his future victims – the Iowa Parole Board were somehow kept in the dark about this, and in October that year, his parole ended; in November, his record in Iowa was sealed.

In the summer of 1971, with help from his mother, Gacy bought a house at 8213 West Summerdale Avenue, where all of his crimes would subsequently take place. Gacy met up again with an old school friend, Carole Hoff, now divorced with two young daughters. 'He swept me off my feet,' she later told *Time* reporters. She married John Gacy on 1 July 1972. By this time, he was already a killer.

John Gacy's first confirmed victim was Timothy McCoy, a sixteen-year-old who was travelling from Michigan to Omaha. Gacy picked him up at the Greyhound terminal and gave him a tour of the town, before offering him a place to stay for the night. According to Gacy, he woke the next day to find Timothy standing at his bedroom door, a kitchen knife in his hand. (Apparently, Timothy had been cooking them breakfast, and had come to tell Gacy, forgetting he was carrying the knife.) Gacy went towards him, and Timothy raised his arms in surrender, tilting the knife upwards, and catching Gacy's forearm with the tip of the blade. Gacy twisted the knife from Timothy and banged the teenager's head against the bedroom wall. Then he kicked him against the wardrobe. Timothy kicked him in the stomach, Gacy grabbed him, pushed him to the floor, then stabbed him repeatedly. It was at that moment, Gacy said later, that 'I realized that death was the ultimate thrill', and he orgasmed as he killed the teenager. He subsequently buried Timothy in the crawl space beneath his home and later covered the spot with concrete.

A week before his wedding, Gacy was in trouble again. On 22 June, he was arrested and charged with aggravated battery and reckless conduct; this time a youth named Jackie Dee claimed Gacy had flashed a sheriff's badge to get him into his car and perform oral sex. The charge was dropped after Jackie tried to blackmail Gacy into paying him so he would retract his claims.

Gacy started his own construction business the same year. PDM ('Painting, Decorating and Maintenance') Contractors became a profitable business over the next six years, and provided Gacy with plenty of the raw material that his sideline as a serial killer would require. He purchased property down in Florida, taking one of his young employees with him to check it out – and raped the boy in their hotel room on the first night. The boy stayed on a beach for the rest of the trip, and when they got back to Chicago, he came round to Gacy's house and tried to beat him up. Gacy's mother-in-law prevented Gacy from being subjected to serious injury, and Gacy claimed that he had been attacked because he had refused to pay the boy for substandard work.

In January 1974, Gacy killed again. The victim was never identified, save as a boy between fourteen and eighteen years old with
medium-brown curly hair. Gacy strangled him and placed him in
his closet before burying him; the corpse leaked fluids from his
mouth and nose onto the closet carpet, and Gacy decided to stuff
cloth rags or the victim's underwear into their mouths in future.

'I do a lot of rotten, horrible things, but I do a lot of good things
too,' Gacy would tell a neighbour round this time. To neighbours
and colleagues (save those who were of an age that Gacy regarded as
a potential target), the next four years saw Gacy become a respected
pillar of the community. He started his annual summer parties in
1974, and re-engaged with the Democratic Party. He became
involved with the local street-lighting committee, and from 1975 to
1978 he was the director of the Chicago Polish Constitution Day
Parade, held each May. In his final year of freedom, he even met
with the First Lady, Rosalynn Carter, and was given the prestigious
'S' pin, which meant he had been given special· clearance by the
Secret Service! He joined the local Moose Club, and became part of
their 'Jolly Joker' clown club, whose members donned clown make-
up to entertain hospitalised children, as well as aid at fundraising
events and parades.

All was not as it seemed on the surface. Gacy had admitted to his
wife Carole that he was bisexual, and on Mother's Day, 11 May 1975,
told her that they would never have sex again. Carole had already
been alarmed by the regular visits of teenage boys to their garage
and finding gay pornography in their house, but maintained the
pretence in public that they were a couple.

Gacy was now effectively free to carry on with his preferred
sexual partners. He was working hard to keep PDM Contractors in
business, but found the time to 'cruise' (his description) for young
men. Not all of them were compliant: fifteen-year-old Anthony
Antonucci was able to turn the tables on Gacy when his boss turned

up at his house. Gacy gave the boy alcohol, then wrestled him to the floor and handcuffed his hands behind his back. However, Anthony was able to get free while Gacy was out of the room, and managed to get the key off Gacy and then cuff the older man – who blustered for a time, then promised to leave if the cuffs were removed.

On 29 July 1975, a week after the incident with Anthony Antonucci, Gacy killed one of his employees, seventeen-year-old John Butkovitch, who had been threatening Gacy over pay he claimed he was owed. Since his wife and stepchildren were away, Gacy invited the boy to come over to his home to discuss it, and while there, he showed John his party piece. First, he would put handcuffs on himself and release them. Then he persuaded John to let him handcuff his hands behind his back – and didn't show him how to release them. He proceeded to sit on the boy's chest for a while, before strangling him, and burying his body beneath the floor of the garage. The teenager's car was found abandoned in a parking lot, with the boy's wallet inside and the keys in the ignition. After John's parents called the police, Gacy claimed that the boy and two friends had come to his home, but they had left after agreeing terms with Gacy. The parents weren't satisfied, and over the next three years made over a hundred calls to the police, convinced that Gacy was involved in their son's 'disappearance'.

In the autumn of 1975, Carole Gacy asked for a divorce, and she and her daughters moved out from the Summerdale home the following February. The divorce was finalised on 2 March 1976. A month later, Gacy killed again – and would keep on killing until he was caught two years later. Neighbours would later claim that Gacy's behaviour became erratic following his divorce, with stories of muffled screaming, shouting and crying in the early hours of the morning, and Gacy keeping unsociable hours.

Eighteen-year-old Darrell Sampson disappeared on 6 April 1976; fifteen-year-old Randall Reffett went missing on 14 May; later that same day, fourteen-year-old Samuel Stapleton was taken by Gacy. All were murdered, the latter two buried together in the crawl space. Seventeen-year-old Michael Bonnin joined them on 3 June. Between 13 June and 6 August, Gacy killed four more young men, only two of whom were identified – William Carroll, aged sixteen, and Rick Johnston, who was seventeen. Of the other two, all that was confirmed was that one was in their twenties, while the other, a teenager, had been strangled to death. All four were buried underneath the kitchen floor.

Some victims managed to get away. Eighteen-year-old David Cram was hired by Gacy to work for PDM in July, and on 21 August moved into the Summerdale house. The next day, Gacy got him drunk, handcuffed him and told him he was going to rape him. David kicked Gacy in the face, and got free – although he stayed living with his attempted rapist. A month later, Gacy tried again, telling Cram, 'Dave, you really don't know who I am. Maybe it would be good if you give me what I want.' The boy again resisted Gacy's attempts, but this time he moved out. (Amazingly, he would continue to work occasionally for Gacy over the next two years.)

Two others were not so lucky. Investigators were able to deduce a timeline for Gacy's murders from the sequence in which bodies were buried in the crawl space, and estimated that a pair of unidentified bodies came from the period between 6 August and 5 October. Three weeks after that, on 24 October, Gacy killed two together – teenage friends Kenneth Parker and Michael Marino – whom he buried in the same grave. On 26 October, yet another PDM employee fell victim: nineteen-year-old William Bundy's final resting place was in a grave dug beneath the master bedroom.

Gacy made his preparations carefully. He arranged for PDM employees to dig trenches in the crawl space beneath his house, and in at least one case – seventeen-year-old Gregory Godzik – he then used it to bury their corpses. Gregory vanished in December 1976, and Gacy told his worried parents that the boy had wanted to run away from home. He even maintained that he had received a message on his answerphone from the youth, although when challenged, he said he had erased it. Gregory was joined in death by his nineteen-year-old friend John Szyc on 20 January 1977 – although, highly unusually, Gacy retained a memento of this particular murder: John's class ring. This he kept in the dresser in the master bedroom.

During all this time, Gacy had a lodger in the house: eighteen-year-old Michael Rossi, another PDM worker, moved in shortly after Cram's departure. Gacy had lured John Szyc to the house on the pretext of buying the young man's car; after the murder, he sold the car to Rossi, saying John had sold it to him because he needed the money to leave town.

Gacy himself had no intention of going anywhere, at least on a permanent basis. PDM's business was increasing, while his murderous tally continued to rise. A twenty-five-year-old man and twenty-year-old Jon Prestidge were killed between December 1976 and March 1977, and another may have followed a few weeks later. There was no doubt this seventeen- to twenty-one-year-old was one of Gacy's victims; however, his placement in the crawl space led to some ambiguity over date.

There was a pause in Gacy's killing spree from March to June 1977; Gacy had begun dating seriously at the start of the year, and when Michael Rossi moved out in April, his girlfriend moved in. She and Gacy were engaged for a short time, but broke it off in June and she moved out. Gacy would try to reconcile with his wife later in the year, but without success; she remarried in 1978.

On 5 July, nineteen-year-old Matthew Bowman became Gacy's next victim, throttled with a rope that the Cook County medical examiner, Dr Robert Stein, would later testify resembled clothesline, knotted and twisted with a small loop at the end. Tightening this around the victim's neck would cut off oxygen and blood to the brain, and the victim would become unconscious, go into convulsions and die.

Between September and the end of the year, a further six were added to Gacy's tally. Robert Gilroy, the eighteen-year-old son of a Chicago police sergeant, was last seen on 15 September although intriguingly Gacy was out of town from 12 to 16 September, leading to speculation that his claims of an accomplice might be true. On 25 September, nineteen-year-old Marine John Mowery disappeared while walking home from his mother's apartment; both youths were strangled and buried in the crawl space. Three weeks passed before twenty-one-year-old Russell Nelson joined them, while mid-November saw both sixteen-year-old Russell Winch and twenty-year-old Tommy Boling strangled and buried in the crawl space, this time beneath the hallway. On 9 December, another nineteen-year-old Marine, David Talsma, was similarly killed and disposed of.

Gacy wound up the year acting very oddly – for him. On 30 December, he abducted Robert Donnelly at gunpoint, took him back to the Summerdale house, and proceeded to rape and torture him – including dunking his head in a bathtub of water until he passed out, then reviving him and starting again. The nineteen-year-old student begged Gacy to kill him, but the serial killer simply said, 'I'm getting round to it.' But instead of strangling the young man and burying him, Gacy drove him to PDM where he let him go. Robert went to the police but, interviewed a week later, Gacy maintained that the episode had been consensual 'slave sex'. Faced with a choice between the apparently upright pillar of the community and the young student, the police elected to believe Gacy, and no charges were filed.

The final victim buried in the crawl space was nineteen-year-old William Kindred, who disappeared on 16 February 1978; Gacy was running out of room. This may explain why he also let his next victim, twenty-six-year-old Jeffrey Rignall, live. Like Robert Donnelly, Jeffrey was raped, tortured, and brought in and out of consciousness (this time with chloroform rather than water). Gacy dumped him in Lincoln Park. He too went to the police but they took no action until Jeffrey was able to give them more evidence: he remembered Gacy's black Oldsmobile, as well as the exit on the Kennedy Expressway that Gacy had used, so he staked that out until he saw Gacy's car. He and his friends then followed Gacy back to Summerdale and provided the police with Gacy's address. Gacy was arrested on 15 July, and was set to be tried for battery against Jeffrey. (It's worth noting that Jeffrey believed there had been a second person in the room when Gacy tortured him; this was also later cited as evidence that Gacy perhaps was telling the truth when he denied responsibility for all the deaths.)

A month before his arrest, Gacy came up with a new idea for body disposal: he would dump the corpses in the Des Plaines River. He had considered using his attic, but remembering the problems with 'leakage' that he had experienced some years earlier, dismissed the idea. He therefore went to the I-55 bridge over the river and threw five corpses into the water (four were later found; one, he believed, had landed on a barge). Timothy O'Rourke was killed in mid-June 1978; the twenty-year-old's body was found on 30 June. Gacy was cautious in the period immediately after his arrest, but began killing again in early November, disposing of nineteen-year-old Frank Landingin's body on the 4th; it was pulled from the river eight days later. Twenty-year-old James Mazzara's body took five weeks to be found; Gacy had killed him on 24 November.

Gacy's last victim was Robert Jerome Piest, who had overheard Gacy mention his firm hired teenage boys when Gacy was discussing a PDM job with a potential client, pharmacist Phil Torf, on 11 December. Robert told his mother that 'some contractor wants to talk to me about a job'. He was never seen alive again. His mother filed a missing person's report which reached Lieutenant Joseph Kozenczak, whose son attended the same high school as Robert. Torf told officers that Gacy was the most likely contractor to whom Robert was referring. Police visited him at home the following evening and Gacy denied offering the boy a job or having any connection to the disappearance. He agreed to come to the police station later that evening; he didn't do so until 3.20 the next morning, and was covered in mud, claiming he had been in a car accident.

Cleaned up, he returned later that day to find the police asking why he had returned to the pharmacy at eight o'clock on the evening of 11 December. Gacy said Torf had called him, saying Gacy had left his appointment book; the police knew Torf had not done so, and asked him for a full statement. It was the beginning of the end for the serial killer. The police learned of both his impending battery charge, as well as his sentence for sodomy in Iowa – the records were unsealed given the gravity of the case – and a search warrant was issued. John Syzc's class ring, handcuffs, assorted driver's licences, books on homosexuality and pederasty, and a piece of two-by-four with holes drilled in the ends were among the many suspicious items found. Gacy's car was impounded along with other PDM vehicles, and a surveillance team set on him – who Gacy tried, unsuccessfully, to charm over the next few days, and then tried to lose.

Evidence continued to mount against him: Michael Rossi and Gacy's ex-wife Carole were questioned, and the class ring was identified. Details of the battery case confirmed a pattern of behaviour and, despite Gacy's consistent denials, the police were sure they were on the right track. On 17 December, a search of Gacy's car by German shepherd search dogs confirmed that Robert Piest's body had been in the vehicle. Early the next morning, Gacy invited the surveillance detectives to join him for breakfast, and, apparently apropos of nothing, noted that 'clowns can get away with murder'. The strain was beginning to tell.

On the afternoon of 18 December, Gacy visited his lawyers to prepare a $750,000 lawsuit against the Des Moines police for harassment. However, the police had been able to track down the provenance of a receipt from the pharmacy where Robert Piest worked which they had found at Gacy's house – it had been given to the teenager by a colleague just before he left to meet the 'contractor'. In a second formal interview, Michael Rossi explained that he had been told to spread ten bags of lime in Gacy's crawl space. The next day, Gacy's lawyers filed their suit, and that afternoon Gacy invited his surveillance detectives inside, and one of them noticed an odd smell, as if of decay, coming from a heating duct.

On the 20th, Rossi told the police he believed Gacy could have buried Robert Piest in the crawl space, and that when he was working in the crawl space, he had been told to do so in very specific areas. David Cram was also interviewed, telling police about Gacy's attempted rapes, and recalling an incident when they had returned to the house and found some mud on the carpet, which had alarmed Gacy. He also confirmed that he too had spread lime in the crawl space and dug trenches – two feet wide by six feet long and two feet deep. The police were now convinced that the crawl space was filled with graves.

The same evening, Gacy went to his lawyers to discuss the civil case – but then told them that Robert Piest was dead. 'He's in a river.' Over several hours, he then verbally confessed to the many murders to his lawyers, Sam Amirante and Leroy Stevens, before passing out from all he had drunk. The next morning he said he had things to do and left.

As the police prepared a request for a second search warrant, Gacy said his goodbyes to various people, including his colleague Ronald Rhode, as well as Rossi and Cram. The latter drove him to another meeting with his lawyers, and then told police that Gacy had told him he had confessed. Gacy visited his father's grave and was acting so erratically that the police worried he might evade justice by committing suicide. He had earlier handed a bag of marijuana to a filling-station attendant, who had passed it to Gacy's surveillance team. This gave them a reason to arrest and hold him while the search warrant was executed.

At 4.30 p.m., the warrant was issued. When they got to Gacy's house, the officers found Gacy had tried to foil them by unplugging his sump pump and flooding the crawl space. However, they simply replaced the plug and waited. Crime scene technician Daniel Genty entered the crawl space once the water was gone and began digging. It took him only a few minutes to find flesh and an arm bone.

Gacy confessed immediately, although he claimed his victims were male runaways or male prostitutes, confirming that he had posed as a sheriff, and that he had got the inspiration for manacling his victims to a two-by-four from the Houston Mass Murderers of 1973. He helpfully provided police with a diagram to show exactly where the bodies were buried in his basement; the next day, he showed them where the bodies in the garage were located, and the spot from where he had thrown the corpses into the Des Plaines River. Gacy would later claim that he was simply showing the police where he had poured concrete, but as prosecutor William Kunkle pointed out, 'He sprayed a stick figure with the orange spray can in the garage – not just a mark – a stick figure showing the orientation of the body. Right underneath that stick figure, exactly where he drew it, pointed in the direction he drew it, was the body of John Butkovich.'

Over the next five months, twenty-nine bodies were exhumed from Gacy's home; Robert Piest's almost 'mummified' body was finally discovered on the edge of the river on 9 April – three pieces of 'paper-like material' had been thrust down his throat while he was still alive, and he had died of suffocation.

John Gacy's home was demolished on 11 April 1979. 'We're going to turn that property back into a pleasant site for the community,' Assistant Cook County State's Attorney Morris Alexander said optimistically. 'We hope the neighbours will eventually forget the horrendous crimes that property has become associated with.'

Gacy spent over 300 hours with doctors at the Menard Correctional Center undergoing psychological tests, and appeared before a panel of psychiatrists, trying to claim he had multiple personality disorder. Three experts believed this was the case and eventually testified for the defence, which was going for a 'not guilty by reason of insanity' verdict.

The trial began on 6 February 1980, with the prosecution setting out to prove Gacy was sane and his crimes were premeditated. Evidence regarding the digging in the crawl space came from Rossi and Cram, while Dr Robert Stein refuted the defence's suggestion that all the 'markedly decomposed, putrefied, skeletalized remains' that were uncovered from the house in an 'archaeological fashion' could possibly be caused by death from accidental erotic asphyxiation. Jeffrey Rignall and Donald Voorhees were both questioned about their torture at Gacy's hands; both were violently ill when they relived their experiences.

The defence did not call Gacy to the stand; Gacy complained about this, and various other matters he saw as prejudicial to a fair trial, to Judge Louis B. Garippo, presiding over the trial, who told him he could testify if he wished. In the end, he didn't. In the closing argument, prosecutor Terry Sullivan claimed 'John Gacy has accounted for more human devastation than many earthly catastrophes, but one must tremble. I tremble when thinking about just how close he came to getting away with it all.' Defence attorney Sam Amirante presented Gacy as 'a man driven by compulsions he was unable to control'. The jury took less than two hours to convict on all thirty-three charges of murder, as well as sexual assault and taking indecent liberties with a child, i.e. Robert Piest. They took a similar length of time the next day to request the death sentence for all the convictions to which it applied.

Speaking sixteen years after the death sentence was carried out, Sam Amirante summed up the necessity for Gacy's execution. 'We were told by the doctors – all the doctors – that if he ever got out again, he would do it again,' he told WBBM Newsradio in Chicago. 'As long as he lived in a structured environment, he'd be OK. But if he ever got out of jail – he could have been in jail for twenty, thirty, forty years – when he got out again, he would have committed another crime.'

Gacy was kept on death row for fourteen years while the various appeals played out. He gave interviews (many of which can be seen on YouTube), and claimed that twenty-eight of the thirty-three murders had been carried out by others who had the keys to his house. Finally, the Illinois Supreme Court set 10 May 1994 as his execution date. Supposedly, his last words before he was given the lethal injection were 'Kiss my ass', although state Corrections Director Howard Peters said that Gacy claimed, 'taking his life would not compensate for the loss of the others and that this was the state murdering him'.

'We were victims here too,' John Mowery's brother Tim Nieder told reporters after news of the execution was confirmed. 'I feel like justice has finally been served, but it's been a long time in the making.'

Ever since Gacy's crimes were revealed, there have been suggestions that the death toll was higher, and that Gacy didn't act alone. As a result of further investigations, a number of other cold cases have been solved that had nothing to do with Gacy's activities. 'There is significant evidence out there that suggests that not only did John Wayne Gacy not operate alone, he may not have been involved in some of the murders, and the fact that he was largely a copycat murderer,' attorney Robert Stephenson told WGN-TV in 2012, although Amirante didn't believe it. There has been little progress on proving others' involvement in the intervening years. There are also ongoing attempts to identify the still-anonymous corpses; an unexpected side effect of this was a DNA test that seemed to prove that the body labelled as Michael Marino was identified in error. Orthodontist Edward Pavlik has stuck by his identification – 'I'm a scientific thinker. I'm telling you that the body and the X-rays given to me as Marino are one and the same without any doubt. I can't make it any clearer than that.'

From Gacy's great evil, some good did come: Sam Amirante authored the Missing Child Recovery Act in 1984, which meant that police no longer had to wait seventy-two hours before they could investigate a missing child, and a state-wide alert could be triggered immediately. It was one of the cornerstones for the Amber Alert system that now operates across the United States.

CHAPTER 24

United States: Ted Bundy

....

'We serial killers are your sons, we are your husbands, we are everywhere. And there will be more of your children dead tomorrow.' One of the best-known quotes from Ted Bundy sums up his cold-hearted approach to what he did. Responsible for at least thirty homicides, one of his own defence team, Polly Nelson, noted that 'Ted was the very definition of heartless evil.' He only fully admitted what he had done when every avenue of escaping execution seemed to have been exhausted. 'His murders were his life's accomplishments,' Nelson wrote in her detailed account of his life and crimes, while according to Revd Fred Lawrence, who administered Bundy's last rites before his execution on 24 January 1989, 'I don't think even he knew . . . how many he killed or why he killed them.'

Piecing together much of Bundy's early life is not helped by the multiple different stories that he told his biographers and lawyers. What is certain is that Bundy was born Theodore Robert Cowell on 24 November 1946 to single mother (Eleanor) Louise Cowell; his father's identity has never been confirmed. He was brought up for the first three years by his grandparents and for many years believed his mother was actually his older sister (a common practice at the time to avoid social stigma on both the mother and child). He only learned the truth much later in life. His mother moved to Tacoma, Washington, in 1950 and met hospital cook Johnny Culpepper Bundy the following year. They married in 1952, with Bundy adopting the five-year-old and bringing him up alongside the four children that he and Louise had together.

As a teenager, Ted Bundy claimed to have been something of a loner, although classmates recalled he was 'well known and well liked'. He was arrested at least a couple of times for burglary and auto theft but, as was customary, the state's record of his misdemeanours was expunged when he reached eighteen. He graduated from Woodrow Wilson High School in 1965 and spent a year each at the University of Puget Sound (UPS) and the University of Washington before dropping out in early 1968. He was involved with a classmate (most commonly referred to by the pseudonym Stephanie Brooks) for a time, but she found him immature and dumped him in the summer of 1968. This upset Bundy considerably and he travelled cross-country for a year, spending a term at Temple University in Philadelphia, and being fired from a job at the Olympic Hotel in Seattle after thefts from lockers. When he returned to Washington state in late 1969, he met divorcee Elizabeth Kloepfer with whom he was in a relationship for seven years. He re-enrolled at the University of Washington as a psychology major, graduating from there in 1972.

It seems that during this period he was an upright citizen. Former police officer Ann Rule, who wrote one of the earliest books about him, worked alongside him at Seattle's suicide hotline crisis centre, and thought he was 'kind, solicitous and empathetic'. He also worked for the HVH Mental Health Center in Seattle, and the Seattle Crime Commission. He graduated in 1972, and helped Governor Daniel J. Evans's re-election campaign before getting further involved with the Republican Party. He studied law at UPS throughout 1973, during which time he once again became involved with 'Stephanie Brooks' but, in January 1974, he broke off the relationship – with many commentators believing that he had deliberately become involved with her again simply so he could get his revenge by being the one to end the relationship this time.

January 1974 also marked his first confirmed attacks on women.

It is pretty certain that Bundy did attack women prior to this time. He claimed to Nelson that he tried kidnapping women in Ocean City, New Jersey, in 1969, and killed for the first time in Seattle two years after; he told psychologist Art Norman that 1969 was marked by the murder of two women in Atlantic City. Detective Robert Keppel was told about a murder in Seattle in 1972 and the death of a hitchhiker in Turnwater, Washington, in 1973 (the FBI noted the latter as his first homicide). He was linked to the death of Ann Marie Burr in Tacoma in 1961, but he vehemently denied any involvement, even writing to her mother from prison in 1986 stating: 'First and foremost I do not know what happened to your daughter Ann Marie. I had nothing to do with her disappearance. You said she disappeared August 31, 1961. At the time I was a normal 14-year-old boy. I did not wander the streets late at night. I did not.' DNA evidence was tested in 2011, but had degraded too much. (It's worth keeping in mind that Bundy denied many of his crimes right up to the day of his execution, hoping that he might be kept alive so he could confess further.)

Bundy was determined not to be caught committing his acts of violence. He knew how to ensure there was little or no evidence at the scenes of the crimes. On 4 January 1974, he attacked an eighteen-year-old dancer and student (referred to as Karen Sparks or Joni Lenz) in her basement bedroom. He beat her up and then tore a rod from the bed and rammed it into her vagina. She was found comatose, but survived, albeit with extensive injuries including brain damage. Four weeks later, at some point on the night of 31 January, he abducted twenty-one-year-old radio announcer and student Lynda Ann Healy from her bedroom, making the bed so it appeared as if all was normal. He had beaten her unconscious then dressed her before carrying her away in a sheet. Her skull and mandible were found at Bundy's dump site on Taylor Mountain in March 1975. Nineteen-year-old Donna Gail Manson was abducted on 12

March while she was heading to a concert in Olympia, sixty miles from Seattle; her body was never found. Eighteen-year-old Susan Rancourt vanished on 17 April after going to a meeting at Central State College in Ellensburg; her skull and mandible were later found at Taylor Mountain, as were those of Roberta Parks, who disappeared from Oregon State University in Corvallis, Oregon, on 6 May while on the way to meet friends for coffee. On 1 June, twenty-two-year-old Brenda Carol Ball left the Flame Tavern in Burien, Washington, and was never seen again; her remains resurfaced at Taylor Mountain, too. Georgann Hawkins disappeared on 11 June while walking down a bright alleyway between her boyfriend's dormitory and her own Kappa Alpha Theta sorority house – Bundy lured her to his car, and strangled her at Issaquah. The next morning, while the police were searching for him, he went back to the alleyway and found her earrings and one of her shoes that he had accidentally left there. No one spotted him.

All that seemed to connect the victims was that the women were white, single, slender in build, were wearing slacks, and had long hair parted in the middle. Police discovered that a number of eyewitnesses had seen a young man who had a plaster cast on either his arm or his leg, who was asking people for assistance in a British or Canadian accent. The man had a Volkswagen Beetle (known as a 'bug').

The final two abductions and murders took place on the same day, 14 July 1974. Bundy approached various women on the crowded beach at Lake Sammamish State Park in Issaquah, twenty miles from Seattle, wearing a tennis outfit but with his arm in a sling, asking for their help getting a sailboat from his bug. Four refused; one got as far as the car and ran when she saw there was no boat; but both twenty-three-year-old probation case worker Janice Anne Ott and eighteen-year-old computer programming student Denise Naslund agreed, four hours apart, going off with Bundy to their deaths. (Bundy did claim that he kept Janice alive until he brought Denise back so one could watch the other die, but retracted that version shortly before his execution.)

Four people recognised the sketch that was produced by witnesses to Janice and Denise's disappearances. Each of them – Elizabeth Kloepfer, Ann Rule, one of Bundy's psychology professors and one of his colleagues where he was working at the Washington State Department of Emergency Services in Olympia – reported their suspicions to the police, but the charming law student, with no adult arrest record, wasn't considered a viable suspect. The skeletons of his most recent two victims were found on 6 September 1974 in Issaquah; Bundy later confirmed that other bones found with them belonged to Georgann Hawkins.

By the time that the skulls and mandibles of the other girls (bar Donna Manson) were found close to a hiking trail that Bundy had frequented on Taylor Mountain, near Issaquah, in March 1975, Bundy had abducted and killed many more victims in a new area. In August 1974 he had been accepted at the University of Utah Law School after dropping out of UPS, and he moved to Salt Lake City. He confessed that he raped and strangled a teenage hitchhiker in Idaho on 2 September; her body was thrown in the nearby Snake River. She was never found or identified. A month later, sixteen-year-old Nancy Wilcox was grabbed in Holladay, near Salt Lake City; Bundy claimed that he wanted to 'de-escalate' his urges, so was going to rape her but release her. However, as he tried to silence her, he strangled her. He said he buried her in Capitol Reef National Park; her remains have never been found. Neither of these crimes were linked to him until Bundy confessed in his last days.

On 27 October, the naked body of Melissa Smith, the daughter of Louis Smith, the police chief of Midvale, Utah, was found. She had vanished nine days earlier and had been raped, sodomised and strangled with nylon stockings. Evidence from the autopsy suggested

THE SERIAL KILLER FILES

she may have been alive for up to a week after she was abducted near a pizza parlour. The same fate befell seventeen-year-old Laura Ann Aime, who vanished on 31 October, and was found on 27 November. Bundy returned to their corpses on multiple occasions, performing sexual acts with the decomposing bodies until putrefaction meant even he could not continue. He applied make-up to Melissa's body, and regularly washed Laura's hair.

One girl did get away: on 8 November, eighteen-year-old Carol DaRonch was approached at a mall in Murray, Utah, by a man claiming to be 'police officer Roseland'. He asked her to come with him back to the police substation as they were holding someone who had tried to break into her car. When she realised that he wasn't driving down the right road, he pulled to the side of the road and tried to handcuff her. Carol 'knew he was going to kill me' but Bundy accidentally put both handcuffs on the same wrist. Carol was able to escape. She would later identify him – 'his eyes were so cold,' she recalled years later. 'There was no expression, just no feeling to them.'

Bundy was determined to have a victim that day, and later that evening he abducted seventeen-year-old drama student Debra Kent. He was spotted hanging around the Viewmont High School theatre, and a key that matched the handcuffs removed from Carol's wrist was found outside the auditorium. All that was ever found of Debra was her kneecap.

Elizabeth Kloepfer reported her suspicions of Bundy to the authorities twice more in the light of these disappearances. However, witnesses from the Lake Sammamish State Park incidents didn't pick him out from a photo line-up, and there was little evidence to tie him to the Utah crimes, bar being in the locality. Come the new year, Bundy would pick a fresh hunting ground.

His first target of 1975 was nurse Caryn Campbell, whom he took on 12 January while she was on a trip with her fiancé and his children to the Wildwood Inn in Snowmass Village, Colorado. She had been walking down a well-lit corridor between the elevator and her room when she was abducted. Her naked, animal-ravaged body was found over a month later, on 17 February, on a dirt road near Aspen; she had been hit with a blunt instrument then raped and murdered. On 15 March, instructor Julie Cunningham was approached by a man on crutches at the ski resort of Vail, Colorado, who asked if she would carry his ski boots to his car. The twenty-six-year-old agreed and was clubbed and handcuffed, before being assaulted and strangled. Bundy said he returned to check her remains at the end of April where he had left them, a hundred miles away in Garfield County, Colorado; he buried them, but they were never found. The body of twenty-five-year-old Denise Oliverson was never returned to her family either: she was abducted while cycling to her parents' home in Grand Junction, Colorado. Her bicycle and sandals were found under a viaduct near a railroad bridge; Bundy said he threw her in the river.

Bundy's youngest victim was Lynette Culver, who was just twelve when he took her from Alameda Junior High School in Pocatello, Idaho. He drowned her, then raped the corpse, and disposed of the body in the Snake River; it was never found. His final victim that summer was only three years older than Lynette: Susan Curtis vanished during a youth conference at Brigham Young University in Provo, Utah. She was buried near Price, Utah, seventy-five miles away – or so Bundy claimed. He couldn't be questioned further about his admission to her murder: he made it only minutes before he was executed.

Bundy's modus operandi throughout this time was pretty consistent. If the urge to kill simply took him, then he would pick up a victim and kill them, disposing of them randomly. (Most of his hitchhiker victims fell under this category.) Most of the time, though, he was in what he described as 'predator' mode: he would preselect a site to dispose of the body, where possible carry out discreet research regarding his victim, prepare all the necessary tools, and then plan the assault carefully so that he knew his means of escape, his alibi and his way of disposing of all evidence. Only once all that was complete would he approach his victim.

He would either fake an injury or claim, as he had to Carol DaRonch, that he was a police officer or other authority figure. This would persuade the unsuspecting victim to accompany him to his Volkswagen, where he had hidden a crowbar near the rear of the car. He would pick that up and hit her over the head, rendering her unconscious. He would then handcuff her and put her in the passenger side of the vehicle, from which he had usually removed the seat. He would drive around for hours with the victim in the car, calming her down by talking to her and claiming that she was disoriented because she had been in an accident and he was taking her to a hospital.

When they reached the dump site, Bundy would hit the girl again then strangle her with a ligature (often nylons) while raping her from behind. This would take place either in front of his car headlights or, if it was a moonlit night, out in the open. Nearly always, he returned to the scene of the crime, after getting rid of anything that might connect him to the incident. (Some of his victims in Utah were taken back to his apartment and he re-enacted pictures from the front of detective magazines using their corpses.)

He buried some of his victims, putting the bodies in graves two to three feet deep, and placing rocks on top. He severed the heads from some, disposing of body and head in different locations, and getting rid of the victims' belongings over a very wide area: some items were found hundreds of miles from the torsos. Some of the heads he took back to his apartment for a time to keep as mementos.

Although it seemed as if Elizabeth Kloepfer's phone calls to the police hadn't led anywhere, they had stuck in the mind of Detective

Jerry Thompson. He recognised the name of Ted Bundy when he was arrested in Granger, a suburb of Salt Lake City, by Sergeant Bob Hayward after failing to stop in his tan Volkswagen bug in the early hours of 16 August 1975. Hayward had seen the car parked in front of the house of people he knew were on vacation, although their teenage daughters were home; when the policeman's lights hit the car, Bundy had driven off in a panic. After he finally pulled to a halt in an abandoned gas station, he produced his licence, and claimed that he had been at a screening of *The Towering Inferno* and had stopped outside the house because he had grown drowsy and thought he shouldn't drive further. Hayward's suspicions grew when he saw the front passenger seat had been taken out and placed in the back. Searching the car's glove compartment, he found a ski mask, a mask made from pantyhose, a crowbar, handcuffs, garbage bags, an ice pick and a coil of rope as well as wire and other tools that suggested he might be planning a burglary. Bundy claimed that he had found the handcuffs, and he liked skiing. When faced with the fact that *The Towering Inferno* wasn't playing at any of the local movie theatres, he changed his story and claimed he had been smoking marijuana and had fled because he wanted to get rid of the evidence. He was arrested for attempting to evade police, and, on 21 August, for possession of burglary tools.

A team of detectives in Washington state had been correlating all the information on the various murders that had taken place the previous year but stopped for no apparent reason. Twenty-six names turned up on four separate lists they had drawn up and, separately, the detectives thought Bundy was a good fit. When they learned that he had been arrested, the team were interested in their colleagues' discoveries, including a guide to Colorado ski resorts found at his apartment with a check mark against the site of Caryn Campbell's disappearance, as well as a brochure for the play performed where Debra Kent had been taken. The handcuffs matched those used on

Carol DaRonch; the crowbar likewise was similar to the tool that Carol's attacker had in his possession.

Suspicion wasn't enough to hold Bundy, and he was released on bail by the Salt Lake City police on 22 August, although he was kept under twenty-four-hour surveillance. Elizabeth Kloepfer was interviewed in Seattle on 16 September, and told detectives about odd items that Bundy had, such as a bag of plaster of Paris (used to create plaster casts), surgical gloves, an oriental knife in a wooden case that he kept in his car's glove compartment, and a sack of women's clothing. He had also got upset when she wanted to change her hair style from the one that his victims sported. Most suspicious of all was the lug wrench that he kept in her own Volkswagen, which he claimed was for 'protection' when he borrowed her car. She was unable to provide him with an alibi for the attacks in the Seattle area, or for the day that Janice Ott and Denise Naslund vanished.

Aware that he was under intense scrutiny, Bundy sold his Volkswagen, which was impounded by the police on 15 October and forensically examined by the FBI. Although this took some time, by 29 January 1976 the experts were able to determine that there were hairs from both Caryn Campbell and Melissa Smith in the vehicle. Long before then, Carol DaRonch had identified the car as her attacker's and agreed to take part in a line-up. Before this took place on 2 October, Bundy cut his hair and parted it in a different way from the style he had adopted the previous year, but Carol had no problem in identifying him. He was arrested and charged with aggravated kidnapping and attempted criminal homicide, and freed on bail on 20 November, after his parents paid $15,000. He moved back to Seattle and stayed with Kloepfer for three weeks, but was kept under close surveillance; he returned to Salt Lake City on 13 December, and made a brief court appearance on New Year's Eve.

In November, representatives from three states – Jerry Thompson from Utah, Robert Keppel from Washington and Michael Fisher from Colorado – got together at a Holiday Inn in Aspen, Colorado, with thirty detectives and prosecutors from five different states to pool their information on the murders. There were considerable circumstantial links between Bundy and the murders: Lynda Ann Healy had known Bundy's cousin; he had spent a lot of time around the areas where the bodies had been found; he had purchased fuel in towns where there had been disappearances (the FBI timeline meticulously sets out the date and time of his credit card purchases); and he had been seen wearing a plaster cast when no one knew of any injury that would account for it. But none of this was enough to charge him with murder. Without solid evidence – which they wouldn't have unless the car search proved positive – they could do little more.

Ted Bundy's four-day trial for the kidnapping of Carol DaRonch began on 23 February 1976 in front of Judge Stewart Hanson Jr. Carol was absolutely clear on the witness stand, and after the judge deliberated over the weekend, he found Bundy guilty on 1 March, and remanded him in custody in Salt Lake City for a psychological evaluation. Those carrying it out thought that Bundy was not 'psychotic, neurotic, the victim of organic brain disease, alcoholic, addicted to drugs, suffering from a character disorder or amnesia, and was not a sexual deviate'. On 6 July, he was sentenced to ten to fifteen years in the Utah State Prison; two weeks earlier, he was convicted of evading police.

In October, Bundy was found with an 'escape kit' (consisting of a road map, a fake social security card and airline schedules) in the bushes in the prison yard, for which he spent weeks in solitary confinement. On 21 October, he was charged with the murder of Caryn Campbell: the crowbar found in his car matched the impressions found on her skull.

Just over three months later, on 28 January 1977, Ted Bundy was transferred to Glenwood Springs, and started to prepare his defence

– he knew that certain leeway was given to prisoners who acted for themselves, such as being allowed not to wear handcuffs and leg shackles during court appearances. On 7 June, he made one such appearance at Pitkin County Courthouse, and asked if he could use the law library during a recess. Permission was granted, and Bundy concealed himself behind a bookcase while a guard waited outside the room (city employee Melinda Severance was quoted in the *Salt Lake Tribune* on 9 June as saying the sheriff's department was 'patently naïve, bordering on criminally stupid, to leave Bundy in the courtroom alone'). Unwatched, he then opened a window and jumped down thirty feet. He sprained his ankle landing, but still managed to evade roadblocks around Aspen, heading onto the mountain. Five miles from the town centre, he broke into a mountain cabin and stole a rifle, as well as food and clothing. He stayed on the run for six days, eventually stealing a car, with some citizens of Aspen – who knew nothing of his murderous ways – almost seeing him as 'some sort of modern Robin Hood'. One local restaurant even offered a 'Bundyburger' – it was a plain roll. 'Open it and see the meat has fled' the sign in the restaurant said. However, with his injured ankle Bundy couldn't drive properly and was picked up, adding charges of escape, burglary and felony theft to his charge sheet. ('I didn't want to go back to jail. It was just too pretty outside,' Bundy told Sergeant Don Davis after he was picked up.)

Bundy spent the next few months in a metal-plated maximum security cell at Glenwood Springs as he continued to fight his case. During pretrial proceedings, the state was not permitted to introduce evidence from Carol DaRonch's case against him as they didn't bear the same 'signature'. Bundy himself claimed he was being kept under inhumane circumstances, with his food so poor that he had lost thirty pounds in weight.

In fact, that weight loss had nothing to do with poor conditions and everything to do with Ted Bundy's desire to escape. On New

Year's Eve – a few days after the trial was transferred to Colorado Springs – he managed to slip through a one-square-foot ceiling panel into the crawl space, thanks to what the El Paso District Attorney Robert Russell described as 'absolute negligence' on the part of the jailers. He then hid in the closet of a jailer's apartment until he knew he could simply walk out. He had been practising getting up into the crawl space for a number of nights, with some prisoners reporting hearing him moving around to guards – who ignored their complaints.

His escape wasn't discovered for fifteen hours. He stole an old MG, which broke down, then hitched a lift to Vail, Colorado, and from there took a bus to Denver, followed by a plane to Chicago, and then a train to Ann Arbor, Michigan. He stole a car there on 3 January 1978 and drove to Atlanta, Georgia, from where he got the bus to Tallahassee, Florida. 'Chris Hagen' had arrived in his new killing ground.

Bundy rented a room under his new alias on 8 January. Four days later, he tried to steal keys for a van from the neighbouring Florida State University campus, but was unsuccessful. On 13 January, he managed to steal another van, and on the night of 14 January, he was seen near the Chi Omega Sorority House. He went drinking at Sharrod's bar, in Tallahassee, leaving there around 2 a.m. before returning to the sorority house around half an hour later.

Around 3.17 a.m., Nita Neary was dropped off at Chi Omega, and was suspicious that the door was open. She heard noises upstairs and then footsteps coming towards the staircase. She hid from view, and a man in a blue knit cap, carrying some sort of log with cloth round it, ran past.

Bundy had got into the house through a rear door with a broken lock. He first attacked twenty-one-year-old Margaret Bowman with a piece of firewood, then strangled her with a nylon stocking. She was not sexually assaulted before or after death. He then went into twenty-year-old Lisa Levy's bedroom, beat her unconscious, strangled her, raped her, bit one of her nipples so hard that it was nearly severed from her chest, bit deeply into her left buttock (in a frenzy, he would later admit) and then assaulted her vagina with a hair-mist bottle. Leaving Lisa, he went into the bedroom of Kathy Kleiner and Karen Chandler: Kathy's jaw was broken and her shoulder lacerated; Karen received a concussion, a broken jaw and a crushed finger.

Police were called at 3.23 a.m. An hour and a quarter later, Bundy went on the attack again, entering the house of Cheryl Thomas, a mere eight blocks away from the sorority house. He dislocated her shoulder, fractured her jaw and broke her skull in five places. On the bed were semen stains and a 'mask' of pantyhose very like the one that had been found when Bundy was arrested, which contained some hairs.

On 8 February, he tried to take a new victim. He had stolen another van from Florida State University, and bought a hunting knife. In Jacksonville, 150 miles east of Tallahassee, around 1.30 p.m. he approached fourteen-year-old Leslie Parmenter – who happened to be the daughter of the local police department's chief of detectives – and claimed to be 'Richard Burton' of the Fire Department. However, when Leslie's older brother came along in his car, Bundy beat a hasty retreat – but the siblings were able to identify both him and the van when their father showed them a picture of the fugitive.

Bundy drove sixty or so miles to Lake City, where he was spotted by a crossing guard as children were heading to school the next day. Around 8.45 a.m. twelve-year-old Kimberly Diane Leach was called to the homeroom to pick up a purse she had left behind; she never returned to her class. Around 8.55, paramedics driving by Lake City Junior High School saw a man leading a young girl by the arm. They were the last, bar her killer, to see Kimberly alive. Her body was found on 7 April, twelve miles from her school, in a state park in Suwannee County, Florida; it was so severely decomposed that forensic experts were unable to achieve much.

By this point, though, Ted Bundy was back in custody. Early on the morning of 14 February, he was driving through West Pensacola in an orange Volkswagen bug that he had stolen in Tallahassee a couple of days earlier. Officer David Lee ran a check on the car and found it had stolen plates; he pursued Bundy when he tried to flee, but then Bundy stopped. Lee told him to get out of the car and to lie down with his hands in front; Bundy kicked his legs out from under him and tried to run. Lee fired a warning shot, which Bundy ignored; he fired again, then ran after the fugitive, tackling him. There was a scuffle before Lee finally got Bundy into handcuffs. He was arrested, and inside the stolen car were three sets of IDs belonging to students, twenty-one stolen credit cards and a stolen TV – as well as the disguise that he had worn in Jacksonville when trying to kidnap Leslie Parmenter. The shirt he was wearing had tears on the sleeve. 'I wish you had killed me,' Bundy muttered as he was taken to jail. Lee had no idea that he had caught one of the FBI's 'Ten Most Wanted Fugitives': Bundy had achieved that distinction just four days earlier.

He was formally identified on 16 February 1978, and kept under close supervision until he could be brought to trial. Florida detectives worked on multiple leads to tie him to the murders in their state, despite his many protestations of innocence. 'Outside of a few minor thefts I have done nothing wrong,' he was quoted as saying in a *New York Times* report on 14 March, which highlighted the fact that 'Police Lack Decisive Evidence'. The van that he had been driving when he kidnapped Kimberly Leach was found and examined: fibres that matched the clothes he was wearing when he was arrested matched those within the vehicle, and there were eyewitnesses who could place him in the van. There were bloodstains on the van carpet which matched Kimberly, as well as semen and Bundy's blood on her underwear. Shoeprints found near her body matched Bundy's; samples of leaves and dirt taken from the fan pointed to the location.

He was charged with Kimberly Leach's murder on 31 July 1978; not long after, prosecutors added the Chi Omega murders to the charge sheet – on 27 April, impressions had been taken of his teeth. 'They line up perfectly, exactly,' dental surgeon Dr Richard R. Souviron explained at a seminar of forensic pathologists in late 1978. 'It is convincing beyond any discussion whatsoever. I'm not saying that this set of teeth killed anybody. I'm seeing that these teeth made those marks [on Lisa Levy's body].'

The trial in the Chi Omega case came up first. Bundy did his best to slow down proceedings by filing various motions, but eventually his trial for the murders and assaults began on 25 June 1979, with Bundy determined to be centre stage. His attorney Polly Nelson later considered that he 'sabotaged the entire defence effort out of spite, distrust and grandiose delusion' because he had to be in charge. He nearly agreed to a deal, where he would agree to killing Lisa Levy, Margaret Bowman and Kimberly Leach in exchange for a seventy-five-year prison sentence. This would mean he avoided the death penalty, and there was a chance that he could finagle a way to move for an acquittal down the line once enough time had elapsed. However, in the end he refused – with at least one member of his defence team considering that it was because he was not willing to admit what he had done.

Time magazine described Bundy as 'handsome, articulate and composed' in court – something the American public could judge for themselves as the trial was one of the first to be televised live. He did his best to get Nita Neary's evidence disallowed from being heard by the jury, and during three and a half hours of cross-examination, she agreed that she had been drinking before she saw him at the sorority house. However, both her testimony and that of her fellow Chi Omega member Connie Hastings, who had seen Bundy hanging around the sorority house on the evening of the murders, were allowed. The evidence from Dr Souviron and his colleague Lowell Levine regarding the bite marks was also damaging. It took the jury less than seven hours to find Bundy guilty of two murders, three attempted first-degree murders and two counts of burglary. Judge Edward Cowart sentenced him to death on 30 July, a week later.

The same sentence was imposed on 10 February 1980 for the abduction and murder of Kimberly Leach. The testimony of the paramedics and the matching fibres were key in obtaining the conviction, alongside the sixty-five witnesses that Assistant State Attorney Bob Dekle was able to call to confirm Bundy's movements. This time Bundy didn't represent himself; his attorneys tried a defence of not guilty by reason of insanity. The jury members weren't swayed.

During the sentencing trial, Bundy asked defence witness Carole Ann Boone – whom he had known for many years – to marry him. Under an obscure Florida law, their verbal promises under oath were binding. Although conjugal visits were not allowed at Raiford Prison where he was held, somehow Bundy and Boone managed to gain some time alone; in October 1982, she gave birth to a daughter, whom she said was Bundy's. For a long time, Carole believed in his innocence. However, when he finally admitted his guilt to investigators, she returned to Washington and wouldn't take his last pre-execution phone call.

There was a long period of appeals before the sentence was carried out, and Bundy gave many conflicting interviews about what he had done. He tried to escape: hacksaw blades were found in his cell in July 1984. He was attacked and possibly gang-raped by other inmates. He also acted as a 'consultant' on serial killers to Robert Keppel with regard to the Green River Killer (see Chapter 28).

The final chance for a stay of execution was the Supreme Court, which denied it on 17 January 1989. In the week before he was executed, Bundy confessed to yet more killings, leading to Robert Keppel and others suggesting that he might well have killed a hundred or more women. He talked of committing suicide to cheat the state of the satisfaction of killing him, but at 7.16 a.m. on 24 January 1989, 2,000 volts of electricity were passed through Ted Bundy at Raiford Prison for the murder of Kimberly Leach. Fireworks were let off when the announcement of the death of the man once described as 'the most competent serial killer in the country, a diabolical genius' was made.

Ted Bundy's Volkswagen bug – or at least the one that he used primarily and in which he was arrested – was on display for years at the National Museum of Crime and Punishment in Washington, DC. After the museum's closure in 2015, the car was moved to the Alcatraz East Crime Museum in Pigeon Forge, Tennessee, to be displayed alongside O. J. Simpson's white Ford Bronco and the former Tennessee electric chair, giving Bundy yet more of the notoriety in death that he revelled in during his near-decade on death row.

CHAPTER 25

United States: Dennis Rader

'If it was a cover, he was extremely good at what he was doing. It's like he had a double personality.' That was the verdict of Kevin Smith, a member of the congregation at the Christ Lutheran Church in Wichita, Kansas, after it was revealed that one of their own was in reality the BTK ('Bind, Torture, Kill') Killer. There is a great deal of literature about serial killers, with many *romans-à-clef* about their deeds. In the case of Dennis Rader – who at his own suggestion became known as the BTK Killer – he was the inspiration for the villain Francis Dolarhyde in Thomas Harris's first book about Dr Hannibal Lecter, *Red Dragon*, while characters in Stephen King's novella (and later movie) *A Good Marriage* echoed elements of the case, particularly in the way that Rader was able to keep his double life so well hidden from his family. Rader was an unusual murderer: unlike most serial killers per the FBI profile, he was able to go for long periods without killing, and although he was arrested in 2005, the most recent crime that could be tied to him took place fourteen years earlier – and it was only because of a thirtieth-anniversary newspaper story of his first crime that he resurfaced.

Dennis Lynn Rader was born in Pittsburg, Kansas, on 9 March 1945, but grew up in the Wichita area, the oldest of four sons born to William Elvin Rader and his wife Dorothea Mae. According to various reports, including a letter he sent to the police, Rader did fit some of the classic profile of a serial killer – he had an interest in killing animals as a youngster, and was responsible for hanging stray cats. 'I strangled dogs and cats,' Rader recalled in his confession. He also had a penchant for hanging himself – aged around eighteen, he used to take photos of himself in his parents' basement, dressed in women's underwear that he had stolen and with a rope tied around his neck. He secretly looked at what he called 'Girly Books' from where he learned about 'S/M & B/D' (sado-masochism, and bondage & domination), and started to fantasise about women in bondage. As the prosecutor would note at his trial, 'All of these incidents, these ten counts, occurred because you wanted to satisfy sexual fantasies.' When he was arrested, police found many such photos alongside the shots of his victims.

He graduated from Heights High School in 1963, and in June 1966 he joined the United States Air Force, and served until August 1970 in Texas, Alabama, Turkey, Greece, South Korea, Okinawa and Tokyo. During that time he admitted that he drew pictures of his fantasies but 'always had to destroy them when I moved from base to base. Would start over again when the feeling starting coming back.' When he was discharged from the USAF, he moved to Park City, Kansas, where he worked in the meat department of the IGA supermarket, alongside his mother, who was a bookkeeper at the store. He started to attend Butler County Community College in El Dorado, graduating from there with an associate degree in electronics in 1973; after that he enrolled at Wichita State University, gaining a bachelor's degree in administration of justice in 1979. By that time he had been married for eight years – he wed Paula Dietz on 22 May 1971. When he graduated, he was also a serial killer, with seven of his acknowledged victims murdered between January 1974 and December 1977.

Rader made various admissions to his crimes – to the police and other authorities after his arrest; in letters that he sent, taunting the police; and then in court. While much of the truth, or otherwise, of his statements can be verified with forensic evidence, his conversations with his victims cannot, and have to be viewed through the prism of a man who was desperately seeking attention, and who survived undiscovered for three decades because of his proficiency at lying.

Thirty-eight-year-old Joseph Otero, his thirty-three-year-old wife Julie and two of their five children – Joseph Jr (aged nine) and Josephine (known as Josie, aged eleven) – were all killed at their home at 803 North Edgemoor Street, Wichita, on the night of 15 January 1974. According to his confession to Ray Lundin, the senior special agent for the Kansas Bureau of Investigation (KBI), Rader found Latina women attractive – 'I guess they just turn me on,' he explained. He had gone to the Puerto Rican Oteros' home, expecting to find just the mother and some of the children there; to his surprise, four family members were present. He crept up to the Oteros' detached garage early that morning and thought through his options. Eventually, at about 8.40 a.m., Joseph Jr. unlocked the door and came out into the yard.

Rader had come prepared, wearing an Air Force parka packed with binding material and weapons. He told the young boy to go back into the house, then held the family at gunpoint, explaining that this was simply a robbery, and if they did as they were told, they would not be harmed. When the dog wouldn't stop barking, Rader ordered Joseph to put the animal outside, which he duly did. Rader told them to go into one of the bedrooms, then proceeded to tie their hands behind their backs. They complained about how tight Rader had tied the bonds, and he gave Joseph Otero Sr, who had a cracked rib from a car accident, a pillow so he could lie down. The older Otero offered Rader his car, and it was at this point, Rader claimed in court, that he decided to 'go ahead and put 'em down'.

He then placed a plastic bag over the head of Joseph Otero and pulled the cords tight. Otero, an airman and former boxer, realised he was in a fight for his life and managed to bite a hole in the bag. As he did so, Rader strangled his wife, and believed he had killed her. He then placed a 'cloth or a T-shirt' over Otero's torn bag, and then put another bag on top of that and tightened it up. He then strangled Josephine until she lost consciousness, and placed a bag over her brother's head.

However, Julie Otero wasn't dead. She regained consciousness to see her son writhing around on the floor, and Rader sitting calmly on a chair watching. She screamed at him to let her son live (and in one version of his story, Rader claimed that he did release Joseph Jr temporarily) but ultimately to no avail. Rader got a rope, and strangled her properly.

Josephine woke up to see the rest of her family dead around her. Rader took her down to the basement and found a sewer pipe that he thought would be strong enough to support the little girl's body. Reassuring her that 'you'll be in heaven tonight with the rest of your family', Rader gagged her and tied her up so that she was hanging by her neck, the tips of her toes just touching the ground. That meant that she was choked to death by the noose. Rader pulled her underwear down, and masturbated while she died. (The traces of semen in the basement would help to convict Rader over three decades later.) After cleaning up the house, cutting the phone line, and pocketing a few items as souvenirs, such as Otero's watch and a radio, he left through the front door and took the Oteros' car over to a Dillons store, where he left it and walked back to his own vehicle.

Rader had a clear idea of what the heaven to which he dispatched Josephine would be like: after he died, all those he killed would serve him in the afterlife. Joseph would be his bodyguard; Julie would bathe him; Joseph Jr would be a 'young sex valet', while his sister was a 'star young maiden'. It's not the vision of heaven that Rader preached when he was president of the Christ Lutheran Church in Park City in the years between the crime and his arrest.

The bodies of the four Oteros were found later that afternoon by the family's other three children, who ran for a neighbour. Police Chief Floyd Hannon said it was 'the most bizarre case I've ever seen,' wondering if there might be a link to something in 'the old country' (Puerto Rico) that had caused it, or a sexual motive. With little evidence to go on – or at least that was usable at the time (prior to the invention of DNA profiling) – the police were unable to make progress.

Rader struck again ten weeks or so later, attacking twenty-one-year-old Kathryn Bright. She was one of his 'PJs', his 'projects', a euphemism for the women he would target and then stalk. Rader was driving through her neighbourhood when he spotted her going into her house, and decided she would make a good potential victim. On 15 April 1974, he dressed in a black stocking cap, camouflage jacket and black gloves, and broke into her house through the back door, waiting for her to come home. He wasn't expecting her to be accompanied by her brother Kevin.

'He told us he was wanted in California and was headed for New York,' Kevin Bright told *Time* magazine in 2005. 'He said all he wanted was money and a car, and he wouldn't hurt us.' It was the same story he had spun to the Oteros, to 'kind of ease them'. Rader forced Kevin to tie his sister to a chair in a back bedroom, then took him to the front and tied him up too. (Rader believed he used materials he found at Kathryn's house – 'if I had brought my stuff and used my stuff, Kevin would probably be dead today,' he told the court in all seriousness.) He pushed Kevin to the floor, but the younger man wasn't going to give in easily. He struggled desperately, but then Rader pulled his handgun and shot him in the head at least twice. Sensibly, Kevin played dead, and when Rader returned to the bedroom to deal with Kathryn, he ran for the door to get help.

Rader wasn't having an easy time with Kathryn either: she too managed to get free from some of her bonds, and fought back 'like a hellcat'. He lost control, and decided he'd had enough of trying to strangle her. He used a knife to stab her 'under the ribs', but then heard a noise from the front as Kevin escaped. Realising that he was in serious danger of being captured, he tried to use some keys to start the Brights' car, but he had the wrong ones. He therefore ran as fast as he could back towards the State University campus where he had parked.

Kathryn crawled to the living room and reached for the phone, and was found holding the receiver when police arrived. She died soon after, but confirmed to police that she had no idea who had done this to her. All Kevin could say was that the killer was an average-size guy, bushy moustache and 'psychotic' eyes. Rader kept a souvenir – the Boy Scout knife that he used to kill Kathryn; it was found in his kitchen pantry when his house was searched.

In October 1974, three people confessed to the murders of the Oteros. None of them was Dennis Rader. 'The three dudes you have in custody are just talking to get publicity for the Otero murders. They know nothing at all. I did it by myself, and with no one's help,' Rader stated in a letter, providing specific details of how the bodies were found – including the location of Josephine's glasses. 'It's hard to control myself. You probably call me "psychotic with sexual perversion hang-up".' He left it in the public library and called a newspaper reporter. It was in this letter that he explained the specific way in which 'the monster' forced him to act. 'The code words for me will be bind them, torture them, kill them. B T K – they will be on the next victim.'

Nothing further happened for nearly three years. Rader continued his PJs, 'trolling' and stalking various women, but, despite saying in his October 1974 letter that he had already chosen his next victim, no one was found. The next woman he killed was twenty-four-year-old Shirley Vian Relford – who wasn't his original target, but that woman, Cheryl Sarkozy, had been out when Rader knocked on her door on the morning of 17 March 1977. (Sarkozy and her roommate Judy Skerl believed that Rader returned the following year, after surprising someone outside their kitchen window late at night.)

Rader used a ruse claiming that he was a private investigator, trying to locate a mother and child; he even had a photo to show people (of his own wife and son, who had been born in 1975). He spotted a young boy, and followed him to his house at 1311 South Hydraulic Street, Wichita. The boy answered the door, and Rader forced his way inside at gunpoint. Rader told the boy's mother that he had 'a problem with sexual fantasies' and that he was going to have to tie her up, and possibly her two children too. He had brought his 'hit kit' with him – rope and duct tape – and he tied the children up first, but they made such a noise that he put the boys in the bathroom with some toys and blankets and tied the door shut. Desperate to placate her attacker, Shirley even helped push the bed against the bathroom door (at least according to Rader) before he tied her up, put a bag over her head and strangled her. The eight-year-old boy who had answered the door managed to escape out of the window for help. His six-year-old brother was able to give police a clear description – but they couldn't be sure of its reliability, given his age. When police checked it three decades later, they found that it was very accurate.

Once Shirley was dead, the phone started to ring, and in a panic Rader made his escape. He later wrote a poem, 'Shirley Locks', about his victim, whom he believed would be his cleaner in the afterlife. Police did wonder if there was a link between Shirley's death and that of the Oteros but there was still insufficient evidence.

Rader's next victim, Nancy Fox, was strangled nine months later, and would prove to be his last for over seven years. He would write a poem about this murder too, entitled 'Oh! Death to Nancy', which he included in his next public letter to the authorities. This was the murder that he was most proud of when he confessed. 'Fox went the way I wanted it,' he said – perhaps justifying things to himself, even though he admitted that Nancy called his sexual bondage fantasies 'ridiculous', and had clawed at his testicles, trying to hurt him.

He did what he described as 'a little homework', checking her mailbox to find out her name, then ascertaining her place of work, and visited her there to 'size her up'. On the night of 8 December 1977, he parked his car about three blocks away from Nancy's home on South Pershing Street, Wichita, and knocked on her front door. As he had anticipated, there was no one in, so he went round the back, cut the phone lines and then broke in to wait for her. Once she arrived home from work at a jewellery store, he 'told her I had a problem, a sexual problem, that I would have to tie her up and have sex with her'. Rader recalled 'she was a little upset' but eventually she agreed to 'get this over with' so she could call the police.

Rader sent her into the bathroom to get undressed, and when she returned to the bedroom, he handcuffed her then strangled her with his belt. He allowed her to regain consciousness, then told her he was BTK, and strangled her again. He then removed the handcuffs and replaced them with pantyhose and then masturbated. 'I was on a high,' Rader recalled. In his delusional state, Rader believed that Nancy would be his primary mistress.

Since Nancy lived alone there was no one likely to report the crime, so Rader did it himself, calling the emergency services at 8.18 a.m. the next day. 'You will find a homicide,' he told the operator, giving Nancy's address and name. He had left the callbox by the time the police arrived.

Two months after that, in February 1978, he sent a package to Wichita TV station KAKE10; it included a letter, a sketch of Nancy and a poem dedicated to her, which featured lines such as 'I'll stuff your jaws till you can't talk, I'll blind [sic] your leg's [sic] till you can't walk', signed BTK. He suggested various names for himself – 'BTK Strangler', 'The Wichita Executioner' – and said he had killed seven people and would strike again. 'How many do I have to kill before I get my name in the paper or some national attention?'

There was great discussion over whether to give BTK the validation but in the end the police decided they would have to warn the public. Police Chief Richard LaMunyon went on local television and admitted, 'We have an individual who apparently has the uncontrollable desire to kill at times . . . Very honestly, we have no solid leads at all.' That broadcast included some subliminal imagery spliced into the videotape and contained words that the behavioural scientists seeking him hoped would be burned into BTK's brain – something that was thought possible at the time. 'NOW CALL THE CHIEF' it read, with a picture of upside-down glasses – matching the sketch that BTK had sent KAKE of Nancy Fox. Panic gripped the city, and one of the companies that benefitted was ADT Security Services. One of their security alarm installers was a mild-mannered gentleman by the name of Dennis Rader, who had started working for ADT in 1974 . . .

Rader continued to target women, and on 28 April 1979, he waited inside a house in South Pinecrest for the owner, sixty-three-year-old Anna Williams, to return home. However, she spent much longer visiting friends than Rader had anticipated, and in the end, he gave up. However, he sent her one of her scarves along with a note. 'Be glad you weren't here,' it read, 'because I was.' However, unlike on previous occasions, he didn't immediately seek out another target. In fact, it was six years before he killed again.

During this time, the police investigations continued. Various tests were tried on the semen samples that Rader had left at the murder scenes, but scientists were only able to narrow down the match to around 15,000 men in Wichita itself – let alone elsewhere in the state. The voice tape was examined in forensic detail but nothing conclusive could be found. In 1983, two teams of detectives came at the evidence with fresh eyes and established 200 prime suspects, 195 of whom voluntarily gave samples; of those seven could not be immediately eliminated from the investigation. The photocopier that BTK used to create the letters he sent was tracked down to the university campus, but it was a public access machine. The poem for Shirley Vian was similar in style and format to one that had just appeared in puzzle magazine *Games*; its subscribers were checked out. But none of these leads brought police to Rader's door.

Rader's next victim was not immediately linked to him by police. He struck much closer to home, and deliberately changed his method of working to throw the investigators off his track. It was, Rader admitted to Sedgwick County sheriff Sergeant Tom Lee, 'his most complicated hit' because of its proximity to his home – although that had made his life much easier in the 'stalking phase'. On the evening of 27 April 1985, he created a fake alibi for himself by getting a taxi back from a local bowling alley, pretending to be a little drunk, and getting the driver to drop him off so he could sober up before he got home. In fact, he went into the home of fifty-three-year-old Marine Hedge and waited for her.

Marine returned home with a male visitor, who left after an hour. Rader waited until the 'wee hours' before putting the lights on and strangling the woman with his bare hands when she started to scream. He then stripped her, put her in a blanket and placed her in the trunk of her car. He then drove to the Christ Lutheran Church – where he was a respected leader of the community and had a key to the basement – and took polaroid photographs of her in various bondage poses. After that, he looked for a place to hide the body; once he had dumped it on East 53rd Street North – a place Rader would later claim was a dumping site for dog carcasses – he covered it in branches. It wasn't found for eight days. Police were unsure whether this was the work of BTK or not.

His next target was also one that wasn't initially connected to him. Twenty-eight-year-old Vicki Wegerle often played the piano at her home on West 13th Street, Wichita, and Rader could hear her on

16 September 1986 when he adopted the disguise of a telephone repairman in order to gain access to her house. Claiming there was something wrong with the phone lines, he entered, then pulled a gun on Vicki, taking her to the back bedroom. Vicki's two-year-old son was there; Rader couldn't decide what he was going to do with the boy. Rader tied up Vicki with leather shoelaces, despite her fighting 'like a hell cat' and scratching him. She begged him to stop, and said a prayer as he throttled her with a nylon sock. Realising that the fight had caused such commotion, Rader left quickly, not realising that he hadn't actually killed Vicki; however, when the paramedics arrived, they were unable to revive her.

At the time the police were unable to do anything with the skin cells found underneath Vicki's fingernails. In 2005, the DNA was matched with that of Dennis Rader. A year earlier, on 19 March 2004, the *Wichita Eagle* received a letter from 'Bill Thomas Killman' who claimed responsibility for Vicki's murder and enclosed a photocopy of her driver's licence and three photographs of her body. It was the first real clue that the investigators had as to the killer's identity.

During the mid-1980s, according to then-Lieutenant Al Stewart, 'We tried a hundred thousand theories. We checked house numbers, the victims' length of residency, the phases of the moon, we read books, looking for arcane connections to mythology, witchcraft and demonology.' None of it gave them any hint as to BTK's identity. On 3 October 1987, fifteen-year-old Shannon Olson's body was found, tied and dumped in a pond in a manner suggestive of BTK's methods.

On New Year's Eve the same year, Mary Fager came back to her home in Wichita to find her husband and her two daughters, aged sixteen and ten, dead. Phillip had been shot; the girls were in the hot tub. They had been strangled. The older girl, Kelli, was nude; Sherri's hands and feet were bound with electrical tape. As far as Mary Fager was concerned, at least, Rader was not responsible. As BTK, he wrote to Mary Fager, saying that he had not committed the crimes, but he was a fan of the person who had. At the time, the police and FBI were confident that the letter was genuine. (A local contractor was arrested and tried for the murders, but was acquitted; however, the police did not consider there were any other suspects.)

Rader's last known victim was sixty-two-year-old Dolores 'Dee' E. Davis, who was strangled by BTK on 19 January 1991. Even as he prepared to hurl a concrete block through Dolores's plate-glass window, he had reservations about proceeding, but went ahead anyway. Dolores was woken by the crash, believing a car had hit her house. Rader claimed he was a fugitive on the run, who just needed 'food, car, warmth'. He handcuffed her, calmed her down, then pretended to get some food together and leave, before coming back, removing her handcuffs, tying her up and strangling her with her own pantyhose. As with Marine Hedge, he bundled the body in a blanket and put it in the trunk of her own car. She was then dumped underneath a bridge.

This wasn't the only similarity between the two murders. Rader had become involved with the Cub Scout movement, and had used a camp-out as an alibi for his murder of Marine Hedge in 1985. Six years later, he was meant to be helping set up a camp at Harvey County Park West, and used the Baptist church where the scouts met – and to which he had a key – to make his preparations. He felt safe.

In many ways, he was justified in feeling that way, but he didn't commit any further crimes. Rader's 'real' life was busy: he stopped working for ADT in 1988, and took a job as a census field operations officer the following year. After that he worked as a dogcatcher and compliance officer for Park City, as well as acting as president of the church council at the Christ Lutheran Church. BTK made no further contact with the police.

Until March 2004. The thirtieth anniversary of the Oteros' murder was marked with a large number of articles in the local and even national press, and it seems that Rader's desire for attention finally got the better of him. Over the next few months he sent eleven separate communications, which finally led to his arrest. The first, sent 19 March, detailed Vicki Wegerle's death. With the FBI and police's advisors concerned that BTK might 'do something diabolical' if he didn't get the attention he craved, the letter received publicity far and wide. It also meant that the DNA sample taken from Vicki's fingernail could be used as the basis for further investigation.

Rader's follow-up, sent on 5 May to KAKE-TV, also made the papers (even if the police kept back various details). This was a three-page letter, which altered some of the contents of a true crime reconstruction of his acts to reflect his views, as well as word puzzles and other taunts to the police (the puzzle included the words 'prowl' 'fantasies' and the name 'Rader'). On 17 June, a letter that included details of the Otero killings was found at Wichita Public Library. Another letter was left in a UPS drop box on 22 October – the thirtieth anniversary of BTK's first communication. On 30 November, the police released some of the information from these letters, which purported to chronicle BTK's life – much of which was pure fiction.

In mid-December, a bag, which contained Nancy Fox's driving licence among many other items supplied by BTK, including a Barbie doll known as PJ with a bag over its head, its hands tied behind its back and the feet bound by pantyhose, was found in Murdock Park. The next month, a package was left on a dirt road; it included various items of jewellery that BTK had taken, as well as a computer disk – Rader even mailed postcards to KAKE-TV telling them where to look, and thanking them for their help.

All of these communications helped the police track down Rader. The computer disk had a deleted document on it whose metadata had been altered and saved by 'Dennis' at the Christ Lutheran Church. His van was spotted on security tapes around the areas where the packages were left. And finally, a DNA sample from his daughter Kerri was obtained without her knowledge from a pap smear specimen she had given five years earlier. It provided the final pieces of evidence.

Dennis Rader was arrested on 25 February 2005 while driving near his home in Park City. His home, vehicles and offices were searched, and the next day, Wichita Police Chief Norman Williams could announce, 'The bottom line: BTK is arrested.' After preliminary hearings, Rader pleaded guilty to ten charges and made a detailed and self-serving admission to the court. He was sentenced to ten consecutive life sentences, with parole available in 2180.

CHAPTER 26

United States: David Berkowitz – Son of Sam

....

Hello from the gutters of N.Y.C. which are filled with dog manure, vomit, stale wine, urine and blood. Hello from the sewers of N.Y.C. which swallow up these delicacies when they are washed away by the sweeper trucks. Hello from the cracks in the sidewalks of N.Y.C. and from the ants that dwell in these cracks and feed in the dried blood of the dead that has settled into the cracks.

Thus began one of the letters sent to *New York Daily News* columnist Jimmy Breslin by the 'Son of Sam', aka David Berkowitz, whose actions kept New York's citizens virtually paralysed for thirteen months, ending in the hot summer of 1977. 'I'm scared,' one Queens girl told *Time* magazine in July that year. 'I used to kiss my boyfriend in front of the house. Now I run in.' Now, apparently having undergone a religious conversion in 1987, Berkowitz remains behind bars, calling himself the 'Son of Hope'. 'Looking back it was all a horrible nightmare and I would do anything if I could undo everything that happened,' he claims on his website. 'Six people lost their lives. Many others suffered at my hand, and will continue to suffer for a lifetime. I am so sorry for that.'

Born Richard David Falco on 1 June 1953, he was put up for adoption by his birth mother, Betty Broder Falco, within a few days of his birth, and adopted by Jewish couple Nathan and Pearl Berkowitz, who reversed his first names and gave him their surname. Young David was told from an early age that he was adopted, and that his mother had died giving birth to him. He was a spoiled child, who might have adored his adopted mother but would frequently hurl abuse at her (because he was adopted, one neighbour said), the worst of which was that he hoped she would die – on the day that she went out to dinner and collapsed from the advanced breast cancer from which she was suffering. She died when he was fourteen, and he felt that he lost everything, never becoming close to his father. This was exacerbated a few years later when his father remarried and retired to Florida.

Berkowitz wasn't a popular teenager – he attended Christopher Columbus High School in the Bronx, and was teased about his weight. He spent some time with the New York City police auxiliary service, where he learned about traffic direction, first aid and rescue-related duties. (On the day of one of his crimes, he helped a couple in distress before going off to shoot two innocent people.) He joined the US Army in 1971, and although he originally failed his rifle-shooting test, went on to become a sharpshooter (the grade between marksman and expert) with the M16 rifle. However, his behaviour started to become abnormal and he was discharged in 1974, spending a short time at Bronx Community College before starting work as a security guard at a warehouse on the docks.

Around this time, he decided to find out something about his birth mother, and was amazed when a group of fellow adoptees told him that many adopting parents claimed the birth mother was dead, in an effort to get the child to bond with them. Berkowitz asked his father for the truth, and learned that his mother was alive – although when he met up with her, he was disappointed that she was 'a frightened and nervous little woman'. He also learned the truth behind his adoption: his mother was having an affair with a married man and he was the unexpected by-product. 'Here I was, never wanting to be born in the first place, miserable, maladjusted, plagued with death fantasies, only to find out that I was unwanted – an accident after all,' he would later write. He maintained some contact with his natural half-sister and her two daughters, but broke off this when the darkness that he had always felt within him threatened their safety. He was, he claimed, getting a very powerful urge to kill his natural family.

Back in New York, Berkowitz met some 'interesting people' at a party – interesting because they were part of a Satanic cult. He went to their meetings in Untermeyer Park, Yonkers, freely offering his life to Lucifer. He claimed that this group were into child pornography and animal sacrifice, all of which appealed to the darkness within him. It would not be long before he started attacking women. 'I lost my ability to love, to have compassion,' Berkowitz said in 1997. 'I became an animal.'

The first assault to which he admitted took place on Christmas Eve 1975, when he attacked two women with a hunting knife. One of these has not been identified, but the other, fourteen-year-old Michelle Forman, was hospitalised with knife wounds; she struggled, fought back, causing Berkowitz to cut himself, and escaped.

That spring, Berkowitz began to obsess about howling dogs that he said were keeping him awake during the day when he was trying to sleep – he often worked night shifts – so he changed jobs, initially becoming a taxi driver and then a postal worker, and found a new apartment. Unfortunately, his new neighbours also had dogs so he would head to the beach to sleep and take long walks to think – and during the course of one such walk, he decided that he must 'slay a woman for revenge purposes for all the suffering, the mental suffering, they had caused me'. He visited his father and stepmother in Florida, where he was seen bashing his head with his hands, and saying no one could help him because it was 'too late'. He visited an old Army comrade in Houston, Texas, where he bought a .44 calibre

Bulldog revolver, supposedly for protection on the long drive back from Houston to New York. He had another use in mind for it.

On 29 July 1976, nineteen-year-old Jody Valenti and her friend, medical technician Donna Lauria, aged eighteen, were sitting in Jody's car outside Donna's apartment on Buhre Avenue in the Bronx, after spending an evening at a disco. Berkowitz drove past them in his 1970 yellow Ford Galaxie, then parked two blocks away. He walked back, his gun inside a brown paper bag. He circled the car – 'like an animal stalking its prey,' he later told psychiatrist David Abrahamsen – and was spotted by Jody. As her friend turned to see what she was looking at, Berkowitz pulled the gun out then crouched down, bracing an elbow on his knee, aimed and fired three times. Jody hit the car horn screaming that her friend had been shot, and Donna's father Michael came out of the apartment to find his daughter dead, killed instantly by the bullet to her head. Jody had been hit in the thigh; the third bullet missed both girls. Berkowitz drove off, singing to himself; he felt more at peace. He hadn't had a physical orgasm, but would later say he had a mental one. Until he saw the headline 'Bronx Girl Slain in Car' in the *New York Post*, he wasn't even sure whether either girl was dead. Jody was able to provide police with a description of the killer, but unable to suggest any reason why she and her friend were attacked.

Berkowitz's next victims were Carl Denaro and Rosemary Keenan, on 23 October. The two were sitting in Carl's car when bullets shattered the windows. Not sure what had happened – 'I felt the car exploded [*sic*],' Carl later told NBC – the long-haired Carl (who police later thought Berkowitz had mistaken for a girl) started the engine and sped off, not realising that he was bleeding from a bullet wound in his head. He would need a metal plate to replace part of his skull. Rosemary was luckier, only receiving injuries from the broken glass. The eighteen-year-old girl's father was a veteran New York cop, so the case received more police time than it might otherwise have done, but to no avail. There was no apparent motive, once again, for the attack, and because it took place in a different area, it wasn't tied to Donna Lauria's death. Although the bullets were identifiable as .44 calibre, they were too damaged to be any further evidential help.

Just over a month later, on 27 November 1976, Berkowitz struck again. This time, his victims weren't in a car, but sitting on the porch of eighteen-year-old Joanne Lomino's home in Bellerose, Queens, chatting after going to the movies. A man in military fatigues came up to Joanne and sixteen-year-old Donna DeMasi and started to ask directions – then broke off, pulled a gun on them, and fired at each girl in turn. As they slumped to the ground, he shot several more times, then ran away. While Donna had been hit in the neck, Joanne's injuries were to her back and she was paralysed from the waist down. Both girls survived.

The opposite sides of Berkowitz's personality were on display on the night of 29–30 January 1977. In the evening, he helped some teenagers get their car out of a snowbank. But at 12.30 a.m. later that night, he chalked up his next victims. Three bullets were fired through the window of the passenger side of John Diel's car as it was parked in front of 1 Station Square, opposite the Forest Hills Inn at the Long Island Rail Road station. Twenty-six year old Wall Street secretary Christine Freund was struck in the head above the ear and in the right shoulder. She died about four hours later at St John's Hospital in Elmhurst. According to John, they had been to see the movie *Rocky* and were waiting for the car's engine to warm up before heading home. Nobody initially replied to John's call for help after the shooting, so he drove to a nearby intersection and blocked the traffic.

It was the first time that the police wondered if there was a connection with previous unexplained attacks. 'We are checking into the possibility that cases with similar circumstances may have occurred in this borough and other boroughs over the past year or so,' Queens District Attorney John J. Santucci told the *New York Times*, 'and whether there are any connections between those possibly similar cases and this one.' The next day, NYPD Sergeant Richard Conlon said the police were 'leaning towards a connection' but that they believed they were looking for 'suspects' – plural – but forensics expert George Simmonds told homicide detective Joe Coffey that they were looking for a 'psycho': the bullets extracted from the Freund murder matched three other shootings.

Another five weeks went by before Berkowitz's impulses led him to commit another murder, just half a block away from his previous crime. Local residents had tried to raise funds to hire security guards to patrol the area after Christine Freund's murder, but they had only been able to amass half of what they needed. The new victim, nineteen-year-old college student Virginia Voskerichian, was killed between 7.30 and 7.45 p.m. on 8 March 1977, as she walked from the Continental Avenue subway station. Initially, police believed she might have been the victim of a robbery gone wrong, although she still had her books and her purse. It transpired that Berkowitz had approached her, and the girl had desperately lifted her books to try to shield herself from her attacker; he had simply fired through the books, killing her. Her body was found lying face down in some shrubbery near the sidewalk in front of 4 Dartmouth Street by policemen responding to a report by a taxi driver that someone had been mugged in the area. New York City Mayor Abe Beame held a press conference alongside the NYPD, and announced that the bullets matched those from Berkowitz's first murder. Berkowitz gained the nickname 'The .44-Cal Killer'.

It was around this time that Berkowitz's irritation with his neighbour and his howling dogs started to crescendo. In early April, he wrote an anonymous letter to Sam Carr, the sixty-four-year-old owner of black Labrador retriever Harvey, saying that he and his wife were finding their lives 'torn apart because of this dog' and they were unable to lead any sort of normal life, 'to sleep late, to make love, to read etc. but the barking and the howling continue and we get no peace'. Carr ignored him.

Police patrols were increased in the areas where Berkowitz had previously killed; however, in the early hours of 17 April 1977, he simply waited until the patrol car had gone by before approaching his next two victims. Twenty-year-old Alexander Esau and eighteen-year-old Valentina Suriani were sitting in a car belonging to Esau's brother on a service road about a block from Valentina's home when Berkowitz fired four shots into their vehicle. Valentina was killed instantly; Alexander was hit twice, once in the head, and was taken to Jacobi Hospital, where he later died. 'There did not seem to be a sensible motivation for these shootings,' John Keenan, Chief of Detectives at the 43rd Precinct, told a press conference the next day. 'It seems to be the work of a psychologically disturbed person.'

There was something different about this killing though: Berkowitz had left a letter near the bodies of the pair, addressed to NYPD Captain Joseph Borrelli. 'I am deeply hurt by your calling me a wemon hater. I am not. But I am a monster. I am the "Son of Sam." I am a little "brat",' it began, mostly written in capitals with numerous misspellings. It was the first time that the Son of Sam name had been mentioned. Elsewhere in the letter he called himself ' "Beelzebub" – the "Chubby Behemouth" '. The letter explained that 'father Sam' commanded him to 'go out and kill'. He warned police, 'to stop me you must kill me. Attention all police: Shoot me first – shoot to kill or else.' And it ended on an ominous note: 'for now I say goodbye and goodnight. Police – Let me haunt you with these words; I'll be back! I'll be back! To be interrpreted as – bang, bang, bang, bank, bang — ugh!! Yours in murder Mr. Monster.' This was described by the *Daily News* as the '1st Solid Clue'.

A task force was set up to coordinate the search for the Son of Sam, and a psychological profile was released on 26 May 1977, based on the letter. Berkowitz was believed to be 'a neurotic, schizophrenic and paranoid, with religious aspects to his thinking process, as well as hintings [*sic*] of demonic possessions and compulsion. He is probably shy and odd, a loner inept at establishing personal relationships, especially with young women.' Every possible lead was investigated – did he hate dark-haired nurses because of something that had happened to his father? Did his modus operandi match that seen on an episode of popular cop drama *Starsky & Hutch*? According to one report, more than 5,000 names were passed on to police for checking – including women naming their husbands and ex-boyfriends. Over the next four months, over 1,500 of these were taken to the next level of investigation, with twelve suspects put under surveillance, over half of which were present or former cops and one was a former FBI agent.

Not long after Valentina Suriani's murder, Berkowitz wrote another letter, this time to Sam Carr, claiming that his life was 'destroyed' and he had nothing to lose. 'I can see that there shall be no peace in my life or my family's life until I end yours. You wicked, evil man – child of the devil – I curse you and your family forever,' he concluded. A week later, Sam Carr's dog Harvey was shot and wounded.

The *Daily News* was at the forefront of the coverage, not missing a chance to whip up fervour. A second letter from the 'Son of Sam' turned up four days after the psychological profile was released, but this time it was sent to *Daily News* columnist Jimmy Breslin. It had been mailed from Englewood, New Jersey, and written on the back of the envelope in four neat lines was: 'Blood and Family – Darkness and Death – Absolute Depravity – .44'. Like the letter to the police, it was written nearly entirely in capitals and misspelled, and noted, 'I am still here. Like a spirit roaming the night. Thirsty, hungry, seldom stopping to rest; anxious to please Som. I love my work. Now, the void has been filled.' He provided what he said were helpful pieces of information for the detectives (whom he encouraged 'to remain . . . I wish them the best of luck'): 'The Duke of Death', 'The Wicked King Wicker', 'The Twenty Two Disciples of Hell', 'John "Wheaties" – Rapist and Suffocator of Young Girls.' Most worryingly, he wrote: 'Tell me, Jim, what will you have for July Twenty-Ninth?' which was the first anniversary of his original killing. Beneath the signature was a small diagram, which Breslin described as 'an X-shaped mark with the biological symbols for male and female, and also a cross and the letter S'.

The paper printed most of the letter on 5 June, under the headline: 'Breslin to .44 Killer: Give Up! It's Only Way Out'. The police reaction was that the Son of Sam 'is taunting us', as they coped with the huge influx of tips based on the material in the newspaper – which had sold over 1.1 million copies of that day's edition. None of them panned out.

On 26 June, Berkowitz notched up two more victims, although both twenty-year-old Sal Lupo and seventeen-year-old Judy Placido survived with just minor injuries. They were shot at as they sat in a car under a large oak tree on 211th Street south of 45th Road – just three blocks from the 11th Precinct stationhouse – after coming out from the Elephas disco. Police thought Berkowitz might have heard the pair talking at the disco and followed them.

Berkowitz didn't strike on the anniversary of Donna Lauria's murder, a date, the *New York Times* commented, 'that was marked by increased patrols, wide publicity and spreading public fears'. Instead, he waited until 31 July, when he shot and critically wounded a young couple as they sat in a car parked under a street light at Shore Parkway and Bay 14th Street on the Brooklyn waterfront, about a mile south of the Verrazano–Narrows Bridge. It was Berkowitz's first crime in Brooklyn and, for once, it was witnessed.

At least two people saw him come out from the shadows of nearby Dyker Beach Park, and walk up behind the car in which clothing-store salesman Robert Violante and secretary Stacy Moskowitz, both aged twenty, were sitting at about 2.50 a.m. According to the witnesses, one of whom – nineteen-year-old Tommy Zaino – saw it all in the rear-view mirror of his car, the Son of Sam crouched, aimed with both hands and fired four shots through the open window on the passenger side. Robert was hit once in the head, Stacy twice. Robert hit the car horn to get help as Berkowitz calmly walked away. The bullet that had hit Robert passed through his head, destroying his left eye and damaging his right; one of the bullets that hit Stacy Moskowitz lodged in her neck, and confirmed the police's suspicions that the Son of Sam was involved. Stacy died after thirty-nine hours.

Multiple witnesses reported seeing a yellow car, most describing it as a Volkswagen Beetle. Roadblocks were set up within an hour of the shooting and the mayor ordered an extra hundred policemen added to the case, as well as the rehiring of 136 who had been laid off. Detective John Falotico was ordered to report to the 60th Precinct station house in Coney Island and given two weeks to work on the case before it would be handed to the Son of Sam task force. It didn't take that long.

Berkowitz wasn't just sending poison pen letters to Sam Carr; the young man who lived in the apartment beneath him was another recipient. Male nurse Craig Glassman received four, which accused him of being a 'demon' and a 'wicked person' who was forcing the writer to kill. 'Sure, I am the killer, but Craig, the killings are at your command,' read one. Two of the letters were received on 6 August; the same day Glassman discovered a fire burning outside his apartment door – and firemen found .22 calibre shells in the ashes.

This brought police attention onto Berkowitz, albeit for the wrong reason. Yonkers police investigated the fire and heard about the letters, correlating them with the ones that Sam Carr had received. These tied in with some of the details in the Son of Sam letters, and the Yonkers detectives began to wonder if the sender just might be the serial killer the whole of the police department was hunting.

Four days after Robert Violante and Stacy Moskowitz were shot, local resident Cacilia Davis came forward. The middle-aged woman was terrified by what she believed she had seen that night. She said she had been out walking her dog, Snowball, near her apartment at 2.30 a.m., the night of the murder. A young man who, she said, 'walked strange, like a cat' approached her on the sidewalk, looked directly at her then passed by. She thought he was holding his right arm down stiffly, as if he had something up his sleeve. Five minutes later, she heard the shots and the car horn. She also remembered a critical fact: a cop had tagged a cream-coloured car parked illegally by a fire hydrant, one block from where the pair were killed.

Patrol officer Michael Cataneo's records were checked, and indeed there was a ticket issued to David Berkowitz, a resident of Yonkers. What was he doing in Brooklyn at 2.30 a.m.? Could he be another critical witness or, indeed, something more? NYPD detective James Justis contacted the Yonkers police and asked them to schedule an interview with Berkowitz; in return, the Yonkers detectives shared their suspicions. (Berkowitz had paid the ticket by mail in the meantime – after all, as he pointed out to his interrogators a few days later, he was a law-abiding citizen.)

The police staked out his apartment at 35 Pine Street, Yonkers, on 10 August 1977, and saw his car parked out front. They could see a rifle butt protruding from an Army duffel bag on the back seat of the car, and a note, printed in the same way as the Son of Sam letters, on the front. As the police waited for a search warrant to arrive, Berkowitz came out of his building at 10.30 p.m., got into his car and started the engine. John Falotico and another officer ran out, guns drawn, and ordered him to switch off the engine and get out.

Berkowitz was smiling broadly at them as he calmly admitted he was Sam. He had brought a manila envelope from his apartment; in it was the .44 calibre pistol that had been used in all the shootings. The search of Berkowitz's apartment turned up the diaries he had been keeping for years, which included details of the many hundreds of fires that he had set throughout the 1970s, as well as another note which read, 'Because Craig is Craig, so must the streets be filled with crime and huge drops of lead poured down upon her head until she was dead – Yet the cats still come out at night to mate and the sparrows still sing in the morning.'

Reporters flocked to 1 Police Plaza where Berkowitz was being questioned, and one (anonymous) detective gave them a few titbits: 'Sam' apparently was 'the dog [that] lives in the house behind this guy. He says the dog commands him. That's the word he used: commands him. He says he understands the dog. The dog commands him to kill.'

But there was one aspect that is rarely mentioned in reports of the case – what Berkowitz intended to do on the night of 10 August. According to Jimmy Breslin's report in the *Daily News*, the same detective told him that Berkowitz

> was going to Riverdale first and get somebody. Then he was going to drive to the Hamptons. Out to Hampton Bays. A discotheque there. He had a .45 semi-automatic and he was going there to kill everybody.
>
> He said he was 'going out in a blaze of glory'. Do you know what that would have done? A machine gun in a discotheque?

(Berkowitz didn't achieve his aim, but the effects would have probably been the same as those that occurred on 12 June 2016, at the Pulse nightclub in Orlando, Florida.)

Mayor Abe Beame came to see Berkowitz for himself (although the pair did not exchange any words) and then held a press conference at 1.40 a.m. 'I am very pleased to announce that the people of the City of New York can rest easy tonight because police have captured a man they believe to be the "Son of Sam",' he told reporters.

The odd smile on Berkowitz's face when he was arrested was still there when he was seen by the public for the first time, when he was being transferred between police stations. He was held in the prison ward at the King's County Hospital, where, according to guards, he slept like a baby and ate like a horse. He was assessed by psychiatrists to see if he was fit to stand trial. 'I had nothing against these victims,' he told them. 'Who were these people to me? They were just people. I didn't hate them. I wasn't angry against them . . . Sam did it through me. He used me. He made me go out there and do it. I did it for him, for blood.' Berkowitz maintained that Sam Carr was 'really . . . a man who lived six thousand years ago . . . Sam is the Devil.'

Berkowitz began to feel suicidal, writing that he was a cursed person, beyond hope. He was ruled fit to stand trial and, in extraordinary scenes in court on 8 May 1978, he went against all legal advice. His lawyer Leon Stern told Judge Corso, 'Mr Berkowitz has indicated to counsel that he wishes to interpose a plea of guilty to his indictment. I want to make it absolutely clear and on the record . . . that this plea is of his own choosing and is contrary to the advice of his counsel.' His defence team believed 'he has a meritorious and valid defence: not guilty by reason of insanity', and that he had the right to his day in court. It was their judgement 'predicated on many months of contact with the defendant, that he is not competent to stand trial, that he is not competent to enter a plea of guilty . . . [He] still suffers from such mental disease and defect he cannot make such a judgement.'

In front of three separate judges, representing the different areas in which he committed his crimes, and after being reminded that he did not need to say anything that incriminated himself, Berkowitz was asked if he aimed his gun ('Yes'), what he did then ('I pulled the trigger'), what his purpose was ('to kill her'/'to kill them'), and if he knew and appreciated his conduct was wrong ('Yes') – along with a few supplementary questions relevant to each case. The Bronx District Attorney, Mario Merola, also noted Berkowitz's admission that between 1974 and 1977 he had set 2,000 fires around the city of New York.

Berkowitz may have accepted his situation at that point, but when it came to his sentencing on 22 May 1978, he was considerably less amenable, breaking free from his straitjacket before being brought into court and then chanting 'Stacy was a whore' continuously during the proceedings. 'That's right!' he screamed at the packed court, which included the relatives of his victims. 'I'd kill her again! I'd kill them all again!' He was dragged, biting and kicking from the room. According to contemporary news reports, he told psychiatrists the outburst was deliberately staged, as he hoped someone would 'kill me and get on with it'.

Berkowitz was brought back on 12 June, considerably calmer. 'It is obviously the intention of the court,' said Queens Supreme Court Justice Nicholas Tsoucalas, 'that this defendant remain incarcerated for the rest of his natural life'. Bronx Justice William Kapelman added: 'It is not my purpose to scold you for the insidious crimes for which you have been sentenced today . . . Let me just say that you grovel in the depth of human degradation.' Berkowitz was formally given six consecutive twenty-five-year-to-life consecutive terms, plus various other sentences for his assaults, totalling 547 years.

After further psychiatric examination, he was sent to the prison at Attica, from where, a year later, he denied all his claims of hearing voices; later in 1979, another inmate tried to kill him, cutting his throat, but Berkowitz wouldn't name his attacker. He was eventually revealed as William E. Hauser, then serving a term for first-degree assault, and currently serving twenty-five years to life for a murder during a 1990 robbery. 'The doctor told David that it was very improbable he would survive. He was cut literally where his jugular was. He was obviously shocked and very frightened of dying. It really was a miracle he survived,' Berkowitz's lawyer Mark J. Heller told the *New York Post*.

Eight years later, he was moved to the Sullivan Correctional Facility, a supermax prison, described by Berkowitz as a place of 'oppressive darkness', and around the same time became a born-again Christian. In 1993, he said the Son of Sam killings were the result of a Satanic plot run by the cult with which he had been involved in the mid-1970s – and he was only responsible for the deaths of three people. 'I honestly didn't know that people were going to die one day,' he told reporters, 'and I'm so very sorry that happened. People that didn't deserve it lost their lives.' He had only pleaded guilty to get out of the cult and to save his family from any retribution.

Berkowitz wrote to New York Governor George Pataki in 2002, expressing remorse, and noting, 'In all honesty I believe that I deserve to be in prison for the rest of my life . . . I have, with God's help, long ago come to terms with my situation and I have accepted my punishment.' His parole application is automatically considered, but he has not made any effort to gain release, not even turning up for the 2014 hearing. 'David told me that the reason he has never sought freedom from the parole board by attending parole hearings is because "Jesus has already freed my heart, soul and mind and has forgiven me,"' Heller told the *New York Post*.

Berkowitz was transferred to a new correctional facility in April 2016.

CHAPTER 27

United States:
Jeffrey Dahmer

....

'He crossed the line with some people – prisoners, prison staff. Some people who are in prison are repentant – but he was not one of them.' That was the verdict of Christopher Scarver, the man who stove in Jeffrey Dahmer's head with a metal bar on 28 November 1994 at Wisconsin's Columbia Correctional Institution, where the cannibal and serial killer was serving his multiple life sentences. It's clear from the interviews with Dahmer – many of which can be watched on YouTube – that his responses to normal human interaction were not what most people would expect, even if he did have a certain degree of self-knowledge. 'I created this horror and it only makes sense I do everything to put an end to it,' he told Detective Patrick Kennedy on 23 July 1991. 'For what I did, I should be dead,' Dahmer told the officers who had arrested him in the early hours of that morning, and there were many who believed that he deserved the death penalty. Much to their chagrin, Wisconsin had abolished capital punishment nearly 140 years earlier.

Jeffrey Dahmer was a 'happy little boy' according to his father, Lionel. Born on 21 May 1960 to Lionel and his wife Joyce after a difficult pregnancy, he loved playing with blocks and stuffed bunnies as well as the family dog, Frisky. He suffered ear, nose and throat infections, but these didn't seem to faze him, although an operation for a double hernia aged six definitely made the boy more introspective, his father recalled. A couple of years earlier at the family home in Iowa, Lionel swept out some animal remains from beneath their home, and noted that his son was 'oddly thrilled by the sound they made. His small hands dug deep into the pile of bones.' It was the start of a fascination with the structure of the body that would last his lifetime.

When Dahmer started first grade, his mother was pregnant with his brother David, and tensions rose between her and her husband. This led to an unhappy home environment, and Dahmer wasn't keen on school either. Just before his seventh birthday, the family moved again, to Bath, Ohio. Dahmer made a friend, Lee, and started to respond well to one of the teachers. (Unfortunately, the teacher gave Lee a bowl of tadpoles that Dahmer had brought in for her; Dahmer went to Lee's garage and poured motor oil into the bowl to kill them.)

Dahmer had an interest in animals from a very early age. He would collect bugs, dragonflies and butterflies, like many young-sters – but he would also pick up roadkill and other animal carcasses, which he would dismember to see how they 'fitted together'. On one occasion, he impaled a dog's head on a stake behind the house. Aged just ten, he asked his father what would happen to chicken bones if placed in bleach; his father, pleased that Dahmer was taking an interest in something rather than just sitting staring blankly at the wall, as he would often do, encouraged him by showing him how to use bleach to clean and preserve bones. Dahmer started to use these techniques on his animal subjects.

Most teens can be moody, answering questions with monosyl-labic grunts, but Dahmer was worse than most, spending much of his time indulging in fantasies in his own mind. He had realised he was homosexual as he hit puberty, but kept this from his parents, whose marriage by then was deteriorating further. He started to drink heavily, taking bottles of gin and beer with him into Revere High School. His teachers regarded him as uncommunicative but polite and intelligent; his fellow students saw him as a class clown, after he started throwing fake fits. However, as he drank increasingly heavily, his grades dropped, and Dahmer graduated in May 1978 having not achieved his potential.

By this time, his father had moved out of the house, and soon after his mother was awarded custody of David and also moved out, leaving Dahmer living by himself. Just three weeks after his graduation, he committed his first murder, aged eighteen. He had entertained ideas of attacking someone a couple of years earlier: he had felt attracted to a male jogger near his home and fantasised about knocking him out and then using his body sexually. He had hidden in a bush, baseball bat in hand, but the jogger took an alternate route, and the urge within Dahmer passed.

This time it wouldn't. On the evening of 18 June 1978, Dahmer picked up eighteen-year-old Steven Mark Hicks, who was hitchhiking to a rock concert. He agreed to come back to Dahmer's place for some beers, but when Steven wanted to leave, Dahmer didn't want him to, and hit him over the head with a ten-pound dumbbell twice from behind. Steven fell to the floor unconscious, and Dahmer used the bar of the dumbbell to strangle him, then stripped him and masturbated over the corpse. Next day, he dissected the body in the crawl-space area, then buried the pieces in the backyard; sometime later (possibly as much as two years), he dug them up, pared the flesh off the bones and dissolved it in acid, and crushed the bones with a sledgehammer. The liquefied flesh was flushed down the toilet, the bits of bone scattered in the nearby woods.

Dahmer's father remarried quickly, and he and his new wife Shari encouraged Dahmer to go to Ohio State University. This was a waste of time – Dahmer spent that period in an alcoholic haze and flunked out. His father gave him an ultimatum: get a job or join the armed forces. Dahmer stayed drunk throughout the holidays, causing problems for the newlyweds. 'He was a gentle person, but when he got drunk it would take four policemen to hold him down,' Shari Dahmer told *Time* magazine shortly after Dahmer's arrest. In January 1979, his father drove him to the recruiting office. Dahmer enlisted in the US Army, training at Fort Sam Houston in San Antonio, Texas, before being deployed to Baumholder in West Germany as a combat medic. During this time, it later transpired that he raped two soldiers: Preston Davis in an armoured personnel carrier after Dahmer drugged him; the other – seventeen-year-old Billy Joe Capshaw – on multiple occasions over a seventeen-month period after he was assigned to a room with Dahmer. 'He was tying me to the bunk with motor pool rope,' Billy Joe recalled in 2013. 'He took all my clothing from me. He would either beat me before he raped me or he would beat me after.' Billy Joe Capshaw complained, but a rape kit that was used to ascertain the truth and the results from it were simply thrown away, with the young soldier sent back to his torturing roommate. Neither incident came out at the time, and indeed Dahmer's apparent good behaviour while in the Army was used by the prosecution at his trial to show that he was sane.

The US Army gave Dahmer an honourable discharge in March 1981 – his alcohol problems had led to a deterioration in performance, but the Army didn't think it would affect him in civilian life – and after six months spent holidaying in Florida, he returned home to Ohio. Despite his father and stepmother's best efforts, he wouldn't control his alcohol intake, and in October, he was given a suspended jail sentence for drunk and disorderly behaviour. Despairing, his father sent him to live with his grandmother in Wisconsin – which did settle him, even if he was still drinking. He held down a job as a phlebotomist for ten months before being laid off, but then remained unemployed for two years. He didn't stay out of trouble, however: he was fined $50 and costs after exposing himself to a crowd of women and children at Wisconsin State Fair Park in August 1982.

At the start of 1985 he found employment again, working night shifts at the Milwaukee Ambrosia Chocolate Factory. His interest in the gay lifestyle also reasserted itself around this time, after he was offered a blow job by a man in the public library (Dahmer refused). He started to spend time in the gay areas of Milwaukee, stealing a male mannequin and using it to stimulate himself in the shower until his grandmother found it and demanded he get rid of it. He then had numerous casual sexual liaisons in bathhouses, although he always preferred that his partners stayed still – he preferred to see 'people as objects of pleasure instead of people'. He therefore started drugging his prospective partners so they would be immobile but, after complaints, his membership of the bathhouses was revoked and he had to use hotel rooms for sex.

His interest in necrophilia also started to build around this time. When he read about the impending funeral of an eighteen-year-old boy, he decided to steal the corpse and take it home. However, when he tried to dig up the coffin, the ground was too hard, so he gave up on the idea.

In August 1986, two months or so after he had started using sedatives on his partners, he was arrested for masturbating in front of two twelve-year-old boys near the Kinnickinnic River. Initially he admitted what he had done, but then changed his story and claimed he had been urinating. He was found guilty of disorderly conduct in March 1987, and given a year's probation and mandatory counselling.

Eight months after his court appearance, Jeffrey Dahmer killed again, over nine years after his first murder. Twenty-five-year-old Steven Tuomi was battered to death in a rented room at the Ambassador Hotel on 20 November 1987; the pair had been drinking in a gay bar and returned to Dahmer's room. Dahmer couldn't remember exactly what happened but he woke to find Steven dead with his chest crushed in and blood on his mouth. Dahmer didn't panic, but went out to buy a large suitcase and used that to transport Steven's body back to his grandmother's, where he masturbated on the body and had sex with it. A few days later he spent two hours dismembering the corpse. He severed the head, arms and legs, filleted the bones, and cut the flesh into small pieces. The flesh went into plastic garbage bags, the bones into a sheet; he then smashed the bones with a sledgehammer. Everything but the head was thrown out; that he kept for a fortnight, wrapped in a blanket, before boiling it in detergent and bleach. He kept the skull as a masturbatory aid until it disintegrated.

This was the first of a trio of deaths over a four-month period. Fourteen-year-old Native American boy James Doxtator agreed to come back to Dahmer's house to pose for nude pictures on 16 January 1988; they had some sexual activity then Dahmer drugged him and strangled him. Again he kept the body for about a week before dismembering and disposing of it. Just over two months later, on 24 March, twenty-two-year-old Mexican Richard Guerrero suffered the same fate – although as with so many victims of gay serial killers, his family refused to believe that Richard was homosexual and therefore could not have been at the Phoenix gay bar for Dahmer to meet him. Richard's body was put in the trash within twenty-four hours of the murder.

It's quite likely that Dahmer's spree would have continued unabated if he hadn't had a shock a month later. On 23 April, he had brought another victim down to the cellar at his grandmother's house. He had already administered the drugged coffee, but the man wasn't yet unconscious when Dahmer's grandmother called out, 'Is that you, Jeff?' Dahmer tried to pretend he was alone, but his grandmother wasn't fooled. Once the young man was unconscious, Dahmer took him to the County General Hospital.

This led to some major changes in Dahmer's lifestyle. Although he didn't stop bringing young men back to drug and have sex with them, he did cease killing them. However, his grandmother eventually had enough both of this behaviour and of the odd smells that were coming from the basement and the garage, and told him to move out. He did so, finding an apartment on North 25th Street, Milwaukee, and moving in on 25 September 1988. The very next day, he was arrested for drugging and sexually fondling a thirteen-year-old Laotian boy, which led to a conviction for second-degree sexual assault and enticing a child for immoral purposes (as with James Doxtator, he wanted the boy to pose nude) in January 1989, although sentencing was suspended until May.

The authorities had no idea that between the conviction and sentencing, Dahmer had killed again, although Assistant District Attorney Gale Shelton probably would not have been surprised. 'In my judgement, it is absolutely crystal clear that the prognosis for treatment of Mr Dahmer within the community is extremely bleak,' she told the court in January. 'His perception that what he did wrong here was choosing too young a victim – and that that's all he did wrong – is a part of the problem . . . He appeared to be cooperative and receptive, but anything that goes below the surface indicates that deep-seated anger and deep-seated psychological problems that he is unwilling or incapable of dealing with.'

Three psychologists agreed with her – they felt Dahmer was manipulative, resistant and evasive – but the court was swayed both by Dahmer's lawyer and Dahmer's own testimony. 'I believe that he was caught before it got the point where it would have gotten worse,' lawyer Gerald Boyle maintained. Dahmer himself said that 'This is a nightmare come true for me. If anything would shock me out of my past behaviour patterns, it's this . . . This enticing a child was the climax of my idiocy.' As a result, he was sentenced to five years' probation and a year in the House of Correction, with work release permitted so he could keep his job. He also had to register as a sex offender.

Two months prior to the sentencing, over the Easter period at the end of March, Dahmer had taken a ten-day vacation and moved back into his grandmother's house. On 25 March, he met twenty-four-year-old model Anthony Sears. Dahmer claimed later that he hadn't been on the hunt for a victim, but Anthony had presented himself at the end of the evening and Dahmer couldn't resist. Anthony came back to Dahmer's grandmother's house where he was drugged and strangled after the pair had engaged in oral sex. Dahmer decapitated the body in the bathtub the next day, stripped the flesh and pulverised the bone as was his habit, but because he found Sears 'exceptionally attractive', he decided to keep a souvenir. He pickled Anthony Sears's head and genitalia in acetone and put them in his work locker. There they stayed until he found a new home in 1990. He painted the skull grey so that it would look like a medical student's model if anyone happened to find it.

Dahmer served ten months in the House of Correction for the assault, and on his release, moved back temporarily with his grand-mother before finding a new apartment on North 25th Street. He moved into Apartment 213 on 14 May 1990 and wasted no time in returning to his old ways. Thirty-two-year-old male prostitute Raymond Smith was enticed back to North 25th Street on 20 May. Dahmer gave him a sedative-laced drink, then strangled him. The next day he bought a polaroid camera and photographed the body in various positions before dismembering him in the bathroom. The legs, arms and pelvis went into a steel kettle and were boiled in detergent, then rinsed in the sink. The rest of Raymond's body, bar the head, was dissolved in acid. The skull was painted grey, and placed next to that of Anthony Sears. Dahmer would masturbate in front of them.

The tables were turned on the killer a week later, when Dahmer accidentally drank the wrong drink, drugging himself rather than his victim. The other man stole clothing, $300 in cash and a watch but didn't otherwise disturb the apartment. Dahmer told his probation officer on 29 May of the robbery, but didn't report it to the police.

Dahmer didn't make that mistake again, and over the next thirteen months, he killed repeatedly, maintaining a ritual of inviting his victims back to the apartment, either to watch pornographic videos with him or for him to take photos of them. He would then drug them, strangle them (either with his bare hands or a leather strap), then have sex with the bodies or masturbate over them. He would photograph the corpses with his polaroid camera and then also visually record the stages of the dismemberment process, before disposing of them with detergent, bleach and a sledgehammer as appropriate. Many of the skulls joined Anthony Sears and Raymond Smith on the shelf. Sometimes he would retain strips of flesh (he decided that he didn't like the taste of human blood, so that wasn't kept), freezing them and trying various seasonings to make them tastier.

Twenty-seven-year-old Edward Smith was drugged and strangled on 14 June; as an experiment, Dahmer kept Edward's skeleton in the freezer, hoping it wouldn't retain moisture. When he put the skull in the oven to dry it out, it exploded. Dahmer said he felt 'rotten' about this murder as he couldn't keep any body parts. Ernest Miller, twenty-two at the time of his death, went willingly with Dahmer on 2 September, but when he asked Dahmer for more money for oral sex, Dahmer slashed his carotid artery with the knife he used on his victims' bodies – he only had two sleeping pills in the apartment at the time. After the usual photos, Dahmer cut off Ernest's head in the bathtub then talked to it and kissed it while he dismembered the rest of the corpse. He retained Ernest's heart, biceps and flesh in the fridge to eat. The rest was disposed of as normal.

David Thomas was the next victim, on 24 September 1990. After Dahmer had given him the sedative drink, he realised that he actually did not feel sexually aroused by his victim, so simply strangled him and dismembered his body, getting rid of all parts of it. That didn't stop him from photographing the process – and those photos would be key in providing identification later.

There was then a gap between killings, but only because Dahmer was unsuccessful in persuading any potential victims to come back with him to North 25th Street. This led to feelings of anxiety and depression, and even suicidal thoughts, as he told his probation officer. However, on 18 February 1991, he approached seventeen-year-old Curtis Straughter at a bus stop, and Curtis agreed to come back to the apartment. Dahmer drugged and strangled him with a leather strap, and then disposed of the body, bar the skull, hands and genitals.

Seven weeks later, on 7 April, Dahmer decided to try something different again. He had been aroused by non-moving sexual partners in the past, and he wondered whether he might be able to induce a permanent unresisting submissive state in his next victim. He would then have someone available for his needs whenever he wanted, rather than risk being rebuffed as he had been the previous year. His target was nineteen-year-old Errol Lindsey, who was waiting to get a key cut when he was approached by Dahmer. Errol was heterosexual, but agreed to go with him. Back at the apartment, Dahmer sedated Errol, then drilled a hole in his skull and poured in muriatic acid – a form of hydrochloric acid that is naturally produced by the stomach during digestion, and is used as an industrial cleaner. Errol woke after this operation and told Dahmer he had a headache then asked the time. Frustrated that he was not gaining the control he sought, Dahmer drugged Errol again, then strangled him. He decapitated the body and flayed the skin off it, putting it in some saline water for weeks in an attempt to preserve it. However, it became brittle and he got rid of it.

Dahmer's activities didn't go unnoticed. There were complaints raised by his neighbours about the smells that came from the apartment and the use of a chainsaw. Sopa Princewill, the manager of the apartments, raised these with Dahmer and was given various excuses, including that his freezer was broken and that his tropical fish had died. No one bar his victims, however, gained access to the apartment. No one, that is, until three police officers – including John Balcerzak and Joseph Gabrish – helped Dahmer take one of his next victims back to the apartment!

On 24 May, Dahmer had inveigled deaf-mute Tony Hughes into posing for photographs, using handwritten notes to communicate. The thirty-one-year-old was sedated and strangled, and his body left on the floor of Dahmer's bedroom for a few days. On 26 May, Dahmer saw a fourteen-year-old boy on Wisconsin Avenue, and invited him to come back to pose for pictures. The lad wasn't originally going to come back, but in the end agreed. After Dahmer took two photos of him, he gave the boy the drugged drink then he drilled a hole in his skull and inserted the acid into the frontal lobe. Dahmer didn't realise it at the time: the youngster was Konerak Sinthasomphone – the younger brother of the Laotian boy who had been the cause of his downfall and incarceration three years earlier.

Dahmer led Konerak into his bedroom – where Tony Hughes's body was still lying decaying – and left him there while he went out drinking, and to buy some beers. Around 2 a.m. Konerak woke and realised he was in trouble. He managed to get out of the apartment, and fled into the street. Naked and bleeding, he stumbled around outside Dahmer's apartment, where he was seen by eighteen-year-olds Sandra Smith and her cousin Nicole Childress. Sandra called 911, and paramedics arrived, putting a blanket around the boy. Dahmer got back around the same time, and told the girls that Konerak was his lover. He tried to lead Konerak back to the apartment, but the boy seemed to struggle. The women explained that they had already called 911, and Dahmer desisted. The police officers duly arrived, and Dahmer spun the same story: Konerak was his nineteen-year-old boyfriend, with whom he had quarrelled when Konerak was drunk. Nicole Childress was sure that Konerak was 'reaching out to me for help', but she and her cousin were told to 'butt out' by the police officers, who believed they were simply in the middle of a domestic tiff. They helped carry Konerak back into the apartment.

According to Dahmer, the apartment was 'smelling like hell' and there were photos of his victims strewn around the place. He showed the officers the pictures of Konerak in his black bikini briefs, and they took a quick look round (Dahmer claimed one of them 'peeked his head around the bedroom but really didn't take a good look'). Advising Dahmer to 'take good care' of Konerak, the officers departed, having not run any sort of check on Dahmer – which would have revealed his conviction for child molestation. As soon as they were gone, Dahmer injected Konerak with muriatic acid again, killing him. He took 28 May off work to dismember both Konerak and Tony Hughes's bodies, keeping both skulls.

The policemen hadn't taken the situation at all seriously. 'Intoxicated Asian, naked male. Was returned to his sober boyfriend,' reported one to the dispatcher according to the transcripts released after an internal investigation was ordered two months later. He noted that his partner 'is going to get deloused'. Sandra Smith's mother, Glenda Cleveland, called the police asking what was being done about the 'child' to be told, 'It wasn't a child, it was an adult . . . It is all taken care of . . . It's a boyfriend–boyfriend thing.' When she read a newspaper article about Konerak's disappearance, she contacted the police department again; they never called her back.

There was just a month until Dahmer's next kill. He travelled to Illinois to attend the Chicago Pride Parade, held on 30 June. At the bus station, he met twenty-year-old Matt Turner who agreed to come back to Milwaukee with Dahmer for a 'professional photo shoot'. Once at Apartment 213, Matt was drugged, strangled and dismembered. Dahmer put his head and his internal organs in separate plastic bags in the freezer for later use.

In Dahmer's own words, he felt 'completely swept along' by a desire to kill. 'It was an incessant and never-ending desire to be with someone at whatever cost,' he told detectives later. 'Someone good looking, really nice looking. It just filled my thoughts all day long.' Interviewed by NBC in 1994 not long before his death, he explained that he wanted to live in a place where 'I could completely control a person – a person that I found physically attractive, and keep them with me as long as possible, even if it meant just keeping a part of them.'

On 5 July 1991, Dahmer returned to Chicago and picked up twenty-three-year-old Jeremiah Weinberger at a bar and brought him back to Milwaukee ostensibly to spend the weekend together. Jeremiah was drugged, but Dahmer was still hopeful of creating a zombie-esque partner, so injected boiling water into his skull. Jeremiah lasted two days before dying – and Dahmer remembered his demise clearly. Jeremiah was the only one of his victims to die with his eyes open. Dahmer decapitated him, leaving the torso in the bathtub.

He now had two torsos to deal with – those of Matt Turner and Jeremiah Weinberger. On 12 July, Dahmer bought a fifty-seven-gallon drum of acid, and placed both of them within it. Three days afterwards, Dahmer met twenty-four-year-old bodybuilder Oliver Lacy in Milwaukee, and went through his usual ritual. However, he still wanted to try keeping his victims alive, so he tried to sedate him with chloroform rather than his usual sleeping-pill-filled drink. This didn't work, so Dahmer strangled him with a leather belt and then had sex with the corpse. He rang his work asking for a day's leave, which was granted. He spent the time dealing with Oliver's body, putting the head and the heart in the fridge and the skeleton in the freezer; the head was to be given pride of place in Dahmer's shrine of skulls that he had been building.

Dahmer didn't go back to work and on 19 July he was informed that he was fired. He went straight out and found yet another victim, this time a father of three from Minnesota who was in town looking for work. Twenty-five-year-old Joseph Bradehoft was to be the last man that Dahmer killed. After strangling him, Dahmer left him on the bed for a couple of days, covered with a sheet – but when this was removed, the head was covered in maggots. Dahmer decapitated him, put the cleaned-up head in the fridge and placed the torso with the others in the blue drum.

On 22 July, Dahmer offered three men $100 to come back to his apartment so he could photograph them. Thirty-two-year-old Tracy Edwards agreed to an evening of photography, beer and company but when he arrived at Dahmer's home, he noticed a dreadful smell and boxes of acid on the floor. Dahmer managed to get a handcuff on him, and took Tracy into the bedroom for the photos. He then threatened Tracy with a knife and, shortly afterwards, placed his head against Tracy's chest and told him he intended to eat Tracy's heart. Tracy persuaded Dahmer to go back in the living room, and took advantage of a brief lull in the other man's concentration to punch him in the face and race out of the front door.

It was now 11.30 p.m. and Tracy managed to flag down two police officers, Rolf Mueller and Robert Rauth, and asked them to remove the handcuffs, explaining what had been happening at the apartment of this 'weird dude'. When their key didn't fit, he agreed to go with them to Dahmer's apartment. Dahmer admitted that he had put the cuffs on Tracy, but didn't say why. Dahmer told officer Mueller the handcuff key was in the bedroom and, at that point, Tracy told the officers that the knife with which he had been threatened was in there.

Mueller entered the bedroom, and saw the knife. He looked in the drawer Dahmer had indicated and also found Dahmer's collection of polaroid photos of his victims. Shocked, Mueller showed them to his partner. Dahmer resisted arrest, but was overpowered and cuffed. While they waited for backup, the policemen checked out the rest of the apartment – and made a shocking discovery in the kitchen. 'There's a fucking head in the refrigerator,' Mueller shouted.

When the investigators forensically checked the apartment, they found a metal stockpot at the back of the closet that had decomposed hands and a penis in it. There were containers of ethyl alcohol, chloroform and formaldehyde, as well as glass jars containing preserved male genitalia. There were three other heads in the kitchen, seven skulls around the apartment, and two human hearts and some arm muscle in the fridge (as well as a tray of blood drippings). The freezer revealed an entire torso, as well as two preserved penises and a scalp. Inside the fifty-seven-gallon drum were the remains of three torsos.

Dahmer felt no need to deny his deeds, and cooperated fully with the authorities. 'As we did the autopsies, we could ask him questions directly about our findings,' chief medical examiner Jeff Jentzen recalled. 'It was interesting to have that kind of access.' Dahmer was interrogated by Detective Patrick Kennedy for over sixty hours over the next fortnight, confessing to all seventeen murders stretching from 1978 to 1991. On 25 July 1991, he was charged with four counts of murder; eleven more charges were added on 22 August; then, on 17 September, Ohio authorities – who had discovered two molars and a vertebra that they could identify during a search of Dahmer's old home – charged him with the murder of Steven Hicks. He was not charged with the murder of Steven Tuomi, nor the attempted murder of Tracy Edwards.

At the first hearing on 13 January 1992, Dahmer was represented by Gerald Boyle, the same lawyer who had helped keep him from severe punishment four years earlier. Against Boyle's advice, Dahmer pleaded guilty but insane, with Boyle telling the court, 'I want to emphasise that the decision to plead guilty is Mr Dahmer's. This case is about his mental condition.' Under Wisconsin law, anyone who pleaded insanity had to first be convicted of the crime, at which time no question of sanity was raised, and then undergo a second separate trial phase on the sanity issue. With Dahmer pleading guilty, it meant the trial would go straight to that part. If he was found guilty but insane, he would go to a mental institution for the criminally insane and, after a year, could start to petition for release every six months; if guilty but sane, he would face a mandatory life sentence.

The trial on the fifteen charges in Wisconsin began on 30 January 1992 with an eight-foot-high, bullet-resistant glass barrier around the defendant. His father and stepmother attended every day, as mental health professionals gave their many differing views on Dahmer's sanity for two weeks. Dahmer's confession ran to 160 pages, read out by two detectives. On 14 February, Gerald Boyle maintained in his closing speech that Dahmer suffered 'a sickness he discovered, not chose' and that he was 'so out of control he could not conform his conduct any more'. Dahmer was 'a runaway train on a track of madness'. District Attorney Michael McCann couldn't disagree more. 'He wasn't a runaway train,' he told the jury. 'He was the engineer! . . . He's fooled a lot of people. Please don't let this murderous killer fool you.'

Two of the jury members dissented from the majority view that Dahmer was sane at the time of each of the fifteen murders. Dahmer's letter prior to sentencing noted that 'I didn't ever want freedom. Frankly, I wanted death for myself. This was a case to tell the world that I did what I did, but not for reasons of hate. I knew I was sick or evil or both. Now I believe I was sick . . . I ask for no consideration.' He received fifteen consecutive life terms. A sixteenth was added at a forty-five minute hearing in Ohio for the murder of Steven Hicks.

Dahmer was kept in solitary confinement for the first year of his sentence, but requested to be placed in a less secure unit. He showed a wry sense of humour, at one point posting a sign on the prison bulletin board for a 'Cannibals Anonymous' meeting. He didn't care about the potential risk to his life, telling his mother, 'It doesn't matter, Mom.' He was attacked by a drug dealer with a homemade shank in the prison chapel, but only received slight scratches. However, he was never going to last long. After Christopher Scarver killed Dahmer on 28 November 1994, his mother, Joyce Flint, raged, 'Now is everybody happy? Now that he's bludgeoned to death, is that good enough for everyone?'

For many, the answer was yes. 'I'm happy and very excited that the monster is finally dead,' Richard Guerrero's sister, Janie Hagen said. 'The devil is gone.' The apartments where he killed twelve of his victims were demolished in November 1992; almost unbelievably, animal rights organisation PETA had plans in 2014 to turn his childhood home into a vegan restaurant named Eat for Life: Home Cooking. Jeffrey Dahmer might well have appreciated the irony of the reason given for abandoning the plans: 'getting zoning for a restaurant on this site is apparently impossible, in part because of issues with the plumbing and waste systems'.

CHAPTER 28

United States: Gary Ridgway – The Green River Killer

....

'The strange thing about Gary Ridgway is if you didn't know the depravity, if you didn't know the evil that this man committed, you would have no clue when you talked on the phone with him,' journalist Charlie Harger wrote in September 2013 after he had finally persuaded the Green River Killer to talk to him. 'This man sounds like he would be a perfect neighbour.' Harger is by no means the first person to make this observation about a serial killer, but in the case of Gary Ridgway, it goes to the heart of how he successfully evaded capture for nearly two decades. It was only because of advances in DNA profiling that he was finally put behind bars; he was convicted of forty-eight murders initially, but he has confessed to around ninety. Even based on that first tally, he is the most prolific American serial killer in terms of confirmed victims.

Gary Leon Ridgway was born on 18 February 1949, in Salt Lake City, Utah, the middle of three brothers. His parents, Mary Rita Steinman and Thomas Newton Ridgway, moved with their young family between Utah and Idaho, finally finding a home in Washington State in 1958, not far from the Pacific Highway and a strip of land that would become the working ground for many prostitutes – a lot of whom Ridgway would hire and sometimes kill. His father was a truck driver – when work was available – while his mother ruled the roost at home, physically dominating her husband and even known to smash a plate over his head at the dinner table.

Ridgway was dyslexic and held back a year at school because of his learning difficulties: he had an IQ of 82 (the average is 100). He was still wetting the bed aged fourteen, and his mother would march him naked to the bathroom and wash him, even at that age, which simultaneously embarrassed and aroused the teenager. Aged sixteen, he stabbed a six-year-old boy through his ribs into his liver after persuading the youngster to come out into the woods with him to build a fort. The boy ran off, hearing Ridgway laughing behind him. 'He was in the wrong place at the wrong time and I was at the right place at the right time, I guess what you'd call it,' Ridgway later told detectives. He had stabbed the boy because he wanted to see how to stab somebody. (The victim told police when he was tracked down nearly four decades later that Ridgway had said, 'I always wanted to know what it felt like to kill somebody.')

He eventually graduated from Tyee High School aged twenty, and married his girlfriend, Claudia Kraig, before joining the Navy and heading out to Vietnam. The marriage didn't last: nineteen-year-old Claudia dated other men, while Ridgway started to become a frequent user of prostitutes, contracting gonorrhoea on more than one occasion. In 1973, on his return from duty, Ridgway met and married Marcia Winslow, and stayed with her for seven years. Marcia thought much about her husband strange: he found religion in a major way, becoming a fanatic proselytiser who would go door to door preaching the Word, and insisting that Marcia do exactly what the church pastor ordered. At the same time, he had an extraordinarily strong carnal appetite, insisting on sexual intercourse multiple times each day, often outside – and he continued to use prostitutes, even though he complained to the police about them being in the area, which led to increased patrols.

And when he started to kill, they made easy targets. He said in his plea-bargain statement:

I picked prostitutes as my victims because I hate most prostitutes, and I did not want to pay them for sex. I also picked
prostitutes as victims because they were easy to pick up without being noticed. I knew they would not be reporting missing right away and might never be reported missing. I picked
prostitutes because I thought I could kill as many of them as
I wanted without getting caught.

On 15 August 1982, Robert Ainsworth was fishing on the Green
River, heading south towards Seattle's city limit, passing by the area
known as Lovers' Lane. To his horror, he realised that what he had
believed was a mannequin in the water was the body of a dead black
woman – and a second one was floating next to it. Detective David
Reichert was one of the first investigating officers on the scene, and
while trying to work out how the killer had got the two bodies into the
water, he pushed through the tall grass beside the river and found a
third body. The first victim was thirty-one-year-old Marcia Chapman,
who had been in the river for about a week; the second was seventeen-year-old Cynthia Hinds, who had been floating for several days;
the third was sixteen-year-old Opal Mills. She had been dead a couple
of days; her blue slacks were knotted around her neck, and her bra
had been pulled up. She had bruises along her legs and arms.

Chief Medical Examiner Donald Reay examined the bodies and
discovered all had been strangled. Marcia and Cynthia's bodies had
been weighted down with pyramid-shaped rocks in their vaginas.
However, this information was kept from the public. 'That is one of
the few things we have in common with the killer right now,' King
County spokesman Pat Ferguson told reporters three days later.
'The killer knows how he or she killed them and so do we, so that
will help when we focus in on a suspect.' Two further recently
discovered bodies were added to the investigation: twenty-three-
year-old Deborah Lynn Bonner had been found slumped over a log

in the river a week earlier, while a month earlier, on 15 July, sixteen-year-old Wendy Lee Coffield was also pulled from the river. One thing connected them all: they had all worked as prostitutes on the strip of the Pacific Highway South near Seattle–Tacoma International Airport. So did the sixth confirmed victim, Gisele Ann Lovvorn, whose decomposed body was found on 25 September around six miles from the river along a bicycle path in underbrush southeast of the airport.

The murderer was quickly dubbed the Green River Killer, and when two more sixteen-year-olds – Kase Ann Lee and Terri Renne Milligan – disappeared at the end of August, police were concerned about their safety. 'There is no evidence . . . to indicate that they are also victims, but the possibility cannot be discounted,' spokesman Frank Kinney said. At that point, Major Richard Kraske, the police's criminal investigation chief, claimed three men were considered suspects, but only one had been questioned (he had raped a prostitute and made reference to the Green River murders); Kinney said there were four, and two had been brought in. (Terri Milligan's body was finally found on 1 April 1984; Kase Ann Lee's never has been, although Ridgway did confess to killing her and leaving her near a drive-in cinema.) Twenty-five officers from various jurisdictions were working on the cases at that point, with Kraske and Reichert leading the task force. They brought aboard FBI serial-killer profiler John Douglas and investigator Robert Keppel who had worked on the Ted Bundy case.

Meat butcher Charles Clinton Clark was arrested in September 1982, and was positively identified by two women who both said that he had picked them up (on separate occasions) in his blue and white truck, then pointed a pistol at their heads, and sexually attacked them. Prostitute Susan Widmark said she had managed to escape after being raped when the driver pulled up at a traffic light; fifteen-year-old Debra Estes was offered a ride by Clark, then handcuffed and forced to give him a blow job at gunpoint before he released her. Clark admitted the rapes, but had alibis for the Green River killings.

A taxi driver became the next focus of police attention, particularly since he matched the profile of the Green River Killer compiled by John Douglas. This included the fact that the killer had deep religious convictions; this proved to be correct, even if some of Douglas's later theories – that there were two killers – did not. The driver remained the main suspect for a long time, until eventually twenty-four-hour surveillance proved that he couldn't have been responsible for later murders.

The bodies started to mount up. Between September 1982 and April 1983, around fourteen girls, aged between fifteen and twenty-three, disappeared; most were known prostitutes from the strip. The last of these was Marie Malvar, who had been seen talking to a potential client on the night of 30 April by her boyfriend; suspicious of the man after he saw Marie arguing with him, her boyfriend followed in his own car, but lost sight of them after he had to stop at an intersection. When Marie failed to return, the boyfriend reported her missing. A week later, he – along with Marie's father and brother – saw the truck once more, and followed it to a house on South 348th Street. They called the police, who visited the house and chatted with the owner. Gary Ridgway denied ever having seen or heard of Marie. Police didn't comment on the way that Ridgway stood against a fence all the time – he was hiding the scratches on his left arm that Marie had inflicted. He denied knowledge of her again when the task force eventually interviewed him over six months later. A similar truck had been seen on another occasion, when sixteen-year-old Kimi-Kai Pitsor vanished, but the reports weren't correlated.

And that was the biggest problem for the investigation. With so many potential victims, the task force was overloaded, and in those pre-computerised days, valuable information was being lost because connections weren't being made (Ridgway's questioning was undertaken by the local Des Moines police but wasn't communicated to the task force for some time, for example). Robert Keppel did his best to suggest ways to improve matters, but it didn't bring the task force nearer capturing the killer. 'Every time you found a body it was like being hit on the head with a baseball bat,' Reichert recalled, while detective Bruce Kalin, who joined the team in 1984, remembered, 'We had mountains of evidence. We even took birds' nests from scenes hoping we would find a hair from the suspect or a piece of jewellery.'

Carol Ann Christensen's body was found on 8 May 1983. She had been strangled and then put on display – her head was covered with a paper bag that hid the fact the killer had placed a fish on top of her neck; there was another fish on her breast, and a bottle between her legs. There was ground beef on her left hand, and at some point she had been in water. Her death was added to the Green River Killer's tally, which mounted throughout the rest of the year. Various 'body dumps' were located and by the end of the year eighteen corpses had been found. The spree continued into 1984: the killer started leaving bodies around Mountain View Cemetery and North Bend near Interstate 90; he had previously been leaving the corpses around Sea–Tac airport and Star Lake.

Not every crime was linked to the Green River Killer. Those for which the task force believed he was responsible were found at the dump sites, and were nude or specifically posed; often he had returned to have sex with the corpses. Most of them were strangled, initially manually, but then with some form of ligature (Ridgway was worried about the bruises the victims were inflicting on his arms). 'I killed some of them outside,' Ridgway would later explain. 'I remember leaving each woman's body in the place where she was found. I killed most of them in my house near Military Road and I killed a lot of them in my truck not far from where I picked them up.'

His method was quite simple: he would gain the women's trust by showing them his wallet, which included a picture of his son, Matthew. Some would go home with him and he would show them his son's bedroom. 'They look in the bedroom, nobody's in there,' he told police. ' "Hey, this guy has a son, he's not gonna hurt anybody." ' When they went with him into his own room, they discovered how far from the truth this was.

The investigators gained help from unlikely sources. Psychic Barbara Kubik-Pattern had a vision of a body near to Interstate 90 in April 1984, and when the police refused to take her seriously, she and her daughter went searching. They found the body – that of Amina Agisheff, a thirty-six-year-old waitress, who seemed not to fit the Green River Killer's normal pattern as she was not a prostitute or runaway, but whom police added to the killer's list. A few months later, Keppel took up an offer made by serial killer Ted Bundy, who was able to provide the team with some insights into the Green River Killer's psychology, although Reichert was aware when he went to talk with Bundy that the serial killer was playing mind games. 'Just to sit across from him and shake hands sent chills,' Reichert recalled. 'You think, "Just how many people's lives have these hands squeezed out?" ' The most useful insights Bundy passed on regarded a serial killer's mentality: he doesn't leave home planning to kill, but does it when the urge comes on him and he feels safe and in control.

The Green River task force was faced with investigating 47,000 tips and 17,000 names; between just 56 law enforcement officers, it was a nigh-on impossible task. The killer continued to evade them, sometimes taunting them in the ways he presented the bodies: twenty-three-year old Denise Bush, who had been kidnapped from the strip in King County, Washington, in October 1982, was found nearly three years later on Bull Mountain – near King City in Washington County, Oregon. 'That was really an in-your-face kind of thing,' Reichert told *Time* magazine. 'It was like, "Are you guys so stupid you can't make the connection?"'

The discovery of Denise's body came as the flood of murders seemed to slow to a trickle. Only two bodies were found between October and December 1984; in the first part of 1985, only the remains of fifteen-year-old Carrie Rois (who had vanished in the summer of 1983) came to light. Denise Bush's body, together with that of nineteen-year-old Shirley Sherrill, was only located because the patch of land where they had been dumped was being bulldozed. Three further victims were found during the winter of 1985, including Kimi-Kai Pitsor – her skull had turned up back in December 1983 in the dump site at Mountain View Cemetery, but the rest of her skeleton was found in Seward Park, Seattle.

Both police and prostitutes knew that anyone working the strip was taking a chance. 'A lot of them think this could only happen to someone else, it will never happen to them,' Seattle police Vice Sergeant Gene Dorman told the Associated Press for a feature on the case at the start of 1986. 'Some of them we've had in this office and given them the little talk about how this could happen to you. And now they're on the missing list. So it probably did happen to them.'

At that point, police were blaming the Green River Killer for the deaths of thirty-four women and the disappearances of eleven others. Working girls believed firmly that if the killer was targeting 'a citizen with a square job' then 'everybody would be out trying to find him. Now they just say, one more [prostitute] off the streets.'

Extra FBI agents were drafted in during January 1986, and a month later, it seemed as if they might have finally got their man. On 6 February, a 'person of interest' was questioned for several hours, and his home and vehicles searched – the term 'person of interest' was defined by task force commander Frank Adamson as 'someone mentioned to the task force in some way as a person police ought to look into'. Although the police and reporters were careful not to name him, neighbours of the house that had been searched gave details that would enabled him to be identified. (It wasn't Gary Ridgway.) One enterprising local even sold popcorn to people watching the suspect's house being searched. However, after the man was freed at 3.30 a.m. to go about his business, Adamson explained, 'I would say [this] is not a major break in the Green River case. It's a little unfortunate so much interest was aroused by this case. If I had my druthers, this would not have occurred.'

Adamson was clearly feeling the pressure from lack of results, particularly after three more bodies were located in the summer of that year. The *Seattle Times* posted a cartoon, showing a policeman looking through binoculars saying, 'He's white male . . . harbours a deep resentment towards the opposite sex . . . and knows these woods inside out.' The second panel showed a small boy in front of a tree house (with a sign that read 'NO GURLS [*sic*] ALLOWED'), surrounded by a bunch of cops yelling, 'Freeze, dog-breath! Green River Task Farce!'

When it became clear that the task force was unlikely to achieve quick results, Adamson was reassigned and Captain James Pompey took over a much-reduced group. Two more bodies turned up in December 1986 in Vancouver, British Columbia – and among their remains were portions of other victims. At the start of the following year, a new 'person of interest' came under the spotlight.

Gary Ridgway hadn't escaped police notice during the investigation. He had been picked up in February 1984 after prostitute Dawn White had reported him over the way that he had tried to solicit her. Questioned about the Green River killings, he passed a polygraph test and was released. (When the evidence was re-examined years later, FBI technicians maintained that he wouldn't have passed under the more stringent guidelines then in force.) Detective Matt Haney decided to investigate Ridgway more closely, and discovered other links between him and the murders. He had been arrested for trying to solicit an undercover police officer in May 1982; he had been disturbed by police with prostitute Keli Kay McGinness on 23 February 1983, four months before Keli disappeared, believed to be a victim of the killer. The place they had been found by police was a dump site for the bodies, behind Sunset Junior High School. In late 1984, Ridgway was questioned after prostitute Rebecca Guay claimed he had tried to strangle her a couple of years earlier, after taking her into the woods and partially undressing her. Ridgway admitted he had been with her, but denied choking her, and claimed she had bitten him.

Haney and his colleagues spoke with Ridgway's second wife, Marie, who explained Ridgway's love for alfresco sex and his high carnal appetite, and also mentioned Ridgway had tried to choke her back in 1972. Another of Ridgway's lovers told police that on Christmas Eve 1981 he had said that he had nearly killed a woman. His work record indicated that on all of the twenty-seven dates and times that they could pinpoint when a victim disappeared, Ridgway was, in the task force's jargon, 'available as a suspect'. On 8 April 1987, a judge signed a warrant allowing the task force to search Ridgway's house and question him; during this, they also took 'bodily samples' of his saliva and hair cuttings. However, they were not able to gain anything further to tie him to the crimes, and he was released.

Captain Pompey died soon after from a heart attack, and his replacement oversaw the gradual winding-down of the task force. Bodies continued to turn up – three boys discovered seventeen-year-old Cindy Ann Smith's remains in June 1987, and other older remains were found over the next year. When a spate of prostitute killings took place in San Diego, California, during 1988, some believed the Green River Killer might be responsible, particularly after William J. Stevens was arrested as a potential suspect in 1989 – he was contemptuous of prostitutes, and had been studying at the University of Washington. However, although Stevens was a burglar and prison escapee, he had an unbreakable alibi for the original Green River killings in 1982.

By July 1991, even David Reichert had been promoted away from the task force, and Tom Jensen was left as the sole investigator. Over $15 million had been spent, apparently all for nothing. Reichert became sheriff of King County in 1997, and in April 2001 he chaired a cold-case review of the Green River killings – given the way technology had improved, he knew there could be benefit in reviewing the evidence. They had semen samples from three of the victims – Opal Mills, Marcia Chapman and Carol Ann Christensen – as well as the saliva from their most viable suspect, Gary Ridgway; all of it was sent to Beverly Himick, a forensic scientist at the Washington State Patrol crime lab. Himick subjected the samples to the new short-tandem-repeat testing DNA analysis, which had only come into use in 1997. It would be used extensively to ascertain the names of the victims of both Bosnian war crimes and in the Twin Towers on 9/11.

The day before America was brought to a standstill by that al-Qaeda operation, Himick rang Reichert with the news. The semen and the saliva samples matched. Reichert and Jensen both broke down in tears when they learned the killer's identity. 'Twenty years is a long time,' Reichert pointed out. 'There was this sense of relief. I always thought the case would be solved, but I did have thoughts that I might not be here.'

Gary Ridgway was arrested on 30 November 2001. Among his possessions was a copy of the book *The Search for the Green River Killer* by reporters Carlton Smith and Tomas Guillen (the pair were rehired by their former employer, the *Seattle Times*, off the back of this). He was held in bail on four counts of murder while investigators pulled apart his life 'with renewed energy', according to Reichert. Ridgway had 'always been among the top five suspects in the case,' Reichert told reporters. 'We're pulling up carpets, looking underneath the carpet, looking through crawl spaces, searching the attic, looking for hair, blood, those types of things,' spokesman Sergeant John Urquhart explained on 3 December 2001. 'A lot of this is potential trace or forensic-type evidence that's going to require a lot of lab work.'

Ridgway was charged with the three murders to which he could be tied by DNA evidence, plus Cynthia Hinds's death given the circumstances, and at his first hearing pleaded innocent to the counts of aggravated first-degree murder. A decision whether to seek the death penalty was delayed during the spring of 2002 after his defence attorneys asked for more time. Three further charges were added on 27 March 2003 after specialised paint found on the bodies of Wendy Coffield and Debra Estes, as well as connected to Debra Bonner, was linked to him – it was used at the truck plant where Ridgway had been working since he was twenty-two years old.

Soon after, his lawyers made an offer – if the death penalty was removed from the equation, he would confess to those seven crimes, as well as many more. On 13 June 2003, the deal was done, and Ridgway duly confessed to forty-eight murders in a plea bargain that spared his life if he helped locate the remains of his victims and provided details of their demise. As to why he had stopped his murderous attacks, in 1985, Ridgway had started to date Judith Mawson, whom he married in 1988; it was around this time that the killings wound down, and Ridgway later admitted that his kill rate had reduced because he truly loved her. (Mawson would later claim that she therefore saved lives.)

There was considerable uproar about the plea bargain that saved Ridgway from execution, but the prosecuting attorney, Norm

Maleng, explained that meant that the families of forty-eight people knew the truth of their deaths. 'Our Green River nightmare is over,' he said in a statement released on 5 November 2003. 'Gary Ridgway does not deserve our mercy. He does not deserve to live. The mercy provided by today's resolution is directed not at Ridgway, but toward the families who have suffered so much.' On 18 December, Judge Richard Jones sentenced Ridgway to forty-eight life sentences with no possibility of parole, and one life sentence to be served consecutively. He was also sentenced to an additional ten years for tampering with evidence for each of the victims.

Ridgway continued to tease the authorities with claims of further victims and in February 2011, after the discovery of the remains of Becky Marrero, a forty-ninth life sentence was added to his count. Searches for the remains still continue and Ridgway offers further clues. But, as reporter Charlie Harger astutely points out,

> Gary Ridgway . . . is playing everybody when he talks. I don't think Gary Ridgway can even comprehend the truth . . . I think he wants to show the world that, 'Here I am, Gary Ridgway, the truck painter from Kenworth, the guy who everybody thought was slow since elementary school, somebody who couldn't hold a candle to Ted Bundy. But, here I am, and I'm the best at something.'

CHAPTER 29

United States: Ray and Faye Copeland

....

The oldest serial killers featured in this volume – and the oldest couple ever sentenced to death in the United States – were responsible for the deaths of five itinerant workers between 1986 and 1989. Chances are there would have been many more if Jack McCormick hadn't evaded death and called the police anonymously, since to Ray and Faye Copeland, it seemed as if they had hit on a scheme that would make them a lot of money very easily. They just needed some scapegoats – and in 1980s America, there was never going to be a short supply of hobos or those down on their luck seeking to make a quick buck.

Ray Copeland was born on 30 December 1914 in Oklahoma and from all accounts had a difficult childhood as his family regularly moved around, finally settling in Ozark Hills, Arkansas. He dropped out of school in fourth grade to help his family but during the Depression years following the Wall Street Crash of 1929, he became a thief. Initially he stole from his immediate family – two hogs from his father, which he sold in another town, and government cheques from his brother – and then graduated to forgery, alongside his livestock thefts. In 1936 he was arrested in Harrison, Arkansas, and jailed for a year. After his release in 1940, he met Faye Della Wilson, who was nearly seven years younger than him. He married her within six months and their first son was born very quickly after. A second son followed the next year, and the young family moved to Fresno County, California, in 1944, where two more sons and a daughter joined the clan. However, they had to move back to Arkansas in 1949, after Copeland was accused of stealing horses from a local farmer; no charges were filed, but it was enough to ruin his reputation.

He lasted just a month back in his wife's home state before being arrested for cattle theft and imprisoned for a year. Once released, they moved to Rocky Comfort, Missouri, but within a few months, Copeland was arrested for the same crime, and this time sentenced to manual labour on the judge's farm. Once free, the Copelands were on the trail again, this time heading to Illinois, where they were constantly on the move: in their eight years in the state from 1953, Copeland was arrested on three separate cases of cheque forgery. In 1961, he paid for twenty head of cattle with a bad cheque, and received a nine-month sentence; undeterred, on his release, he bought nineteen more at an auction, also with a bad cheque, and got a further nine months.

In 1966, aged fifty-one, Copeland moved to Missouri, and the following year, the family bought a forty-acre farm in Mooresville, Missouri – a tiny village in Livingston County, whose population was only 131 at the time of the 1970 census. He still needed money, and had no intention of getting it legally. He therefore came up with a scheme to use passing workers: he would get them to sign his name on a cheque, so that if he were questioned when a cheque was refused, he could claim he knew nothing about it since it wasn't in his handwriting. He got away with this for a time until one drifter named Gerald Perkins was caught by the police, and the truth was uncovered. As a result, Copeland spent a further two years in prison. The plan clearly needed some refinement, and Copeland realised that the weak link was the unemployed man who signed the cheque – the only person who knew Copeland was involved. If he could be got rid of . . .

The final version of the scheme, as outlined at the Copelands' trial, saw Copeland enlist the help of a series of transients from a nearby homeless shelter. He would bring the man to live at the couple's home, and then Copeland would take him to various nearby towns, where the homeless man would open a post office box and a checking account, using the Copelands' money. He would then be taken to various livestock auctions where he would buy the cattle that Copeland wanted, using the cheques from the accounts that had just been opened. However, there wouldn't be sufficient funds in the accounts to cover the value of the cheques, but that didn't matter to Copeland – he sold the cattle straight after the purchase, and pocketed the proceeds . . . then killed the homeless man before the cheques bounced and any investigation began.

Fifty-six year-old Jack McCormick would have been the Copelands' sixth victim, if all had gone according to their plan. He was a recovering alcoholic who described himself as a 'common gutter tramp and drunk'. He was living at the Victory Mission in Springfield, Missouri, in July 1989 when Copeland arrived, offering him a $50-a-day job. He claimed that he was hard of hearing and needed help at the cattle auction. Jack was happy to help, and went with Copeland to Brookfield, Missouri, to open a checking account and get some starter cheques. Faye Copeland asked Jack to sign a blank starter cheque, and then he and Ray Copeland went to the various cattle auctions.

On 6 August, Jack McCormick was killing time at the Copelands' farm, and went for a walk behind the barn. There he saw what he thought was a human skull and either a leg or arm bone protruding from the ground. Faye wasn't at all happy that he had been back there, and told him that the area was out of bounds. Two days later, the proper cheques arrived, and Jack and Ray Copeland went to get them; the pair then went to a sale at Green City, Missouri. When they got back to the farm, Ray berated Jack in front of Faye, saying he was no use at buying cattle; already unhappy after his discoveries earlier in the week, Jack decided he had seen enough and he wanted out. He asked Ray to take him to Brookfield so they could close the bank account.

The next morning, 9 August, Faye left the farm early, claiming she was going to a part-time job at the local Holiday Inn. Ray called Jack McCormick into the barn, asking him to help find a racoon. Jack wasn't initially suspicious that Ray was carrying a .22 calibre rifle, but then he saw that a tractor had been backed up near the barn. On the trailer attached to it were a shovel and a piece of plastic. When he looked up from poking a stick in a hole in the floor, Jack found Ray pointing the rifle directly at him. Jack thought fast, and was able to persuade Ray to take him into Brookfield, although Ray insisted on going to the courthouse at Chillicothe first. There they found Faye waiting – who seemed more than a little surprised to see Jack. The three of them went to Brookfield that afternoon and closed the account, even though a cheque for over $1,100 was still outstanding. The Copelands said they would take Jack home to collect his belongings. He refused to go with them.

Instead, Jack went to a bar and met Rose Clevenger, who agreed to go with him to collect his belongings. When they got to the farm, the Copelands came out and swore at Jack, who claimed Clevenger was his sister. Faye didn't believe him, and made Clevenger give her real name, and took note of her licence plate. Jack McCormick got his stuff, and carried on his travels. Two weeks – and, the court transcript notes, 'much liquor' – later, he was in Nebraska. He called a local 'crime stoppers' hotline, and reported seeing three or four bodies on the Copelands' farm. He was later arrested in Oregon for the bad cheque he had written in Green City, and for car theft.

As far as the Copelands were concerned, it was good riddance to bad rubbish, and they moved on to the next potential victim. In August 1989, Ray Copeland found his next mark, Lothar Borner, at the Souls Harbor Mission in Joplin, Missouri; however, Borner had problems opening a post office box and a checking account.

Concerned at the emphasis that Copeland was putting on this, Borner decided to return to the Mission.

The following month, the Copelands found a new transient: James Page. However, he too had trouble getting a post office box; eventually, after failure in Sedalia, James was able to obtain one in Gallatin. As with McCormick, he was given starter cheques, one of which he signed and gave to Ray. This time it was Faye who accompanied their mark to the auction, telling him to say that she was his wife if anyone asked. They went to various auctions – but before James outlived his usefulness, events overtook the Copelands.

The police had taken the 'crime stoppers' tip from Jack McCormick seriously. Well aware of the Copelands' criminal activities, they came out to the farm with a search warrant. 'You'll find nothing on my place,' Copeland told them, and, certainly, they didn't find any bodies – at least, of humans – when they dug up the ground. However, they found plenty of other incriminating material: there was a lot of clothing in different sizes in the guest-bedroom closet (later identified as belonging to the victims); likewise, there was plenty of other people's luggage. There was also a list of names hidden in a Polaroid camera case; against three names was an 'X'.

After nine days of fruitless searching for bodies, the sheriff brought Jack to the farm and asked him where he had seen the bones. Jack changed his story, and said that he had got it wrong.

Undeterred, the police went to a farm near Ludlow, Missouri, where they had been told by local residents that Ray Copeland had done odd jobs. In a barn, they found several shallow graves, in which were buried Jimmie Dale Harvey, Paul Cowart and John Freeman wrapped in blankets and laid head to toe. All had last been seen working for Copeland; all had written bad cheques; all of them were on the list, in Faye's handwriting, marked with an X. On another farm, they found two more bodies. Wayne Warner had been buried in a shallow grave underneath thousands of large bales of hay. Six weeks later, Dennis Murphy's body was found chained to a forty-pound concrete block at the bottom of a well – Murphy was one of their first victims, disappearing in 1986.

Ray Copeland denied everything. He claimed the transients had palmed off bad cheques on him too; and he said that he had seen Jack McCormick dumping a body into the well. However, all the men had been killed with a gunshot to the head. One of the bullets inside a skull matched the .22 calibre rifle that Ray Copeland owned.

The case against Ray was clear, but there were question marks over Faye's involvement, with some believing that she lived in fear of her husband and would have done what she was told. However, a quilt was found in the house. Faye had made it from the clothing of the dead men.

Faye was sent to trial first, facing a jury on 1 November 1990. She continued to maintain that she knew nothing, but after two and a half hours' deliberation, she was found guilty of four counts of murder and one of manslaughter. After a further three hours, she was given the death penalty. Ray's reaction was reported as being 'Well, those things happen to some, you know.' It happened to him too at his trial: he received the death penalty in March 1991.

Neither Copeland was executed. Ray Copeland died of natural causes on 19 October 1993. Faye Copeland appealed her conviction in August 1996, but the Supreme Court of Missouri denied her a rehearing on 17 September. On 6 August 1999, federal judge Ortrie Smith commuted the sentence to life imprisonment without parole; on 10 August 2002 she became paralysed after a stroke and the following month the state governor granted her medical parole. She was moved to a nursing home, where she died on 23 December 2003.

CHAPTER 30

United States:
Aileen Wuornos

‘I killed those men, robbed them as cold as ice. And I'd do it again, too,' Aileen Wuornos told the court as she asked to be put to death for her crimes. 'There's no chance in keeping me alive or anything, because I'd kill again. I have hate crawling through my system.' Wuornos was an exception to many of the FBI's own rules on serial killers – even Robert Ressler, who coined the term, saw her as an aberration. A rare female serial killer that wasn't part of a 'team', Wuornos was the inspiration for Charlize Theron's award-winning performance in the movie *Monster*.

Aileen Carol Pittman was born on 29 February 1956, the second child of Leo Dale Pittman and Finnish-American Diane Wuornos, who was only fourteen when they married two years earlier. Aileen never knew her father – he was already in prison when she was born and later was convicted of sex crimes against children. He hanged himself in prison on 30 January 1969; some sources say he was strangled. In January 1960, just before Aileen's fourth birthday, her mother left her and her brother Keith with her parents, Lauri and Britta Wuornos, in Troy, Michigan; they legally adopted the pair in March 1960 and brought them up alongside their own children. Aileen wasn't aware that she and her brother were the Wuornos's grandchildren rather than children until she was aged twelve or so, at which point both children rebelled against their grandfather's strict regime. (Aileen's uncle Barry would later tell the court that her stories about this were false: 'We were a pretty straight and normal family – very little trouble in the family.')

Wuornos was already a precocious child: she was involved sexually with her brother, and would exchange sexual favours for cigarettes, drugs or food at school. She later claimed her grandfather assaulted her when she was a child, and she blamed a friend of his for getting her pregnant, aged fourteen. She was put in a home for unwed mothers, where she was uncooperative and hostile; she gave birth to a baby boy on 23 March 1971. He was immediately placed for adoption.

Her grandmother died in the summer of 1971 from liver failure, and Wuornos's grandfather threw her out of the house. Her mother offered that she and her brother could come and stay with her, but the teenager refused, living in the woods near her old house and making a living from prostitution. Aged eighteen, she was arrested in Colorado for driving under the influence, disorderly conduct and firing a pistol from a moving vehicle; she failed to turn up to answer the charges.

In 1976, Aileen Wuornos hitchhiked down to Florida and met yacht club president Lewis Gratz Fell. The sixty-nine-year-old fell under Wuornos's spell and asked her to marry him, with all the attendant notices in the local society pages. The problem was that Wuornos didn't really want to settle down – Fell was a meal ticket – and was constantly in trouble. She was jailed for assault after a confrontation in a local bar, and the marriage was short-lived: after only nine weeks, it was annulled on 21 July. By that point Wuornos had already returned to Michigan, where she was arrested for throwing a cue ball at a bartender's head. Four days before the annulment – and the restraining order that Fell obtained against her after she hit him with his own cane – Wuornos came into money of her own: her brother Keith died of oesophageal cancer, leaving her $10,000 on his life insurance.

It didn't take Aileen Wuornos long to get through that, buying – and shortly afterwards, wrecking – a new car, and living the high life. She made her way back to Florida, where she spent the next decade in a hand-to-mouth existence, earning from prostitution and occasional small-time crimes. She was arrested in May 1981 for robbing $35 and two packs of cigarettes from a convenience store; she was released in June 1983. A month later, she was arrested on forgery charges, in November 1985 she was named as a suspect for the theft of a revolver and ammunition. In January 1986 she was arrested for car theft, resisting arrest and obstruction of justice; a .38-calibre revolver and ammunition were found in the stolen car; six months later, sheriffs questioned her after a man claimed she had pulled a gun on him and demanded $200. She had spare ammunition on her, and a .22 pistol was under the seat of the car.

In June 1986, Wuornos met hotel maid Tyria Moore at a gay bar in Daytona, and the pair moved in together to wherever Wuornos was earning her living – Moore even gave up her job. In her own words, Wuornos was an 'exit to exit' hooker on the interstate, and supplemented the income with various scams under various pseudonyms: she claimed she was assaulted by a Daytona Beach bus driver to try to gain compensation. Her behaviour became increasingly erratic to go along with the 'poor' attitude that police officers commented on when she was arrested; she waged a verbal war with a supermarket after a problem with lottery tickets, and kept getting in fights.

Fifty-one-year-old Richard Mallory was her first murder victim. He was last seen by his co-workers at the Clearwater, Florida, electronics store that he ran on 30 November 1989, although nobody was too surprised that he had vanished for a time: Richard often went on alcoholic binges. Even when his car was found on 1 December, it wasn't necessarily an indication that something was wrong, although his wallet, personal papers, several condoms and a half-bottle of vodka were scattered nearby. Eventually, his fully dressed body was found several miles away in a nearby wood; it had been wrapped in a carpet. Fingerprints showed it was Richard, and he had died from two gunshot wounds to the left lung. Although it seemed as if Richard had lived a sleazy life, there were no obvious suspects. The trail went cold.

On 5 May 1990, a naked male body was found in Brooks County, Georgia, close to Interstate 75 – just over the state line from Florida. There were two .22-calibre bullets in the body. On 1 June 1990, David Spears's naked body was found along Highway 19 in Citrus County, Florida, forty miles north of Tampa. He had been shot six times, and had not been seen since May 19 when he had gone to visit his ex-wife; his truck had been spotted near Interstate 75 on 25 May. The truck was found shortly after David was identified on 7 June.

A day earlier, yet another naked male body was found not far from Interstate 75; it was in such a bad state of decomposition thanks to the Florida climate that it couldn't be identified from fingerprints. The man had been shot nine times with a .22-calibre weapon. The detective investigating the case, Tom Muck, got in touch with his colleagues investigating Spears's death and the unidentified Georgia killing, but there wasn't sufficient evidence linking the crimes as yet. On 7 June, a car belonging to rodeo worker Charles Carskaddon was found in Marion County; his .45 automatic and various other items had been taken from the vehicle. Charles had been missing since 31 May while on the way to visit his fiancée.

Sixty-five-year-old Peter Siems was a retired merchant seaman who helped with a Christian outreach ministry. He left his home in Jupiter, Florida, to visit relatives in Arkansas on 7 June; he never got there, and a missing person's report was filed on 22 June. On 4 July, his car was found: two women – one blonde, one brunette – had climbed from it after it had spun off State Road 315 near Orange Springs, Florida. Eyewitness Rhonda Bailey saw them throw beer cans in a bush and swear at each other; the blonde woman, whose arm was bleeding, asked Bailey not to report them to the police before managing to reverse the car back onto the road. It was too badly damaged, however, and they soon abandoned it. When the police investigated it, they found bloodstains throughout the vehicle, including a palm print in the trunk. (A fire officer also encountered the pair as they walked along the road; they denied the vehicle was anything to do with them.)

Troy Burress disappeared on 30 July while on his delivery route for Gilchrist Sausage. The fifty-year-old was reported missing at 2 a.m. the next day, and his truck was found very shortly afterwards on the side of Highway 19, twenty miles east of Ocala. On 4 August, a family out for a summer picnic found his body in a clearing off Highway 19, about eight miles from where his truck had been located. He had been shot twice with a .22-calibre pistol, in the back and chest. Not far from his severely decomposed body, police found his credit cards, clipboard, business receipts and an empty cash bag from a local bank. Hitchhiker Curtis Michael Blankenship came under suspicion, but was soon cleared.

Former police chief Dick Humphreys vanished on 11 September 1990, the day after his thirty-fifth wedding anniversary. He had been celebrating his last day at work as a protective investigator specialising in abused and injured children at the Sumterville office of Florida's Department of Health and Rehabilitative Services prior to starting a new job in Ocala. His body was found the next day, shot seven times with a .22-calibre pistol; his car turned up a week later, its licence plates gone, behind an abandoned service station in Suwannee County. However, it wasn't linked to him until 13 October, the same day that his badge and other items were found seventy miles from where his corpse was discovered.

Reserve police officer Walter Gino Antonio was found in the woods north-west of Cross City on 19 November. He had been shot three times in the back and once in the head, and his body stripped – except for his socks. The sixty-year-old truck-driver's car was found some distance away, in Brevard County, five days later.

The media were reporting the latest murders and the police finally went public with their investigations – and that the two women found with Peter Siems's car were the likely suspects. They ran a story on 30 November 1990 via Reuters press agency that included police sketches based on descriptions given by the eyewitnesses to the crash. Over the next three weeks, four separate people identified the women as Tyria Moore and Lee Blahovec – one of Wuornos's aliases.

Port Orange police were able to provide a great deal of assistance: they knew that the pair had stayed at the Fairview Hotel in Harbor Oaks, or in an apartment nearby. In Daytona, they discovered that 'Cammie Marsh Greene' had pawned a camera and a radar detector (belonging to Richard Mallory) on 6 December; the same day she got rid of a box of Spears's tools, leaving a thumbprint on the receipt. The following day she pawned Antonio's distinctive gold ring in Volusia County. The thumbprint was matched with fingerprint records in Volusia County and belonged to a Lori Grady, wanted on a concealed weapons charge. The palm print in Peter Siems's car went with the fingerprints, and a National Crime Information Center request came back with confirmation of matches in Michigan, Florida and Colorado: all the associated aliases belonged to Aileen Carol Wuornos.

On 5 January 1991 officers began combing the streets for Wuornos. Two of them – Mike Joyner and Dick Martin – posed as 'Bucket' and 'Drums', two drug dealers from Georgia. They found Wuornos on the evening of 8 January at the Port Orange pub, and had to rapidly prevent two local cops from arresting her prematurely. Then, as Wuornos walked down the road towards another bar, Florida Department of Law Enforcement officers started to follow her; again 'Bucket' and 'Drums' had to get them off their suspect's tail. They didn't as yet have a solid case against her and needed to ensure that they did so before making the collar. Wuornos went to a biker bar, the Last Resort, where Bucket and Drums started to gain her confidence.

The next afternoon, they all met up again – Wuornos had spent the night at the bar – and the undercover cops asked her if she wanted to get cleaned up at their motel room. She agreed, and when she was outside the bar, she was arrested as Lori Grady on the outstanding weapons charge. However, in order to make murder charges stick, they needed something stronger.

On 10 January, the day after Wuornos was arrested, the police tracked down Tyria Moore, who was staying with her sister in Pittston, Pennsylvania. Two detectives flew up to question her; she was read her rights but not charged with any offences. Moore immediately said that she knew about the murders. As she explained in court, she and Wuornos were sitting in their apartment drinking beer on 1 December 1989, when Wuornos said she had to tell her something. 'She said she had shot and killed a man,' Moore recalled. 'She said she had put the body in the woods under a rug.' Wuornos had kept a box with some of Richard Mallory's personal possessions in it, and showed Moore a photograph of her victim. 'I remember seeing the name Richard on a piece of paper,' Moore said while Wuornos was 'going through the stuff, throwing some away.'

Moore told the detectives that she hadn't wanted to hear about the murder, 'And then any time she would come home after that and say certain things, telling me about where she got something, I'd say I don't want to hear it.' She admitted she was scared of what Wuornos might do to her. 'She always said she'd never hurt me, but then you can't believe her.' She agreed to help the detectives elicit a confession from her former partner: they put her in a motel where the plan was she would speak with Wuornos in jail and say she was worried that the murders would be pinned on her rather than Wuornos.

When the two women spoke on 14 January, Wuornos seemed convinced that the police had no idea who they had really got. 'I wasn't one of those little suspects,' she told Moore. 'I think somebody at work – where you worked at – said something that it looked like us. And it isn't us, see? It's a case of mistaken identity.'

The police were convinced that this wasn't the case, and Moore kept pressure on Wuornos to clear her of any involvement. In the end Wuornos said, 'I will cover for you, because you're innocent. I'm not going to let you go to jail. Listen: if I have to confess, I will.'

And she did, on 16 January 1991. Not that it was her fault, of course. 'I shot 'em 'cause to me it was like a self-defending thing,' she maintained. 'Because I felt if I didn't shoot 'em and didn't kill 'em, first of all . . . if they had survived my ass would be getting in trouble for attempted murder, so I'm up shit's creek on that one anyway, and if I didn't kill 'em, you know, of course, I mean I had to kill 'em . . . or it's like retaliation too. It's like, You bastards, you were going to hurt me.'

She was charged with the murder of Richard Mallory on 17 January. Property belonging to seven of the missing men was found in a storage unit she had rented, and prosecutors in four Florida counties worked on additional charges against her. 'We want to clear up as many homicides as possible,' Captain Steve Binegar told the press. 'We believe she pretty much meets the guideline of a serial killer.'

Wuornos's trial opened on 13 January 1992. During the year she had been incarcerated there had been assorted unusual developments – Wuornos's story was told in all forms of media, and she was adopted by forty-four-year-old born-again Christian, Arlene Pralle, who became her advocate in all but the legal sense, presenting a picture of a battered woman pushed to extremes. Meanwhile, her lawyers tried to arrange a plea bargain, whereby she would plead guilty to six charges and receive six consecutive life terms. However, the state attorneys didn't go for it – they wanted her to receive the death penalty.

She was only on trial for one case, but Florida law allowed for some evidence to be admitted if it showed a pattern. Some of Moore's testimony was excluded, but parts of Wuornos's videotaped confession could be shown – including the telling line, 'I took a life . . . I am willing to give up my life because I killed people . . . I deserve to die.'

That was in stark contrast to her performance on the witness stand straight after the jury saw that video. For three hours she answered questions, stating 'I'm the innocent victim, not him.' Her work as a prostitute was all Moore's fault: she demanded money from Wuornos. Moore 'was my pimp, and I was her white slave. She wanted money and clothes and a place to live.' Moore sent her out to work as a hooker, and if Wuornos didn't, 'she would break up with me, and find another girl that would definitely take care of her. I did it because I loved her to the max.'

According to her, Richard Mallory picked her up under a freeway bridge in Tampa, and they drove to Daytona Beach, stopping at a spot where Wuornos admitted she initiated sex for money. Mallory choked her, tied her hands together behind her back, then held her down on the front seat of his car and raped her. She claimed she thought he was going to kill her, and yelled at him, but 'The more I yelled the rougher he got.' She decided she wasn't going to die, so 'I finally jerked my hand loose, grabbed my gun from my bag, whipped it out in front of me, and I shot him. Then I shot him again.' Mallory crawled out of the car and went round to the other side, but 'I had to shoot him again, 'cause he just kept coming.' She took the Fifth Amendment more than two dozen times during cross-examination, and got tangled in her various stories. On the stand, she claimed that her time with Richard Mallory involved anal rape and torture; she hadn't mentioned that to the police. As local reporter Jeff Brazil commented in his report on her testimony: 'The defence in the Aileen Wuornos murder case called its one and only witness. In the end it may have been one witness too many.'

Wuornos testified on Friday, January 24; on the afternoon of Monday 27, Judge Uriel Blount sent the jury out to consider their verdict. It took them ninety-five minutes to reach a conclusion. She was found guilty. 'I'm innocent! I was raped!' she screamed. 'I hope you get raped! Scumbags of America!' The next day, the penalty phase began, with psychologist Elizabeth McMahon testifying that Wuornos had an 'angry, self-destructive personality that operates at a child's level'. The jury weren't swayed; on 30 January, they unanimously recommended that she be sent to the electric chair. 'Every time I began to think about her, I thought about those men she killed,' juror Gary Degayner told the media after the trial was over. 'They didn't have a chance to say anything.'

On 31 January, the judge followed their recommendation despite Wuornos tearfully maintaining, 'I'm no serial killer.' She was also given a ten-year sentence for armed robbery. The other cases against her were not contested: she was given three more death sentences on 15 May for the murders of Dick Humphreys, Troy Burress and David Spears. In June she pleaded guilty to Charles Caskaddon's murder, for which she was given a death sentence in November 1992; three months later, she was sentenced to die for the murder of Walter Gino Antonio. No charge was ever brought regarding Peter Siems; his body was never found, despite Wuornos taking investigators to show them the site where she left him.

Dateline NBC investigated Mallory's murder and discovered that he had served a ten-year prison sentence for rape – something the police had singularly failed to check with the FBI. However, it transpired that the defence had been aware of Mallory's violent past and chosen not to call his girlfriend from the time.

The appeals process dragged on while Wuornos was kept on death row, but in 2001, she petitioned the Florida Supreme Court to dismiss her counsel and terminate all pending appeals. She spent some time in her final weeks talking with filmmaker Nick Broomfield, and complaining that the staff were trying to poison her. She was executed on 9 October 2002; her last words were suitably off-kilter: 'I would just like to say I'm sailing with the rock and I'll be back, like *Independence Day*, with Jesus. June 6, like the movie. Big mother ship and all. I'll be back, I'll be back.'

Primary Sources

CHAPTER 1: IVAN MILAT

Real Crime Daily, 'Ivan Milat's nephew claims his uncle was framed for the Backpacker Murders' (28 February 2016).

Daily Telegraph (Sydney), 'Ivan Milat: Disappearance of teenage girls linked to Australia's worst serial killer' (10 August 2016).

News.com.au, 'Explosive details of the violent crime a young Ivan Milat allegedly got away with' (26 April 2015).

Sydney Morning Herald, 'Back into heart of darkness' (5 September 2010).

Sydney Morning Herald, 'Friends born of sorrow' (24 April 2006).

Australian, 'The nine bodies found in Belanglo Forest' (22 November 2010).

Australian Institute of Criminology, 'Investigating homicide: New responses for an old crime', paper presented at the 4th National Outlook Symposium on Crime in Australia (June 2001).

Herald Sun, 'Backpacker murders; How backpacker Paul Onions survived a close encounter with evil Ivan Milat' (January 1997; reprinted 15 May 2015).

Sunday Mail (Queensland), 'Backpacker who escaped Ivan Milat to return to Australia' (31 January 2010).

Daily Mail, 'Trophies of a serial killer: New photographs from inside Ivan Milat's house as Australia's most notorious murderer marks 20 years in prison' (21 May 2014).

Dispatch, 'Suspected charged in seven murders' (31 May 1994).

Hansard, Legislative Assembly of New South Wales, 'Maitland Correctional Centre Escape Attempt' (20 May 1997) (worth reading for the way in which the minister deals with his parliamentary colleagues!).

Supreme Court of New South Wales, 'Regina v. Milat Matter No. Cca 60438/96 [1998] NSWSC 795' (26 February 1998).

News.com.au, 'Inside the life and mind of Australia's most infamous serial killer: letters from Ivan Milat' (12 March 2016), http://www.news.com.au/national/crime/inside-the-life-and-mind-of-australias-most-infamous-serial-killer-letters-from-ivan-milat/news-story/67a972cc48e03c2109c175b7805bb8fb

CHAPTER 2: PAUL CHARLES DENYER

Herald Sun, 'Special handwriting analysis provides an insight into the mind of serial killer Paul Denyer' (6 April 2013).

ABC, 'Murderer's sex change request sparks rights debate' (9 January 2004).

Trevor Marriott, *The Evil Within* (John Blake, 2013).

Herald Sun, 'The urges that drove serial killer Paul Charles Denyer to murder had been building since age 14' (9 April 2013).

Herald Sun, 'Serial killer Paul Denyer is a monster with no remorse' (9 April 2013).

Daily Telegraph (Sydney), 'Family of Paul Denyer tell of killer's death threat' (22 July 2011):.

Herald Sun, 'Denyers tell of killer's death threat' (22 July 2011).

Age, 'Stop pandering to "sicko", says Doyle' (28 June 2004).

The Pursuit of Justice: 25 Years of the DPP in Victoria (Director of Public Prosecutions, Victoria, 2008).

Forensic Investigators, Season 1, Episode 1 (September 2004).

CHAPTER 3: MICHAEL WAYNE MCGRAY

Globe and Mail, ' "I'm a sociopath," man says in explaining why he killed cellmate' (30 October 2012).

Globe and Mail, ' "I got very good at it," killer says' (24 March 2000).

National Post, 'Prison couldn't keep Michael Wayne McGray from killing – just like he said it wouldn't' (29 November 2011).

Globe and Mail, 'Community wants coroner's inquest' (15 November 1993).

Globe and Mail, 'Nova Scotia man claims to be Canada's worst serial killer'(21 March 2009).

Globe and Mail, 'Killer should have been isolated, mother of slain man tells inquest' (30 October 2012).

Crime Stories, 'The Homicidal Drifter', Season 3, Episode 2 (17 March 2006).

CHAPTER 4: PEDRO ALONSO LÓPEZ

Daily Record, 'Inside the mind of a serial killer' (10 February 2001).

Biography, 'Pedro Alonso López: The Monster of the Andes' (2004).

CHAPTER 5: DANIEL CAMARGO BARBOSA

Hoy, 'La infancia y la virginidad: Dos vertientes del crimen' (15 November 1994).

Hoy, 'Cronologia de los asesinatos de Camargo Barbosa' (15 November 1994).

El Pais, 'El sádico del Chanquito' (2 February 1988).

El Tiempo, 'Terminó historia de terror en Ecuador' (15 November 1994), http://www.eltiempo.com/archivo/documento/MAM-250868.

CHAPTER 6: LUIS ALFREDO GARAVITO CUBILLOS

Irene Baron Chilito et al., 'Estructura de la personalidad de Luis Alfredo Garavito', Congreso Latinoamericano Psicología Jurídica e Forense (undated), http://psicologiajuridica.org/psj311.html.

El Tiempo, 'Ecuador pidió envío de Luis Alfredo Garavito' (28 May 2011).

Emol Mundo, 'Colombia: Condenan a 1.853 años de cárcel a asesino de 172 niños' (3 November 2001).

M. Benecke, A. Mätzler, M. Rodriquez and A. Zabeck. 'Two homosexual pedophile sadistic serial killers: Jürgen Bartsch (Germany, 1946–1976) and Luis Alfredo Garavito Cubillos (Colombia, 1957)', *Minerva Medicolegale* (September 2005): 153–69.

CNN, 'Man admits killing 140 children in Colombia' (30 October 1999).

BBC News, 'World: Americas: Colombian child killer confesses' (30 October 1999).

Attorney General, '172 niños víctimas de Luis Alfredo Garavito', press release (1999), http://web.archive.org/web/20070928043238/ http://www.fiscalia.gov.co/pag/divulga/InfEsp/Garavito.htm.

CHAPTER 7: JACK THE RIPPER – THE WHITECHAPEL MURDERS

Metropolitan Police: 'Jack the Ripper', http://content.met.police.uk/ Site/jacktheripper.

Casebook: Jack the Ripper, http://www.casebook.org.

People, 'Horrible affair in Whitechapel: outrage, robbery, and murder' (8 April 1888).

Star, 'The Whitechapel tragedy: Verdict of the coroner's jury on the revolting murder' (24 August 1888).

Daily Telegraph, 'The Whitechapel murders' (24 September 1888).

The Times, 'The Whitechapel murder' (3 September 1888).

The Times, 'The Whitechapel murder' (14 September 1888).

CHAPTER 8: JOHN CHRISTIE

BBC, 'On this day: 1953: Christie to hang for wife's murder' (25 June 2005).

Glasgow Herald, 'Pathologist's evidence on four murdered women' (30 April 1953).

Glasgow Herald, 'Defence of insanity in Christie trial' (23 June 1953).

Glasgow Herald, 'No question of wrong man being hanged' (24 June 1953).

Glasgow Herald, 'Christie's defence of insanity fails' (26 June 1953).

High Court of Justice, Queen's Bench Division, Divisional Court, Mary Westlake v. Criminal Cases Review Commission (17 November 2004).

J. Scott Henderson QC, *Report of an inquiry into certain matters arising out of the deaths of Mrs Beryl Evans and of Geraldine Evans and out of* the conviction of Timothy John Evans of the murder of Geraldine Evans (HMSO, July 1953).

Hon. Mr Justice Brabin, *The Case of Timothy John Evans: Report of an Inquiry by the Hon. Mr Justice Brabin* (HMSO, October 1966).

Ludovic Kennedy, *Ten Rillington Place* (HarperCollins, 1971).

Edward Marston, *Crime Archive: John Christie* (National Archive, 2007).

CHAPTER 9: JOHN GEORGE HAIGH – THE ACID BATH MURDERER

James H. Hodge (ed.), *Famous Trials 6* (Penguin, 1962).

K. Ramsland, 'John George Haigh: a malingerer's legacy', *Forensic Examiner* (December 2006).

The Trial of John George Haigh (The Acid Bath Murder), Notable British Trials vol. 78 (W. Hodge, 1953).

The Times, court reports (9 and 26 March 1949; 29 July 1949; 19 January 1951).

Time, 'The press: I was a vampire' (1 August 1949).

Time, 'The press: Wicked character' (4 April 1949).

Time, 'Foreign news: A glass of blood' (25 July 1949).

Letter from John Haigh to his girlfriend Barbara Stevens (4 March 1949), available at http://www.nationalarchives.gov.uk/releases/2005/highlights_july/july10/popup/pcom_9_818doc1.htm.

Letter from John Haigh to Messrs Eagen & Sons (26 July 1949), available at http://www.nationalarchives.gov.uk/releases/2005/highlights_july/july10/popup/pcom_9_818doc4.htm.

Neil Root, *Frenzy! Heath, Haigh & Christie* (Arrow, 2012).

Professor Keith Simpson, *Forty Years of Murder* (Harrap, 1978).

CHAPTER 10: IAN BRADY AND MYRA HINDLEY – THE MOORS MURDERERS

Time, 'World: A most unusual trial' (29 April 1966).

Time, 'World: The maximum sentence' (13 May 1966).

Glasgow Herald, 'Coroner commends police after Moors verdict' (13 April 1988).

Glasgow Herald, 'Police tell inquest of finding girl's body on moor' (3 August 1987).

Meriden Morning Record, 'Strange, savage twist hits Britain's moorland trial' (21 April 1966).

Glasgow Herald, 'Clothing on moor body identified' (23 October 1965).

Age, 'Moors murders lawyers given guard' (22 April 1966).

Glasgow Herald, 'Crown counsel tells court of sex element' (21 April 1966).

Glasgow Herald, 'Police questions on picture of boy's grave' (29 April 1966).

Evening Independent, 'Mom says clothes slain son's' (28 April 1966).

Lodi News-Sentinel, 'More bodies are hunted by officers' (25 October 1965).

Daily Telegraph, 'Revealed: The schoolgirl who escaped the clutches of the Moors Murderers' (30 December 2005).

Glasgow Herald, 'Brady and Hindley sent for trial' (21 December 1965).

Glasgow Herald, 'Forensic expert questioned on Smith's stick' (26 April 1966).

Glasgow Herald, 'Dawn phone call by two frightened people' (20 April 1966).

Glasgow Herald, 'Crown witness describes axe killing' (22 April 1966).

Glasgow Herald, 'Witness admits interest in conviction' (23 April 1966).

Glasgow Herald, 'Court hears tape-recording of three voices' (27 April 1966); warning: this report includes an almost complete transcript of the Lesley Ann Downey tape.

Glasgow Herald, 'Police evidence on interview with Brady' (28 April 1966).

Glasgow Herald, 'Ian Brady admits hitting Evans' (30 April 1966).

Glasgow Herald, 'Myra Hindley cross-examined on Evans's death' (4 May 1966).

Glasgow Herald, 'QC tells jury of 8 "trade marks of murder"' (5 May 1966).

Glasgow Herald, 'The judge sums up in "this horrible case"' (6 May 1966).

Glasgow Herald, 'Guilty verdicts in moors case' (7 May 1966).

Guardian, 'Funeral pariah' (21 November 2002).

CHAPTER 11: FRED AND ROSEMARY WEST

Hereford Times, 'Fred West's brother denies incest claims' (7 November 2014).

Daily Record, 'TV documentary reveals how serial killer Fred West was chased from Glasgow by razor-wielding lynch mob' (1 June 2014).

BBC News, 'Fred West "admitted killing waitress"' (25 March 1998).

Gloucestershire Live, 'Did Fred West murder Mary Bastholm – the detective's story Part 1' (28 December 2011).

Independent, 'Young women tell of attacks by Fred West' (3 November 1995).

North Devon Journal, 'Serial killer's tortured Northam childhood' (7 July 2011).

Observer, 'There's nobody home . . .' (15 February 2004).

Independent, 'I survived Fred and Rose West' (8 September 1998).

Daily Mail, 'Glamorising of an evil nobody' (5 September 2011).

Martin Amis, *Experience* (Jonathan Cape, 2000).

Independent, 'The bodies: Litany of sadness: The lives of West's twelve female victims' (2 January 1995).

Herald Scotland, 'Prosecution tells how young girls were abducted and abused "in most appalling way". The victims of depravity' (7 October 1995).

Graham McGredy-Hunt, *Searching for Suzy* (Lulu, 2012).

Herald Scotland, 'History of perversion that lay behind John West's serial rape charges. A family steeped in evil' (29 November 1996).

Herald Scotland, 'Brother of Fred West "knew about murders"' (21 April 1997).

Daily Mirror, 'Serial killer Rose West cuts her own hair amid fears she will be attacked by prison inmates' (22 February 2015).

Gordon Burn, *Happy Like Murderers* (Faber & Faber, 1998).

CHAPTER 12: DR HAROLD SHIPMAN

Dame Janet Smith, *The Shipman Inquiry, First Report: Volume One: Death Disguised* (HMSO, 19 July 2002).

Dame Janet Smith, *The Shipman Inquiry, Sixth Report: Shipman, The Final Report* (27 January 2005).

Dame Janet Smith, *The Shipman Inquiry, Second Report: The Police Investigation of March 1998* (July 2003).

Guardian, 'Shipman may have killed young girl' (27 January 2005).

Manchester Evening News, 'Shipman killed 15 as junior doctor' (30 June 2005).

BBC News, '"I feel guilty over Shipman killings"' (30 September 2003).

BBC News, 'Shipman defence attacks morphine theory' (10 November 1999).

BBC News, 'Shipman takes the stand' (26 November 1999).

BBC News, 'Murder trial doctor weeps' (1 December 1999).

BBC News, 'Final evidence in Shipman trial' (December 13, 1999).

BBC News, '"No case" against Shipman' (7 January 2000).

Tameside Metropolitan Borough, 'Garden of Tranquillity [*sic*] opens in Hyde Park', press release (July 2005).

Panorama, 'The Man Who Played God', BBC TV (31 January 2000).

CHAPTER 13: PETER SUTCLIFFE – THE YORKSHIRE RIPPER

Daily Mail, 'Return of the Ripper hunter' (11 January 1980).

High Court of Justice, Queen's Bench Division, R. v. Peter Coonan (formerly Sutcliffe) (16 July 2010).

Keighley News, 'Death of "ripper survivor" at 75' (25 April 2008).

Daily Mail, 'Yorkshire Ripper may face more murder charges' (6 December 2015).

Daily Mail, 'Haunted to the end' (11 April 2011).

People, 'Crime People: I survived the Ripper' (16 January 2000).

Home Office, 'Sir Lawrence Byford report into the police handling of the Yorkshire Ripper case' (written 1981; released 1 June 2006).

Daily Mirror, 'Let Yorkshire Ripper die in jail: Families' fury at Peter Sutcliffe freedom bid' (2 March 2010).

Huddersfield Daily Examiner, 'My Ripper hell' (4 May 2006).

Daily Mirror, 'Yorkshire Ripper hoaxer Wearside Jack speaks for first time about "prank" that derailed serial killer investigation' (14 July 2013).

Confession Statement: Statement of Peter William Sutcliffe (4 January 1981).

Chapter 14: Dennis Nilsen – The Coleherne I

Russell Coffey, *Dennis Nilsen: Conversations with Britain's Most Evil Serial Killer* (John Blake, 2013).

Brian Masters, *Killing for Company: The Case of Dennis Nilsen* (Random House, 1985).

Dennis Nilsen, 'Dennis Nilsen's autobiography' (2013), http://dennis-nilsen.blogspot.co.uk.

Daily Telegraph, 'Nilsen describes how he murdered his first victim' (10 November 2006).

Glasgow Herald, 'Nilsen "confessed he had no tears for his victims"' (26 October 1983).

Glasgow Herald, 'Nilsen not insane, says psychiatrist' (27 October 1983).

Glasgow Herald, 'Jury told Nilsen took on role of "quasi-God"' (25 October 1983).

Glasgow Herald, 'A life sentence' (5 November 1983).

Glasgow Herald, 'Nilsen to serve at least 25 years' (5 November 1983).

Glasgow Herald, 'Judge quizzes psychiatrist in Nilsen trial' (28 October 1983).

Glasgow Herald, 'Nilsen "like man drowning in nightmares," jury told' (29 October 1983).

Crown Prosecution Service, 'Dennis Nilsen – CPS decision about first victim', press release (6 December 2006).

CHAPTER 15: MICHAEL LUPO – THE COLEHERNE II

David Stafford and Caroline Stafford, *Cupid Stunts: The Life and Radio Times of Kenny Everett* (Omnibus, 2013).

Independent, 'Serial killer with HIV virus dies in jail' (18 February 1995).

Guardian, 'Gay cruiser who strangled four men in a "cold rage"' (11 July 1987).

Ben Campkin and Rosie Cox (eds), *Dirt: New Geographies of Cleanliness and Contamination* (I. B. Tauris, 2012).

LBC/IRN, 'Homosexual killer Michael Lupo case' (11 July 1987).

Crimen Real, 'El Lobo del Londres – Michael Lupo' (2014), accessed via YouTube.

CHAPTER 16: COLIN IRELAND – THE COLEHERNE III

Independent, 'Serial killer locked up for life' (21 December, 1993).

People, 'A killer stalks gay London' (12 July 1993).

Daily Mirror, 'Death of a serial killer: "Gay Slayer" who tortured five men to death dies in jail' (21 February 2012).

Guardian, 'Officers' homophobia hampered murder investigations, says review' (15 May 2007).

Real Crime, Colin Ireland, ITV (2008).

Pink News, 'Exercise yard fall contributed to death of "Gay Slayer", inquest hears' (29 February 2012).

Robert K. Ressler and Tom Shachtman, *I Have Lived in the Monster* (St Martin's Press, 1997).

CHAPTER 17: STEVE WRIGHT

Guardian, 'My anger is buried deep inside' (21 February 2008).

Guardian, 'Girlfriend insists new suspect is innocent as forensic teams search their home' (20 December 2006).

BBC Suffolk, 'Suffolk murders 2006: Profile of a serial killer' (February 2008).

Daily Telegraph, 'Steve Wright: A real Jekyll and Hyde' (21 February 2008).

BBC News, 'How Steve Wright's trial unfolded' (21 February 2008).

Crown Prosecution Service, 'Steve Wright guilty of murders of five women', press release (21 February 2008).

Sunday Mirror, 'Ripper hunt exclusive: The suspect' (17 December 2006).

Chronicle Live, 'Dad of murdered Paula Clennell welcomes life-term ruling for serial killer Steve Wright' (23 February 2014).

BBC News, 'Killer steeped in world of vice' (21 February 2008).

BBC News, 'Serial killer drops appeal case' (2 February 2009).

Daily Mail, 'The other suspect who said: Suffolk Strangler may be me' (14 February 2008).

Daily Telegraph, 'The school nerd who liked to help vice girls' (19 December 2006).

CHAPTER 18: AHMAD SURADJI

BBC News, 'Indonesian sorcerer sentenced to death' (27 April 1998).

CNN, 'Indonesian executed for killing 42 females' (11 July 2008).

Crime Investigation Asia, 'Indonesia's Sorcerer from Hell' (2012)

Dusan AS – fictionalised dramatization featuring interview with Suradji (2012).

CHAPTER 19: ALI ASGHAR BORUJERDI

Cyrus Schayegh, 'Serial Murder in Tehran: Crime, Science, and the Formation of Modern State and Society in Interwar Iran', *Society for Comparative Study of Society and History* 47: 4 (October 2005), pp. 836–62.

H. Enayat, *Law, State and Society In Modern Iran* (AIAA, 2013).

CHAPTER 20: HADJ MOHAMMED MESFEWI

Times and Democrat, 'An awful fate' (28 June 1906).

St John Daily, 'He has murdered thirty-six women' (1 May 1906).

Queanbeyan Age, 'Moroccan murderers' (6 September 1907).
Home Daily Sentinel, 'Murderer walled up alive' (16 June 1906).

CHAPTER 21: VASILI KOMAROFF

'Serial Killer Crime Index: KOMAROFF, Vasili', Crimezzz.net (2005), http://www.crimezzz.net/serialkillers/K/KOMAROFF_vassili. php.
Sasha, 'Komarov, Vasily (Rus.), Serial-Killers.ru (undated).
Alina Maximova, 'Shabolovsky Murderer Vasili Komaroff', All-Kriminal. ru (undated).

CHAPTER 22: MOSES SITHOLE

Independent, 'SA serial killer suspect caught' (19 October 1995).
IOL, 'Serial killer put in his place' (8 November 2012), http://www.iol. co.za/news/crime-courts/serial-killer-put-in-his-place-1419729.

CHAPTER 23: JOHN WAYNE GACY

FBI File Number 62-5154, Subject John Wayne Gacy (assorted documents), accessed at vault.fbi.gov.
Press-Courier, 'Youthful victims buried alive, expert speculates' (19 February 1980).
Hour, 'Authorities level John Gacy home' (12 April 1979).
CBS Chicago, 'Movie, documentary could be adapted from book by Gacy's lawyer' (21 December 2011).
Desert News, 'Serial Killer Executed by Injection in Illinois' (10 May 1994).
Chicago Tribune, 'Woman's attorneys say DNA proves Gacy victim was not her missing son' (26 October 2012).
Time, 'Nation: "I do rotten, horrible things"' (8 January 1979)
Time, 'Serial killer John Wayne Gacy may have had accomplices' (13 February 2012).

Sam L. Amirante and Danny Broderick, *John Wayne Gacy: Defending a Monster* (Skyhorse Publishing, 2011).

Tim Cahill, *Buried Dreams: Inside the Mind of a Serial Killer* (Bantam Books, 1986).

Joseph R. Kozenczak and Karen Henrikson, *The Chicago Killer: The Hunt for Serial Killer John Wayne Gacy* (Xlibris, 2003).

Clifford L. Linedecker, *The Man Who Killed Boys: A True Story of Mass Murder in a Chicago Suburb* (St Martin's Press, 1986).

Robert Ressler and Tom Schactman, *Whoever Fights Monsters: My Twenty Years Hunting Serial Killers for the FBI* (St Martin's Press, 1992).

Terry Sullivan and Peter T. Maiken, *Killer Clown: The John Wayne Gacy Murders* (Pinnacle, 2000).

Records and Archives of the Circuit Court, County Cook, Illinois (available online); the full twenty-two boxes of evidence can be viewed although the court warns 'Much of the written and visual material is extremely graphic in nature.'

CHAPTER 24: TED BUNDY

Huffington Post, 'DNA evidence fails to link Ted Bundy to Ann Marie Burr' (10 October 2011).

Ted Bundy to Beverly Burr, letter (8 June 1986).

Desert News, 'Officer recalls Bundy's '75 capture' (20 August 2000).

Salt Lake Tribune, 'Back in courtroom, dead-tired Bundy hears new charges' (14 June 1977).

Salt Lake Tribune, 'Inmates heard Bundy "preparing" escape?' (4 January 1978).

Salt Lake Tribune, 'Jailers raked in Bundy escape' (5 January 1978).

Time, 'Press: Knocking on death's door' (27 February 1989).

New York Times, 'Florida inmate a suspect in killings of 36 women, but police lack decisive evidence' (14 March 1978).

Time, 'Nation: The case of the Chi Omega killer' (16 July 1979).

Time, 'I deserve punishment: Ted Bundy' (6 February 1989).

Elizabeth Kendall, *The Phantom Prince: My Life with Ted Bundy* (Madrona, 1981).

Stephen G. Michaud and Hugh Aynesworth, *Ted Bundy: Conversations with a Killer* (Authorlink, 2000).

Polly Nelson, *Defending the Devil: My Story as Ted Bundy's Last Lawyer* (William Morrow, 1994).

Ann Rule, *The Stranger Beside Me* (Penguin, 1989).

FBI files on Ted Bundy, accessed at vault.fbi.gov.

CHAPTER 25: DENNIS RADER

Wichita Eagle, 'Investigators tell of grisly crimes, Rader's delight' (18 August 2005).

Wichita Eagle, 'BTK describes his own crimes' (16 July 2005).

Chicago Tribune, 'Baffled church supports, prays for BTK suspect' (28 February 2005).

Washington Post, 'From DNA of family, a tool to make arrests' (21 April 2008).

'The BTK Story', TruTV (contemporary news reports).

John Douglas and Johnny Dodd, *Inside the Mind of BTK* (John Wiley & Sons, 2003).

Robert Beattie, *Nightmare in Wichita* (NAL, 2005).

CHAPTER 26: DAVID BERKOWITZ – SON OF SAM

Independent, 'Timothy Dowd: New York cop who caught "Son of Sam" killer David Berkowitz dies' (30 December 2014).

New York Post, 'Bronx girl slain in car' (29 July 1976).

New York Post, 'Summer of insanity as killer terrorized City: Mad gunman's spree panicked young lovers' (27 June 1999).

NBC Dateline, 'Did "Son of Sam" really act alone?' (2 July 2004).

New York Times, 'Woman dies in mystery shooting' (31 January 1977).

New York Post, 'Shots fired into car kill her in embrace' (31 January 1977).

New York Times, 'Columbia coed, 19, is slain on street in Forest Hills' (9 March 1977).

New York Times, 'Fourth woman slain by same gun' (18 April 1977).

New York Daily News, '.44-cal slayer kills girl, beau' (18 April 1977).

New York Daily News, 'Killer to cops: "I'll do it again"' (19 April 1977).

New York Daily News, 'Breslin to .44 killer: Give up! It's only way out' (5 June 1977).

New York Times, '".44-Caliber Killer" wounds two in car parked on Queens Street' (27 June 1977).

New York Times, '.44-killer wounds 12th and 13th victims' (1 August 1977).

New York Times, 'Suspect in "Son of Sam" murders arrested in Yonkers; Police say .44 caliber weapon is recovered' (11 August 1977).

New York Daily News, 'Breslin: A dog told Berkowitz to do it' (11 August 1977).

New York Daily News, 'Nab mailman as .44 killer' (11 August 1977).

Time, 'Behavior: Son of Sam is not sleeping' (11 July 1977).

Time, 'Crime: The man hunt for Son of Sam goes on' (8 August 1977).

Time, 'Nation: Sam told me to do it . . . Sam is the Devil' (22 August 1977).

USA Today, '"Son of Sam" serial killer denied parole' (9 July 2002).

New York Post, '"Son of Sam" skips parole hearing, in prison at least 2 more years' (14 May 2014).

New York Post, '"Son of Sam" throat-slashing suspect revealed' (27 July 2015).

New York Post, 'Killer who slashed Son of Sam in jail is denied parole' (25 February 2016).

Ariseandshine.org (Berkowitz's own website).

New York Daily News, 'Berkowitz gets 547 years but . . .' (13 June 1978).

Huffington Post, '"Son of Sam" David Berkowitz denied parole, but says Jesus has forgiven him' (13 May 2014).

CHAPTER 27: JEFFREY DAHMER

New York Post, 'Why I killed Jeffrey Dahmer' (28 April 2015).

Independent, 'Soldiers, sexual abuse – and the serial killer: The US military's secret sexual assaults' (28 June 2013).

Time, 'The little flat of horrors' (5 August 1991).

Time, 'Milwaukee murders: Did they all have to die?' (12 August 1991).

New York Times, 'Milwaukee police once queried suspect' (27 July 1991).

Times-News, 'Officers were in Dahmer's apartment' (2 August 1991).

Limelight, 'Medicine at Michigan: Faculty profile: Jeff Jentzen: Examining forensic medicine' (Spring 2009).

Reading Eagle, 'Dahmer, guilty, insane' (13 January 1992).

Anne E. Schwartz, *The Man Who Could Not Kill Enough: The Secret Murders of Milwaukee's Jeffrey Dahmer* (Birch Lane Press, 1992).

Don Davis, *Milwaukee Murders, Nightmare in Apartment 213: The True Story* (St Martin's Paperbacks, 1995).

People, 'The final victim' (12 December 1994).

Time, 'PETA won't be turning serial killer's house into vegan restaurant after all' (9 April 2014).

Time, 'Trials: Do mad acts a madman make?' (3 February 1992).

Brian Masters, *The Shrine of Jeffrey Dahmer* (Hodder & Stoughton, 1993).

CHAPTER 28: GARY RIDGWAY – THE GREEN RIVER KILLER

KOMO News, 'Voice of Evil: The Green River Killer breaks his silence' (13 September 2013).

Walla-Walla Union Bulletin, 'Police begin to unravel the death of three prostitutes' (19 August 1982).

Walla-Walla Union Bulletin, 'Police fear for lives of two missing teens' (29 September 1982).

Evening Sun, 'Police mum on investigation of the Green River killings' (1 October 1982).

Defiance Crescent News, 'Seattle slayer sought' (4 October 1982).

Walla-Walla Union Bulletin, 'Fear goes with territory prostitutes, killer share' (5 January 1986).

Walla-Walla Union Bulletin, 'Task force questions "person of interest"' (7 February 1986).

Walla-Walla Union Bulletin, 'Coverage of Green River incident intense' (9 February 1986).

Walla-Walla Union Bulletin, 'Serial slayings suspect nabbed' (2 December 2001).

Walla-Walla Union Bulletin, 'Search of 2 of Ridgway's homes complete' (4 December 2001).

Robert Keppel, *The Riverman* (Pocket Books, 1995).

Carlton Smith and Tomas Guillen, *The Search for the Green River Killer* (Penguin, 1991).

Time, 'River of death' (27 February 2003).

King County, Washington, 'Statement of Norm Maleng on Ridgway Plea', press release (5 November 2003).

Nancy Grace, 'When Serial Killers Strike: The Green River Killer' (8 July 2013).

CHAPTER 29: RAY AND FAYE COPELAND

State of Missouri, Respondent v. Faye Copeland, Appellant 928 S.W.2d (1996) No. 73774 (17 September 1996).

Daily News, 'The case of the vanishing vagrants' (25 March 2008).

Tom Miller, *The Copeland Killings* (Pinnacle Books, 1993).

Charlotte Greig, *Evil Serial Killers: In the Minds of Monsters* (Capella, 2005).

Medical Detectives, 'Killer's "Cattle" Log', Series 6, Episode 15 (2001).

CHAPTER 30: AILEEN WUORNOS

CNN, 'Wuornos' last words: "I'll be back"' (15 October 2002).

Panama City News Herald, 'Wuornos' childhood abuse contradicted' (30 January 1992).

Chicago Daily Herald Suburban, 'Police arrest suspect in Florida highway slayings' (18 January 1991).

Panama City News Herald, 'Former lover relates Wuornos' admission' (17 January 1992).

Orange County Register, 'Serial killing suspect: "I'm victim"' (25 January 1992).

Winnipeg Free Press, 'Defence gambles on hooker's testimony' (26 January 1992).

Panama City News Herald, 'Wuornos convicted of highway slaying' (28 January 1992).

Northwest Florida Daily News, 'Jury to make life-or-death decision on killer' (29 January 1992).

Panama City News Herald, 'Highway killer cries as jury recommends death penalty' (31 January 1992).

Northwest Florida Daily News, 'Condemned "highway killer" exclaims to court "I'm no serial killer"' (1 February 1992).

Acknowledgements

This book has taken rather longer to go from commissioning to publication than any of us expected, and my thanks are particularly due on this occasion to Duncan Proudfoot at Little, Brown for his patience and faith in the project, as well as to my original editor Clive Hebard who was expecting a manuscript at Halloween 2015, and his successor Amanda Keats, all of whom have had rather a long wait. Thanks as ever are due to my copy-editor Howard Watson, who has ensured that I've not made any avoidable errors – any that remain in the text are strictly my responsibility.

Very special thanks are owed to surgeon Chris Williams and osteopath Alexandra Luzzato, without whom sitting at the laptop to write twenty words a day wouldn't have been possible, let alone the two-thousand-plus this book needed! Special thanks also to my father, Ian Howden-Simpson, for stepping in to ensure that the original carpal tunnel operation I required could happen as speedily as needed, and to Isabelle Cannon for taking off some of the pressure during my recuperation.

Thanks to my willing band of helpers who have shared their talents and helped with tracking down or translating source material in other countries and languages, particularly Maria Cebotari and David Kines; and those who suggested cases that might be worth investigating, some of whom have requested anonymity, but including Steve Scott, Joan de la Haye and my daughter Sophie (who worked her way through many previously published collections and commented on a number of anomalies between accounts). Thanks to those who have helped locate material here: Eve Woodlands,

Monica Derwent, Adina Mihaela Roman, Patricia Hythe and Amanda Wing.

Thanks as ever to those who have kept the wheels of commerce going in recent times – Marc Gascoigne, Phil Jourdan, David Moore, Jonathan Oliver, Emma Capron, Gary Smailes, Madeleine Vasaly, Kate Fox, Charlotte MacDonald, Sophie Orme, Grace Paul and Albert DePetrillo, and to Amanda Rutter for the bovine aero introduction!

Thanks to the members of All the Right Notes Choir, and the 2015/16 Year 6 at St Wilfrid's School for the musical distractions, and to Rani and Rodo, my faithful terriers, for their unswerving dedication to ensuring that I can only write for ten minutes at a time without being interrupted for some reason that only they understand – but who also made sure that I never got too lost in all of this.

Last but most definitely not least, to my partner Barbara and my daughter Sophie. This book has taken me into some dark places, and your love and support have kept me (moderately) sane and sensible.

Index

....